Human Fertilisation and Embryology:
Reproducing Regulation

The UK has been at the forefront of regulation and legislation of assisted reproduction since the enactment of the Human Fertilisation and Embryology Act 1990. However, as technology continues to advance, so the academic, political and ethical debates around assisted reproduction flourish. This book highlights and critically analyses contemporary issues associated with assisted reproduction and embryology, many of which were either not considered or not anticipated when the Human Fertilisation and Embryology Act (HFE Act) was passed in 1990. The book aims to identify and evaluate areas that have provoked debate and where further or renewed regulation is needed. While it will primarily be of interest to a UK readership, it is expected that it will also be of interest to academics, students and practitioners elsewhere in the world.

Dr Kirsty Horsey is a Lecturer in Law at the University of Kent. She is reproduction editor of BioNews, a web and email based service of news, information and comment on assisted reproduction and human genetics.

Hazel Biggs is Professor of Medical Law at Lancaster University. Previously she was Director of Medical Law at the University of Kent. Her work encompasses most areas of medical law with a particular emphasis on autonomy, choice and informed decision-making. She is an editor for *Medical Law Review* and is affiliated to the Centre for the Economic and Social Aspects of Genomics (CESAGen) at Lancaster University.

Biomedical Law and Ethics Library
Series Editor: Sheila A.M. McLean

Scientific and clinical advances, social and political developments and the impact of healthcare on our lives raise profound ethical and legal questions. Medical law and ethics have become central to our understanding of these problems, and are important tools for the analysis and resolution of problems – real or imagined.

In this series, scholars at the forefront of biomedical law and ethics contribute to the debates in this area, with accessible, thought-provoking, and sometimes controversial ideas. Each book in the series develops an independent hypothesis and argues cogently for a particular position. One of the major contributions of this series is the extent to which both law and ethics are utilised in the content of the books, and the shape of the series itself.

The books in this series are analytical, with a key target audience of lawyers, doctors, nurses, and the intelligent lay public.

Forthcoming titles:

Horsey and Biggs, *Human Fertilisation and Embryology* (2007)
McLean and Williamson, *Impairment and Disability* (2007)
Gavaghan, *Defending the Genetic Supermarket* (2007)
Priaulx, *The Harm Paradox* (2007)
Downie and Macnaughton, *Bioethics and the Humanities* (2007)
McLean, *Assisted Dying* (2007)
Huxtable, *Euthanasia, Ethics and the Law* (2007)
Elliston, *Best Interests of the Child in Healthcare* (2007)

About the Series Editor:

Professor Sheila McLean is International Bar Association Professor of Law and Ethics in Medicine and Director of the Institute of Law and Ethics in Medicine at the University of Glasgow.

Human Fertilisation and Embryology:

Reproducing Regulation

Edited by Kirsty Horsey and
Hazel Biggs

Routledge
Taylor & Francis Group
LONDON AND NEW YORK

First published 2007 by Routledge-Cavendish

This edition published 2013 by Routledge
2 Park Square, Milton Park, Abingdon, Oxon OX14 4RN

Simultaneously published in the USA and Canada
by Routledge
711 Third Avenue, New York, NY 10017

*Routledge is an imprint of the Taylor & Francis Group, an
informa business*

© 2007 Kirsty Horsey and Hazel Biggs

Typeset in Times New Roman by
RefineCatch Limited, Bungay, Suffolk

British Library Cataloguing in Publication Data
A catalogue record for this book is available from the British Library

Library of Congress Cataloging in Publication Data
A catalog record for this book has been requested

ISBN10: 1-84472-090-X (pbk)
ISBN10: 1-84472-091-8 (hbk)

ISBN13: 978-1-84472-090-3 (pbk)
ISBN13: 978-1-84472-091-0 (hbk)

Contents

Contributors

Hazel Biggs was appointed Professor of Medical Law at Lancaster University in April 2005, prior to which she was Director of Medical Law at the University of Kent. The focus of her research is medical law and ethics with the main emphasis being end of life decision-making, human reproduction and clinical research and she has published widely in these areas.

Eric Blyth is Professor of Social Work at the University of Huddersfield and holds an adjunct professorship at the University of Alberta. He is chair of the Project Group on Assisted Reproduction (PROGAR) and has acted as an advisor on assisted conception to professional bodies, governmental departments and regulatory bodies in various countries. His research has included surrogacy arrangements, egg donation, egg sharing and donor insemination (DI).

Dr Jess Buxton is a geneticist who works for Progress Educational Trust, a UK charity that provides information and debate on the ethical, legal and social issues raised by assisted reproduction, genetics and embryo research. She is genetics editor of BioNews, a weekly web and email based service providing news, information and comment on these areas of science.

Dr Heather Draper is a Reader in Biomedical Ethics in the Centre for Biomedical Ethics at Birmingham University. Her research interests focus on the medicalisation of pregnancy and childbirth including the use of reproductive technologies. Although she is interested in many aspects of biomedical ethics (from tissue transplantation to gender re-assignment, from confidentiality to cosmetic surgery), reproduction remains her main area of research. She is particularly interested in what makes someone a parent and what, specifically, parental obligations to born and unborn children are.

Dr Kirsty Horsey is a Lecturer in Law at the University of Kent. She is also reproduction editor of BioNews, a weekly web and email based service of news, information and comment on assisted reproduction and human genetics, published by Progress Educational Trust. Her primary research interests focus on family law aspects of assisted reproductive technologies.

Emily Jackson is Professor of Medical Law at Queen Mary, University of London. She has previously taught at LSE, Birkbeck and St Catharine's College, Cambridge. She is the author of *Regulating Reproduction* (Hart, 2001) and *Medical Law: Text, Cases and Materials* (Oxford University Press, 2006).

Dr Ellie Lee is a Senior Lecturer in Social Policy at the University of Kent. She previously worked at Southampton University as a lecturer, and then as research fellow working on a study about teenagers and abortion for the Joseph Rowntree Foundation. She is the author of *Abortion, Motherhood, and Mental Health: Medicalizing Reproduction in the US and Britain* (Transaction, 2003) and has written many articles about abortion, contraception and reproductive technologies. Her most recent study is of mothers' experiences of feeding their babies in the early weeks. She is the co-ordinator of Pro-Choice Forum.

Dr Fiona MacCallum is a Lecturer in Psychology at the University of Warwick, specialising in the psychological effects of creating families through new reproductive technologies.

Robin Mackenzie is Director of Medical Ethics and the Law at the University of Kent. She has taught law in New Zealand, Scotland and England and has published in the field of medical law and ethics as this applies to reproduction, genetics, death and dying, intellectual property and feminist thought.

Dr Nicolette Priaulx is a Lecturer in Law at Keele University. Her main research interests are in the areas of tort law and medical law, with specific concerns around the ethics of compensation and the nature and construction of compensable harm. Following a series of articles exploring these themes in the context of the reproductive torts, she is now finalising her monograph entitled *The Harm Paradox: Tort Law and the Unwanted Child*, which is due to be published with Routledge-Cavendish in 2007.

Laura Riley is Press and Public Policy Manager for BPAS, the sexual healthcare charity previously known as the British Pregnancy Advisory Service. Prior to this she was Director of Progress Educational Trust and commissioning editor at BioNews, with a background in television documentaries primarily in BBC Religion & Ethics and BBC Science departments. She holds an MA in Medical Law and Ethics from Kings College London.

Preface

Human fertilisation and embryology and issues associated with the use of technology in family formation and the treatment of infertility have long been the subject of political and social controversy. This collection of essays draws attention to the ongoing debate of scientific interference in the process of reproduction and, more particularly, the scope and shape of the regulation of assisted reproduction technology.

In the 1980s, the novelty of the development and use of technologies associated with human reproduction resulted in calls for a single piece of all-encompassing legislation to regulate these new and developing practices. Together, the prospect of researching on human embryos and the potential to produce new forms of family led to concerns and imaginings about what might in future become technically possible. Many commentators were reluctant to embrace the new reproductive technologies. Some feminists claimed that they represented the technical domination of men (as doctors and scientists) over the bodies of women. Other critics claimed that they evidenced a move towards 'Franken-science' and that we should not tamper with Nature or 'play God'.

While the response to the introduction of assisted reproductive technology (ART) was not entirely negative, in 1982 the Government of the day was moved to commission an inquiry into assisted reproduction and embryology, chaired by philosopher Mary Warnock. Over a period of two years, the Commission heard evidence from many of the actors involved in assisted reproduction clinical practice, research and social and academic study. The Warnock Committee Report was published in July 1984 and immediately prompted parliamentary discussions on human fertilisation and embryology, culminating in the enactment of legislation in 1990.

The years between the publication of the Warnock Report and the passing of the Human Fertilisation and Embryology Act in 1990 saw the establishment of the Voluntary Licensing Authority (VLA, later the Interim Licensing Authority, or ILA). As a joint venture between the Medical Research Council and the Royal College of Obstetricians and Gynaecologists, its main role was to monitor developments in assisted reproduction. The VLA would therefore consider research applications and could grant licenses for research and clinical practice. Although it was not a statutory body and in effect had no legal power, the VLA illustrated the potential for the operation of a regulatory body in the field of assisted reproduction.

In 1985, Enoch Powell's Unborn Children (Protection) Bill was put before Parliament. If passed, the Bill would have prohibited any further research into assisted reproduction technologies, as it proposed that the manipulation of any embryo would be an offence except when that embryo was used in actual infertility treatments. Powell's Bill had a great deal of support and progressed easily to its third reading. In response, supporters of embryo research launched a counterattack; groups of scientists, clinicians, politicians and others who supported embryo research and assisted reproduction began concerted lobbying of the House of Commons, seeking to campaign against the Bill through increased public understanding and awareness of embryo research. After many heated debates and its opponents' efforts at filibustering, the Bill ran out of time and was defeated. Meanwhile, the VLA issued embryology guidelines in accordance with the recommendations made in the Warnock Report, setting a 14-day limit on embryo research and requiring signed consent from the 'parents' before research could be authorised. In 1986, Ken Hargreaves MP introduced another version of the Unborn Children (Protection) Bill, arguing that there was still great support in Parliament for the prohibition of embryo research. The Bill had little chance of being enacted but served to keep the debate firmly in the public eye. Outside Parliament, the pro-research lobby continued to expand and both sides maintained pressure on the Government for realistic legislation. In November 1987, the Government at last responded to the Warnock recommendations and published a White Paper on Human Fertilisation and Embryology which outlined a framework for such legislation.[1]

The Human Fertilisation and Embryology Act (HFE Act) was eventually enacted and became law in 1990. Morgan and Lee say that the Act was passed because, following the Warnock Report and subsequent developments, a universal piece of legislation was required to 'regulate research on embryos, to protect the integrity of reproductive medicine and to protect scientists and clinicians from legal action and sanction'.[2] Although the Act deals mainly with issues surrounding specific medicalised infertility treatments and issues in embryology, it also provided for the establishment of the Human Fertilisation and Embryology Authority, a statutory body to monitor and

---

1 *Human Fertilisation and Embryology: A Framework for Legislation* Cm 259 (1987) London: HMSO. A full account of the development of the debate around reproductive technologies and embryo research can be found in Jack Challoner, *The Baby Makers: The History of Artificial Conception* (1999) London: Channel 4 Books, Chapter 6.

2 Morgan, D and Lee, R *The Human Fertilisation and Embryology Act 1990* (1991) London: Blackstone Press.

control the provision of infertility treatments. Section 5 of the HFE Act required the setting up of the Authority to replace the Interim Licensing Authority on 1 August 1991.

For many years, the Human Fertilisation and Embryology Act has stood as a benchmark piece of legislation and, indeed, it has been used as a model or template for legislation in other jurisdictions. However, science and technological development have a tendency to move faster than the law. Legislative drafting can never be sufficiently flexible to keep pace with the rate of scientific progress in this area. For this reason, recent years have witnessed a number of challenges to the Act and the regulatory authority it created. There are areas of modern assisted reproduction that fall outside the Act, such as sex selection of children without the use of embryo technology or the operation of internet-based donor sperm providers. The use of reproductive technology to create 'saviour siblings', as the media would have them called, has challenged the law and its ability to treat the use of new developments consistently and fairly (for example, see *Quintavalle (on behalf of Comment on Reproductive Ethics) v HFEA* [2005] UKHL 28). The Human Fertilisation and Embryology Authority (HFEA) has also been called upon to respond not only to the implications of scientific advances but also to the differences in legislative approaches in other jurisdictions, leading it to appear inconsistent in its application of the law as it stands. For example, the requirement in the Act that couples obtain 'treatment together' in order to be recognised as the legal parents of the child produced has recently been the subject of legal challenge, as has the interpretation of the law on consent.

The increasing number of challenges to the Act and the Authority and its operation makes it clear that reform may be necessary (for example, see *In Re D (A Child Appearing by Her Guardian ad Litem) (Respondent)* [2005] UKHL 33; *The Leeds Teaching Hospitals NHS Trust v Mr A, Mrs A and Others* [2003] EWCA 259 (QBD); and *Evans v Amicus Healthcare Ltd and Others* [2004] EWCA (Civ) 727; later *Evans v United Kingdom* (App. no. 6339/05)). In 2004, the Government announced that a full review of the legislation would take place, and shortly afterwards the House of Commons Science and Technology Committee established its own enquiry into the operation of the law, reporting its findings, which contain many recommendations for change, in March 2005.[3] The essence of the Committee's report seems to be that a more liberal interpretation of the regulation of assisted reproduction should be attempted, allowing for more patient choice and control over the matters and methods by which they choose to create their families in line with health policy more generally. The HFEA itself has reviewed a number of areas with which it is concerned: the welfare provisions contained within the 1990 Act

---

3 Fifth Report from the House of Commons Science and Technology Committee (2005), *Human Reproductive Technologies and the Law*, Session 2004–5: HC 7-I.

and detailed in the Authority's Code of Practice and the donation and use of sperm, eggs and embryos are just two of these. In August 2005, the Department of Health launched its own public consultation into the operation of the law, which closed in November 2005, seeking views on whether and how it might be updated given the 'rise of new technologies, changes in societal attitudes, international developments and the need to ensure effective regulation'.[4]

These developments mean that this book is both important and timely. It highlights and critically analyses some of the contemporary issues in assisted reproduction and embryology in the light of the ongoing review of legislation in this area. Its contributors focus on areas regarded as 'hot topics', both politically and academically, with particular emphasis on those that were either not considered or were under-considered when the Human Fertilisation and Embryology Act was passed in 1990. Issues arising from scientific and technological development unforeseen at the time of the legislation are debated alongside those that to some remain unresolved, such as the regulation of surrogacy arrangements, the status and operation of the 'welfare principle', the designation of parenthood, access to infertility treatment and reproductive autonomy in terms of abortion.

The main aim of the book is to look at areas that either need re-regulation or are likely to provoke public and academic debate, discussion and lobbying. The editors hope that the contributors' discussions and recommendations will complement the parliamentary reviews of the Act and encourage further debate before any redrafting of the law. It is anticipated, however, that, as with other reforms, many of the issues raised will continue to be debated even after the new legislation is formulated. In addition, while the UK is at the forefront of legislation in this area, other nations continue to debate (both politically and academically) how the regulation of human fertilisation and embryology should proceed. Therefore, while the book will primarily be of interest to a UK readership, it is expected that academics elsewhere will also be interested in many of the issues discussed.

4 Department of Health, *Review of the Human Fertilisation and Embryology Act: A Public Consultation* (2005), Foreword.

Chapter 1

The quest for a perfect child

How far should the law intervene?

Hazel Biggs

INTRODUCTION

After the birth of Louise Brown in 1978, the news that *in vitro* fertilisation (IVF) had succeeded in producing a child provoked widespread debate about the safety and morality of the procedure and calls for legislation. The early response of the UK Parliament was to institute the Warnock Committee in 1982 to investigate 'recent and potential developments in medicine and science related to human fertilisation and embryology' and 'to consider what policies and safeguards should be applied, including consideration of the social, ethical and legal implications of these developments' (Cmnd 9314, 1984: 4). Its subsequent Report formed the basis of the Human Fertilisation and Embryology Act 1990, which is today the subject of a Department of Health review. Assisted reproductive technologies (ARTs) are more heavily regulated than any other medical intervention and it is within this context that this book considers the operation of the Human Fertilisation and Embryology Act (the 1990 Act) and broader issues connected with the regulation of assisted conception techniques.

Drawing on the work of other contributors to this collection and contemporary analysis of the issues, this introductory chapter will scrutinise the ethical and legal implications of permitting free individual choice over how reproductive technology is used to produce a child that conforms to the ideals of each individual potential parent: the perfect child. The present Department of Health review of the operation of the 1990 Act (Department of Health, 2005) provides an opportunity to assess the scope and shape of that regulation and to ask how far the law should intervene in the quest for the perfect child. Generally the discussions in the individual chapters are not couched within the parameters or language of the 'perfect child'; however, the device provides a useful conceptual framework within which to critique not only these chapters but also the review of the 1990 Act more broadly. This chapter will first explain what is meant by this terminology before proceeding to investigate what, if anything, is wrong with the quest for the perfect child. It will examine the extent to which there is a genuine need to regulate assisted reproductive technologies and suggest some alternatives to the current legislative framework before briefly focusing on an area associated with the use of ARTs that has not been assessed by the other authors in the collection, namely postmenopausal pregnancy.

WHAT IS WRONG WITH THE QUEST FOR THE PERFECT CHILD?

The age in which we live permits choice over most aspects of life, and death. Increasingly therefore, patients are becoming healthcare consumers seeking specialist treatments and healthcare interventions that suit their personal needs and agendas. With regard to reproduction and the use of reproductive technology, however, much of the commentary condemns the intervention of exploitation, consumerism and reproductive tourism, generating the pejorative terminology associated with the 'designer baby' debate and denigrating reproductive choice where it is associated with the quest for perfection (Brazier, 1999; Lee, 2002). But perfection can be construed in many ways, and I will commence with some apposite interpretations of perfection and an appraisal of what the perfect child might represent for those who seek it. Accordingly, 'perfection' will be characterised as a subjective assessment which may, or may not, have wide-ranging implications with regard to reproductive freedom and choice.

It is only relatively recently that medical science has developed the ability to intervene in what has hitherto been regarded as a natural process in order to produce a perfect child, and the success rates of the available interventions remain limited (see Riley, Chapter 5, and Buxton, Chapter 6, in this volume). Yet, while the advent of reproductive technology and reprogenetics has undoubtedly raised awareness of new possibilities, the desire for perfection in a child is not a new phenomenon, hence the traditional first questions of new parents: 'what is it?' concerning the sex of the offspring, and 'is it all right?' in relation to its being physically whole and suffering from no immediately obvious abnormality. In addition, it is claimed that 'parents have always tried to determine their children's genes. Aristotle advised men to tie off their left testicle to guarantee a male child' (*The Economist*, 2001, p 16). However, prior to the availability of innovations in reproductive medicine, the expectations of prospective parents were more limited than today. If attempts to conceive a child failed in the past, the mechanisms available to assist nature were relatively few, requiring either acceptance of childlessness or applications to become adoptive parents. Once a pregnancy was confirmed, ante-natal interventions were minimal and people were generally relieved at the time of delivery to discover that they had a 'perfect child'. The advent of ante-natal blood testing, screening techniques and the widespread introduction of ultrasound scanning to detect foetal abnormalities in the 1970s and

1980s, coupled with the availability of legal termination of pregnancy after 1967, may be regarded as a prelude to today's pursuit of the perfect child.

The use of the terminology of perfection in this chapter is not intended to denote discrimination or discriminatory tendencies but rather to mirror the social impact of advanced reproductive medicine on the process of becoming a parent. To understand what would constitute a perfect child for individual people requires knowledge of the particular circumstances of those concerned. For example, economic or professional imperatives may dictate that for some the perfect child is one born at the perfect time, perhaps to coincide with specific social or financial commitments, and, up to a point, increased access to improved methods of contraception has permitted this in recent decades. Alternatively, such a child may be conceived of the union with a perfect sexual partner, where perfection is constructed according to genetic or social compatibility or basic physical attraction. Or it may be a child of a particular sex in order to balance the family or avoid a sex-linked inherited condition. More usually in relation to the use of fertility treatment, however, the perfect child may simply represent a longed-for child previously thought impossible because of impaired fertility. Here it is important to note that fertility may be impaired for a variety of reasons ranging from physical to medical deficiency, resulting perhaps from disease, hormonal insufficiency or congenital malformation. There may also be social reasons for a failure to conceive, possibly due to delays in attempts to become pregnant because of career priorities or the fact that one's sexual partner is of the same gender.

In any sphere of life, perfection is a highly subjective concept whose definition is largely dependent upon individual preferences, needs and desires. The perception of what constitutes perfection in a child will therefore reflect the aspirations of the parent or prospective parent and may be represented by a multitude of different characteristics. For example, the perfect child may be physically and mentally complete, or may possess specific physical, intellectual and emotional attributes. Of course, at present it is largely technically impossible to select for most of these features in advance of pregnancy or birth, but it is the prospect of perhaps being able to do so in the future that has led to the controversies surrounding so-called 'designer babies'. In addition, the few known examples of this practice, such as the deliberate selection of a deaf sperm donor by Sharon Duchesneau and Candy McCullough in a successful attempt to create a hearing-impaired child, have fuelled popular condemnation (Teather, 2002). This couple's perfect child is a deaf child who will share their culture as part of a hearing impaired community. They regard deafness as a positive aspect of their lives rather than a disability that will disadvantage their offspring, but they have been widely castigated in the media as a result (*The Sunday Times*, 2002).

It is true, however, that since Louise Brown was born, IVF and some other forms of assisted reproduction have moved from experimental and audacious to commonplace, almost mundane. In the UK alone, IVF was responsible for the births of more than 50,000 babies between 1978 and 1999, the majority of which were born after 1995 (HFEA, 2000). The numbers continue to increase as the reliability of the technology improves and it is estimated that currently around 1 per cent of babies born in the UK are the result of assisted reproduction. Around the world, approximately 300,000 children are thought to have been the product of ART (Peterson, 2005). However, despite the apparently everyday nature of assisted conception techniques, they, and the ways in which they are regulated, are not without their critics. The controversy is perhaps unsurprising, particularly as traditional notions of family creation and what it means to be a parent are necessarily disrupted by scientific intervention in the process of reproduction. The political and social debate that preceded the enactment of the HFE Act 1990 shaped the law as we know it today and in the intervening years the assumptions that underscored those debates and fashioned the Act have been extensively critiqued. Many of the concerns expressed in this book have developed from that critique. Some of the legal and social controversies, such as the definitions of 'mother' and 'father', were anticipated prior to the enactment of the 1990 Act and addressed in the legislation, while others, such as those associated with techniques like preimplantation genetic diagnosis (PGD), postmenopausal conception and cloning, were largely the stuff of science fiction at that time. And, while in many regards the use of reproductive technologies has been embraced and generally accepted, some of the uses and potential uses of the technology remain contentious. Furthermore, as science advances and more novel ways of making perfect babies are developed, new and different controversies arise. The ability to screen embryos for genetic conditions and compatibility with existing children, for instance, has provoked heated debate and stretched existing regulation to breaking point (see, for example, *Quintavalle (on behalf of Comment on Reproductive Ethics) v HFEA* [2005] UKHL 28).

Some aspects of the detailed operation of the 1990 Act have generated more academic debate than others in recent years. The so-called 'welfare principle' enshrined in s 13(5), for example, remains the object of heated discussion, not least in this volume (Blyth, Chapter 2, and Jackson, Chapter 3, in this volume). Emily Jackson (Chapter 3) examines the assumptions that underlie the welfare principle and the ways in which it might be applied to assess the suitability of potential recipients of fertility treatment to become parents. She details the obvious difficulties involved in evaluating the welfare of a child that does not yet exist and points out the tensions between the application of the welfare principle and the reasoning in the 'wrongful life' cases, which rely upon established arguments that it is always better to be born than not ever to come into existence (Farsides and Dunlop, 2001). Despite accepting those arguments as valid, Eric Blyth finds it inconceivable that any revised legislation would not include an explicit commitment to the welfare interests of potential children and favours the retention of some form of welfare assessment. His analysis draws attention to the little utilised provision that concerns 'the effect of a new baby or babies upon any existing child of the family' (HFEA, 2004: 3.3 (v) (e)) and he uses this to argue that 'there are grounds for retaining an explicit commitment to the interests both of children conceived as a result of assisted conception and of any other child who may be affected by the birth, but that the focus of s 13(5) should be redirected from imprecise requirements to take account of children's welfare towards a more explicit focus on protecting them from foreseeable significant harm' (Blyth, Chapter 2, p 18). In the context of research and development, he also explains that, despite the centrality of the welfare provision to clinical decisions on whether and when to provide fertility treatment to particular patients, evidence from clinicians reveals that 'considerations other than the interests of children conceived through therapeutic interventions have been the major drivers of technological development' (p 34).

Perhaps even more contentious than the welfare provision, surrogacy has provoked a great deal of social, legal and ethical debate in recent years. Many of the issues, including how best to assign parenthood in surrogacy arrangements, how to avoid exploitation and how such arrangements might be rendered enforceable, remain to be satisfactorily resolved. Robin Mackenzie's chapter (Chapter 9 in this volume) addresses some of these issues and concludes that both the HFE Act 1990 and the Surrogacy Arrangements Act 1985 should be amended to facilitate private ordering and reproductive autonomy where surrogacy is concerned. She contends that the fact that today an increasingly broad range of familial relationships is being recognised by the law as it adapts to social change represents a growing acceptance of private ordering in family formation. The assignment of guardianship, parental responsibility, residency orders and child support obligations to a wider and more diverse range of family members is cited as evidence of this trend. With this in mind, she also advocates that in order to enhance reproductive autonomy, those involved in a surrogacy arrangement should be able to choose the type of family they seek to create. For example, they may desire an extended family with continuing contact between all potential parents and children or one with none. Rather than selecting a perfect child, these people are pursuing their perfect family and should be afforded legal recognition and protection in their quest. Mackenzie therefore argues, '[I]n my view, protection of the parties would involve providing mechanisms whereby the wishes of the adults, the varieties of current families and the interests of the children all received legal recognition' (Mackenzie, p 200). With regard to enforceability, she proposes that surrogacy agreements of this nature should be subjected to the scrutiny and approval of the court prior to the conception of a child. The agreement could then be underpinned by a presumption of enforceability that is rebuttable in cases where disagreement subsequently arises, so that the court may still assign legal parenthood on the basis of the best interests of the child.

Kirsty Horsey (Chapter 8 in this volume) also discusses cases involving surrogacy arrangements, using their example as one vehicle to analyse the premises and assumptions that underpin the legal definitions of mother and father in the 1990 Act, and suggests that a better way to designate parenthood would be to base it upon the intention to create and parent a child produced through assisted reproduction. Using recent case law, she extends the principle to other aspects of ART to illustrate its efficacy in ensuring that parenthood is assigned in a way that accords with social reality. In her view, those whose quest for the perfect child has involved the successful use of reproductive technologies and interventions with the intention of bringing a child into the world should automatically be recognised as its legal parents.

The condemnation of surrogacy frequently revolves around its potential to commodify the offspring produced, which in turn raises concerns about causing damage to their psychological wellbeing as they develop (Ketchum, 1989; Verny, 1994). In her chapter on the payment of gamete donors, Heather Draper (Chapter 4 in this volume) examines related concerns about 'trade' in human gametes. Beginning with an assessment of the extent of parental responsibility owed to children born of donated gametes by those who provided the genetic material, she reveals that the current legal framework operates in a way that assumes parental responsibility is inalienable in these circumstances. Effectively, if a person has a biological connection to the child produced, some residual parental relationship persists even if socially and legally the ties are severed. This, she says, seems to be culturally embedded and forms the basis of the potential harm that might be wrought on children created in this way. The argument relies upon the assumption that gamete donors who receive cash or 'in kind' rewards for providing gametes are responsible for any psychological harm that might be caused to the resulting children because they are their biological parents. Given, among other things, the difficulties associated with demonstrating the harm that these children, or potential children, might suffer (Jackson, Chapter 3 in this volume) and of securely identifying gamete donors as 'parents', Draper finds this morally unconvincing as an argument against paying donors for their contribution.

In considering the quest for the perfect child, debates around abortion law and the legal timeframe within which abortion may be lawfully performed may at first sight appear out of step with the discussion of technological interventions to alleviate fertility problems. Abortion is in some respects 'the other side of that coin', but while it appeared to be 'a settled question' (Lee, Chapter 11 in this volume, p 232) it has re-emerged as the subject of extreme controversy, particularly surrounding the current time limit of 24 weeks and the availability of 'late abortion'. The issue falls within the remit of this book because the Human Fertilisation and Embryology Act 1990 (s 37) introduced amendments to the Abortion Act 1967 reducing the legal availability of abortion in line with foetal viability from 28 weeks to 24, except where there is 'substantial risk that if the child were born it would suffer from such physical or mental abnormalities as to be seriously handicapped' (s 1(1)(d)), when it can be performed at any stage. It is therefore appropriate that the law surrounding the availability of abortion in the later stages of pregnancy is being debated in and around Parliament with a view to further reform of the 1990 Act. Here Ellie Lee (Chapter 11 in this volume) assesses the reasons for the recent revitalisation of abortion as a live concern. She associates the recent resurgence of opposition to later termination of pregnancy with the development of new imaging techniques and rightly argues that these interventions change nothing in the nature of the debate. Technological advances in methods of ultrasound imaging describe the developing foetus in ways that are more accessible and comprehensible to the lay public but surely add nothing to the general understanding of the nature and characteristics of a post-24-week foetus. It seems completely improbable that those who meet the legal criteria for late abortion involving labour and delivery contemplate it without a sound understanding of the fact that the foetus is in the advanced stages of development and would be viable and what that means in practice.

Nicolette Priaulx (Chapter 10 in this volume) also discusses abortion law, examining the premises that underpin the foetal abnormality ground for abortion and questioning whether there are sound justifications for it. She finds the assumption that underpins s 1(1)(d) of the Abortion Act 1967 to permit abortion on grounds of foetal abnormality 'deeply problematic' and advocates instead a move towards a law founded on reproductive autonomy. Removing the gestatory time limit and replacing it with choice for women will, she believes, assist in alleviating some of the more discriminatory aspects of the current law and provide 'the best way forward for both feminist and disability equality activists seeking to reframe existing abortion law' (Priaulx, Chapter 10, p 227).

While the authors mentioned above focus on issues that have proven problematic in the existing legislation, Jess Buxton and Fiona MacCallum problematise specific issues with regard to processes that are not explicitly addressed in the 1990 Act but now need to be included in any reformed regulatory framework. Jess Buxton (Chapter 6 in this volume) discusses prenatal diagnosis (PND), PGD and preimplantation genetic screening (PGS) and provides insights into the scientific methods involved. She discusses the legal and ethical issues associated with the use of these techniques in detail before recommending that, far from requiring policing by the law, decisions about when and how they are used are best left to those who will be most closely affected by them, namely the prospective parents. Fiona MacCallum (Chapter 7 in this volume) considers the status of embryos that are donated for procreative purposes in the light of suggestions that embryo donation might be treated in the same way as adoption to permit the donating couple to have some influence on who receives their embryo. The experience of parenthood for those who have received donated embryos is, she argues, likely to differ from that of adoptive parents because of the way the process is regulated; embryo donation parents will be regarded as legal parents from birth. Her concerns turn on the emphasis that should be placed on genetic heritage in this context, given that adopted children are entitled to locate their genetic parents and anonymity for gamete donors has recently been withdrawn. She acknowledges that there are important distinctions between adoption and embryo donation, but in her view that does not justify the differences in the way that welfare considerations are assessed. She therefore suggests that a clearer definition is needed in relation to embryo donation as this would 'benefit assisted reproduction practitioners and would-be parents, as well as the children conceived through these treatments' (MacCallum, Chapter 7, p 152).

These commentators address many of the central issues under consideration in the current review and public consultation of the HFE Act 1990. There are, however, some highly controversial aspects of the debate that are not covered elsewhere in this volume, namely postmenopausal pregnancy, sex selection and human cloning. Issues like these lead some critics to complain that the quest for the perfect child is not fuelled simply by the art of the possible and the fact that medical technology now offers opportunities that were previously not available, but also by 'the rise of the "want" society – one in which it has become fashionable to seek the fulfilment of wants and to accept far less readily, if at all, that some desires cannot, should not, or even must not be satisfied or satiated' (Lee and Morgan, 2001, p 26). Indeed, it has been noted elsewhere in this work (Priaulx, Chapter 10) that deciding what kind of children to have is 'one of the most controversial components of reproductive freedom' (Buchanan *et al*, 2000, p 210). Reproductive cloning and sex selection may be regarded by some as extreme uses of reproductive technology which exemplify the nature of the controversy that surrounds the so-called designer baby debate and the assumptions and fears that underpin it. Space precludes a detailed discussion of them here, but suffice to say that cloning has been extensively debated and is expressly precluded from review in the public consultation under the Department of Health's terms (para 1.13), while sex selection is expressly included (s 5, especially para 5.28 onwards) and was also controversially reported on by the Science and Technology Committee (HC 491). Instead, the remainder of this chapter will focus on the provision of reproductive technology to older women to evaluate whether the implications for parents, children and society indicate that the law should pay special attention to this application of fertility treatment (see Department of Health Consultation paras 3.16–3.17). It will be argued that so long as the procedures and techniques used are demonstrably safe, the decision to use reproductive technology should be personal to the individuals concerned and legal intervention in that process should be minimal. It is acknowledged that many of the current restrictions on the availability of reproductive technologies are imposed due to the limited resources endemic in a publicly funded healthcare system. Other authors in this collection have addressed that issue (see Jackson, Chapter 3; Draper, Chapter 4; Riley, Chapter 5), but this chapter will focus on the underlying principles and not engage specifically with concerns about the allocation of scarce resources.

FERTILITY TREATMENT AND THE OLDER WOMAN

The phenomenon of older women becoming mothers has generated extreme public concern that was reinvigorated in the UK in July 2006 with the birth of a son to 62-year-old child psychiatrist Patti Rashbrook. More specifically, women of advanced biological age announcing the birth of a child have been vilified in the press and electronic media (Mutler, 2005; *Telegraph*, 2005; BioNews, 2005; Foggo and Rogers, 2006). At issue here is whether that condemnation is justified and, if so, how far it should influence the law and regulation of assisted reproductive technologies.

The term commonly used to describe pregnancy in older women is post-menopausal pregnancy. The term is not strictly accurate, however, since some women experience premature menopause and therefore seek fertility treatment and 'postmenopausal pregnancy' while still within the usual child-bearing age range. This discussion will centre on the use of reproductive technology by women who seek to become pregnant when they are beyond the 'natural' child-bearing age range, typically women in their fifties and sixties, but similar arguments often are applied to women in their forties. Commentators tend to argue that pregnancy and motherhood in women who are older than the 'normal' age of reproduction is selfish and unnatural, and that these women will not be well suited to caring for a child because they lack the stamina and vigour of younger women. In addition, concerns are raised about the prospect of children being orphaned at a relatively young age. Each of these concerns contributes to the moral outrage expressed over postmenopausal pregnancy, but none is well founded.

It is, on the face of it, true that using ARTs to enable women who are too old to reproduce to become pregnant is unnatural, but that in itself does not make the procedure, or its outcome, morally wrong such that it should be outlawed. Indeed, if it did, the same reasoning would require that we condemn any medical intervention (Singer and Wells, 1983). Further, those medical interventions that involve the use of 'non-natural' products such as manufactured chemical pharmaceutical agents, or surgical procedures that 'naturally' do more harm than good, should surely be prohibited by law. Similarly, as de Wert points out, naturally occurring phenomena like spontaneous abortion or reduction of pregnancy 'do not morally justify interventions such as a selective abortion or a multifetal pregnancy reduction' (de Wert, 1998, p 223). It clearly is unnatural to use medicines to prevent pregnancy or to use reproductive technology to facilitate pregnancy in postmenopausal women, but it is equally unnatural to use pharmaceutical interventions and reproductive technology to produce any pregnancy. What then makes a postmenopausal pregnancy less acceptable than a technology-induced pregnancy in a younger woman?

A strong argument is related to the welfare of the potential child and suggests that an older mother will be less able to meet the needs of caring for a child because she will be less physically fit and agile and have less vigour than a younger counterpart. This is, of course, a massive generalisation and one that could readily be addressed by good medical practice rather than defined as part of the legal welfare test, as will be discussed later. Individual parents of whatever age exhibit a range of physical attributes and tolerances that mirror the make-up of society. They parent their children according to their own abilities and proclivities. In addition, older women have always cared for and nurtured children either as grandparents or as naturally conceiving older mothers. The average age of menopause is 52, which means that a proportion of women remain fertile into their late forties and early fifties and, albeit rarely, pregnancies do occur in the older age ranges (Fisher and Sommerville, 1998, p 207). There does not seem to be any evidence that their children come to harm because they lack vitality. In addition, if parental stamina is such an important factor for the welfare of a child, it is interesting to note that similarly condemnatory arguments are not generally used when older men embark upon parenthood, as they frequently do. Rather, these men tend to be congratulated and applauded (recent examples include David Jason, Des O'Connor and Paul McCartney). Worryingly, however, recent evidence suggests that, as with older women, the quality of male gametes is also affected by age and that there is a higher than average incidence of genetic disorders in the biological children of older fathers, which is compounded when both parents are in the older age ranges (BioNews, 2005; Zhu *et al*, 2005). In relation to the physical welfare of children, those who are born to older postmenopausal women as a result of using artificial reproductive technologies are less likely to be disadvantaged in this way because gametes donated by younger women must be used. This also means that their chances of achieving a pregnancy are often greater than those for women in their late thirties and early forties using their own eggs, because 'pregnancy success rates are most strongly correlated with the age of the ova, donated or otherwise' (Peterson, 2005, p 284).

It is also often claimed that women who become mothers in their fifties and sixties are more likely to leave a child orphaned early in life. Intuitively this may be the case, but it must be balanced against the fact that any child could be orphaned regardless of the age of her parents. Tragedies like illness and accident befall many people and some children will inevitably be left without one or both parents during their formative years. Yet, even where the early death of a potential parent might be predicted, actuarially at least, as in the case of those suffering terminal disease or engaging in dangerous pursuits, society does not regulate to prevent them having children naturally. Further, it is statistically demonstrable that in England people generally are living longer, and that women are living longer than men (Fisher and Sommerville, 1998), making it more probable that older parents will survive to see their offspring grow to maturity.

Part of the antipathy associated with postmenopausal pregnancy is based on the assumption that women who seek pregnancy then have done so by choice, usually because they have favoured career over family, which, although often regarded as selfish, may be an entirely reasonable course of action in order to provide the child with economic security. There may be other reasons, however. Perhaps an individual woman's personal moral views would not permit her to embark on pregnancy earlier in life because she had not met a suitable partner. Or it may be that she had dedicated her life to caring for an elderly relative or a sibling and was simply unable to care for a child as well. Or this is a 'second family' with a new partner later in life. Any of these may be cited as reasons for delaying pregnancy and childrearing in individual cases but none have a real bearing on whether or not the potential child's welfare will be threatened. A woman, or couple, who elects to start a family later in life using reproductive technology is likely to do so with the same good intentions as any other woman or couple and their suitability should be assessed according to the same criteria. In terms of the welfare principle, Emily Jackson has argued convincingly that this should be founded on a consideration of whether it would plausibly be better not to be conceived and born than to have parents such as these (Jackson, Chapter 3 in this volume). Such a judgement would be based on a risk assessment of the possibility that the would-be parents might cause harm to the child, their ability to care for it in a stable environment and their commitment to bringing up a child once one has been born (HFEA, 2004, 3.12). Given that many of those who seek pregnancy at this time of life argue that they regard it as an opportunity to dedicate themselves to bringing up a child in an environment where it will be financially secure and not competing with the time pressures associated with career progression, these criteria might appear to be readily satisfied.

However, despite the fact that each of these objections to postmenopausal pregnancy can be readily contested, the current regulatory framework adopts a position that appears to mirror them. The National Institute for Health and Clinical Excellence (NICE) is a special health authority and independent organisation with responsibility for providing guidance on the prevention and treatment of ill health and the promotion of good health. Its guidance on the provision of fertility treatment stipulates, '[T]his guidance does not include the management of people who are outside this definition . . . couples who are using contraception, (for example where one partner has been sterilised), and couples outside the reproductive age range' (NICE, 2004, p 2). Furthermore, alongside its guidance on how many embryos should be transferred per cycle and the number of cycles permitted in IVF treatment, 'recommendations about the optimal age range for IVF treatment' are included (NICE, 2004, p 1). It is, of course, perfectly acceptable, even necessary, for regulation and legislation to reflect the values of society. However, those values and beliefs must surely be based upon firm foundations rather than anecdote and prejudice. The furore around postmenopausal pregnancy mirrors the early alarm and apprehension expressed about the use of ARTs generally (e.g. Warnock, 1984), all of which have been demonstrated to be unsound (Kovacs, 1996; Golombok *et al*, 2001). In the absence of evidence supporting concerns that postmenopausal pregnancy will be harmful to children conceived through its use, the case for its prohibition seems weak.

Alongside concerns for the welfare of the potential child it is, of course, also important that the physical safety of a postmenopausal woman seeking to become pregnant and bear a child should be assured. The usual screening, checks and tests associated with 'normal' pregnancies tend to be redoubled in the case of artificially induced pregnancy, but because of the perceived risks of pre-eclampsia, hypertension and other complications associated with pregnancy and birth in older women, these are likely to be more stringently applied here. Indeed, there is an argument that because 'older women are such unusual candidates for fertility treatment . . . the screening and assessment they receive vastly exceeds that provided for younger women' (Fisher and Sommerville, 1998, p 212). That being so, it is difficult to conclude that postmenopausal women who seek pregnancy through ART should be denied on medical grounds.

With regard to the provision of healthcare services more generally, individual choice founded on the key ethical principle of autonomy plays a central role in determining what facilities are made available. Within established confines of clinical need and the therapeutic encounter, patients are encouraged to be self-determining in the doctor–patient partnership so that, according to Beauchamp, aside from matters of resource allocation, the circumstances in which individual autonomy should be constrained are limited to those where 'an individual's choices endanger the public health, (or) potentially harm another party' (Beauchamp, 1999 (parenthesis added)). Having discounted the likelihood of harm to the welfare of the potential child, it is difficult to anticipate who else might suffer such harm as a result of postmenopausal pregnancy as to lead it to be banned. Therefore, aside from the obvious safety and resource limitations, if postmenopausal pregnancy is the only mechanism through which some people can have their perfect child, I cannot envisage circumstances in which the law should legitimately prevent it.

CONCLUSIONS

The concept of the perfect child is inextricably connected to the pejorative terminology of 'designer babies', which implies the making of ethically unacceptable reproductive choices. In addition, to suggest that a child is wanted only if it is perfect and that imperfection will be rejected hints at eugenics and commodification, which may be rightly regarded as the undesirable face of a modern consumer society. Without overtly using the terminology of the perfect child, the contributors to this book consider aspects of human fertilisation and embryology that relate to the quests of those who need to use ARTs to produce their perfect child. Frequently, the arguments revolve around the interaction between reproductive autonomy and self-determination, since it is at this interface that the law tends to intervene to limit choice.

The extent of the legal regulation of reproductive medicine is not only of academic interest but is also relevant to everyone who seeks parenthood or has an interest in the social implications of scientific progress. According to Peterson, the Warnock Report, upon which the Human Fertilisation and Embryology Act 1990 is based, promulgated the position that in the modern age, when medicine treats not only life-threatening conditions but all malfunctions, 'whether childbearing is considered a "wish" or a "need" is irrelevant' (Peterson, 2005, p 31). The current legal position does not reflect this position. It is therefore important to question why the use of reproductive technology differs from other medical interventions to such an extent that it requires specific and proscriptive legislation.

In this age of individual autonomy and choice, and now that most of the procedures involved in artificial reproduction have become commonplace, certainly 'mainstream' and acceptable, it is appropriate to permit these interventions to be negotiated between the patients and doctors concerned, as with other medical treatment. Of course, there exists no defined 'right' to treatment of this type and in a publicly funded healthcare system it cannot be easily argued that any form of therapy be given priority over any other. However, the availability of all effective forms of treatment should be determined according to transparent and legitimate criteria (Riley, Chapter 5 in this volume).

Concerns around the welfare of the potential child are self-evidently important, but the ways in which welfare is interpreted and protected under the 1990 Act and the Code of Practice have been soundly discredited (see Blyth, Chapter 2, and Jackson, Chapter 3, in this volume). Thus, in keeping with arguments and themes that pervade this collection of essays, I argue that there must be sound and transparent reasons for preventing or restricting choice in reproduction (Draper, Chapter 4, Mackenzie, Chapter 9, and Priaulx, Chapter 10, in this volume). The only caveat is that of quality control and quality assurance, such that the techniques must be safe and adequate and appropriate research must be conducted to demonstrate safety and efficacy. The law need only intervene to that extent; otherwise, those who need to use reproductive technologies to produce their perfect child ought properly to be left to decide for themselves on the basis of medical need and through the process of clinical consultation which interventions are best for them and their potential offspring. In some circumstances this may be difficult to achieve; for example, obtaining useful data on risks and benefits associated with postmenopausal pregnancy is likely to prove difficult due to the small number of women becoming pregnant in this age range. Nevertheless, given the controversy associated with pregnancy in older women, it is imperative here, as in relation to any medical treatment, that good evidence is generated to support claims about safety and effectiveness.

REFERENCES

Beauchamp, TL (1999) 'Ethical theory in bioethics' in Beauchamp, TL and Walters, L (eds) *Contemporary Issues in Bioethics*, 3rd edn Wadsworth, pp 1–32

BioNews (2005) 'Older father link to birth defects', 21 July www.bionews.org.uk/new.lasso?storyid=2663

Brazier, M (1999) 'Regulating the reproduction business' 7 *Medical Law Review* 166

Buchanan, A, Brock, D, Daniels, N and Winkler, D (2000) *From Chance to Choice, Genetics & Justice* Cambridge: Cambridge University Press

Department of Health (2005) *Review of the Human Fertilisation and Embryology Act: A Public Consultation* London: HMSO

Farsides, B and Dunlop, RJ (2001) 'Is there such a thing as a life not worth living?' 322 *British Medical Journal* 481

Fisher, F and Sommerville, A (1998) 'To everything there is a season? Are there medical grounds for refusing fertility treatment to older women?' in Harris, J and Holm, S (eds) *The Future of Human Reproduction* Oxford: Oxford University Press

Foggo, D and Rogers, L (2006) 'Fertility experts urge end to "selfish" late motherhood' *The Times*, 9 July http://www.timesonline.co.uk/article/0,,2087–2261943,00.html

Golombok, S, MacCallum, F and Goodman, E (2001) 'The "test-tube" generation: parent–child relationships and the psychological wellbeing of in vitro fertilisation children at adolescence' 72 *Child Development* 599–608

House of Commons Science and Technology Committee (2005) *Inquiry into Human Reproductive Technologies and the Law: 8th Report of Session 2004–5*, HC 491

Human Fertilisation and Embryology Authority (2000) '*Over 50,000 babies born following IVF treatment in the UK since first success in 1978*' Press release, 13 December

Jackson, E (2001) *Regulation Reproduction* Oxford: Hart Publishing

Ketchum, S (1989) 'Selling babies and selling bodies' 3 *Hypatia* 116

Kovacs, G (1996) 'Assisted reproduction: a reassuring picture' 164 *Medical Journal of Australia* 628–30

Lee, E (ed) (2002) *Designer Babies: Where Should We Draw the Line?* London: Hodder and Stoughton

Lee, RG and Morgan, D (2001) *Human Fertilisation and Embryology: Regulating the Reproductive Revolution* London: Blackstone Press

Mutler, A (2005) 'Children's author becomes oldest woman to give birth' *The Independent Online*, 17 January http://news.independent.co.uk/europe/article15364.ece

NICE (2004) *Fertility: Assessment and Treatment for People with Fertility Problems* London: RCOG Press

Peterson, MM (2005) 'Assisted reproductive technologies and equity of access issues' 31 *Journal of Medical Ethics* 280–5

Singer, P and Wells, D (1983) 'In vitro fertilisation: the major issues' 9 *Journal of Medical Ethics* 192–5

Teather, D (2002) 'Lesbian couple have deaf baby by choice' *Guardian*, 8 April

Telegraph (2005) 'Groups criticise mother who gave birth at 67' Leader column, 17 January www.telegraph.co.uk/news/main.jhtml?xml=/news/2005/01/17/umother.xml&sSheet=/portal/2005/01/17/ixportaltop.html

The Economist (2001) 'Perfect?' Leader column, 14 April 16

The Sunday Times (2002) 'This is Margarette Driscoll: "Why we chose deafness for our children" ' *The Sunday Times*, 14 April

Verny, T (1994) 'The stork in the lab: biological, psychological, ethical, social and legal aspects of third party conceptions' 9 *Pre- and Perinatal Psychology Journal* 57

Warnock, M (1984) *Report of the Committee of Inquiry into Human Fertilisation and Embryology* Cmnd 9134 London: HMSO

de Wert, G (1998) 'The post-menopause: playground for reproductive technology?' in Harris, J and Holm, S (eds) *The Future of Human Reproduction* Oxford: Oxford University Press, p 223

Zhu, JL, Madsen, KM, Vestergaard, M, Olesen, AV, Basso, O and Olsen, J (2005) 'Paternal age and congenital malformations' 10.1093 *Human Reproduction Online* http://humrep.oxfordjournals.org/cgi/content/abstract/dei186v1

Chapter 2

Conceptions of welfare

Eric Blyth

INTRODUCTION

The UK was one of the first countries to introduce legislation providing a framework for the systematic regulation of assisted conception services, one that has been identified as providing a model regulatory system that other countries may usefully emulate (Blank, 1998). However, the requirement that:

> a woman shall not be provided with treatment services unless account has been taken of the welfare of any child who may be born as a result of the treatment (including the need of that child for a father), and of any other child who may be affected by the birth
> (Human Fertilisation and Embryology (HFE) Act 1990, s 13(5))

is perceived as one of the Act's most controversial provisions. Some critics have argued for its removal from the regulatory framework (see, for example, Jackson, 2002).

In 2005, the UK regulatory body, the Human Fertilisation and Embryology Authority (HFEA), undertook a consultation exercise on the operationalisation of s 13(5) (HFEA, 2005a, b, d); the entire Act has been reviewed by the House of Commons Science and Technology Select Committee (2005) and at the time of writing is under review by the Department of Health (Department of Health, 2005; People Science & Policy, 2006). All three reviews have facilitated the articulation of divergent viewpoints concerning the welfare of the child, and are drawn upon in this chapter.[1]

---

1 Following its review, the HFEA revised its Code of Practice, to take effect from 1 January 2006, implementing a 'more focused interpretation' of the Act's welfare provision to provide a 'reasonable, proportionate, fair and practical system' for undertaking welfare of the child assessments, which should be predicated in a presumption to provide assisted conception services 'unless there is evidence that the child to be born would face a risk of serious medical, physical or psychological harm' (HFEA, 2005d). In evidence to the House of Commons Science and Technology Select Committee, Caroline Flint MP, Minister of State for Public

While the Human Fertilisation and Embryology Bill first presented to Parliament in 1989 contained no explicit provision for safeguarding the welfare of children, and the implementation of s 13(5) has proved problematic, it would be stretching credibility to imagine that s 13(5), or at least an amended version of it, will not feature in any revised legislation. Clearly, no government would wish to be perceived as abandoning an existing commitment to safeguard the welfare of children. Indeed, the then Minister of State for Public Health, Melanie Johnson MP, stated in evidence to the House of Commons Science and Technology Select Committee: 'I believe that the single most important factor is the welfare of the child' (Johnson, 2005), an assertion which – as noted by one of the Committee members (Harris, 2005) – appears to bestow higher priority to the welfare of the child than is actually afforded by s 13(5).

Given the criticisms of s 13(5), this chapter considers whether such sentiments can be translated into workable and fair policies and practices that will better serve the interests of people conceived as a result of assisted conception procedures, or whether they are destined to be little more than comfortable-sounding rhetoric which confounds the efforts of regulators and service providers and does nothing to serve the interests of those it is designed to safeguard. The chapter concludes that there are grounds for retaining an explicit commitment to the interests both of children conceived as a result of assisted conception and, indeed, of any other child who may be affected by the birth, but that the focus of s 13(5) should be redirected from imprecise requirements to take account of children's welfare towards a more explicit focus on protecting them from foreseeable significant harm.[2]

THE HFE ACT AND THE WELFARE OF THE CHILD – A SALUTARY TALE OF GOOD INTENTIONS?

To understand current issues concerning s 13(5), it is necessary to consider the origins of the HFE Act's welfare of the child requirement and how legislators expected their intentions to be implemented in practice.

For practical convenience, I will start this brief historical foray with the Report of the Warnock Committee, appointed by the Government in 1982 to 'consider recent and potential developments in medicine and science related

---

Health, indicated that the Government was wondering whether a case still existed to retain the 'need for a father requirement' (Flint, 2006) – see also later discussion.

2 Since this chapter was first drafted, such a refocusing has been recommended by the House of Commons Science and Technology Select Committee (2005, p 107), and the HFEA in its proposals for 'welfare assessments' to be undertaken by treatment centres within the current legislative framework (HFEA, 2005d).

to human fertilisation and embryology; to consider what policies and safe-guards should be applied, including consideration of the social, ethical and legal implications of these developments; and to make recommendations' (Department of Health and Social Security, 1984).

Arguably, the Committee's Report, and subsequent debate, gave more consideration to the status and interests of embryos than to children; the Report's only specific references to the welfare of children concerned surrogacy arrangements (which most members considered were inherently inconsistent with a regard for the child's welfare) and its view that it would be 'morally wrong' deliberately to create single-parent families. But while the Committee asserted that children generally fared better living in a two-parent heterosexual household, it shied away from prescribing criteria for the assessment of potential parents on the grounds that it would not be possible to 'draw up comprehensive [social] criteria that would be sensitive to the circumstances of every case' (Department of Health and Social Security, 1984: 2.13; 13.5).

In response to the Warnock Report, the Government published a Consultation Paper (Department of Health and Social Security, 1986), followed by a White Paper (Department of Health and Social Security, 1987). The sole explicit reference to the welfare of children in either of these documents was in the latter's discussion of surrogacy arrangements, which noted: 'it is widely accepted that the interests of the child are paramount' (Department of Health and Social Security, 1987, p 12) – although providing no further discussion on how this might be reflected in either regulation or practice. (It should be noted that, as regards surrogacy arrangements, very soon after publication of the Warnock Report, Parliament passed the Surrogacy Arrangements Act 1985 – a 'rapid response' measure prohibiting certain activities concerned with commercial surrogacy arrangements in the light of the so-called 'Baby Cotton' case (Cotton and Winn, 1985) – although this made no reference to the welfare of children either). Echoing Warnock, the White Paper expressed the Government's view that it was neither appropriate nor practical to devise a statutory procedure to establish criteria for eligibility to assisted conception services (Department of Health and Social Security, 1987, p 77).

In a lecture delivered in 1987, Baroness Warnock made explicit the Committee's difficulty in trying to get to grips with the concept of the welfare of the child: the first public acknowledgement that omission of a clear steer from the Committee had been deliberate:

> When we called on the good of the child as our justifying principle, we were as often as not attempting to prop ourselves up by clutching at something about to give way . . . if we do make such judgements for the sake of the child we are hard put to it to support them by factual evidence. We are surreptitiously making moral judgements.
>
> (Warnock, 1987, pp 20–21)

In hindsight, history might have taken a different turn had the Warnock Committee itself articulated the problems both of conceptualising and operationalising a child welfare principle, rather than Baroness Warnock sharing them three years later with an audience composed mostly of social workers and other welfare professionals, or had these concerns been raised in parliamentary debate during the passage of the HFE Bill in 1989 and 1990. At least, the Government and legislators would have been warned that comfortable-sounding rhetoric might be less effective in practice. As it was, the HFE Bill presented to the House of Lords in 1989 made no explicit reference to the welfare of the child at all.

At this point, it is necessary to backtrack a little in time in order to provide a more thorough contextualisaton of how what emerged as s 13(5) came to be included in the legislation (while also acknowledging that any such account and analysis are necessarily limited by reliance on information that is in the public domain). When the Warnock Committee was established, it invited submission of evidence from interested parties. One such group had been the All Party Lords and Commons Family and Child Protection Group; in its evidence, the Group claimed that 'the interests and well being of any possible child must be the *principal* consideration' (All Party Lords and Commons Family and Child Protection Group, 1983 – my emphasis). Further, the All Party Group made reference to 'the undesirability from the child's point of view of making AID[3] available to single women, whether unmarried, widowed or divorced, and lesbians'. While the Warnock Committee chose not to incorporate the All Party Group's views in its own recommendations, the Group's members, of course, had a further opportunity to influence the final shape of the legislation as it proceeded through Parliament. At the time, Jill Knight MP was both Chairman of the All Party Group and a member of the House of Commons Standing Committee that undertook detailed consideration of the HFE Bill; it was during the Committee stage that – after several attempts to compose an amendment that would satisfy at least a majority on the Conservative-dominated Committee – what became s 13(5) emerged. Here it is important to note – particularly with regard to the controversy that s 13(5) has subsequently generated – that the process by which the welfare requirement became incorporated into the Act effectively bypassed all extra-parliamentary debate. Because so little explicit reference to the welfare of children conceived through assisted conception had been made between publication of the Warnock Report in 1984 and introduction of the Bill in 1989, it had not featured as a major issue for debate. And, as I noted earlier, no parliamentarians publicly questioned how the welfare requirement might work in practice.

---

3 AID (artificial insemination by donor) being the conventional term then in use to describe what is now more commonly described as 'donor insemination' or simply 'DI'.

Section 13(5)'s allusion to the All Party Group's initial aspirations meant that it had secured a means of impeding access to assisted conception services by lesbians and single women (especially when taken with s 28 of the HFE Act, which defines situations in which a child would become legally, although, of course, not biologically, fatherless) – even if it was unable to secure the Government's unequivocal endorsement of a complete prohibition.

The Government's decision was based on legal advice that a complete prohibition would risk contravening the European Convention on Human Rights and Fundamental Freedoms, to which the UK was a signatory (Bottomley, 1990),[4] as well as fears that excluded individuals might seek assisted conception services outside the proposed regulatory system, thus placing at risk any child born as a result of unlicensed services (Standing Committee, 1990; Mackay, 1990a). The Government claimed that affording the welfare of the child paramountcy similarly risked contravening the European Convention and in any event could conflict with the rights and welfare of others, not least those of any other child who might be affected by the birth of the child conceived following assisted conception (Standing Committee, 1990).

Once the Government had committed itself to incorporating within the Act a specific requirement to consider children's welfare, ministers (Bottomley, 1990a; Mackay, 1990b) commended a definition of the welfare of the child originally outlined by New Zealand judge Michael Hardie-Boys:

> Welfare is an all-encompassing word. It includes material welfare, both in the sense of adequacy of resources to provide a pleasant home and comfortable standards of living and in the sense of adequacy of care to ensure that good health and due personal pride are maintained. However, while material considerations have their place, they are secondary matters. More important are the stability and security, the loving and understanding care and guidance, the warm compassionate relationship, that are essential for the full development of the child's own character, personality and talents.
>
> (Hardie-Boys, 1981)

What is important to note is that this concept was taken from family law, which requires courts to make decisions regarding the care and upbringing of existing children – indeed, the Lord Chancellor, Lord Mackay, had made similar reference to Hardie-Boys' judgement in parliamentary debate on the then Children Bill (subsequently the Children Act 1989); here, uniquely, it was being applied to children who do not yet exist. (It should be noted that

---

4 However, it was a close call, since an amendment to the Bill in the House of Lords restricting assisted conception services to married couples only was defeated by a single vote: Official Report, House of Lords, 6 February 1990 col 787.

this was not an attempt to afford human rights to embryos, but to anticipate the interests of children once they were born. Such a distinction is inherent throughout the discussion in this chapter.)

Lord Mackay articulated a further connection between the child's welfare and parental circumstances:

> among the factors which clinicians should take into account will be the material circumstances in which the child is likely to be brought up and also the stability and love which he or she is likely to enjoy. Such stability is clearly linked to the marital position of the woman and in particular whether a husband or long term partner can play a full part in providing the child with a permanent family setting in the fullest sense of that term, including financial provision . . . With the child and welfare amendments we have just discussed there is a likelihood that through counselling and discussion with those responsible for treatment [single women seeking assisted conception services] may be dissuaded from having children once they have fully considered the implications of the environment into which their child would be born or its future welfare.
>
> (Mackay, 1990a)

So the Government's intention was clear enough: women without a male partner should be 'discouraged' from conceiving children by means of assisted conception.

Since the HFE Act did not define the welfare of the child, it was left to the HFEA to issue guidance to treatment centres on operationalising the welfare requirement (s 25(2)). However, while the HFEA did not provide a definition either, it is not surprising that guidance contained in its Code of Practice (HFEA, 1992, 1993, 1995, 1998, 2001, 2004a, 2005d) drew heavily on the Government's emphasis on parenting competence and the suitability of those seeking assisted conception services. In particular, it interpreted 'taking account' as undertaking a 'welfare assessment'. So, although the HFEA's guidance has always included assessment of risks of harm to the child, including inherited disorders, transmissible disease and multiple births as sources of risk of harm to children, it does so only in the context of an 'assessment . . . relating to patients' rather than through consideration of the intrinsic characteristics of specific assisted conception procedures – in particular, multiple embryo transfer. The recent revisions to the Code of Practice, while removing 'vague and subjective social questions' and focusing on 'serious harm' to the child, do not change this basic orientation to implementation of s 13(5) (HFEA, 2005e).

The HFEA's guidance to treatment centres on taking account of the welfare of the child changed little between its original formulation in 1992 and 2005. Current guidance outlines both core criteria that centres should consider and additional criteria where (a) donated gametes or embryos are used, (b) the child will have no legal father or (c) the child will be conceived as a result of a surrogacy arrangement.

Given the inherent capacity for discrimination contained in s 13(5), the HFEA has attempted to steer a clear course in its guidance to centres to be even-handed:

- Centres should avoid adopting any policy or criteria that may appear arbitrary or discriminatory (HFEA, 2001: 3.3);[5]
- Centre staff are expected to be aware of the need to show both care and sensitivity in this decision making process (HFEA, 2004a: 3.1);
- Those seeking treatment are entitled to a fair assessment. Treatment centres are expected to conduct the assessment with skill and care, and have regard to the wishes and sensitivities of all those involved (HFEA, 2005d: 3.7);
- Patient(s) are expected to be given the opportunity to respond to adverse comments and objections before a final decision is made (HFEA, 2005d: 3.17);
- Where treatment is refused treatment centres are expected to:
    (i) explain the reasons for such refusal to the woman and, where appropriate, her partner, together with any circumstances which may cause the treatment centre to reconsider its decision and
    (ii) explain any remaining options and
    (iii) explain opportunities for obtaining appropriate counselling (HFEA, 2005d: 3.19).

THE WELFARE OF THE CHILD – A CRITIQUE

While there is some overlap between specific criticisms of s 13(5) – and the welfare of the child concept more generally – the key challenges that have been posed are that it is overly bureaucratic, unnecessary, ineffective, ambiguous, discriminatory and irrelevant. Each of these criticisms is reviewed below. Finally, in this section I consider a largely overlooked element in current debates concerning s 13(5), the requirement to take account of 'any other child who may be affected by the birth'.

In evidence to the Science and Technology Select Committee, Professor Neil McClure estimated that about 7,000 children were born in the UK annually as a result of IVF. With a success rate of one in four, that meant

---

5 This phrase was included in all editions of the Code of Practice up to and including the fifth edition – but is not included in the current, sixth, edition.

approximately 28,000–30,000 welfare of the child assessments – 'a huge amount of work'. He added:

> How often do we identify problems? How often do we stop treatment based on welfare of the child concerns? We reckoned the hit rate . . . was between zero and 0.3 per cent. So we have this draconian procedure which makes us all feel nice and comfortable that we are guaranteeing that children are going to be born into a satisfactory environment . . . There is something radically wrong here in our approach to this.
>
> (McClure, 2004)

The HFEA has confirmed that people are 'rarely turned down' by assisted conception centres for welfare reasons. The main grounds are: medical (because the person requesting services is receiving treatment for cancer or has an infectious disease); psychiatric (because the person requesting services has a mental illness or misuses alcohol or drugs); or social (because a couple requesting services are not living together) (HFEA, 2005a, p 9). McClure's estimated 'hit rate' needs to be interpreted as a ballpark figure rather than as a precise statistic, although the Science and Technology Committee used these figures to suggest that around 10 children annually could be exposed to potential harm if the welfare of the child provision were abolished (House of Commons Science and Technology Select Committee, 2005, p 96). Meanwhile, at a consultation meeting on 10 February 2005 organised by the HFEA as part of its review of guidance on the welfare of the child (HFEA, 2005c), Tony Rutherford, a clinician from Leeds, said that his clinic had come across three previous sex offenders for whom treatment had been refused.

As McClure's comments show, the low prevalence of exclusion has been used to argue that the level of current scrutiny is excessive. Conversely, however, it might be argued that, far from being 'draconian', 'radically wrong' or 'disproportionate to the benefit gained' (HFEA 2005a, p 9), the system is, in principle, working by withholding services from people considered not able properly to undertake the care of a child, and that the effort invested is justified. Consider, for example, the likely implications for the child (self-evidently the principal consideration), the clinic and the integrity of the system as a whole of a single instance in which a child conceived through assisted conception was subsequently subjected to abuse by his or her parents – especially where prior investigation might have indicated the existence of possible risk to the child. While we might conclude that such a child would still have 'a life worth living' (see below for further discussion of this concept), providing assisted conception services in such circumstances seems to me a wholly dubious enterprise.

Claims that the requirement is unnecessary are also made by service providers. In evidence to the Science and Technology Select Committee, both the Royal College of Obstetricians and Gynaecologists (RCOG) and the British

Fertility Society (BFS) considered that spelling out the requirement in legislation or regulations was unnecessary because 'it is good medical practice' (Templeton, 2004a) and 'part of the normal consultation process' (Kennedy, 2004). In other words, doctors are taking account of the welfare of the child already, and need to be told neither to do it nor how to do it. It should be noted that, even before the introduction of statutory regulation in the UK, the Interim Licensing Authority for Human In Vitro Fertilisation and Embryology claimed that it had '*always* said that the welfare of the child must be paramount' (Interim Licensing Authority, 1991, p 87 – my emphasis).[6]

However, in further evidence to the Committee, clinicians and scientists acknowledged that 'good medical practice' may not always be implemented, thus implicitly conceding that it may not always be appropriate to leave professionals to their own devices (see below for further discussion).

Charges of ineffectiveness primarily relate to the Act's requirement that 'account' only needs to be taken of the child's welfare. From this, it may be concluded that any specific decision made by a treatment centre either to offer or withhold services that it justifies by asserting that the welfare of the child has been taken into account is largely immune to effective challenge.

The British Fertility Society (1999) alluded to the ambiguity of the welfare of the child which, in the absence of a definition, had become 'the subject of confusion and debate'. Previously, I have noted that such ambiguity has been used by both advocates and opponents of donor anonymity in assisted conception to argue their case from a child welfare perspective and drawing, in particular, on the United Nations Convention on the Rights of the Child (Blyth, 1998, 2002; Blyth and Farrand, 2004; United Nations Committee

---

6 Anticipating implementation of the Warnock Committee's recommendation to establish a statutory regulator, the Voluntary Licensing Authority for Human In Vitro Fertilisation and Embryology (VLA) was established jointly by the Medical Research Council and the Royal College of Obstetricians and Gynaecologists in 1985. Given considerable opposition – especially by some faith communities and legislators – to Warnock's approval of limited embryo experimentation, the VLA's explicit aim was to ensure that 'all those involved in human in vitro fertilisation will work with the Authority to achieve a consensus view on the acceptability of their programme in order to allay any public anxiety' (Voluntary Licensing Authority, 1986, p 33). In 1989, frustrated at the Government's failure to act on Warnock's recommendations, the VLA re-invented itself as the *Interim* Licensing Authority for Human In Vitro Fertilisation and Embryology (ILA). The reference to the ILA's endorsement of the welfare of the child was made in response to publication of the HFEA's draft Code of Practice. In fact, this claim is hard to substantiate since the VLA/ILA had made first reference to the welfare of the child only in its fourth annual report (Voluntary Licensing Authority, 1989) – and this was in respect of ethics committee deliberations rather than clinical practice. The VLA/ILA never specified the need to take account of the welfare of the child in its guidelines for clinical practice.

on the Rights of the Child, 1993, 1994a, b, 1995, 2002; Government of Norway, 2002).

I have already made reference to s 13(5)'s (at least implicit) potential for discrimination in respect of marital status and sexual orientation by inclusion of the 'need for a father' requirement. Early studies of the operation of s 13(5) indicated that women were being refused services by some centres on the grounds not only of marital status and sexual orientation but also on those of age, although other centres were willing to offer a service in similar circumstances; thus, welfare assessments undertaken in different centres were resulting in quite different outcomes (see, for example, Douglas, 1993; Blyth, 1995). Given that studies undertaken before implementation of the HFE Act reported similar practices, it may be that the Act did not fundamentally change the way in which centres were operating (see, for example, Steinberg, 1986; Douglas, 1992; Douglas and Young, 1992). While the HFEA does not cite a woman's marital status or sexual orientation as a reason for the refusal of assisted conception services on welfare grounds (HFEA, 2005d), support/campaign groups for single women and lesbians report that these constitute continuing grounds for discrimination (see, for example, Saffron, 2004), and it is at least questionable whether the child's 'need for a father' is compatible with the spirit of more recent legislation such as the Adoption and Children Act 2002 (England and Wales) and the Civil Partnerships Act 2004, which have expressly outlawed discrimination on the basis of marital status or sexual orientation. However, it is important to note that there is still evident support for an eligibility test on the basis of a woman's marital status or sexual orientation (see, for example, All-Party Parliamentary Pro-life Group, 2004; Catholic Bishops' Conference of England and Wales and the Linacre Centre for Healthcare Ethics, 2004;[7] Church of England Community and Public Affairs Unit, 2004).[8]

A more fundamental claim of discrimination inherent in s 13(5) is that it selects out for special treatment (that is, pre-conceptual assessment of parenting ability) those people who are unable to conceive without medical assistance (or, even more insidiously, those who have no fertility problem themselves but whose partner does) – an imposition that is not placed on the fertile population, even those with a history of proven child abuse. Furthermore, assessment of parenting capacity is not made on the basis of the actual needs of an existing child but on the assumed needs of a child-yet-to-be-born when there are no reliable and accepted measures for predicting future parenting capacity (see, for example, Jackson, 2001, 2002). In fact, s 13(5) is even

---

7 The Catholic Bishops' Conference of England and Wales and the Linacre Centre for Healthcare Ethics similarly also disapproved of the posthumous use of gametes or embryos because death terminated the marriage relationship.

8 However, as noted above, the Government appears to be considering whether such a requirement should be retained in revised legislation.

more focused, since it applies only to those seeking a procedure that is licensed under the HFE Act or any procedure provided by a licensed treatment centre. In addition to marital status and sexual orientation, which the Government clearly intended to be taken into account, other potential 'contraindications' of eligibility for assisted conception services that have been identified include: 'advanced' maternal age; a serious mental health condition; a life-threatening illness; a significant learning or physical disability; alcohol or drug misuse; conviction for a sexual or violent crime; child protection measures taken regarding an existing child or children (see, for example, Mumford *et al*, 1998; Brazier, 2004; Shakespeare, 2004). A recent additional ground for disqualification for donor procedures has been proposed if the prospective parent(s) refuse(s) to enter into a prior commitment to tell their child about his or her conception (Donor Conception Network, 2004).[9]

Those who claim that s 13(5) and the welfare of the child assessment more generally is irrelevant not infrequently also indict it on one or more of the charges already discussed, but go further than others in demanding its wholescale abandonment (see, for example, Jackson, 2001, 2002, also Chapter 3 in this volume; Wilkinson, 2003; Harris, 2004; Savulescu, 2004). Typically, the starting point for these critics is reference to claims to reproductive rights and reproductive autonomy which themselves are based on international conventions, such as the Universal Declaration of Human Rights (United Nations, 1948) and the European Convention on Human Rights and Fundamental Freedoms (Council of Europe, 1950) and national legislation, the Human Rights Act 1998, which enumerate the right to 'respect for private and family life' (UDHR Art 12; ECHR Art 8; HRA s 8) and the right 'to marry and found a family' (UDHR Art 16.1; ECHR Art 12; HRA s 12).

However, such rights have not generally been interpreted to support an individual's absolute or 'positive' right to marry anyone he or she chooses, to have children or to receive assistance to conceive a child. O'Neill (2002) also argues that claims to reproductive autonomy have been overstated and fail to take account of the obligation to take responsibility for any ensuing children. The closest that any agreed formulation of rights comes to making a case for a positive right to access to assisted conception is the United Nations' definition of reproductive health:

> Reproductive health is a state of complete physical, mental and social well-being and not merely the absence of disease or infirmity, in all matters relating to the reproductive system and to its functions and processes. Reproductive health therefore implies that people ... have the

---

9 DC Network subsequently acknowledged that such a requirement could not be enforced in practice (Merricks, 2004).

capability to reproduce and the freedom to decide if, when and how often to do so . . . and the right of access to appropriate health-care services that will enable women to go safely through pregnancy and childbirth and provide couples with the best chance of having a healthy infant.

(United Nations, 1994, 7.2)

Thus, many jurisdictions legally restrict those who may marry through the imposition of age limitations, proscribed relationships and prohibitions on same-sex marriages. And no jurisdiction formally affords a legal right to anyone to have a child, either through natural conception or by means of assisted conception. Consequently, it is generally accepted that a person's wish to conceive and rear a child is a 'negative' right; so, while this obligates no one to provide the means or services by which the right may be actively pursued, it should be free from unjustifiable external interference, whether from the State or anyone else (see, for example, Ethics Committee of the American Society for Reproductive Medicine, 2004). From this perspective, it is argued that the only appropriate basis for restricting adults' procreative autonomy is that of serious harm to others. Reference to John Stuart Mill's (Mill, 1859) claim that '[t]he only purpose for which power can rightfully be exercised over any member of a civilised community against his will is to prevent harm to others' is frequently made in this regard and, at face value, the prevention of 'harm to others' – in this case the child – would allow for some form of 'welfare test'. However, the rationale for any such test is undermined by the assertion that there are hardly any circumstances into which a child could be born that would make him or her better off by not having been born in the first place:

Since reproductive technologies select which children will come into existence, even if those children have worse lives than average, that is not a reason to restrict the technology since they would not have otherwise have existed.

(Savulescu, 2004)

From this perspective, there is only one legitimate welfare question: 'Would this particular child be wronged by allowing him or her to be born?'. To which Harris provides the following answer: 'To give the highest priority to the welfare of the child is always to let that child come into existence, unless existence overall will be a burden rather than a benefit' (Harris, 2004, p 77).

Wilkinson (2003, p 157), arguing from a similar ideological position to that of Harris, claims that preventing the conception of children who 'could be significantly compromised physically or emotionally [is] astonishingly illiberal', which, if it were ever implemented, would amount to something akin to a 'procreative police state'. Wilkinson contemplates the 'logical conclusion' of policies designed to minimise (by reducing to zero) the chances of any child being harmed, which is essentially an argument for discontinuation of the species. Alternatively, if applied selectively, restrictions on the reproductive autonomy of people seeking assisted conception procedures are an 'invidious and opportunistic invasion of [their] privacy' (Jackson, 2002, p 182).

A possible remedy to counter concerns that assisted conception services may be provided to potential child abusers – or others considered 'unsuitable' to undertake the care of a child – and that any resultant child might be placed at risk of harm has been suggested that would not prevent the child's conception and birth. If, in a particular case, a treatment centre had concerns about the care with which a child might be provided, it could notify the social services department, which could then take any necessary action to safeguard the child under child protection legislation – a recommendation made by the House of Commons Science and Technology Select Committee (2005, p 103).

Section 13(5)'s requirement to take account of the welfare of 'any other child affected by the birth' is a much-neglected provision. Until recent revision of the HFEA's Code of Practice, consideration of existing children was confined to 'the effect of a new baby or babies upon any existing child of the family' (HFEA, 2004a: 3.3 (v) (e)) and to treatment being refused if the centre concluded that it would not be in the interests of any other child (HFEA, 2004a: 3.23 (ii)). In relation to surrogacy, the Code of Practice placed an expectation on centres to assess 'where possible' the effect of a proposed surrogacy arrangement on an existing child or children of either the surrogate or of commissioning parents (HFEA, 2004a: 3.16). In its consultation on the operation of s 13(5), the HFEA made no reference to 'any other child' other than to reiterate the relevant references in the HFE Act itself and the Code of Practice and invited no specific comments on it (HFEA, 2005a). Some changes have, nevertheless, been made in the revised welfare provisions which require centres to consider factors that are likely to cause 'serious physical, psychological or medical harm, either to the child to be born or to any existing child of the family', and reference is made in the revised requirements to the care of existing children as a possible guide to assessing future risks (HFEA, 2005d: 3.8). As regards surrogacy, concerns for existing children in the surrogate's family are now restricted to taking account only of the effect of a possible breakdown in the arrangement (HFEA, 2005d: 3.10), although no explanation for apparently reducing the scope for considering the interests of existing children has been provided.

This neglect is reflected in the research community, since no studies appear to have investigated the 'any other child' requirement either. In research on surrogacy arrangements, Blyth (1994) and Jadva *et al* (2003) provide accounts of surrogates' perceptions of their children's responses to the surrogacy arrangement, but no specific research into the impact of a surrogacy arrangement on surrogates' children has been undertaken. Perhaps the 'saviour sibling' phenomenon (discussed below) will generate fresh interest in the 'any other child' consideration.

SO IS A CHILD WELFARE REQUIREMENT NECESSARY?

The libertarian promotion of reproductive autonomy renders any 'welfare test' redundant. Children's interests are always best served by being conceived and born, since non-existence can never be better than existence. A countervailing approach is that children's welfare can be promoted by preventing the birth of some children in some circumstances. Advocates dispute that this harms the child who has not yet been conceived: 'By not bringing them into being we do no harm to a child, since none exists' (Brazier *et al*, 1998: 4.28).

This approach takes the view that what sets apart assisted conception from other forms of medical intervention and legitimates consideration of interests in addition to those of the individual or couple seeking assisted conception services – not least a professional responsibility to prevent harm wherever possible – is that the intended outcome is the birth of a child who would otherwise not be born. Consequently, differential treatment and restricting individual reproductive autonomy are justified in principle, although not as rationalisations for arbitrary, capricious or unfair treatment. While the very concept of child welfare invites paternalism, what must not be overlooked is the potential vulnerability of children within assisted conception as the only parties who are unable to consent to the procedure.

At this point, a key limitation on both the conceptualisation and the operationalisation of the welfare of the child principle within the UK context needs to be made explicit. As I illustrated earlier, the exclusive focus on the social and psychological wellbeing of the child was at least understandable, given the messages from government. However, as Lord Mackay acknowledged, welfare also encompasses 'good health'. If the WHO definition of health as 'a state of complete physical, mental and social wellbeing, and not merely the absence of disease or infirmity' (World Health Organisation, undated) is applied (on the basis that this has become a universally accepted definition), it is possible to envisage a considerably different framework for conceptualising the welfare of the child, one that is not focused exclusively or inappropriately on trying to predict future parenting competence. This model of child welfare puts the onus on those providing assisted conception services to do their best not only to ensure the birth of a healthy child but to try to ensure that the circumstances of the child's conception promote his or her health.

So, for example, given what we know about donor-assisted conception and the experiences of people who have been conceived as a result of anonymous donation (see various accounts in Donor Conception Support Group of Australia Inc., 1997; Lorbach, 2003; Daniels, 2004), we might well ask how far anonymous donation is consistent with promotion of the donor-conceived person's health.[10] Here, Feinberg's (1992) notion of the child's right to an 'open future' is helpful:

> the mature adult that the child will become, like all free citizens, has a right to self-determination, and that right is violated in advance if certain crucial and irrevocable decisions concerning the course of his life are made by anyone else before he [*sic*] has the capacity of self-determination himself.
>
> (Feinberg, 1992, p 91)

Feinberg illustrates his argument with examples where parents' rights to control their child's upbringing, to determine their own general lifestyle or to practise their own religion have been constrained by the State because they have been perceived as compromising the child's future interests. In advancing the general principle, Feinberg argues that the child has a right 'to have these future options kept open until he [*sic*] is a fully formed, self-determining adult capable of deciding among them' (Feinberg, 1992, p 77).

So, as regards assisted conception, Feinberg's ideas could be applied to the child conceived through anonymous donor-assisted conception who is destined to have limited (if any) information about his or her donor, other people to whom he or she may be genetically related and genetic history; to the child conceived following intracytoplasmic sperm injection (ICSI) who may have an increased risk of imprinting disorders and reduced future fertility (see, for example, Ponjaert-Kristoffersen *et al*, 2004; Sutcliffe, 2004; Bonduelle *et al*, 2005); and to the child conceived through multiple embryo replacement who may be exposed to increased physical health risks through prematurity, low birth weight and disability and to death (see, for example, European Society for Human Reproduction and Embryology, 2000; Schieve *et al*, 2002) and to the loss of one or more siblings.[11]

The potential relevance of Feinberg's ideas for considering children's interests in assisted conception is illustrated in oral evidence given by some of Britain's foremost scientific and clinical specialists in assisted conception to the House of Commons Science and Technology Committee on 24 November and 8 December 2004.

In the first of these sessions, Professors Henry Leese and Robert Edwards expressed their approval for a 'proceed with caution' approach to the development of technology, while acknowledging that adherence to such an

---

10 Indeed, British government health ministers took the view that donor anonymity was inconsistent with the general welfare of donor-conceived people – a view that led to the abolition of donor anonymity in the UK with effect from April 2005 (Blears, 2003; Johnson, 2004).

11 While there have been studies of twin bereavement and loss (see, for example, Woodward (1998)), I have been unable to locate any research into the psychological impact of surviving foetal reduction.

approach has not always been evident. According to Leese, '. . . there is general recognition the evidence base is not as robust as it should be. The field has been largely techniques driven . . . and the underlying science has to catch up, and we were struggling against the lack of good evidence, of safety and efficacy' (Leese, 2004). Edwards described the 'accidental' discovery of ICSI '. . . and within three months it was crossing the world . . . I was amazed that it worked – I still am but it does work. There was never any foresight in what might happen to that' (Edwards, 2004).

The health and development of children conceived as a result of ICSI are now being systematically followed up through collaborative multicentre international studies (see, for example, Barnes et al, 2004; Sutcliffe, 2004; Ponjaert-Kristoffersen et al, 2004; Bonduelle et al, 2005). However, in practice, ICSI has become a standard procedure for male factor infertility, as well as being routinely used in the absence of a diagnosis of male factor infertility (Centers for Disease Control and Prevention, 2005), while still subject to ongoing evaluation.

Furthermore, Edwards' charge of a lack of 'foresight' applies not only to ICSI. Both IVF and DI were introduced, and have been routinely practised, with no attempt to undertake any effective evaluation of their long-term health outcomes until comparatively recently. The prevalence of IVF is such that it accounts for approximately 1 per cent of all children born in the UK – and for an even higher proportion of total births in Nordic countries – 3.9 per cent of all births in Denmark, 3.2 per cent of all births in Sweden, 2.8 per cent of all births in Iceland and 2.4 per cent of all births in Finland (Andersen et al, 2005).

DI has been practised for years without any attempt to evaluate its outcomes. Indeed, for much of its history, accepted medical 'wisdom' was that any potential adverse outcomes were best avoided by keeping recourse to DI secret. Until 1987, prospective recipients of DI in the UK were being advised: 'unless you reveal [DI conception] to your child, there is no reason for him or her ever to know that he or she was conceived by donor insemination' (Royal College of Obstetricians and Gynaecologists, 1987, p 3). This is hardly an approach that is either supported by, or enhances, evidence-based practice; over a century since the medical use of DI was first reported, the lack of evidence on which to establish policies that command broad community acceptance (the preservation or removal of donor anonymity is a case in point) remains a major difficulty. As regards more recent, high-tech assisted conception procedures, few children conceived through these have yet reached maturity and even fewer have themselves become parents. Consequently, the long-term impact of assisted conception procedures on children – and certainly any intergenerational implications of manipulation or cryopreservation of gametes and embryos, and the use of 'sub-optimal' sperm – remains unknown (see also Brinton et al (2004) for a recent discussion on the possible susceptibility to cancer of children conceived through assisted conception).

In its session on 8 December 2004, the House of Commons Science and Technology Committee heard evidence from two fertility specialists, Professor Alan Templeton (President of the Royal College of Obstetricians and Gynaecologists) and Professor Lesley Regan (former member of the Royal College of Obstetricians and Gynaecologists Scientific Advisory Committee). In an earlier part of his evidence, Templeton had described focus on welfare of the child assessments as 'a distortion of clinical practice . . . All the time it was going on, of course, we were having multiple births – triplet births and so on – around the country, *and if you want to talk about the welfare of the child start talking about 28-weekers being born in triplet births*' (Templeton, 2004b, my emphasis).

Dr Evan Harris MP subsequently asked why the HFEA had taken so long to limit embryo transfer if welfare of the child issues had been 'so obvious'. Templeton replied:

> Do not ask me. I have been writing about it since 1995. The RCOG guideline in 1996 recommended two embryos, and the BFS guidelines at that time. It has taken until two years ago for the HFEA to catch up with what was recommended clinical practice . . . I think it is a big issue and I think we have to ask ourselves why it did not happen more quickly. Certainly the HFEA could have made it happen more quickly but I think they were very concerned about legal challenges; they were very concerned that there was a society view out there that patients were willing to take the risk. That was quite erroneous, in my view.
>
> (Templeton, 2004c)

Regan (2004) added that one of the reasons for the delay in limiting multiple embryo transfer had been 'an enormous drive from the private funding sector', an assessment supported by Jones and Cohen (2004), who note that the prevalence of multiple embryo transfer is a particular problem in the United States – where assisted conception services are largely unregulated (except for professional guidance issued by the American Society for Reproductive Medicine) and are exclusively provided by profit-making enterprises. Of children born in the United States in 2001 following IVF, ICSI, GIFT and ZIFT, 54 per cent were multiple births, compared with 3 per cent in the general population during the same period. The twin rate was 45 per cent, 15 times higher than in the general population (3 per cent); the triplet and higher order multiples rate was 8 per cent, 42 times higher than in the general population (0.2 per cent). These procedures accounted for 16 per cent of America's multiple births, 14 per cent of all twin births and 42 per cent of all triplet and higher order multiple births (Wright *et al*, 2004). Jones and Cohen conclude that 'the problem has yet to be solved, particularly in the United States where factors on the part of the patient and the ART program seem to require acceptance of an undesirably high multiple pregnancy rate' (Jones and Cohen, 2004, S22).

So there is substantial evidence from the testimony of leading clinicians and scientists that considerations other than the interests of children conceived through therapeutic interventions have been the major drivers of technological development; arguably, whether they have been good for children (and the fact that so far, at least, there have been few reported misadventures as a result of the technology *per se*) has had more to do with chance than purposeful strategy.

The rate of technical development since passage of the HFE Act has been considerable. As a consequence, procedures that might have appeared at the time destined to remain within the domain of science fiction (if indeed they were ever contemplated at all) now appear considerably less implausible. The technology now exists to create new life from ovarian or testicular tissue and by using eggs from aborted foetuses, which carry considerable potential implications for any individual were he or she to be conceived as a result of their use. Two fairly recent uses of technology have generated considerable debate – including child welfare issues – preimplantation genetic diagnosis (PGD) and Human leucocyte antigen (HLA) tissue-typing, which allows the conception of a so-called 'saviour sibling'.

PGD allows an embryo to be tested for a number of conditions and so has potential therapeutic value in identifying embryos that might have a life-threatening inherited condition – especially where there is a family history (more details of the procedures involved are given by Buxton, Chapter 5 in this volume). Currently, the more esoteric characteristics for which an embryo could be screened – thus giving rise to the (emotive and misleading) phenomenon of the so-called 'designer baby' – remain theoretical, but that is not to say they always will be. Furthermore, PGD could be used to screen out disabling conditions that are not life-threatening. This possibility raises major ethical issues, but discussion of these is clearly beyond the scope of this chapter. PGD does enable the sex of an embryo to be determined; consequently, a particular embryo could be implanted – or discarded – on the basis of its sex alone. While the HFEA has permitted sex selection on medical grounds to prevent the conception of a child with a life-threatening or life-shortening condition, it has consistently refused to permit PGD for selecting the sex of an embryo for social reasons only – for example for 'family balancing' – a policy that appears to command majority public support (HFEA, 2004b). So, while medical reasons are privileged, there will be continuing debate on distinguishing between 'serious' and 'minor' conditions as technology allows the detection of an ever-increasing number of characteristics in early-stage embryos.

I have previously referred to the neglect of the 'any other child' requirement in s 13(5) – a clause that appears ready made for 'saviour siblings'. HLA tissue-typing enables embryo selection for implantation on the basis that the resulting child could become a donor of umbilical cord blood stem cells for treating an existing sibling with a life-threatening illness. In principle, the new child could also become a donor of bone-marrow, tissue or organs. The varying views on the acceptability of conceiving a 'saviour sibling', which has clear child welfare considerations, have been illustrated by the way in which the different instances have been handled in the UK (BBC News Online, 2003, 2004a, b). Space precludes a discussion of the ethics of 'saviour siblings'. These are more fully explored in – for example – Robertson *et al* (2002); Pennings (2004); Sheldon and Wilkinson (2004).

Here I will limit my observations to highlighting the importance of welfare of the child considerations – and in particular the formulation of s 13(5) – in respect of 'saviour siblings': first, concern for the welfare of 'any other child'; second, that there are existing children whose welfare can be taken into account;[12] and third, the conception of children for the specific purposes of tissue-matching and acting as a donor for another person (whether in practice this is another child or an adult).

What I have attempted to show in this section is that there are distinct medical and psychosocial risk factors for children associated with assisted conception procedures that justify the establishment of explicit legislative and regulatory requirements to protect children from harm. In the final section of this chapter, I make some proposals as to how these might be framed.

PROTECTING CHILDREN FROM HARM – A REVISED FRAMEWORK

Unlike the HFE Act, the ideological base underpinning current and proposed legislation regulating assisted conception in some other countries is identified in key principles. Legislation in Canada, New Zealand, South Australia, Victoria and Western Australia, and proposed legislation in New South Wales specify 'principles', 'objects' or 'purposes and principles', which contain references to children's 'welfare' (Reproductive Technology Act 1988: South Australia; Human Reproductive Technology Act 1991: Western Australia); children's 'welfare and interests' (Infertility Treatment Act 1995: Victoria); children's 'health and well-being' (Assisted Human Reproduction Act 2004: Canada); children's 'interests' (Assisted Reproductive Technology Bill 2003: New South Wales); and children's 'health and well-being' (Human Assisted Reproductive Technology Act 2004: New Zealand).

While there is insufficient space to discuss the detail of any such guiding principles that might be used to draft revised legislation for the UK, it will need to be consistent with the European Convention on Human Rights and Fundamental Freedoms (as required by the provisions of the Human Rights

---

12 As was acknowledged by Manse LJ in *R (Quintavalle) v Human Fertilisation and Embryology Authority* [2003] EWCA Civ 667 at 122 and 133.

Act 1998) – and, as I have shown, the Government took legal advice on the implications of the European Convention when drafting s 13(5) in the first place. That much the Government is obliged to do. Another key international convention to which the Government is formally committed – and which provides an almost global agreement on basic principles – is the United Nations Convention on the Rights of the Child. The UN Convention's principal requirement is that:

> In all actions concerning children, whether undertaken by public or private social welfare institutions, courts of law, administrative authorities or legislative bodies, the best interests of the child shall be a primary consideration.
>
> (Art 3,1)

It follows from this that any action undertaken by public or private social welfare institutions, etc. that disregarded the rights outlined in the Convention would, by definition, contravene the child's 'best interests', and although the UK is not obligated to have regard to the UN Convention in the same way as the European Convention, internal and external scrutiny on implementation of the Convention mean that any action inconsistent with the Convention is likely to be highlighted, as occurred previously in respect of donor anonymity (United Nations Committee on the Rights of the Child, 2002). It is also worth noting that the National Assembly in Wales has formally adopted the UN Convention as a basis for policy-making on matters affecting children and young people (Davidson, 2004).

Although the Convention itself uses the imprecise term 'best interests', it moves a step closer to fleshing out what the child's 'best interests' mean in practice by linking these to a list of specified rights. At the same time, a rights-based approach itself moves away from the indeterminacy, subjectivity and emphasis on children's dependence on adults to define their needs that are inherent in notions of children's 'welfare' and 'best interests'.

Some general principles that follow from the Convention afford all children the right to protection against discrimination, either against oneself or one's parents (Art 2); to life, survival and development (Art 6); as far as possible, to know and be cared for by his or her parents (Art 7); to preservation of his or her identity (Art 8); and to the highest attainable standard of health (Art 24).

Further provisions in the Convention identify the central responsibilities of parents (or substitute carers) to include the provision of a safe, loving and secure family environment (Preamble); the provision of appropriate guidance and direction to a child in the exercise of his or her rights (Art 5); an obligation to ensure a child's best interests (Art 18(2)); an obligation to ensure the child's upbringing and development (Art 18(2)); protection against harm (Art 19); and the 'primary obligation' to secure, within their abilities and financial capacities, the conditions of living necessary for the child's development

(Art 27(2)), including the provision of adequate nutrition, clothing and housing (Art 27(3)).

It should be noted that the Convention does not require that the best interests of the child must be the primary consideration; and so the HFE Act's current emphasis, which allows the interests of others – including other children, and in particular sick children for whom the new child may be an intended donor – to be given consideration also, maintains a balance that should be retained.

With the two Conventions forming a basis for establishing some guiding principles, we can then begin to flesh out some general expectations that would be consistent with protecting children's rights as outlined in the UN Convention. In particular, it will be possible to identify on the basis of empirical evidence some factors that may compromise potential parents' capacity to safeguard the rights of any children for whom they may have a responsibility.

For a start, this means we can discount those factors that in themselves are known to have no bearing on parenting competence – marital status and sexual orientation. The current 'need for a father' requirement in s 13(5) is anachronistic, out of tune with the reality of contemporary family life, inconsistent with recent legislation that has explicitly proscribed discrimination on the grounds of marital status or sexuality and has no foundation in available empirical evidence. If the Government wishes to prevent single women and lesbians from accessing assisted conception services, then it must justify this by reasons other than using the child's interests or rights as convenient, but disingenuous, cover.

The key safety provision in revised legislation should be the avoidance of foreseeable, significant harm to the child. An important philosophical element in this formulation is that the child, and not his or her parent(s), is the focus of decision-making. Such a requirement should include reference to the safety of the proposed procedure and should form the only basis on which assessment of the circumstances into which any child would be born should be undertaken. This means that issues that comprise part of the current welfare assessment that are more properly considered to be supportive and educational functions in assisting people to prepare for what may be fairly unconventional forms of parenthood would be removed from the assessment framework altogether. This should not be taken to mean that centres should not be providing this support, only that it should not be part of a welfare assessment process.

Assessment of parenting competence itself would be placed on the same footing as current standards in child protection; it should be transparent, non-discriminatory, non-arbitrary and based on evidence. Where a decision is made not to offer a service (whether on the grounds of predicted harm to the child or for any other reason), the centre should have in place a system for review or appeal independent of the individual(s) making that decision, thus extending the provisions already identified by the HFEA when treatment is refused (HFEA, 2004a: 3.24). Therefore, there should be no routine intrusive vetting of people seeking assisted conception services for their future child-drearing abilities. Clearly, where the history of the individual(s) seeking assisted conception services reveals evidence of any 'contraindications', a thorough assessment – including the possible risk to any child – should be undertaken. As a matter of principle, each case should be assessed on its intrinsic merits.

This is not to suggest that simply importing child protection practices and procedures will solve all the problems associated with the current welfare assessments. There remains an element of prediction and the risk being assessed is still that to a child who does not yet exist, both of which are imbued with an inevitable uncertainty. Current practice wisdom from child protection is that assessments should be underpinned by 'respectful uncertainty' and 'healthy scepticism' (Laming, 2003, p 205). If the child protection model is to be applied to assisted conception, the Department of Health Social Services Inspectorate offers a useful comment on assessment that probably reflects the ideal better than it does the reality of current practice. Nevertheless, it outlines the relationship that service providers should aim to establish with those seeking services in order to complete a meaningful assessment:

> Assessment is a participatory process. It necessarily involves establishing trust and understanding if meaningful information is to be obtained. The most effective way of achieving understanding may be to enable people to describe their situation in their own words using their preferred language and at their own pace. Assessment should be a process of working alongside people. They should not be passive recipients of a potentially humiliating service.
>
> (Social Services Inspectorate, 1991, p 14)

CONCLUSION

In this chapter I have attempted to provide a detailed critique of the current requirement in the HFE Act for treatment providers to take account of the welfare of the child. I have tried to show that s 13(5) is a product of the political landscape of Britain in the late 1980s and early 1990s – a political landscape that has changed considerably in the intervening period. It is hard to imagine that, were Parliament now proposing to regulate assisted conception for the first time, s 13(5) would retain its present form. I have proposed that while s 13(5) is in need of a fundamental reorientation, it should not be abolished. The interests of children who will be conceived as a result of assisted conception procedures and the interests of other children (and the adults that they will become) demand that these are recognised in legislation.

These interests would be better served in revised legislation that is grounded in the European Convention on Human Rights and Fundamental Freedoms and the United Nations Convention on the Rights of the Child and in which the current requirement to take account of the child's welfare is replaced by a focus on avoiding foreseeable, significant harm.

REFERENCES

All Party Lords and Commons Family and Child Protection Group (1983) *Evidence to the Warnock Committee* London: House of Commons, 3 February

All-Party Parliamentary Pro-life Group (2004) *Memorandum from the All-Party Parliamentary Pro-life Group to the House of Commons Science and Technology Select Committee: Human Reproductive Technologies and the Law*, Appendix 11. Ev 225. In House of Commons Science and Technology Committee (2005) *Human Reproductive Technologies and the Law. Fifth Report of Session 2004–05*. Vol II: Oral and written evidence http://www.publications.parliament.uk/pa/cm200405/cmselect/cmsctech/7/7ii.pdf

Andersen, AN, Gianaroli, L, Felberbaum, R, de Mouzon, J and Nygren, KG (2005) 'Assisted reproductive technology in Europe, 2001. Results generated from European registers by ESHRE' 20 *Human Reproduction* 1158–76

Barnes, J, Sutcliffe, A, Kristoffersen, I, Loft, A, Wennerholm, U, Tarlatzis, B, Kantaris, X, Nekkebroeck, J, Hagberg, B, Madsen, S and Bonduelle, M (2004) 'The influence of assisted reproduction on family functioning and children's socio-emotional development: results from a European study' 19 *Human Reproduction* 1480–7

BBC News Online (2003) ' "Designer baby" ban quashed', 8 April http://news.bbc.co.uk/1/hi/health/2928655.stm

BBC News Online (2004a) 'Brother's tissue "cures" sick boy', 20 October http://news.bbc.co.uk/1/hi/health/3756556.stm

BBC News Online (2004b) 'Mother carrying "designer baby" ', 29 November http://news.bbc.co.uk/1/hi/northern_ireland/4050989.stm

Blank, R (1998) 'Regulation of donor insemination' in Daniels, K and Haimes, E (eds) *Donor Insemination: Social Sciences Perspectives* Cambridge: Cambridge University Press

Blears, H (2003) Keynote speech to the Human Fertilisation and Embryology Authority Annual Conference, Royal College of Surgeons, London, 28 January

Blyth, E (1994) 'I wanted to be interesting. I wanted to be able to say "I've done something interesting with my life": interviews with surrogate mothers in Britain' 12 *Journal of Reproductive and Infant Psychology* 189–98

Blyth, E (1995) 'The United Kingdom's Human Fertilisation and Embryology Act 1990 and the welfare of the child: a critique' 9 *International Journal of Children's Rights* 417–38

Blyth, E (1998) 'Donor assisted conception and donor offspring rights to genetic origins information' 6 *International Journal of Children's Rights* 237–53

Blyth, E (2002) 'Information on genetic origins information in donor-assisted conception: is knowing who you are a human rights issue?' 5 *Human Fertility* 185–92

Blyth, E and Farrand, A (2004) 'Anonymity in donor-assisted conception and the UN Convention on the Rights of the Child' 12 *International Journal of Children's Rights* 89–104

Bonduelle, M, Wennerholm, U-B, Loft, A, Tarlatzis, BC, Peters, C, Henriet, S, Mau, C, Victorin-Cederquist, A, Van Steirteghem, A, Balaska, A, Emberson, JR and Sutcliffe, AG (2005) 'A multi-centre cohort study of the physical health of 5-year-old children conceived after intracytoplasmic sperm injection, in vitro fertilization and natural conception' 20 *Human Reproduction* 413–19

Bottomley, V (1990) *Official Report*, House of Commons, 20 June col 1030

Brazier, M (2004) *Minutes of Evidence taken before the House of Commons Science and Technology Select Committee: Human Reproductive Technologies and the Law*, 27 October. Ev 119. In House of Commons Science and Technology Committee (2005) op cit

Brazier, M, Golombok, S and Campbell, A (1998) *Surrogacy: Review for Health Ministers of Current Arrangements for Payments and Regulation – Report of the Review Team* London: The Stationery Office

Brinton, L, Kjær, S, Thomsen, B, Sharif, H, Graubard, B, Olsen, J and Bock, J (2004) 'Childhood tumor risk after treatment with ovulation-stimulating drugs' 81 *Fertility and Sterility* 1083–91

British Fertility Society (1999) 'Recommendations for good practice – welfare of the child' 2 *Human Fertility* 85

Catholic Bishops' Conference of England and Wales and the Linacre Centre for Healthcare Ethics (2004) *Memorandum from the Catholic Bishops' Conference of England and Wales and the Linacre Centre for Healthcare Ethics to the House of Commons Science and Technology Select Committee: Human Reproductive Technologies and the Law*, Appendix 38. Ev 319. In House of Commons Science and Technology Committee (2005) op cit

Centers for Disease Control and Prevention (2005) *2003 Assisted Reproductive Technology Success Rates: National Summary and Fertility Clinic Reports* Atlanta, GA: US Department of Health and Human Services Centers for Disease Control and Prevention http://www.cdc.gov/ART/ART2003/PDF/ART2003.pdf

Church of England Community and Public Affairs Unit (2004) *Memorandum from the Church of England Community and Public Affairs Unit to the House of Commons Science and Technology Select Committee: Human Reproductive Technologies and the Law*, Appendix 17. Ev 245. In House of Commons Science and Technology Committee (2005) op cit

Cotton, K and Winn, D (1985) *Baby Cotton: for Love and Money* London: Dorling Kindersley

Council of Europe (1950) *Convention for the Protection of Human Rights and Fundamental Freedoms* Strasbourg: Council of Europe

Daniels, K (2004) *Building a Family with the Assistance of Donor Insemination* Palmerston: Dunmore Press

Davidson, J (2004) *Embedding Children and Young People's Participation across all Assembly Government activity*. December http://www.wales.gov.uk/organicabinet/SubCmteeMeetings/children/papers/cyp(04–05)15.pdf

Department of Health (2005) *Review of the Human Fertilisation and Embryology Act: A Public Consultation* http://www.dh.gov.uk/assetRoot/04/11/78/72/04117872.pdf

Department of Health and Social Security (1984) *Human Fertilisation and Embryology* (The Warnock Report), Cmnd 9314, London: HMSO

Department of Health and Social Security (1986) *Legislation on Human Infertility Services and Embryo Research*, Cm 46, London: HMSO

Department of Health and Social Security (1987) *Human Fertilisation and Embryology: A Framework for Legislation*, Cm 259, London: HMSO

Donor Conception Network (2004) *Memorandum from the Donor Conception Network to the House of Commons Science and Technology Select Committee: Human Reproductive Technologies and the Law*, Appendix 47. Ev 334. In House of Commons Science and Technology Committee (2005) op cit

Donor Conception Support Group of Australia Inc. (1997) *Let the Offspring Speak: Discussions on Donor Conception* Georges Hall, New South Wales: Donor Conception Support Group of Australia Inc.

Douglas, G (1992) 'Access to assisted reproduction: legal and other criteria for eligibility. Report of a survey funded by the Nuffield Foundation' Unpublished report Cardiff: Cardiff Law School

Douglas, G (1993) 'Assisted reproduction and the welfare of the child' in Freeman, M and Hepple, B (eds) 46 *Current Legal Problems* 53–7

Douglas, G and Young, C (1992) 'Findings from a survey of Issue members' unpublished report Cardiff: University of Wales

Edwards, R (2004) *Minutes of Evidence taken before the House of Commons Science and Technology Committee: Human Reproductive Technologies and the Law*, 24 November. Ev 148. In House of Commons Science and Technology Committee (2005) op cit

Ethics Committee of the American Society for Reproductive Medicine (2004) 'Child-rearing ability and the provision of fertility services' 82 *Fertility and Sterility* 564–7

European Society for Human Reproduction and Embryology (2000) 'Capri Workshop Group. Multiple gestation pregnancy' 15 *Human Reproduction* 1856–64

Feinberg, J (1992) 'The child's right to an open future' in Feinberg, J *Freedom and Fulfilment: Philosophical Essays* Princeton: Princeton University Press

Flint, C (2006) Evidence to the House of Commons Science and Technology Committee, 12 July. http//www.parliamentlive.tv

Government of Norway (2002) *Human Rights 2002. Annual Report of Norway's Efforts to Promote Human Rights* 5.8.1. Ministry of Foreign Affairs http://odin.dep.no/filarkiv/196882/Human_Rights

Hardie-Boys, M (1981) 'Walker v Walker and Harrison' *NZ Recent Law* 257 Cited by Law Commission Working Paper No 6 *Custody* (1985) para 6.1

Harris, E. (2005) *Minutes of Evidence taken before the House of Commons Science and Technology Committee: Human Reproductive Technologies and the Law*, 19 January. Ev 185. In House of Commons Science and Technology Committee (2005) op cit

Harris, J (2004) *On Cloning: Thinking in Action* London: Routledge

House of Commons Science and Technology Committee (2005) *Human Reproductive Technologies and the Law. Fifth Report of Session 2004–05*. Vol I http://www.publications.parliament.uk/pa/cm200405/cmselect/cmsctech/7/7i.pdf

Human Fertilisation and Embryology Authority (1992) *Code of Practice* London: HFEA   http://www.hfea.gov.uk/cps/rde/xbcr/SID-3F57D79B-0FA672DF/hfea/1st_Edition_Code_of_Practice_1991.pdf

Human Fertilisation and Embryology Authority (1993) *Code of Practice*, 2nd edn London: HFEA   http://www.hfea.gov.uk/cps/rde/xbcr/SID-3F57D79B-0FA672DF/hfea/2nd_Edition_Code_of_Practice_1993-06.pdf

Human Fertilisation and Embryology Authority (1995) *Code of Practice*, 3rd edn London: HFEA   http://www.hfea.gov.uk/cps/rde/xbcr/SID-3F57D79B-0FA672DF/hfea/3rd_Edition_Code_of_Practice_1995-12.pdf

Human Fertilisation and Embryology Authority (1998) *Code of Practice*, 4th edn London: HFEA   http://www.hfea.gov.uk/cps/rde/xbcr/SID-3F57D79B-0FA672DF/hfea/4th_Edition_Code_of_Practice_1998-07_.pdf

Human Fertilisation and Embryology Authority (2001) *Code of Practice*, 5th edn London: HFEA   http://www.hfea.gov.uk/cps/rde/xbcr/SID-3F57D79B-0FA672DF/hfea/5th_Edition_Code_of_Practice_2001-03_.pdf

Human Fertilisation and Embryology Authority (2004a) *Code of Practice*, 6th edn London: HFEA   http://www.hfea.gov.uk/cps/rde/xbcr/SID-3F57D79B-0FA672DF/hfea/Code_of_Practice_Sixth_Edition_-_final.pdf

Human Fertilisation and Embryology Authority (2004b) *Sex Selection: Options for Regulation* London: HFEA

Human Fertilisation and Embryology Authority (2005a) *Tomorrow's Children: A Consultation on Guidance to Licensed Fertility Clinics on Taking in Account the Welfare of Children to be Born of Assisted Conception Treatment* London: HFEA http://www.hfea.gov.uk/cps/rde/xbcr/SID-3F57D79B-0FA672DF/hfea/consultation_document.pdf

Human Fertilisation and Embryology Authority (2005b) *Tomorrow's Children: Report of the Policy Review of Welfare of the Child Assessments in Licensed Assisted Conception Treatment* London: HFEA http://www.hfea.gov.uk/cps/rde/xbcr/SID-3F57D79B-0FA672DF/hfea/TomorrowsChildren.pdf

Human Fertilisation and Embryology Authority (2005c) *Consultation Meeting: Tomorrow's Children: A Consultation on Guidance to Licensed Fertility Clinics on Taking in Account the Welfare of Children to be born of Assisted Conception Treatment*, 10 February London: HFEA

Human Fertilisation and Embryology Authority (2005d) *New Guidance on Welfare of the Child Assessments* London: HFEA http://www.hfea.gov.uk/cps/rde/xbcr/SID-3F57D79B-0FA672DF/hfea/Revised_Guidance.pdf

Human Fertilisation and Embryology Authority (2005e) 'Improved welfare checks system will be better, fairer and clearer for fertility patients, GPs and clinics' Press release,   2   November   http://www.hfea.gov.uk/cps/rde/xchg/SID-3F57D79B-45C70FD0/hfea/hs.xsl/1113.html

Interim Licensing Authority (1991) *The Sixth Report of the Interim Licensing Authority for Human In Vitro Fertilisation and Embryology* London: Interim Licensing Authority

Jackson, E (2001) *Regulating Reproduction: Law, Technology and Autonomy* Oxford: Hart Publishing

Jackson, E (2002) 'Consent and the irrelevance of the welfare principle' 65 *Modern Law Review* 176–203

Jadva, V, Murray, C, Lycett, E, MacCallum, F and Golombok, S (2003) 'Surrogacy: the experiences of surrogate mothers' 18 *Human Reproduction* 2196–204

Johnson, M (2004) Keynote speech to the Human Fertilisation and Embryology Authority Annual Conference, Royal College of Surgeons, London, 21 January

Johnson, M (2005) *Minutes of Evidence taken before the House of Commons Science and Technology Committee: Human Reproductive Technologies and the Law*, 19 January. Ev 185. In House of Commons Science and Technology Committee (2005) op cit

Jones, H and Cohen, J (2004) 'IFFS Surveillance 04' 81 (5) Suppl 4 *Fertility and Sterility*

Kennedy, R (2004) *Minutes of Evidence taken before the House of Commons Science and Technology Committee: Human Reproductive Technologies and the Law*, 8 December. Ev 168. In House of Commons Science and Technology Committee (2005) op cit

Laming Report (2003) *The Victoria Climbié Inquiry: Report of an Inquiry by Lord Laming* Norwich: The Stationery Office

Leese, H (2004) *Minutes of Evidence taken before the House of Commons Science and Technology Committee: Human Reproductive Technologies and the Law*, 24 November. Ev 147. In House of Commons Science and Technology Committee (2005) op cit

Lorbach, C (2003) *Experiences of Donor Conception: Parents, Offspring and Donors Through the Years* London: Jessica Kingsley Publishers

Mackay, Lord (Lord Chancellor) (1990a) *Official Report*, House of Lords, 6 March col 1098

Mackay, Lord (Lord Chancellor) (1990b) *Official Report*, House of Lords, 6 March col 1097

McClure, N (2004) *Minutes of Evidence taken before the House of Commons Science and Technology Committee: Human Reproductive Technologies and the Law*, 14 June. Ev 12. In House of Commons Science and Technology Committee (2005) op cit

Merricks, W (2004) *Minutes of Evidence taken before the House of Commons Science and Technology Committee: Human Reproductive Technologies and the Law*, 30 June. Ev 32. In House of Commons Science and Technology Committee (2005) op cit

Mill, JS (1859) *On Liberty* Oxford: Oxford University Press (cited in Jackson, 2001 op cit, p 320)

Mumford, SE, Corrigan, E and Hull, MGR (1998) 'Access to assisted conception: a framework of regulation' 13 *Human Reproduction* 2349–55

O'Neill, O (2002) *Autonomy and Trust in Bioethics* Cambridge: Cambridge University Press

Pennings, G (2004) 'Saviour siblings: using preimplantation genetic diagnosis for tissue typing' in Daya, S, Harrison, R and Kempers, R (eds) *Advances in Fertility and Reproductive Medicine: International Congress Series 1266* Amsterdam: Elsevier

People Science & Policy Ltd (2006) *Report on the Consultation on the Review of the Human Fertilisation & Embryology Act 1990* London: People Science & Policy Ltd http://www.peoplescienceandpolicy.com/downloads/DH_consultation.pdf

Ponjaert-Kristoffersen, IT, Tjus, T, Nekkebroeck, J, Squires, J, Verte, D, Heimann, M, Bonduelle, M, Palermo, G and Wennerholm, U-B (2004) 'Psychological follow-up study of 5-year-old ICSI children' 19 *Human Reproduction* 2791–7

Regan, L (2004) *Minutes of Evidence taken before the House of Commons Science and Technology Committee: Human Reproductive Technologies and the Law*,

8 December. Ev 169. In House of Commons Science and Technology Committee (2005) op cit

Robertson, JA, Kahn, J and Wagner, J (2002) 'Conception to obtain hematopoietic stem cells' 32 *Hastings Center Report* 34–40

Royal College of Obstetricians and Gynaecologists (1987) *Donor Insemination* London: RCOG

Saffron, L (2004) *Minutes of Evidence taken before the House of Commons Science and Technology Select Committee: Human Reproductive Technologies and the Law*, 30 June. Ev 43. In House of Commons Science and Technology Committee (2005) op cit

Savulescu, J (2004) *Memorandum from Professor Julian Savulescu to the House of Commons Science and Technology Committee: Human Reproductive Technologies and the Law*, Appendix 62. Ev 359. In House of Commons Science and Technology Committee (2005) op cit

Schieve, LA, Meikle, SF, Ferre, C, Peterson, HB, Jeng, G and Wilcox, LS (2002) 'Low and very low birth weight in infants conceived with use of assisted reproductive technology' 346 *New England Journal of Medicine* 731–7

Shakespeare, T (2004) *Memorandum from Dr Tom Shakespeare to the House of Commons Science and Technology Select Committee: Human Reproductive Technologies and the Law*, Appendix 65. Ev 362. In House of Commons Science and Technology Committee (2005) op cit

Sheldon, S and Wilkinson, S (2004) 'Should selecting saviour siblings be banned?' 30 *Journal of Medical Ethics* 533–7

Social Services Inspectorate (1991) *Getting the Message Across. A Guide to Developing and Communicating Policies, Principles and Procedures on Assessment* London: HMSO; Standing Committee (1990) Official Report, House of Commons Standing Committee B, 15th May

Steinberg, DL (1986) 'Research in progress: a report on policies of access to AID as a medical treatment in the UK' 9 *Women's Studies International Forum* 551–4

Sutcliffe, A G (2004) 'The long-term paediatric outcome of assisted reproductive therapies' in Daya, S, Harrison, R and Kempers, R (eds) *Advances in Fertility and Reproductive Medicine: International Congress Series 1266* Amsterdam: Elsevier

Templeton, A (2004a) *Minutes of Evidence taken before the House of Commons Science and Technology Committee: Human Reproductive Technologies and the Law*, 8 December. Ev 167. In House of Commons Science and Technology Committee (2005) op cit

Templeton, A (2004b) ibid. Ev 168

Templeton, A (2004c) ibid. Ev 169

United Nations (1948) *Universal Declaration of Human Rights* Geneva: United Nations

United Nations (1994) *International Conference on Population and Development. Programme of Action of the UN ICPD: Reproductive Rights and Reproductive Health* Geneva: United Nations

United Nations Committee on the Rights of the Child (1993) *Consideration of Reports Submitted by States Parties Under Article 44 of the Convention: France* CRC/C/3/Add15, 4 June Geneva: United Nations

United Nations Committee on the Rights of the Child (1994a) *Consideration of Reports Submitted by States Parties Under Article 44 of the Convention: Concluding Observations: France* CRC/C/15/Add20, 25 April. Geneva: United Nations

United Nations Committee on the Rights of the Child (1994b) *Consideration of Reports Submitted by States Parties Under Article 44 of the Convention: Concluding Observations: Norway* CRC/C/15/Add23, 25 April. Geneva: United Nations

United Nations Committee on the Rights of the Child (1995) *Consideration of Reports Submitted by States Parties Under Article 44 of the Convention: Concluding Observations: Denmark* CRC/C/15/Add33, 15 February. Geneva: United Nations

United Nations Committee on the Rights of the Child (2002) *Consideration of Reports Submitted by States Parties Under Article 44 of the Convention: Concluding Observations: United Kingdom of Great Britain and Northern Ireland* CRC/C/15/Add188, 9 October. Geneva: United Nations

Voluntary Licensing Authority (1986) *The First Report of the Voluntary Licensing Authority for Human In Vitro Fertilisation and Embryology* London: Voluntary Licensing Authority

Voluntary Licensing Authority (1989) *The Fourth Report of the Voluntary Licensing Authority for Human In Vitro Fertilisation and Embryology* London: Voluntary Licensing Authority

Warnock, M (1987) 'Ethics, decision-making and social policy' 685 *Community Care* 18–23

Wilkinson, S (2003) *Bodies for Sale: Ethics and Exploitation in the Human Body Trade* London: Routledge

Woodward, J (1998) *The Lone Twin: Understanding Twin Bereavement and Loss* London: Free Association Books

World Health Organisation (undated) *Constitution of the World Health Organisation* http://w3.whosea.org/aboutsearo/const.htm

Wright, VC, Schieve, LA, Reynolds, MA, Jeng, G and Kissin, D (2004) 'Assisted Reproductive Technology Surveillance – United States, 2001: surveillance summaries' 53 (SS–1) *Morbidity and Mortality Weekly Report* 1–20 http://www.cdc.gov/mmwr/PDF/SS/SS5301.pdf

Chapter 3

Rethinking the pre-conception welfare principle[1]

Emily Jackson

INTRODUCTION

This chapter is a revised version of an article I wrote some years ago which questioned the prevailing assumption that a principle derived from family law should inform legal involvement in decisions taken prior to a child's conception. The Government's announcement, in January 2004, that it planned a 'root and branch' review of the Human Fertilisation and Embryology Act 1990 offers an opportunity to go back to first principles and consider whether the 'welfare principle' contained in the 1990 Act offers a sensible and effective way to protect children conceived through fertility treatment. In 2005, the Human Fertilisation and Embryology Authority, following a public consultation on the welfare of the child, set out new guidance to clinicians which embodies a 'lighter touch', risk-based approach to assessing the welfare of children. At the time of writing, it remains to be seen whether the Government's proposed new legislation will stick with the status quo or revise the welfare principle. In this chapter, I explain why, for a number of reasons, I believe that substantial revision may be desirable.

In the parliamentary debates leading up to the passage of the Human Fertilisation and Embryology Act in 1990, the inclusion of a welfare principle was neither challenged nor defended. Instead, it was simply assumed to be self-evidently true that their future children's welfare ought to be taken into account before a couple are offered assistance with conception, and this assumption undoubtedly persists today. In this chapter I suggest that there are, in fact, several compelling reasons to reflect critically upon the welfare principle's colonisation of reproductive choice.

Before I begin, some clarification is necessary. I am not concerned here with the question of whether a particular assisted conception technique is *safe* when I acknowledge both that doctors have special expertise in evaluating its

---

1 This is an updated and reworked version of a paper which was published in the *Modern Law Review* in 2002: 'Conception and the Irrelevance of the Welfare Principle' (2002) 65 *Modern Law Review* 176–203.

impact upon future children and that they should be under a duty to take this into account when making treatment decisions. If this were the sole purpose of the pre-conception welfare principle, it would be as uncontentious as basing the decision not to prescribe a particular medicine to pregnant women upon evidence of its propensity to cause birth defects. The welfare principle that I criticise here is not, however, a statutory adaptation of clinicians' common law duty of care. Rather, its principal purpose has been to ensure that prospective patients are judged fit people to bring a child into the world prior to acceptance onto an infertility clinic's treatment programme.

Of course, for the vast majority of people, deciding whether or not to conceive is not susceptible to legal control. People who conceive through heterosexual sexual intercourse do so without any external scrutiny of the merit or otherwise of their decision. Monitoring these exceptionally personal choices in order to identify ill-judged or improper conception decisions would be unreservedly condemned as an unacceptably intrusive abuse of state power because, as Alexander Capron has observed,

> whatever advice one might be justified in giving friends who are making a selfish, rash or otherwise irresponsible choice about reproduction, or whatever moral criticism one might properly mount of such con-duct, the consequences of giving legal effect to a judgment of parental irresponsibility seem unacceptable both for the individuals involved and for society.
>
> (Capron, 1997, p 665)

Certainly, during the second half of the twentieth century, the 'science' of eugenics was resoundingly denounced for its assumption that the State has a legitimate interest in vetting the quality of potential parents.

In this chapter, I largely take for granted that there are good reasons for not imposing a child welfare filter upon the decision to conceive through hetero-sexual intercourse, even when the choice would-be parents have made may seem foolish or disturbing. At the outset, it is worth spelling out precisely what these reasons consist in. I would suggest that there are broadly two different justifications for the presumption that normally exists in favour of privacy in procreative decision-making. First, interfering with a particular individual's decision to conceive a child would usually involve violating their bodily integ-rity and sexual privacy. We do not sterilise people who have been convicted of violent offences against children because, however gruesome their crime, their body must remain inviolate. The second and I would argue equally important reason for respecting people's conception choices is that the freedom to decide for oneself whether or not to reproduce is integral to a person's sense of being, in some important sense, the author of their own life plan. For most people, these two justifications for reproductive privacy mesh together in the requirement that we treat both their body and their life plan with respect.

We should, however, remember that those individuals whose procreative preferences can be disregarded without simultaneously violating their bodily integrity and sexual privacy nevertheless retain their interest in being able to make exceptionally personal and important decisions according to their own conception of the good.

There are a number of strands to my argument. I begin by trying to work out what the pre-conception welfare principle actually means. How could it be possible to base a decision upon whether to try to bring a child into the world upon an assessment of *that child's* best interests? Second, I suggest that it may be unfair to deprive some people of the zone of privacy that surrounds most individuals' reproductive decision-making. Next, I contrast the use of the welfare principle in pre-conception decision-making with the judgments in tort for what have become known as 'wrongful life' actions. I argue that the application of a pre-conception welfare principle sits rather uneasily with the normal judicial presumption that existence must invariably be preferred to non-existence. Finally, I point to the potentially absurd consequences of applying the 'welfare principle' to *any* medical intervention which might assist a couple to conceive. If IVF must be preceded by an assessment of any potential child's future welfare, why not impose the same criteria upon the supply of ovulation predictor kits, or the carrying out of investigations into the causes of a couple's apparent infertility?

Before I explain more fully why I believe that the child welfare filter upon access to fertility treatment is fundamentally problematic, I first describe the mechanism through which this pre-conception welfare principle is currently incorporated into the law.

THE WELFARE PRINCIPLE

In many countries, access to assisted conception services is confined to married or cohabiting heterosexual couples. On the face of it, the British legislation appears far more liberal. The Human Fertilisation and Embryology Act 1990 contains no statutory bars upon the treatment of any competent adult, so single, lesbian or postmenopausal women may all lawfully receive assisted conception services in British clinics.

It would, however, be a mistake to equate the absence of a statutory prohibition upon the treatment of women without male partners with official endorsement of the assisted creation of unconventional families. On the contrary, at the time of the passage of the 1990 Act, there was intense political concern about the social and economic problems believed to result from lone parenthood, and the then Conservative Government had been explicitly pursuing a legislative agenda based upon the promotion of traditional family values. As a result, while the Act may not formally *prohibit* clinics from assisting single or lesbian women to conceive, it does contain an oblique presumption against their treatment through its incorporation of a modified 'welfare principle'.

Section 13(5) of the Human Fertilisation and Embryology Act 1990 provides that:

> a woman shall not be provided with treatment services unless account has been taken of the welfare of any child who may be born as a result of the treatment (including the need of that child for a father) . . .

This section has to be read in conjunction with the rules governing the paternity of children born following assisted conception. Because under s 28 of the 1990 Act children born to single or lesbian women treated in licensed clinics with donated sperm will be legally father*less*, clinics' duty to consider their child's *need for a father* translates into a statutory obligation to take into account the undesirability of single or lesbian motherhood. Compelling criticism could, of course, be mounted of this prevailing presumption, explicit in many other countries and implicit within the UK's regulatory framework, that women without male partners should not have straightforward access to assisted conception services. However, my concern here is not with s 13(5)'s uneven impact upon single or lesbian patients; rather it is with the appeal to children's welfare itself.

When s 13(5) was debated in Parliament, the only matter of contention was the question of single or lesbian women's access to treatment. In contrast, the wisdom of including a welfare principle was never doubted. When he introduced the amendment which became s 13(5), Lord Mackay, the then Lord Chancellor, said:

> A fundamental principle to our law about children . . . is that the welfare of children is of paramount consideration. I think that it is . . . entirely right that the Bill should be amended to add that concept.[2]

The incorporation of a welfare principle was 'greatly welcomed'[3] by every peer who expressed an opinion. Lord McGregor, for example, described it as 'a happy extension of a principle which has now been part of English law for more than half a century'.[4] For Baroness Warnock, it was axiomatic that 'the good of the child . . . must be considered and taken into account'. When the relevant clause came before the House of Commons three months later, a similar consensus was evident. Ann Winterton MP asserted that 'the interests

---

2 HL Deb vol 516 col 1097 6 March 1990.
3 Lord Ennals; Lord McGregor, HL Deb vol 516 col 1100 6 March 1990. See also Lord Robertson, HL Deb vol 516 col 1100 6 March 1990.
4 Lord McGregor, HL Deb vol 516 col 1100 6 March 1990.

of the child in matters of artificial insemination should be paramount'.[5] Virginia Bottomley MP said 'it must be right and proper for consideration to be given to the welfare of [the] child'.[6] Even Jo Richardson MP, who was concerned that the needs of the 'client' should also be relevant, agreed that the clinician ought to 'tak[e] account of the welfare of the child'.[7] Across the political spectrum, then, the assumption appeared to be that because 'we are all concerned with the welfare of the child',[8] we should not hesitate to include a statutory direction to that effect whenever possible. But just because the welfare principle has been judged an appropriate test for deciding, for example, where a child should live after her parents' divorce, it does not necessarily follow that it makes sense to use it to determine whether a child is conceived.

Indeed, it is worth noting that the dominance of the welfare principle within family law itself is not without its critics (Reece, 1996). Section 1(1) of the Children Act makes a child's welfare the courts' paramount consideration in any decision affecting his upbringing, and in recent years criticism has focused upon its potential incompatibility with Art 8 of the European Convention on Human Rights, now incorporated into English law by the Human Rights Act 1998. Article 8 protects every person's right to family life, without setting any *a priori* hierarchy of protected interests. Hence, under the Human Rights Act, children's welfare will not always necessarily take priority over the interests of other family members (Fortin, 1999). David Bonner, Helen Fenwick and Sonia Harris-Short go so far as to suggest that unless parents' interests are given greater weight, the welfare principle itself might be subject to a declaration of incompatibility with the Human Rights Act:

> It could certainly be argued following the implementation of the HRA that the welfare principle, as traditionally understood under English law, would have to be reinterpreted under section 3 to give greater recognition to the parent's interests, failing which, it would probably fall victim to a declaration of incompatibility under section 4.
>
> (Bonner *et al*, 2003, p 575)

But regardless of existing controversy over the legitimacy of the paramountcy principle within family law, the critical difference between s 1 of the Children Act 1989 and the welfare principle under consideration here is that it applies to decisions that affect children who already exist, and who therefore already have interests that can be weighed in the balance when making a decision. Where the Human Fertilisation and Embryology Act's welfare principle

---

5 HC Deb vol 174 col 1021 20 June 1990.   6 HC Deb vol 174 col 1031 20 June 1990.
7 HC Deb vol 174 col 1028 20 June 1990.
8 Lord Ennals, HL Deb vol 516 col 1100 6 March 1990.

differs is that it purports to make a child's best interests relevant to a judgement made *prior to that child's conception*.

But how could a clinician take into account the welfare of any child who might be born following the use of assisted conception and decide, as a result, not to offer treatment to a particular couple or individual? For the purposes of this chapter, I propose to contrast a 'thick' and a 'thin' interpretation of the direction to clinics contained in s 13(5). The thin version of the welfare principle could be used to deny access to infertility treatment only if we can envisage circumstances in which non-existence would be preferable to the life that would be led by these would-be parents' offspring. So, to decide that it would be better not to be born than to have parents such as these is to find that a particular couple or individual present an immediate threat to their offspring so grave that not being conceived could plausibly be considered preferable. It is difficult and perhaps even impossible to imagine what such circumstances might consist in.

Despite being the more literal interpretation of the words in s 13(5), this 'thin' version has not taken hold, and instead it is generally agreed that what I propose to call the 'thick' interpretation obtains. According to the thick version of the welfare principle, the clinic is charged with doing more than simply vetting potential patients to ensure that they reach a minimal level of parental adequacy, judged by whether it could conceivably be better not to exist than to have these people as parents. Rather, the thick interpretation – as proposed in Parliament[9] and set out in the Human Fertilisation and Embryology Authority's previous guidance to clinics – directs clinicians to take into account factors such as the would-be parents' commitment to having and bringing up a child; their ability to provide a stable and supportive environment; their future ability to look after or provide for a child's needs; and the possibility of any risk of harm to their child (HFEA, 2004: 3.12). This, interestingly, looks very similar to the checklist of factors which informs the courts' assessments of children's welfare in care proceedings or disputes over residence and contact arrangements (Children Act 1989, s 1(3)).

The 2005 guidance dilutes this thick interpretation and focuses instead upon whether the potential parents pose a risk to their as yet unconceived child. Clinics are supposed to base the decision to offer treatment upon factors such as whether either prospective patient has ever had any mental health problems; whether they have had a child taken into local authority care; and whether either of them has a criminal record, particularly relating to offences involving violence and/or children. Nevertheless, unlike other people who might be contemplating actions which could lead to the female partner becoming pregnant, anyone who cannot conceive without assistance

9 HL Deb vol 516 col 1098 6 March 1990.

must still have their parental aptitude assessed prior to conception. In what follows I suggest that this is in practice an almost impossible task, and that it is understandably and justifiably resented by many infertile couples.

Ineffective

The most compelling reason to doubt the wisdom of reproducing the substance of s 13(5) in any future legislation is that it is, in practice, incapable of distinguishing between adequate and inadequate parents. If its purpose is to ensure that children are born into families which are likely to offer an acceptably safe and supportive environment, and if it cannot achieve this end, it may be time to rethink whether it is sensible to force clinics and patients to undergo an assessment process which will not in fact improve outcomes for children.

Clinics can only provide the vast majority of assisted conception services if they have a licence granted by the Human Fertilisation and Embryology Authority (HFEA). Licence renewal is contingent upon compliance with both the terms of the legislation and the HFEA's Code of Practice (HFEA, 2004). Clinics that were blatantly ignoring the injunction to consider the child's welfare could therefore face revocation or non-renewal of their licences. Yet, because there is no direct prohibition upon the treatment of specific categories of would-be patient, it would be difficult for a licence committee to decide in any particular case that a clinic had exceeded the discretion that it undoubtedly has to assist any adult to conceive. In practice, to satisfy the HFEA there must be a procedure in place to demonstrate that the welfare of the child has been considered.

But even where the process through which the welfare of the child is evaluated is comparatively rigorous, it is not clear that it will necessarily be able to identify inadequate parents. Infertility clinicians do not receive training in assessing future parenting ability and nor will they have access to the sort of detailed information that might be necessary to make such a complicated assessment. Research consistently demonstrates that better outcomes for children are associated with their parents' warmth, sensitivity and responsiveness (Golombok, 2000). This means that if we are really attempting to enhance the welfare of children through the application of s 13(5), prior to treatment clinicians should be attempting to anticipate the quality of the *relationship* that is likely to develop between this couple or individual and any child that they might conceive.

But it is, of course, not easy to predict whether a childless couple are capable of offering a child unconditional love and a stimulating environment. Unlike adoption agencies, infertility clinics do not conduct rigorous investigations into the backgrounds and lifestyles of would-be parents. They do not make home visits over a sustained period of time, nor do they interview other family members. And if those seeking treatment already have children, when evidence of their parenting ability might appear to be more readily obtainable, clinicians will not interview the child, nor will they seek reports from teachers or other individuals who might be in a position to comment upon their parenting skills. Gillian Douglas has suggested that s 33 of the Human Fertilisation and Embryology Act – which places restrictions upon the disclosure of information about patients' treatment – has led some clinics to assume that they are prohibited from communicating directly with third parties about people seeking assistance with conception (Douglas, 1993, p 65). If s 13(5) is genuinely directed towards judging the adequacy of would-be parents, we are expecting infertility clinics to make extraordinarily difficult appraisals with very little information.

In its Consultation Document *Tomorrow's Children*, the HFEA laid out three different approaches to taking into account the welfare of children: a maximum welfare principle, under which treatment would be provided only to ideal parents; a reasonable welfare principle, which would confine treatment to parents who will offer the child a reasonably happy life; and a minimum threshold principle, where the emphasis is on protecting the child from serious harm (HFEA, 2005). Despite their obvious differences, all three standards of assessment require clinicians to have access to clear and reliable evidence of future parenting ability. In the end, the HFEA opted for the minimum threshold standard, recasting the welfare of the child assessment as a welfare of the child *risk* assessment. Even under this comparatively light-touch assessment of parental adequacy, it is still necessary for clinicians to be able to predict with some degree of certainty whether a serious risk of harm exists in any particular case. Without access to much more information than can ordinarily be gleaned from, for example, the patients' GP, and without specialist expertise in the prediction of future behaviour, this is by no means a straightforward task.

Were the purpose of s 13(5) really to safeguard, in any meaningful sense, the future wellbeing of children born following assisted conception, a far more intensive and exacting scrutiny of prospective patients would be necessary. Since this does not happen, it could plausibly be argued that s 13(5) is in practice an essentially cosmetic provision. There were perhaps two reasons for its inclusion in the Human Fertilisation and Embryology Bill in 1990. First, it was supposed to address, at least in theory, the concerns of MPs who were alarmed by the possibility that infertility treatment might routinely be provided to single or lesbian women. In the debates in both Houses of Parliament this was a recurring concern, and an amendment that would have prohibited the treatment of such women was defeated by the narrowest possible margin.[10] Given the extent of this hostility to the creation of 'fatherless' children, some concession was needed in order to neutralise parliamentary

10 HL Deb vol 515 col 787 6 February 1990.

opposition to the Bill. Hence s 13(5)'s specific mention of the child's 'need for a father'. So, s 13(5)'s principal purpose was to obstruct the treatment of women without male partners (Douglas, 1993, p 58) rather than to institute a system of vetting future parents.

Second, it would simply have been politically unthinkable *not* to support the inclusion of a welfare principle. Since concern for children's wellbeing is universal, bolting a welfare principle onto any new policy instantly both adds to its appeal and inhibits effective criticism. But while the welfare principle may be a useful political device, it is important to critically reflect upon what it is supposed to achieve. If its purpose is genuinely to identify inadequate parents prior to conception, there would have to be a far more rigorous investigative process than is envisaged by s 13(5) and the HFEA's guidance to clinics.

Of course, it could be argued that if the Human Fertilisation and Embryology Act's pre-conception welfare principle is merely 'window dressing', then my criticism of it is misplaced. If it has little practical impact upon people's access to infertility treatment, why not simply ignore it? However, because infertile individuals often experience the pre-conception welfare assessment as unfair and discriminatory, and because it may be inconsistent with certain basic legal principles, its functional inefficacy gives us good grounds to question the wisdom of its retention in its present form in any new piece of legislation.

Unfairness

The obvious rejoinder to my contention that it is unfair to subject only those who cannot conceive naturally to this pre-conception welfare principle would be that there is a very clear difference between respecting people's freedom to engage in unprotected sexual intercourse and offering individuals or couples assisted conception services. This is undoubtedly true, but it does not necessarily follow that this factual difference justifies the imposition of a *child welfare* filter upon access to treatment. I am certainly not advocating wholly unrestricted access to assisted conception services. There may indeed be many good reasons for refusing to offer a particular couple or individual services that might enable them to conceive. If the requested treatment might pose an unacceptable risk to health, for example, a clinician might be justified in withholding it. Or if providing assisted conception services would significantly impede a health authority's capacity to offer a comprehensive health service to the rest of the community, it could legitimately restrict access to publicly funded treatment.

Unlike factors that go to the heart of whether infertility treatment is, for example, clinically advisable or publicly affordable, the pre-conception welfare principle is an attempt to distinguish between fit and unfit parents. In the next sections, I suggest that this may treat infertile people unfairly. It is, however, important to acknowledge that certain additional complicating factors inform decisions about access to treatment within the National Health Service. For the sake of clarity, I therefore discuss private and public treatment separately.

Privately funded treatment

Of course, that a patient is prepared to pay for their own treatment does not give them an absolute right to demand that a doctor carries out any medical procedure that they might desire. Medical practitioners are not mere technicians, rather they also bring their clinical and ethical judgement to bear upon treatment decisions. As a result, there are times when a clinician might refuse to treat an individual regardless of her willingness to pay for the treatment herself. Private patients who have sought the amputation of healthy limbs, for example, have encountered opposition from doctors who believe that psychotherapy offers a better solution to their problem.

It is clearly possible to imagine circumstances when a doctor's ethical responsibility might prompt her to refuse a request for privately funded infertility treatment. Obvious examples might be if the would-be patient was herself a child or was otherwise incapable of giving a valid consent to medical treatment, when a clinician might plausibly judge that infertility treatment, with its associated physical discomfort and unpleasant side-effects, was not in the patient's best interests. But what if the doctor does not want to treat someone because she thinks that they would be an inadequate parent? As we have seen, the statute specifies that their future children's welfare must be taken into account when deciding whether to treat a particular patient, so clearly a doctor would be acting lawfully by refusing treatment on child welfare grounds. A clinician's concern for the wellbeing of children created with her assistance is, of course, entirely understandable, and it is easy to imagine circumstances in which a doctor would be extremely reluctant to offer infertility treatment to a particular couple or individual. We should, however, be wary of endowing a clinician's instinctive negative reaction to a prospective patient with perhaps unwarranted authority. As I have argued above, it is not clear that doctors have either sufficient expertise or information to judge parental fitness fairly and objectively.

Let us imagine two hypothetical couples, couple A and couple B, both of whom have decided to abandon contraception in order to start a family. The female partner in couple A conceives within a few months, whereas the female partner in couple B has still not conceived 18 months later, at which point medical advice is sought. Tests reveal that the female partner in couple B has blocked fallopian tubes and *in vitro* fertilisation (IVF) is recommended. For the sake of clarity, let us assume that couple B will meet the full costs of any treatment themselves. Nevertheless, before their first IVF cycle can be started, couple B must have their parental adequacy judged by the clinic, and third parties, such as their GP, might be consulted to ensure that they are not known to present any risks to their future offspring. Thus we have two couples, both of which have made the life-changing decision to become parents. Couple A can, as a result of their biological good luck, have a baby without anyone scrutinising their parental adequacy. Conversely, couple B's biological misfortune means that they must be judged fit people to bring a child into the world prior to conception. Now, of course, there is no reason to suppose that couple B are more likely to be inadequate parents than couple A. Couple A could be crack-addicts and known child abusers, who have had all of their previous six children taken into the care of the local authority, and yet their conception decision-making would still lie within the zone of privacy which is denied to couple B. Their child might be taken into care immediately after birth, but we cannot, and therefore do not prevent that child's conception. Provided that a couple's reproductive organs are functioning normally, they may have as many children as they like. We exercise *no* control over the reproductive decision-making of fertile individuals who are likely to mistreat any child they might have because protecting their bodily integrity and sexual privacy trumps our concern about the risk of harm they present to future children. In this hierarchy of protected interests, the welfare of future children thus occupies a curious middle ground, in which it is always *less* important than fertile couples' bodily integrity and sexual privacy and *more* important than infertile couples' decisional privacy.

One obvious reason for drawing this distinction between fertile and infertile couples might be found in the difference between positive and negative liberty. If the freedom to have children is essentially a negative liberty, then the State's obligation is simply to refrain from placing obstacles in the path of individuals who wish to conceive, rather than positively providing them with the services that might be necessary in order to overcome their biological incapacity. So couple A cannot be prevented from conceiving normally, but there is no obligation to positively assist couple B. Remember, however, that couple B are not asking the State to provide them with assisted conception services. In these circumstances, I would argue that their negative liberty is also at stake, although admittedly its content is slightly different from that of couple A. Couple B's privacy interest is in making the *decision* to start a family. All of the available treatments may turn out to be clinically inappropriate for them, but we invade their decisional privacy when we judge the *wisdom* of couple B's reproductive decision-making.

In essence, my argument is that the decision to try to conceive a child should lie within a realm of decisional privacy. By this, I mean that there are some aspects of one's life where the interest in making decisions for oneself, according to one's own values and priorities, is of overwhelming importance. Arguing for decisional privacy is not the same as saying that a couple are entitled to have their desire for a child *satisfied*. Instead, I suggest that while there may be a number of factors that might reasonably be invoked in order to deny a couple access to infertility treatment, the wisdom or otherwise of their decision to try to start a family is not necessarily one of them.

By defending the privacy of a couple's reproductive decision-making, am I resurrecting the idea of a separate 'private sphere' as a haven from State intrusion? Perhaps surprisingly in the light of feminism's thoroughgoing trashing of the public/private distinction (MacKinnon, 1987, p 100; 1989, p 191), I do find myself sympathetic to the idea that there are some aspects of our lives that are enriched by our freedom to shield them from public scrutiny. Of course, privacy is not an absolute or an unqualified good (Allen, 1999, p 725). Historically, the privacy of the domestic sphere has facilitated the concealment and trivialisation of violence and abuse. But just as it would be a mistake to abandon the concept of freedom just because it has sometimes been invoked in order to defend exploitative or oppressive practices, so privacy may deserve a more nuanced account (Sennett, 1977; Elshtain, 1981; Allen, 1988; Schneider, 1991; Gavison, 1992; Cohen, 1997).

In particular, it might be worth drawing attention to privacy's uneven distribution within society: some people's domestic arrangements have always been more private than others. Single parents, for example, have often been subjected to public scrutiny and criticism, at times again justified by concern for the 'best interests of the child' (Fineman, 1991; Jackson, 1997). Homeless people, or those who live in institutions, commonly find their lack of privacy one of the most humiliating and demeaning aspects of their situation. Dismissing privacy out of hand misses, therefore, the intrinsic importance to us all of having a space – physical or metaphoric – into which the State cannot intrude without compelling reasons. It also obscures the valuable political insight that this 'space' has tended to be jealously guarded *only* if individuals conform to dominant familial or behavioural norms. Outside of the 'natural' family, privacy becomes a scarce resource, but one which is no less important for the individuals to whom it has been denied. In relation to the argument pursued here, it is perhaps infertile couples' *unnatural* failure to conceive that strips them of the privacy to which they would otherwise be entitled when deciding to start a family.

There is a parallel here with Drucilla Cornell's elaboration of the importance for each individual of possessing the 'psychic space' to shape her own intimate life free from State scrutiny (Cornell, 1995, 1998). An individual needs this 'imaginary domain', according to Cornell, so that she can 'claim herself as the "self-authenticating source" of what the good life is for her' (Cornell, 1998, pp 37–8). If the State imposes limits upon people's capacity to make 'personality-defining' decisions about how they organise their intimate lives, it fails to treat those individuals with the equivalent respect that Cornell argues is due to each citizen. Cornell draws particular attention to the harm caused by the law's tendency both to privilege one form of family life and to pathologise unconventional arrangements. One consequence of this historically uneven distribution of familial privacy is that members of the 'normal' majority (for my purposes, fertile heterosexual couples) tend to take for granted their own right to be free from State intrusion, while simultaneously assuming that scrutiny of the 'abnormal' minority (here, those who cannot conceive without assistance) is self-evidently legitimate (Cornell, 1998, p 176).

My critics might argue that we should view the opportunity infertility offers for scrutinising parental adequacy in a different and more positive light. It could, for example, be argued that our inability to assess most people's parental fitness prior to conception is a regrettable consequence of the priority accorded to bodily integrity. On this analysis, if we *can* ensure that individuals meet some minimum level of parental adequacy before they conceive, then our concern for children's wellbeing should lead us to seize this opportunity. Yet this sort of justification for the welfare principle has much in common with the arguments popular among eugenicists in the first half of the twentieth century. Just as eugenicists argued that society would be improved if 'defective' individuals were discouraged from reproducing, so s 13(5) is intended to weed out 'unfit' parents from assisted conception services in order to enhance children's welfare. The pre-conception welfare principle may be directed towards improving the quality of *individual* children's lives, rather than the health of *society* as a whole, but it nevertheless rests upon the assumption that it is the business of government to dissuade certain individuals from conceiving. But we do not only reject eugenic principles because in practice strategies such as compulsory sterilisation of the 'unfit' violated those individuals' bodily integrity. Another equally important reason for condemning eugenic selection is the belief that it is not appropriate for the State to make judgements about who should and who should not be permitted to reproduce.

There is something else wrong with the argument that we should tolerate mildly intrusive scrutiny of *all* infertile couples in order to exclude the tiny proportion of would-be parents who might represent a danger to their children. Invoking an extreme example, such as a couple who would be likely to have their child taken into care immediately after birth, in order to justify subjecting *every* infertile couple to the humiliating experience of having to justify their parental adequacy prior to conception could apply equally to fertile couples. If the claim is that we should be prepared to put up with a degree of inconvenience and embarrassment in order to protect a small number of children from significant harm, then there is no reason why this should apply only to would-be parents who happen to be infertile.

Publicly funded treatment

Offering people infertility treatment at public expense is, of course, a rather different matter. The National Health Service is plainly incapable of providing infertility treatment on demand to anyone who thinks that it would improve the quality of her life. The NHS simply does not have enough money to pay for every medical procedure that patients might want, or even need, and taxpayers are evidently not prepared to give up the proportion of their income which would be necessary to satisfy all of our health-related preferences. Providing the whole population with optimum access to medical care would probably absorb *all* of a country's resources (Hall, 1994, p 694). Indeed, one study estimated that providing all the healthcare that could be beneficial to each French citizen would cost five and a half times France's gross national product (Lamm, 1992, p 1512).

Obviously, the criteria used to make rationing decisions must satisfy some threshold level of fairness. It would, for example, plainly be unlawful to refuse to treat a particular patient on the grounds of race.[11] But while some factors – like the colour of a patient's skin – are plainly irrelevant, and others – such as the likelihood that treatment will be futile – are undoubtedly important considerations, there is a grey area where considerable disagreement exists. For instance, some people believe that a person's alcoholism should be a relevant factor when deciding whether to offer them a liver transplant (Neuberger *et al*, 1998), whereas others consider that the difficulties in isolating a single causal factor for liver failure, and the violations of privacy that would be necessary to identify voluntary risk-takers, might themselves create substantial injustice (Beauchamp and Childress, 2001, pp 247–8).

Distinguishing between fair and unfair rationing criteria is essentially a question of distributive justice. At the risk of drastic oversimplification, let us briefly outline two possible approaches: consequentialism and egalitarianism (Beauchamp and Childress, 2001, pp 264–5). A consequentialist strategy decides whether a patient should be provided with medical treatment on the basis of its likely outcome. Here it is important to further differentiate between considerations of medical and social utility. Giving priority to a patient whose treatment is more likely to be successful is an example of *medical* utility, whereas treating a doctor in preference to a drug trafficker involves taking the *social* utility of treatment into account. Egalitarianism, on the other hand, is principally concerned with the *justice* of a particular distribution rather than its consequences. I cannot improve upon Amy Gutmann's summary of what is demanded by a principle of equal access to healthcare:

> The principle requires that if anyone within a society has an opportunity to receive a service or good that satisfies a health need, then everyone who shares the same type and degree of health need must be given an equally effective chance of receiving that service or good.
>
> (Gutmann, 1981, p 543)

Here the emphasis is on facially neutral rationing criteria which treat each

---

11 See the comments of Schiemann J in *R v Ethical Committee of St Mary's Hospital (Manchester) ex parte Harriott* [1988] 1 FLR 512.

patient with equivalent concern and respect; an example might be taking into account the length of time spent on a waiting list.

A set of fair rationing criteria would, I argue, normally consist in a mixture of egalitarian principles and considerations of medical utility. Only in the most exceptional circumstances could it be fair to distinguish between patients according to the *social* utility of their treatment. A hypothetical example offered by Beauchamp and Childress is the decision to inoculate doctors and nurses first following the outbreak of a highly infectious disease (Beauchamp and Childress, 2001, p 271). But apart from the extreme example of preserving the lives of skilled rescuers during a disaster, there are sound practical and ideological reasons for excluding considerations of social utility from the rationing of scarce healthcare resources. Not only does judging individuals' comparative social worth offend the egalitarian principle that each person's life must be assumed to be equally valuable, but it would also simply be impossible to carry out this sort of assessment with any degree of certainty, objectivity or fairness. Without divine foresight, how could we claim to know that patient X will make a richer contribution to society than patient Y? Placing doctors under a duty to make treatment decisions according to their assessment of a patient's social value would also have a profoundly negative impact upon the doctor/patient relationship.

If a just rationing system can be informed only by egalitarian standards and considerations of medical utility, how might this lead us to distribute publicly funded infertility treatment? Factors such as the urgency of clinical need may be helpful when rationing life-saving treatments such as liver transplants, but are plainly of no assistance to the distribution of infertility treatment. Taking medical utility into account would therefore generally mean evaluating the chance of a successful outcome. In practice, this would probably lead to an upper age limit for female patients, such as that suggested by the National Institute of Clinical Excellence in their recommendation that women under the age of 40 should have access to three cycles of IVF at public expense. Where medical utility is roughly equal, other neutral criteria which treat all would-be patients with equivalent respect must be devised; an example might be the number of cycles of treatment that an individual has already had at public expense.

Section 13(5) might be described as a consequentialist rationing device, but opinion will differ over whether its concern is with the medical or the social utility of treatment. To interpret the child's wellbeing as an indicator of a successful *clinical* outcome requires a rather strained interpretation, and it might be more accurate to describe s 13(5) as an attempt to take the *social* utility of treatment into account, which as we have seen is generally believed to be prima facie illegitimate.

However, regardless of whether the child's welfare is described as a medical or a social outcome, for several interconnected reasons I believe that attempting to ration treatment using s 13(5) is unsatisfactory. First, if the alternative is non-existence, it will in fact invariably be in the particular future child's best interests to be conceived. Distributing assisted conception services according to whether a child's welfare will be served *by her own conception* is clearly nonsensical. Instead, invoking s 13(5) as a rationing device must, logically, involve claiming two things: (a) that denying couple X the opportunity to bring baby X into the world will enable treatment to be provided to couple Y, and (b) that baby Y is likely to have a much better life than baby X. We thereby increase the aggregate of children's wellbeing by refusing to treat couple X and diverting our resources instead to couple Y. This consequential-ist analysis rests upon two dubious assumptions. First, that it is possible to forecast with some degree of certainty whether a particular child is likely to flourish before she is conceived, and second, that it is clinicians who are especially well equipped to make this sort of prediction. Because if we admit that vague speculation about future children's future wellbeing will frequently be wildly inaccurate (Douglas, 1993, p 70), then the justification for s 13(5) must collapse. It cannot be acceptable to point to a statistical correlation between certain parental characteristics – such as poverty – and children's impaired life chances in order to deny publicly funded infertility treatment to all poor people. This is precisely the sort of probabilistic calculation that was invoked by eugenicists, and it is, as Gillian Douglas has noted, 'not satisfac-tory to have a statutory provision used . . . to sanction what ultimately amounts to discrimination' (Douglas, 1993, p 69). Finally, it is not clear that the doctor/patient relationship is enhanced by giving clinicians the power to determine who *deserves* to become a parent (which is undoubtedly not a question that requires specialist *clinical* expertise).

Incoherent

I turn now to my third criticism of the pre-conception welfare principle, namely that it is inconsistent with judicial attitudes to what are known as 'wrongful life' actions. These are cases brought by a child whose claim is that, 'but for' the defendant's negligence, she would not have been born and her injury – that is, her painful life – would have been avoided. In the definitive English case, Mary McKay claimed that she had suffered damage by 'entry into a life in which her injuries are highly debilitating' after her mother's doctor failed to diagnose and treat the rubella infection she had contracted during pregnancy (*McKay v Essex Area Health Authority* [1982] QB 1166). Because the doctor in this case had not caused Mary's injuries, but had just failed to offer Mrs McKay the opportunity to terminate her pregnancy, the Court of Appeal found that the gist of Mary's complaint was that she was allowed to be born at all. Thus, to assess compensation, they would have to compare the value of non-existence (of which she had been deprived by the doctor) and existence in a disabled state.

Ackner LJ was simply not prepared to countenance such a balancing exercise. He asked, 'how can a court begin to evaluate non-existence, the undiscovered country from whose bourn no traveller returns?'. And his conclusion was simple: '[n]o comparison is possible' (at 1189). Stephenson LJ also rejected Mary McKay's claim, but his reasoning was slightly different. He appeared to argue that if the choice is between entering into life with a disability and not entering it at all, then living should *almost always* be considered preferable. There is an obvious inconsistency between these two judgments. Ackner LJ argues that it is simply *impossible* to evaluate non-existence, whereas Stephenson LJ contends that existence must almost always be judged preferable to non-existence. Clearly, we can only arrive at Stephenson LJ's assessment of the relative merit of existence and non-existence if we have evaluated, albeit crudely, the value of non-existence. Stephenson LJ's judgment should perhaps be preferred because it is also plainly not true that the courts are *incapable* of deciding that non-existence would be preferable to (or at least no worse than) existence, since this is precisely the assessment that has sometimes been made when authorising the non-treatment of very severely disabled neonates (*Re B (a minor)* [1981] 1 WLR 1421; *Re J (A Minor) (Wardship: Medical Treatment)* [1990] 3 All ER 930; *National Health Service Trust v D* [2000] 2 FLR 677). If existence is *always* to be preferred, then it would be difficult to justify denying any premature baby, however terrible her injuries, life-prolonging treatment.

Despite the existence of these differences, both judgments sit rather uneasily with the pre-conception welfare principle. Let us consider Ackner LJ's judgment first. As we have seen, when a clinician decides whether to offer treatment to would-be parents, she is charged with weighing up whether or not the welfare of any child that they might have would be best served by coming into being. So although Ackner LJ states that it is simply *impossible* to compare existence with non-existence, s 13(5) of the Human Fertilisation and Embryology Act demands that clinicians should engage in precisely this balancing exercise in order to work out whether existence or non-existence would be in a particular future child's best interests.

Stephenson LJ's acknowledgement that existence must almost always be preferred to non-existence does, of course, leave open the possibility that there could be some rare circumstances in which it would be possible to conclude that non-existence would be preferable. An example might be an exceptionally severely disabled neonate who would derive no benefit from her continued existence. If this reasoning were applied to s 13(5), it would constitute what I referred to previously as the 'thin' interpretation, that is, that any child conceived by these parents would have a life so short, painful or insensate that it would probably be better for them never to exist. Indubitably, there are very few, if any, potential parents who could plausibly be refused treatment on these grounds.

Yet s 13(5) rests upon the assumption that assessing the welfare of any child that might be born to particular parents is not merely a filter to exclude individuals whose baby is inevitably going to lead a very short and painful life. Rather, it is directed towards judging a couple or individual's likely parenting ability before deciding whether to offer them treatment. However, this 'thick' version of the welfare principle is plainly inconsistent with the judgments of both Stephenson and Ackner LJJ.

There is insufficient space here to also consider in any detail potential tensions between the pre-conception welfare principle and decisions in so-called 'wrongful birth' and 'wrongful conception' claims. It is, however, worth noting that the principal reason why parents have been barred from recovering the costs associated with an unplanned child's maintenance is that it would be unseemly and contrary to public morality to compensate parents for the birth of a healthy child. The 'inarticulate premise' underlying the House of Lords' judgment in *McFarlane v Tayside Health Board* [1999] 3 WLR 1301, for example, was that the birth of a healthy baby is always a blessing and an occasion for joy. So again we find the judiciary troubled by the idea that not being conceived could ever be judged preferable to conception. Yet the assumption underpinning s 13(5) is precisely that there might be circumstances in which it would *not* be in a potential child's best interests to be conceived. Effectively, this must mean that there are circumstances in which, based upon an assessment of the child's best interests, non-life is the preferred option. If the law always treats conceiving a child as beneficial, how could it at the same time enjoin infertility clinics to weed out would-be parents on the grounds that *their* child's conception would *not* be beneficial?

Potential absurdity

In defence of the pre-conception welfare principle, it might be argued that positively assisting people to conceive children is entirely different from ordinary sexual conception and that it is perfectly legitimate for anyone who acts positively to help someone to conceive to assume some responsibility for the wellbeing of the resulting offspring. Under the 1990 Act, s 13(5) applies whenever a woman is provided with 'treatment services' in a licensed clinic. Treatment services are defined in s 2(1) as 'medical, surgical or obstetric services provided to the public or a section of the public for the purpose of assisting women to carry children'. While the meaning of surgical and obstetric services seems fairly clear, how broadly should 'medical services' be defined? Might preliminary investigations into the causes of a couple's apparent infertility qualify as 'medical services . . . for the purpose of assisting women to carry children'? Could the supply of an ovulation predictor kit by a licensed clinic count as such a 'medical service'? If medical services were to receive a very broad interpretation, then clearly the pre-conception welfare principle would apply much more widely than people have tended to assume.

Surely we would not want to suggest that no doctor should carry out investigations into the causes of infertility without first assessing a couple's fitness to parent. Nor would it seem sensible to suggest that supplying ovulation testing kits which might help a couple to conceive should be illegitimate unless consideration has first been given to the welfare of any child who might be conceived. But why is it that these examples seem self-evidently absurd, while the pre-conception assessment of couples undergoing IVF or donor insemination is widely agreed to be acceptable? I would suggest that the legitimacy of the status quo – under which people seeking fertility treatment must first have their parental adequacy judged – has been taken for granted for so long that the suggestion that would-be parents should *not* be subject to any sort of scrutiny seems both shocking and profoundly irresponsible.

My purpose in this chapter is to encourage a slightly more reflective analysis. If we think we need to judge parental fitness when doctors do *some* things which help women to become pregnant but not others, we need to be able to explain why. Given that medical assistance with conception exists on a continuum, from some very low-tech and simple interventions to other highly complex techniques, we need to be able to justify any line that we intend to draw between those where pre-conception assessment of parents is required and those where it is not. For example, we could say that assessment is necessary only when doctors create a new life *in vitro*, but of course this would rule out the application of s 13(5) prior to donor insemination, when the creation of any new life will happen naturally *in vivo*. When considering which point on the spectrum of medical services which may facilitate or enable conception should trigger a pre-conception welfare assessment, I must admit to being at a loss to see any logical reason to draw the line in any one place rather than another.

CONCLUSION

It is important to reiterate that I am not arguing that everyone has a right to be provided with the treatment that may be necessary for them to conceive. Plainly, there is a crucial difference between negative liberty or freedom from external constraints – which is the sort of freedom sexually active, fertile, heterosexual couples have in relation to reproduction – and positive liberty – that is, the positive provision of resources, which might be what infertile people need in order to conceive. Positive rights to resources are always claimed against a background of relative scarcity and there are therefore inherent limitations upon their satisfaction (Fried, 1978, p 108).

Of course, publicly funded fertility treatment cannot be available indefinitely upon request and rationing is clearly inevitable. And, although I believe that treatment should be available within the NHS, I accept that infertility is not life-threatening and that a health authority could legitimately decide to restrict access to publicly funded assisted conception services. Where treatment is available but rationed, criteria such as the chance of a successful outcome and the number of cycles that a patient has already had at public expense may be relevant. What should not be relevant, in my opinion, is a largely perfunctory attempt to judge their parental adequacy.

If a patient intends to pay for their own treatment, there are fewer grounds upon which their request may legitimately be refused. These might be confined to cases in which providing treatment would be contrary to a doctor's clinical or ethical judgment. If super-ovulatory drugs would cause a woman lasting physical damage, or if the request was made by a minor, then clinicians might be entitled to conclude that treatment should not be provided. The conscientious objection clause in s 38(1) of the Human Fertilisation and Embryology Act already offers some protection for healthcare professionals who are uncomfortable with the provision of assisted conception services. This would normally be invoked by medical professionals who object to the *procedures* involved in treatment rather than to the prospect of treating particular patients. But if the removal of s 13(5) from the statutory scheme proved wholly unacceptable to a clinician, it is important to remember that she would continue to be entitled to invoke the conscientious objection clause and my proposal would therefore not automatically recast her as a mere clinical technician. Forcing doctors who wish to make moral judgements about an individual's fitness for parenthood to exercise their right to conscientious objection would lend the law greater transparency and coherence because any reluctance to offer treatment services would be admitted to lie within the doctor's subjective moral sensibilities, rather than arising from the sort of objective and non-discriminatory pre-conception assessment of parenting ability which may in practice be impossible and for which infertility clinicians undoubtedly lack the necessary information and expertise.

If s 13(5) is genuinely directed towards safeguarding the interests of future children, it is a haphazard and inefficacious sort of child protection. Haphazard, because only dangerously inadequate parents who *also* happen to be infertile can be prevented from wreaking havoc upon their children's lives by bringing them into the world. And inefficacious, because in practice, judgements are made with partial and inevitably inadequate evidence. Once the pre-conception welfare principle that is supposed to control access to infertility treatment is subjected to scrutiny, it is revealed to be muddled and ineffective. Our shared concern for the welfare of children should not, I argue, lead us to be wholly unreflective about the practical and ethical difficulties in assessing the welfare of children who do not yet exist.

REFERENCES

Allen, A (1988) *Uneasy Access: Privacy for Women in a Free Society* Totowa, NJ: Rowman and Littlefield

Allen, A (1999) 'Coercing privacy' 40 *William and Mary Law Review* 723

Beauchamp, TL and Childress, JF (2001) *Principles of Biomedical Ethics*, 5th edn Oxford: Oxford University Press

Bonner, D, Fenwick, H and Harris-Short, S (2003) 'Judicial approaches to the Human Rights Act' 52 *International and Comparative Law Quarterly* 549

Capron, AM (1997) 'Tort liability in genetic counseling' 79 *Columbia Law Review* 618

Cohen, JL (1997) 'Rethinking privacy: autonomy, identity and the abortion controversy' in Weintraub, J and Kumar, K (eds) *Public and Private in Thought and Practice: Perspectives on a Grand Dichotomy* Chicago: University of Chicago Press

Cornell, D (1995) *The Imaginary Domain: Abortion, Pornography and Sexual Harassment* London: Routledge

Cornell, D (1998) *At the Heart of Freedom: Feminism, Sex and Equality* Princeton, NJ: Princeton University Press

Douglas, G (1993) 'Assisted conception and the welfare of the child' 46 *Current Legal Problems* 53

Elshtain, JB (1981) *Public Man, Private Woman* Princeton, NJ: Princeton University Press

Fineman, M (1991) 'Intimacy outside of the natural family; the limits of privacy' 23 *Connecticut Law Review* 955

Fortin, J (1999) 'The HRA's impact on litigation involving children and their families' 11 *Child and Family Law Quarterly* 237

Fried, C (1978) *Right and Wrong* Cambridge, Mass: Harvard University Press

Gavison, R (1992) 'Feminism and the public/private distinction' 45 *Stanford Law Review* 1

Golombok, S (2000) *Parenting: What Really Counts?* London: Routledge

Gutmann, A (1981) 'For and against equal access to health care' 59 *Milbank Memorial Fund Quarterly/Health and Society* 542

Hall, MA (1994) 'Rationing health care at the bedside' 69 *New York University Law Review* 693

Human Fertilisation and Embryology Authority (2004) *Code of Practice*, 6th edn London: HFEA

Human Fertilisation and Embryology Authority (2005) *Tomorrow's Children: A Consultation on Guidance to Licensed Fertility Clinics on Taking into Account the Welfare of Children to be Born of Assisted Conception Treatment* London: HFEA

Jackson, E (1997) 'Fractured values: law, ideology and the family' 17 *Studies in Law, Politics*

Lamm, RD (1992) 'Rationing of health care: inevitable and desirable' 140 *University of Pennsylvania Law Review* 1511

MacKinnon, C (1987) *Feminism Unmodified: Discourses on Life and Law* Cambridge, Mass: Harvard University Press

MacKinnon, C (1989) *Toward a Feminist Theory of the State* Cambridge, Mass: Harvard University Press

Neuberger, J *et al* (1998) 'Assessing priorities for allocation of donor liver grafts: survey of public and clinicians' 317 *British Medical Journal* 172

Reece, H (1996) 'The paramountcy principle: consensus or construct' 49 *Current Legal Problems*

Schneider, EM (1991) 'The violence of privacy' 23 *Connecticut Law Review* 973

Sennett, R (1977) *The Fall of Public Man* Cambridge: Cambridge University Press

Chapter 4

Paying gamete donors does not wrong the future child

Heather Draper

INTRODUCTION

There are many different concerns raised about trade in human tissue, includ-ing human gametes. Some concerns centre on the potential for exploiting the poor and vulnerable (see Hughes, 1998), others on the argument that trade in human body parts is contrary to human dignity. There are also arguments about whether the human body can be treated as a form of property (see Dickinson, 2001). Some writers are concerned that payment for tissue or gametes may undermine autonomy (see, for instance, the World Medical Association *Statement on Human Organ and Tissue Donation and Transplan-tation*), while others disagree, arguing that prohibiting payment is unduly paternalistic and harmful (see Radcliffe-Richards *et al*, 1998). Some argue that payment undermines altruism (see Titmass, 1970), others are concerned that payment has implications for the just allocation of resources (see Erin and Harris, 2003), and still others argue that regulating the market is the best protection against abuse (see Resnik, 2001).

All of these arguments have a bearing on whether those donating gametes should be paid for the actual gametes they give, only compensated for the discomfort and inconvenience of donating, or merely given expenses (though what this means is also controversial – does it include loss of earnings, regard-less of how great or small those earnings might be, for instance?). In this chapter, however, I will not look at these well-rehearsed arguments. Instead, I will concentrate on concerns for the welfare of the future child, particularly the contention that the child might legitimately claim to have been wronged if the gametes from which she was conceived were sold rather than donated altruistically.

Following the response to its public consultation in 1998, the Human Fertilisation and Embryology Authority (HFEA) was persuaded not to abol-ish all payments and benefits to gamete donors, as was originally intended (HFEA, 1998). These payments were quite small on the whole, but the controversial practice of egg sharing also continues to be tolerated.[1] This practice, where those willing to donate eggs can get IVF treatment at a reduced cost, was clearly a much greater benefit in kind than the £15 per donation offered to sperm donors, although the cumulative financial benefit of donating sperm can amount to several hundreds of pounds. Neither was perceived by the HFEA to be payment for gametes *per se*.

The HFEA has now completed its SEED (Sperm, Egg and Embryo Donation) review, part of which re-visited the issue of compensating gamete donors and published its *SEED Report* (HFEA, 2006). The SEED review was partly prompted by two legislative developments: the lifting of donor anonymity in the UK and a European Union (EU) Tissue and Cells Directive requiring Member States to limit compensation for any tissue donation to expenses and inconvenience. The EU Directive came into force in April 2006. There is, however, existing legislation governing payments for gametes and embryos: s 12(e) of the Human Fertilisation and Embryology Act 1990 states that '. . . no money or other benefit shall be given or received in respect of any supply of gametes or embryos unless authorised by directions'.

This section does permit the HFEA to authorise payments to gamete donors but the Authority has consistently argued for altruistic donation, guided by two principles that were restated in the public consultation for the SEED review. First, that fully informed consent, free from any inducement and pressure, is fundamental to gamete donation and, second, that the potential for human life inherent in a donation made with the specific intent of producing children should be respected (HFEA, 2004, p 5). The HFEA is concerned, then, that offering payments may undermine the voluntariness of the donor's decision, but it is also concerned that payments 'might result in the children so produced being perceived as commodities'.

This statement reflects the view that gametes are a special kind of tissue because using them can result in inherently valuable entities – children. Some of the HFEA's concerns about payment reflect, therefore, a concern to avoid harming those who may result from gamete (or embryo) donation. The general concern that children might be perceived as commodities has, however, been combined with a more specific concern that individual children might be

---

1 Nor, it appears, has the HFEA changed its mind on this issue following its latest review of payment. Its *SEED Report*, a report published in January 2006 following a review of sperm, egg and embryo donation in the UK, recommended that donors receive up to £250 for each course of sperm donation or egg donation cycle, plus reasonable expenses, which includes compensation for loss of earnings pegged to that of the per diem rate for jury service. Egg sharing also continues to be legitimate in the Authority's eyes. However, the Department of Health, which is currently reviewing the Human Fertilisation and Embryology Act, asks whether the HFEA is the right body to make decisions on payment or whether it should be a matter for Parliament (Department of Health, *Review of the Human Fertilisation and Embryology Act: A Public Consultation* (16 August 2005) s 4).

harmed by the thought that their donor *sold* the gametes that led to their creation. People conceived as a result of gametes donated since April 2005 will have enough identifiable information to trace a donor, if they so wish (although donor-conceived individuals will not be able to gain access to this information until they are 18 years old). In theory, then, they will be able to question the donor about their motives for donating. There is a concern that donor-conceived individuals will be psychologically damaged if they learn that this motivation was purely financial rather than altruistic, either from their parents (the recipients) or from the donor in person.

It is not clear that donor-conceived individuals will be psychologically damaged if they discover their donor was paid – the evidence to make a confident assertion one way or the other does not yet exist. There is evidence that donor-conceived individuals are not harmed if their parents are open about the circumstances of their conception (see, for example, Turner, 1993; Golombok, 1998; Vanfraussen *et al*, 2001) and likewise evidence that they may be harmed if they are not told (see Clamar, 1989; Snowden, 1993; Daniels and Taylor, 1993; Donor Conception Support Group of Australia Inc., 1997). Nevertheless, there is also considerable resistance to honesty and openness from the recipients (see Robinson *et al*, 1991; Gottlieb *et al*, 2000; Klock *et al*, 1996; Cook *et al*, 1995; Brewaeys *et al*, 1993, 1997; Soderstorm-Antilla *et al*, 1998; Lycett *et al*, 2005), which suggests that only a significant minority of donor-conceived people will ever know that they are donor-conceived. It is too soon to know whether the lifting of anonymity in the UK will promote or hinder greater openness, but it is clear that donor-conceived individuals can only trace a donor and be harmed or benefited by a relationship or interaction with that donor if they know that they are donor-conceived to begin with. As things stand, they are more likely not to be told than to be told. But the lack of evidence of psychological damage and the secrecy surrounding gamete donation do not mean that there is nothing further to discuss about payment. We can ask, for instance, whether donor-conceived children can in principle claim to have been wronged by their donor if he or she was financially rather than altruistically motivated, drawing a distinction between claims to have been harmed and claims to have been wronged. Not all harms are also wrongs, and one might be wronged without experiencing a harm. One way that a harm can become a wrong is if it is inflicted unjustly: there is a difference between serving a custodial sentence for a crime for which one was justly convicted and being kidnapped, for instance, even though both involve the harm of the loss of freedom. A distinction can also be drawn between an uncomfortable or distressing feeling and a wrong. A person may feel harmed by the knowledge that their donor sold her gametes, but this feeling might be unjustified. We can also ask whether it would be better not to exist than to experience some psychological damage, whether or not this harm is also a wrong.

BETTER NEVER TO EXIST THAN TO RESULT FROM TRADED GAMETES?

If payment for gametes is prohibited on the grounds that the resulting children would be harmed, many of the children who would have been created as a result will never come into being. Their existence will have been prohibited in their own interests, the prohibition being based on a judgement that it is better not to come into being than it is to live with the knowledge that one resulted from a trade in gametes. This looks like a very weak argument: some psychological damage, while undesirable, does not seem too great a price to pay for existence. But those who never come into being are not harmed by their non-existence. Different children – children who will not be at risk of this psychological damage – will exist instead, and it could be argued that given the choice between bringing into being a child who may have psychological damage and one who will not, it is better to choose the least harmful option. This argument is, however, based on the utilitarian principle that we should aim to maximise happiness and minimise suffering where we can, rather than solely on the interests of the future child, since the interests of the future child as an individual (rather than a net contributor to general happiness) are best served by coming into existence, provided that once in existence that child would not consider non-existence preferable to existence (see Harris, 1998, Chapters 3 and 4). All restrictions on reproduction in the interests of the future child face this kind of problem. Ironically, at the same time as reviewing arrangements for donors, the HFEA conducted a review of provisions to protect the future child under s 13(5) of the 1990 Act and will have to address these very problems.

Of course, it is not impossible that some of the same children could exist despite the prohibition on trade. Those who would have sold their gametes might decide instead to donate them, just as some donors, under the current arrangements, when offered payment may refuse it. But it is most likely that a prohibition on trade will result in different children being conceived, and given the general shortage of gametes for donation, perhaps fewer children will come into being too. But if a prohibition on trade is to be justified on the grounds that it best maximises happiness, the reduction in the number of lives created is also significant and must also be weighed in the balance for a proper utilitarian calculation to be made. In this case, the good of the additional lives is likely to outweigh the potential for psychological damage in some individuals.

Harris (1998, pp 109–10) has drawn an important distinction between harming and wronging in the context of the disabilities a child might be born with, for instance impairments like genetic disorders. He starts with the assumption that any kind of impairment is a harm:

> A condition that is harmful . . . is one in which the individual is disabled

or suffering in some way or in which his interests or rights are frustrated. The disability or suffering may be slight, just as harms may be trivial. And of course what constitutes a disability may have to be defined relative to a particular population ... In the particular circumstances of the case, such a condition may be advantageous to the individual ... But it is still something disabling and hurtful, it still counts as being in a harmed condition.

But although he argues that it is generally in the interests of an individual to exist rather than not to exist (and so, for the reasons outlined above, the child cannot claim to have been wronged), this does not mean that parents do no wrong in choosing to bring children with impairments into existence when they could have chosen otherwise. The wrong they do is that of:

> ... choosing deliberately to increase unnecessarily the amount of harm or suffering in the world or of choosing a world with more suffering rather than choosing a world with less.
>
> (Harris, 1998, p 111)

This distinction is helpful in that it clarifies the wrongs that can be attributed to a decision to disadvantage a possible future child in some way. While the child cannot claim to have been wronged by being brought into existence, her parents may have done wrong by not choosing to create a different child instead. Accordingly, in the case of trade in gametes, recipients do wrong if they choose to buy gametes knowing that the future child might be damaged as a result. But, if we apply Harris's argument faithfully, this blame is not unconditional; the recipients have to be in a position to choose – between using bought gametes and using donated ones. If no donated gametes are available, then using bought ones is not wrong. This is partly because the harm could not have been avoided (by using donated gametes) and partly because:

> If children are wanted it is better to have healthy children than to have disabled children where there are alternatives, and it is better to have children with disabilities than to have no children at all.
>
> (Harris, 1998, p 91)

This suggests that the arguments about the welfare of the future child might not be decisive in preventing potential recipients from purchasing gametes where donated ones are unavailable: the child is not wronged and the recipients do no wrong.

One objection to Harris's argument is that his view that any impairment is a definite harm, however slight, is not correct. This is not the place to explore the arguments for and against Harris's argument in respect of impairment and harm. What is relevant to establish here is whether the potential psycho-logical damage in question is a harm that it would be wrong to inflict, bearing in mind the point made above: there is a difference between justly and unjustly feeling badly about something, however unpleasant the experience. An academic, for instance, may be psychologically damaged by an honest reviewer's report and subsequent refusal of a journal to accept a paper for publication, but the rightness or wrongness of both the report and the editor's decision turns not on this damage, but on the quality of the paper submitted. Given that the recipients (when they have no alternative) do no wrong in using purchased gametes, does the wrong lie with the donor who sells these gametes? After all, it is the donor whose motivation might be the cause of the psychological damage for the possible future child.

DONORS AND PARENTAL RESPONSIBILITIES

To show that the future child would be justified in feeling harmed by the knowledge that they were conceived from traded gametes, an argument has to be made for why it is wrong to trade gametes that justified this sense of harm. As I understand the argument from harm, this feeling of harm comes either from some sense of being a commodity – someone sold to the recipient by the donor – or from the closely related sense that the intention of the donation was not that a child would come into being but that there was money to be made. The moral significance of these feelings is grounded in an understand-ing of the moral importance of genetic connectedness and the significance of genetic connectedness to an understanding of who our parents are. Where a genetic connection is central to an understanding of what it means to be a parent, these two potential sources for the feelings of harm could be reformu-lated as either 'it is wrong for parents willingly to sell their children' or 'it is wrong for parents to conceive children for money'. In either formulation, the resulting individual has a just grievance against the donor for trading his or her gametes, and because the grievance is just, they are right to feel harmed as a result because the donor has wronged them. The wrong in both cases depends upon the view that *donors are correctly identified as parents*. Clearly, however, a gamete is not a child, so selling a gamete is significantly not like selling a child. But let us grant for the sake of exploring this argument further that the continuum between the gamete and the child is sufficiently close to justify the sense that future children are being conceived for money or traded.

Few people would argue that genetic connectedness is necessary for one to be a parent. Adoption has long been recognised as a means of acquiring parental rights and responsibilities and as a legitimate means of becoming a mother or father to a child. Gamete donation, though a more recent arrival, is similarly perceived. While the law recognises both as a means of acquiring parental responsibilities, it is also clear that the genetic connection remains important, even in law. By enabling children by adoption and, more recently, children by donation to trace their genetic origins, the law gives a mixed message on parenting: it is possible to acquire rights and responsibilities through adoption and receiving gametes, but completely divorcing oneself from parental responsibilities through adoption or donation is a different matter. The law reflects a widely held view that it is 'only natural' for children to want to know who their 'real' (genetic) parents are. Indeed, it has been suggested that children have a right to know their genetic origins (for instance by Melanie Johnson when announcing the lifting of gamete donor anonymity in the UK (Johnson, 2004), and also see McWhinnie (2001), who argues that depriving those created as a result of sperm donation of information about the donor contravenes Arts 7 and 8 of the United Nations Conventions on the Rights of the Child).

Although these 'real', 'natural', 'genetic' or 'birth' (the terms used vary) parents are protected from any direct financial or childrearing responsibilities, they are not protected from the apparently legitimate expectation of children to know who they are, a desire to meet them or questions about their motivations for alienating themselves from their parental rights and responsibilities. The justification for this position seems to be that while genetic connectedness is not *necessary* for one to be a parent, it is certainly *sufficient*: one is the parent – in some sense – of any child who results from one's gametes. For this reason, one is never completely alienated from one's parental responsibilities, for while the social and financial aspects of parenting (particularly minors) can be transferred, the genetic fact of one's being the parent cannot be transferred or denied. The importance of this genetic link seems to be culturally embedded, although philosophical justifications have been offered.

David Benatar (1999), for instance, considers that the responsibility for genetically related children springs from the concept of reproductive autonomy:

> Having reproductive autonomy entails having certain rights and responsibilities. One is entitled to make certain reproductive decisions. For example, antecedent to any contracts or agreements, one is entitled to reproduce or fail to reproduce and one has rights to the children one produces. One also bears responsibilities for one's reproductive conduct. One is responsible not only for what one explicitly decides but also for failing to decide, as in cases where one engages in unreflective reproductive conduct. Thus if one's passions lead to contraceptive sex . . . and one fails to abort, the resultant child is one's responsibility even if one did not explicitly decide to have a child.
>
> (Benatar, 1999, p 174)

According to Benatar, donors are parents, parents who have transferred responsibility for rearing their offspring to others but parents by virtue of the genetic connection nonetheless. Benatar goes on to argue that donation is almost always wrong because donors generally transfer their responsibilities too lightly. He believes that donors rarely consider, or have sufficient information to consider, how good at rearing children those who receive their gametes will be. Those who consider the recipients' parenting skills at all are likely, he believes, to take 'the over optimistic view' (Benatar, 1999, p 176) that most people do a reasonably good job of rearing children and gamete recipients are unlikely to be an exception, whereas in reality not all parents do an equally good job. For donation not to be wrong, according to Benatar, the donors would have to be confident of the parenting skills of the recipients because, in short, donors are responsible for the children that exist as a result of their donation.

Several things follow from Benatar's line of argument. The first is that if donors do not exercise their responsibilities seriously enough, the resulting children have a legitimate reason to complain. So, if a donor-conceived child does end up with bad parents, this is at least partly the donor's fault for not vetting the recipients properly or donating via an organisation that does undertake proper vetting. Second, donating simply for money is wrong if it encourages light (as opposed to serious) transferring of parental responsibility. While there might be weighty or lifesaving reasons for wanting the money, such cases will be rare, and even then donors would still be obliged to ensure the proficiency of those to whom the responsibilities for childrearing are transferred. This is unlikely to be the case if they have their minds focused on the financial benefits. Benatar equates a willingness to transfer responsibilities *per se* with 'a lack of seriousness about them' (1999, p 177). Indeed, he argues that parental responsibilities are such that being assured of a competent recipient alone will not suffice to justify a transfer of responsibility, and the lack of consideration on behalf of donors regarding their parental responsibilities to their children amounts to betrayal. 'Commercial concerns' are, according to Benatar, one of the many 'paltry reasons to transfer weighty responsibilities' (1999, p 179).

Nelson (1991) fixes the responsibility more closely to the actual genetics than Benatar, arguing that those who provide the gametes are causally responsible for the child: without their gametes, the child would not exist. As Bayne (2003) notes, the stronger version of the causation argument must be connected directly to a particular identity passed though genes. Any other version of the argument would be too broad, including, for instance, the clinicians whose skills in assisted conception are also a causal link in the creation of the child. Bayne describes this distinction as 'causes-who' rather than 'causes-that' (Baynes 2003, p 81). Nelson, like Benatar, is suspicious about the transfer of parental responsibilities. In his view, only the best interests of the child justify such a transfer, and a further problem with gamete donors is that they intend to transfer responsibility at the outset; they never intend to fulfil the responsibilities that are created along with the child.

Both Benatar and Nelson seem to be arguing that gamete donors have moral (if not legal) parental responsibility by virtue of the genetic connection, be this justified by reference to reproductive autonomy or causation. The question of whether, how and why these responsibilities can be transferred is a thorny one, which has attracted much comment (see, for instance, Bayne (2003) and Fuscaldo (2006)). It does, however, resonate with the concerns of the HFEA that the child will be harmed by the discovery that her donor was financially motivated. This suggests that the future child will also be concerned with the issue of transfer of parental responsibility, for which there are 'good' and 'bad' motivations. A good, though perhaps misplaced, motivation is an altruistic desire to help others; a bad motivation is seizing an opportunity to generate income.

According to the arguments of Benatar and Nelson, donors do something wrong when they sell their gametes because of the relationship between gametes and parental responsibility. On this interpretation, however, it is not so much that the children are justified in feeling commodified by their donor, nor that the donor donated for money as such. Rather, the wrong lies in the casual or unwarranted transfer of parental responsibility, which remains casual or unwarranted however much of a good job the recipients do in rearing the donor-conceived child. This wrong could only be exacerbated by the introduction of a financial motive. Both arguments, however, would generally tell against donation *per se* and not just paid donation, a conclusion that might not be supported by those objecting only to trade in gametes and not donation *per se*.

DONORS DO NOT HAVE PARENTAL RESPONSIBILITIES

Suppose a man dies carrying a donor card that states that any of his organs can be taken for transplantation, including his testicles. His wishes are followed and several of his organs are transplanted into recipients, including both of his testicles, one each to two recipients. Now also suppose that, several years later, a woman reports a violent sexual attack on her by the first recipient. Semen samples are collected and the DNA is identical to that of the organ donor. And suppose that another woman claims that the second recipient is the father of her child and a paternity test connects the child to the organ donor. What sense does it make to argue that while the first recipient must be the rapist, the organ donor and not the second recipient is the father of the child, as arguments about the sufficiency of genetic connectedness would seem to suggest?

We seem to be struggling with a way to reconcile our norms about how parental responsibilities are generated in natural conception with practices like gamete donation in assisted conception. In natural conception, paternity testing – the use of genetic connectedness – is used to confirm parental responsibilities, particularly financial ones, when there is any uncertainty about whose obligations these are. Likewise, paternity tests have been used to disrupt parental relationships with children, for instance when a divorcing spouse paternity tests his children and then disowns them if they are not genetically related, regardless of previous years of fathering them; or a disgruntled ex-partner uses a negative paternity test to prevent a man from having any access to, or rights with respect to, children he has been fathering for years. It is perhaps not surprising that genetic tests of this kind have been labelled 'paternity' tests, rather than 'parentity' tests: as the old saying goes, 'it is a wise father who knows his own children', whereas for women biological experience has traditionally confirmed their maternity.[2] Equating parental responsibility with genetic connectedness has run into difficulties with the emergence of assisted conception. The 'Leeds' case[3] counterintuitively suggested, for example, that parental responsibilities are forthcoming even when children are the result of negligence on behalf of a clinic that results in non-consensual 'donation' of gametes, whereas another child was declared legally fatherless even though the man who consented to treatment with donated sperm was willing to be the father, irrespective of the fact that his ex-partner has continued with infertility treatment without his knowledge and even though the same ex-partner was agreeable.[4]

Use of donated gametes in particular has tended to focus attention on intent to parent as the relevant criterion for parental responsibilities: the donor does not have parental responsibilities because he or she did not intend to have the child but rather intended that it would be the child of the recipients, who themselves used donated gametes with the intention of becoming parents.[5] This creates inevitable problems, however, when attempting to produce a coherent account of parental responsibilities that includes both assisted and natural conception. In the case of the latter, absence of intent is no defence against paternity. Men cannot argue that they did not intend a pregnancy to result from a sexual encounter to avoid paternity; neither can they cite contraceptive failure, nor drunkenness or other mental impairment, nor their own willingness – encouragement even – for a termination of pregnancy.

2 But with gamete donation, this may change: indeed, it may be that it is a wise child who knows her parents, and given the view that individuals have a right to know their genetic origins (a view to which I do not subscribe – see Draper (2005, pp 70–87)), paternity tests may yet be renamed parentity tests.
3 *The Leeds Teaching Hospital NHS Trust v (1) Mrs A; (2) Mr B (3) YA and (4) ZA (by their Litigation Friend, the Official Solicitor); (5) The Human Fertilisation and Embryology Authority; (6) Mr B and (7) Mrs B* [2003] EWCA 259 (QBD).
4 *Re R (a child)* [2003] 2 All ER 131 – now upheld in the House of Lords – *In Re D (A Child Appearing by Her Guardian ad Litem)* [2005] UKHL 33.
5 This is supported by the provisions re parenthood and sperm donors in s 27 of the HFE Act – but shows big inconsistencies when compared to egg donors.

Indeed, not even statutory rape is sufficient to protect a man from unwanted parental responsibilities (Morgan, 1999). One response to these problems is to argue that assisted conception has highlighted some injustices in the way that parental responsibilities fall on men. Sheldon, for instance, has mounted a compelling argument that it is unjust to foist paternity on unwilling men who would, if it had been their decision, have terminated a pregnancy (Sheldon, 2003). Another response has been to recognise that moral responsibility flows not just from intention but also from that which we can reasonably foresee will be the result of our voluntary actions, whether these consequences are intended or not (Fuscaldo, 2006). This account, however, would once again include gamete donors and begs the question of why it is that gamete donors can (relatively easily) transfer parental responsibility but unwilling fathers by natural conception cannot.

My own view is that the question about *who* is a parent can only be answered by asking *what* a parent is, and questions about what generates parental responsibilities have to be answered with reference to what it is that we value about reproductive rights or liberties. The short answer to the question 'what is a parent?' is that a parent is the person putting good parenting into action: it is essentially about what has been described as social parenting (to distinguish it from biological or genetic parenting). In my view, it is no coincidence that a common response to tales of child abuse is 'what kind of parent would do such a thing?' – the clear inference being that no kind of parent would do such a thing; our understanding of what it is to be a parent cannot accommodate such behaviour. Being a parent is not an honorary title, as those who are transfixed by genetic connectedness seem to suppose, it is a title that one earns by doing the business of parenting.

But as the previous discussions have indicated, parenting is also a moral relationship: being a parent means having certain responsibilities (as well as rights, which we have no time to discuss here). We need, therefore, to connect the definition of what a parent is to a specific individual who is obliged to put good parenting into action. At this point, my argument has something in common with Benatar's: the responsibilities are connected with reproductive rights or liberties. Reproductive rights or liberties are important for two reasons: first, they protect individuals from unwelcome bodily intrusion, and second, they enable individuals to have unfettered access to the good of parenting, for this is surely why voluntary reproduction is a good. As Harris puts it:

> . . . anyone denied the opportunity to have children which they want is denied something almost universally acknowledged to be one of the most worthwhile experiences and important benefits of life.
>
> (Harris, 1985, p 152)

But what makes having children 'one of the most worthwhile experiences and important benefits of life' is that one becomes a parent to them, not that one procreates then walks away.

What distinguishes gamete donors from unwilling fathers (or mothers) by natural conception, then, is that their actions are in no way associated with a *personal* parental project (by act or omission). The act of donation is not an act of reproductive rights or liberties, properly understood, at all, even though it involves their reproductive systems. It is the recipients who are attempting to exercise their reproductive liberty, properly understood, to share in the universally acknowledged, most worthwhile and important benefit of having children. It is their personal parental project, not the donor's.

The gamete donor, like the donor of a testicle or ovary, donates the opportunity for someone else to enter into a personal parental project. They are no more the parent of any resulting child than the organ donor is a father or a rapist in the examples above. Accordingly, a donor-conceived individual cannot claim to have been wronged by the actions of the donor who sells gametes if the claim to have been wronged is located in a sense of betrayal by a parent. It is not the donors who have responsibility for the use to which their gametes are put but the recipients who have responsibility for a child who results from their personal parental project and the exercise of their interest in the good of parenting that flows from reproductive liberty.

CONCLUSION

The argument against trade in gametes based on the potential psychological harm for the future child is not convincing on several grounds. It is difficult to argue that such children are so harmed that non-existence would be preferable to existence, so it is difficult for an argument to be successfully mounted that they have been wronged by being brought into existence. While there is a shortage of donated gametes, recipients cannot be blamed for having children using traded gametes. Finally, the claim that donor-conceived individuals are wronged by the actions of the donor in selling his or her gametes also fails because it is not clear that trade in this context is a failure of parental responsibility to the future child since it is far from clear that donors – whether or not they sell their gametes – are, in any morally meaningful sense, parents of the individuals created from their gametes.

It is more than unlikely that the review of the Human Fertilisation and Embryology Act 1990 will recommend a return to donor anonymity, nor is it likely, because of the EU Tissues and Cells Directive, to recommend that people should be free to sell their gametes. What this chapter shows is that there are reasons to doubt the rationale for the lifting of donor anonymity and reasons to question the arguments against the sale of gametes that are based on assertions about the welfare of the future child, arguments that may well be forced back into play when considering the extent to which donors should be compensated or reimbursed their expenses, including loss of income.

REFERENCES

Bayne, T (2003) 'Gamete donation and parental responsibility' 20 *Journal of Applied Philosophy* 77–87

Benatar, D (1999) 'The unbearable lightness of bringing into being' 16 *Journal of Applied Philosophy* 174

Brewaeys, A *et al* (1993) 'Children from anonymous donors: an inquiry into heterosexual and homosexual parents' attitudes' 14 *Journal of Psychosomatic Obstetrics & Gynaecology* 23–35

Brewaeys, A *et al* (1997) 'DI: child development and family functioning in lesbian mother families' 12 *Human Reproduction* 1349–59

Clamar, A (1989) 'Psychological implications of the anonymous pregnancy' in Offerman-Zuckerberg, J (ed) *Families in Transition: A New Frontier* New York: Plenum Press

Cook, R *et al* (1995) 'Keeping secrets: a controlled study of parental attitudes towards telling about donor insemination' 65 *American Journal of Orthopsychiatry* 549–59

Daniels, K and Taylor, K (1993) 'Secrecy and openness in donor insemination' 12 *Politics and the Life Sciences* 155–70

Dickinson, DL (2001) 'Property and women's alienation from their own reproductive labour' 15 *Bioethics* 205–17

Donor Conception Support Group of Australia Inc. (1997) *Let the Offspring Speak: Discussions on Donor Conception* Georges Hall, New South Wales: Donor Conception Support Group of Australia Inc.

Draper, H (2005) 'Why there is no right to know one's genetic origins' in Athanssoulis, N (ed) *Philosophical Reflections on Medical Ethics* London: Palgrave/Macmillan

Erin, CA and Harris, J (2003) 'An ethical market in human organs' 29 *Journal of Medical Ethics* 137–8

Fuscaldo, G (2006) 'Genetic ties: are they morally binding?' 20 *Bioethics* 64–76

Golombok, S (1998) 'New families, old values: considerations regarding the welfare of the child' 13 *Human Reproduction* 2342–7

Gottlieb, C *et al* (2000) 'Disclosure of DI to the child' 15 *Human Reproduction* 2052–6

Harris, J (1985) *The Value of Life* London: Routledge & Kegan Paul

Harris, J (1998) *Clones, Genes and Immortality* Oxford: Oxford University Press

Hughes, P (1998) 'Exploitation, autonomy and the case for organ sales' 12 *International Journal of Applied Philosophy*

Human Fertilisation and Embryology Authority (1998) *Consultation on the Implementation of Withdrawal of Payments to Donors* London: HFEA

Human Fertilisation and Embryology Authority (2004) *The Regulation of Donor-Assisted Conception: A Consultation on Policy and Regulatory Measures Affecting Sperm, Egg and Embryo Donation in the United Kingdom* London: HFEA

Human Fertilisation and Embryology Authority (2006) *The SEED Report* London: HFEA

Johnson, M (2004) 'Donor anonymity and review', 21 January London: Department of Health, available at www.dh.gov.uk/NewsHome/Speeches/SpeechesList/SpeechesArticle/fs/en?CONTENT_ID=4071490&chk=zLzthb

Klock, S *et al* (1996) 'A comparison of single and married recipients of DI' 11 *Human Reproduction* 2554–7

Lycett, E *et al* (2005) 'School-aged children of donor insemination: a study of parents' disclosure patterns' 20 *Human Reproduction* 810–19

McWhinnie, A (2001) 'Gamete donation and anonymity' 16 *Human Reproduction* 807–17

Morgan, LW (1999) 'It's ten o'clock: do you know where your sperm are?' Online: available at: www.supportguidelines.com/articles/art199903.html

Nelson JL (1991) 'Parental responsibilities and the ethics of surrogacy: a causal perspective' 5 *Public Affairs Quarterly* 49–61

Radcliffe-Richards, J *et al* (1998) 'The case for allowing kidney sales' 351 *The Lancet* 1950–2

Resnik, DB (2001) 'Regulating the market for human eggs' 1 *Bioethics* 1–25

Robinson, J *et al* (1991) 'Attitudes of donors and recipients to gamete donation' 6 *Human Reproduction* 307–9

Sheldon, S (2003) 'Unwilling fathers and abortion: terminating men's child support obligations' 66 *Modern Law Review* 175–94

Snowden, R (1993) 'Sharing information about DI in the UK' 12 *Politics and the Life Sciences* 194–5

Soderstorm-Antilla, V *et al* (1998) 'Embryo donation: outcome and attitudes among embryo donors and recipients' 16 *Human Reproduction* 1120–8

The EU Tissues and Cells Directive. Available at: www.hfea.gov.uk/AboutHFEA/HFEApolicy/EUTissuesandCellsDirective

Titmass, R (1970) *The Gift Relationship: From Human Blood to Social Policy* London: Allen and Unwin

Turner, C (1993) 'A call for openness in donor insemination' 12 *Politics and the Life Sciences* 197–9

Vanfraussen, K, Ponjaert-Kristoffersen, I and Brewaeys, A (2001) 'An attempt to reconstruct children's donor concept: a comparison between children's and lesbian parents' attitudes towards donor anonymity' 16 *Human Reproduction* 2019–25

World Medical Association *Statement on Human Organ and Tissue Donation and Transplantation*

Chapter 5

Equality of access to NHS-funded IVF treatment in England and Wales

Laura Riley

INTRODUCTION

In the UK, approximately one in seven couples, or 3.5 million people, are affected by fertility problems. However, most heterosexual couples (about 84 per cent) having regular unprotected sexual intercourse (two or three times a week) will conceive within one year and 94 per cent of couples will conceive within two years. For the remainder, 'infertility' is defined as failure to conceive after regular sexual intercourse for two years in the absence of known reproductive pathology (National Institute for Clinical Excellence, 2004a). The distress caused by unwanted infertility is well documented and, after pregnancy itself, infertility is recognised as the commonest reason for women aged 20–45 to see their general practitioner (GP).

In vitro fertilisation (IVF), an established method of infertility treatment, still has a remarkably low success rate in producing babies. The 2006–07 Human Fertilisation and Embryology Authority Guide to Infertility gives new clinic data based on 38,264 cycles of treatment given to 29,688 women between 1 April 2003 and 31 March 2004. During this period, there were 8,251 births giving rise to 10,242 children. This represents an overall live birth rate per treatment cycle for all IVF of 21.6 per cent, up from 20.4 per cent in the previous year.

Where the woman's own eggs are fertilised and the embryos transferred to her without being previously frozen, the pregnancy success rate in the UK is 28.2 per cent if she is under 35 years old, 23.6 per cent if she is aged 35–37, 18.3 per cent aged 38–39 and 10.6 per cent for women aged 40–42 (Human Fertilisation and Embryology Authority, 2006). A 'cycle' of IVF is the term for the process in which a woman's ovaries are stimulated with drugs to produce a number of eggs. The eggs are surgically collected and mixed with sperm and the resulting embryos then transferred back to the woman, with the aim of establishing a pregnancy. Viable embryos created in this process but not transferred at that stage may be frozen and transferred to the woman at a later date, which can be several years later. IVF is around 22 per cent effective with one cycle and 50 per cent effective after three cycles. At present, about 1 per cent of all births in the UK are as a result of IVF or donor insemination, another widespread method of infertility treatment.

IVF is a relatively expensive medical treatment and in a straightforward private treatment cycle costs perhaps between £3,000 and £6,000 per cycle, plus consultation costs, blood tests, other tests and drugs which can cost £500 – £750 per cycle. If any of the embryos created are to be frozen and stored for thawed transfer to the woman at a later date, this is separately chargeable. HFEA fees chargeable to clinics, both National Health Service (NHS) and private, towards the costs of being regulated and inspected are currently £102 for each cycle of IVF and £51 for each donor insemination cycle. The issue of repeated opportunities to undergo NHS funded IVF treatment is thus of crucial importance to many people needing to attempt pregnancy using these services.

People for whom IVF is indicated may face a greater or lesser difficulty in accessing treatment depending on their financial, medical and social circumstances. In this chapter I have attempted to assess the legal aspects of some of the wide range of responses the NHS has made to those in this position. I also consider the impact that the National Institute for Clinical Excellence's 'Clinical Guideline 11' (NICE, 2004a) may have in creating a more equitable approach to treatment provision in England and Wales within the constraints of limited NHS resources.

IVF PROVISION IN ENGLAND AND WALES BEFORE APRIL 2005

There are 85 Human Fertilisation and Embryology Authority (HFEA) licensed fertility clinics, 52 of which will see NHS patients. All UK NHS and private IVF clinics are required by the Human Fertilisation and Embryology Act 1990 (HFE Act) to be licensed and regulated by the HFEA, which the HFE Act also constituted. In 2005, only about 25 per cent of IVF treatment in the UK was funded by the NHS. In Scotland since 2000, NHS Health Boards have been implementing guidance from the Expert Advisory Group on Infertility Services in Scotland (EAGISS) on the provision of NHS-funded IVF, and in Northern Ireland, work is ongoing to decide on the extent and nature of their NHS-funded infertility services.

English NHS fertility services including IVF were originally commissioned by fewer than 100 Health Authorities with different policies ranging from funding no treatment at all to funding a maximum of two cycles of IVF. From April 2002, with the abolition of Health Authorities, NHS fertility treatment provision in England became subject to the spending decisions of over 300 Primary Care Trusts (PCTs), where IVF provision varied considerably. In Wales, five Health Authorities (and from April 2003 the 22 Local Health Boards which replaced them) offered fertility treatments ranging from no IVF treatment to a maximum of two cycles.

The All Party Parliamentary Group (APPG) on Infertility and the National Infertility Awareness Campaign (NIAC) surveyed all 302 English PCTs in February 2005 to establish the extent and nature of English NHS IVF provision prior to 1 April 2005. The survey had about a 70 per cent response rate, with the responses received estimated to cover 214 PCTs, as some responses were given by one PCT on behalf of PCT consortia. Of the 214 PCTs, 26 funded no form of infertility service, a further 20 reporting funding infertility treatment in exceptional circumstances only (APPG on Infertility, 2005). At the opposite end of the spectrum, Central Manchester Primary Care NHS Trust gained press attention in 2004 after a baby was born there using sperm cryopreserved for a record-breaking 21 years. This was after an exceptional four cycles of NHS-funded IVF, although this level of NHS funding support is thought to be unique to the couple concerned (Boseley, 2004; Hall, 2004).

The 'postcode lottery' has become the colloquial term for a differing availability and standards of treatment offered to patients depending on which NHS funding area they are resident in. A minority of commentators have defended the right of local decision-makers to respond to known local needs when commissioning (Ashcroft, 2003). The historical variation in NHS fertility service provision may stem partly from the fact that professionals with different interests have been responsible for commissioning in PCTs. These range from directors of public health or service redevelopment to heads of family planning or consultants in reproductive medicine, as the charity Infertility Network UK found in their 2004 PCT survey of IVF provision (Infertility Network UK, 2004).

Where an NHS purchaser routinely funds IVF treatment, it is accompanied by local clinical and social eligibility criteria for treatment. NHS purchasers' discretion to impose their own criteria in lieu of stipulations issued elsewhere could be extrapolated by the observation in *R v Sheffield Health Authority, ex p Seale* (1994) 25 BMLR 1 that there is no 'Direction by the Secretary of State, or . . . imposition by her, of a limitation on the provision of such a[n IVF] service'.

An APPG on Infertility and NIAC survey of all 302 English PCTs in February 2005 gives the most recent available reporting on local eligibility clinical criteria. The survey found that 'Policies on maximum body mass index (BMI) [and] smoking are very patchy . . . Only a third of PCTs have a policy on the duration of unexplained infertility'. Prior to 1 April 2005, little consistency was shown in the PCTs' policies on eligible female age ranges. One hundred and twenty-one PCTs (more than half of respondents) reported having a policy on maximum female age range, but only 35 per cent of these were fixed at age 39, as recommended by NICE clinical guidance. The most frequently given age range was 'under 37 years old' (in 24 PCTs), followed by '23–39' years old (in 21 PCTs). However, two PCTs had an upper age limit of 'under 34 years old', while one PCT reported treating of women of 40 years old as their upper limit.

Three PCTs fixed limits for the youngest age at which a woman could begin funded treatment at 30, 32, and 36 years old. While particularly harsh for women with infertility confirmed during their twenties, this also takes no account of dwindling IVF success for women aged over 30. Fewer PCTs specified male age ranges. None had lower limits, but upper limits for men ranged from 45 to 56 years old. The male upper limit appears to be based on a social judgement, as there is no significant overall increased risk of birth defects associated with increasing paternal age. However, the risk of children being born with specific congenital conditions (Down syndrome and syndromes involving multiple body systems or limb malformations) does appear to increase with the father's age over 35, probably due to genetic mutations in sperm caused by biological or environmental factors (Zhu *et al*, 2005).

The decision in *Seale* indicates that rationing policies resulting in the exclusion of patient groups, or offering only limited funding, are not illegal when based on indicators of clinical effectiveness such as the patient's age. Mrs Seale, aged 37, had received a letter from her Health Authority (HA) stating that due to her age, treatment was not offered owing to limited resources and a high demand for IVF. The HA had a cut-off point for treatment at 35 years old to make optimum use of resources by limiting treatment to those more likely to benefit. Auld J found the cut-off at 35 years not to be irrational because clinical evidence at that time held that IVF treatment was generally less effective for women aged over 35. Auld J stated that it was not 'unreasonable' for an HA to adopt a general policy based on current evidence about effectiveness of a treatment in a certain age group. However, he added that:

> [a] clinical decision on a case-by-case basis is clearly desirable . . . However, it is reasonable, or it is at least not *Wednesbury* unreasonable of an authority to look at the matter in the context of the financial resources available to it, to provide this and many other services for which it is responsible under National Health Service legislation.

Disparities in individual clinics' and PCTs' interpretation of the requirements at s 13(5) of the HFE Act have created difficulty for some single women and lesbian couples in accessing fertility treatment. Section 13(5) states that as a condition of licensed treatment,

> [a] woman shall not be provided with treatment services unless account has been taken of the welfare of any child who may be born as a result of the treatment (including the need of that child for a father), and of any other child who may be affected by the birth.

Some clinics have accordingly excluded single women and lesbian couples from treatment completely. Others create their own requirement for a minimum length of relationship before treating unmarried couples.

The HFE Act requires the HFEA to produce a Code of Practice (HFEA, 2003). This gives guidance as to assessing patients under s 13(5), including taking into account different specified factors which might affect the welfare of the child born as a result of treatment. Since the implementation of revised guidance in January 2006, in which clinics were encouraged to 'remove vague and subjective social questions from their assessment', clinics are no longer obliged to write automatically to each patient's general practitioner (GP) to ask whether, from medical records, the GP has reason to believe that a resulting child might be at risk, although they remain free to do so. If patients refuse consent for approaching their GP, this can be taken into account in their assessment. The HFEA does not publish details of the exact assessment procedure that each clinic requires, so the evidence remains anecdotal on this.

In 2004–5, the HFEA conducted its first review of Code of Practice guidance to clinics on interpreting s 13(5), with the resulting guidance announced in November 2005. The HFEA's revision of the guidance on Welfare of the Child specifically excluded the re-examination of their advice on the consideration that clinicians are required to make regarding the potential child's 'need for a father'. The HFEA also does not publicise details of which clinics will accept lesbian couples or single women for treatment, some of whom must find a clinic by word of mouth, or trial and error. Lesbian parents Maria Hurley and Lisa Saffron (Director of Pink Parents, a national support group for lesbian, gay and bisexual parents and families) gave oral evidence of their experiences to the House of Commons Science and Technology Select Committee inquiry on 'Human Reproductive Technologies and the Law' (House of Commons, 2004). In reply to Question 342, Ms Hurley said:

> My partner and I were refused treatment on the ground that we were lesbians. The only information that the clinic had was my name, age and the fact that I had been in a lesbian relationship for nine years. They considered that to be adequate information on which to refuse twice. We have now taken that to appeal. During the appeal, very little was said. They did not talk to us about our views and the provision we had made for male role models for any children we might be lucky enough to have. Their refusal was because of staff who had religious views and did not want us in their clinic.

Members of staff with religious or other views refusing to participate in treatment procedures because they object to lesbian couples having fertility treatment are not protected by the HFE Act. The 'conscientious objection' section in the HFE Act serves a similar purpose to s 4 of the Abortion Act 1967, which allows doctors to refuse to participate in abortions. Section 38(1) of the HFE Act states that 'no person who has a conscientious objection to participating in any activity governed by this Act shall be under any duty, however arising, to do so'. This section allows for refusal to participate in an entire activity, such as IVF treatment or embryo research. However, it does not sanction the acceptance or refusal of particular individuals or patient groups solely on the grounds of personal prejudice or religious conviction.

In her oral evidence, Ms Saffron revealed one demeaning interpretation of the s 13(5) requirement regarding the child's 'need for a father' in reply to Q345:

> . . . another clinic [had] just started to accept lesbians on condition that each couple bring a letter from a man saying that he would vouch for them.
>
> *Chairman*:   A letter from a man?
> *Ms Saffron*: Any man. They did not have to meet the man; they just wanted the letter signed by a man. People were calling me at Pink Parents asking if the clinic had the right to require this.
>
> *Chairman*:   No pictures or anything? Just a letter.
> *Ms Saffron*: No. It could have been written by the woman herself and signed.
>
> *Chairman*:   Absolutely; of course.
> *Ms Saffron*: The clinic felt they were discharging their duties in regard to taking account of the welfare of the child.

Fundamentally, the HFE Act is now under review by the Department of Health, including the requirements of s 13(5). A new HFE Bill is predicted to be debated in Parliament by 2007, with the new Act to be implemented in 2008. Evidence given in July 2006 to the House of Commons Science and Technology Committee by Caroline Flint, the Minister of State for Public Health, indicated that the Government would be minded to recommend the removal of the 'need for a father' formulation in its present form, although any changes to the current statute will rely on a vote in Parliament (BBC News Online, 2006).

Many patients, clinicians and others since 1990 have urged that s 13(5) be substantially revised. Many recommended that the 'need for a father' part be removed, including the then Chair of the HFEA and the House of Commons Science and Technology Committee (House of Commons, 2005). Others have argued that there should be no legislative requirement for welfare assessment, thus removing an intrusive process with little power to predict or prevent future harm and equalising access to fertility treatment (see, for example, Jackson, 2002 and Chapter 3 in this volume).

Additional to the statutory obligations of s 13(5), many NHS providers impose their own social criteria for treatment to enable prioritisation in the allocation of IVF. The APPG on Infertility and NIAC survey from March 2005 found that 'almost half of PCTs have a policy on existing children, with 58 per cent of them barring [from treatment] all couples that have a child from either partner, adopted or otherwise'. Since 2000, this has been pre-requisite for NHS IVF treatment in Scotland, following advice on 'Eligibility criteria for assisted conception' from EAGISS in 1999.

Some of the PCTs in the survey required a specific duration of the couples' relationship, ranging from one to three years. Thirteen PCTs required the relationship to be 'stable' – however that may be quantified. The survey revealed other social criteria, 19 PCTs specifically stating that they would not fund same-sex couples, two requiring the couple to come with a positive recommendation from their GP and four requiring residency in the local area for between 1 and 2 years. One PCT rather disturbingly takes into account unspecified 'religious/financial/social/intellectual reasons'.

Prior to the NICE 'Clinical Guideline 11, Fertility: assessment and treatment for people with fertility problems', published in February 2004, no national review had examined the clinical or cost effectiveness of NHS fertility treatment. In 2000, Alan Milburn, Secretary of State for Health, announced the Department of Health and Welsh Assembly Government's commission of NICE to look at fertility treatment:

> Unfortunately NHS fertility services vary massively around the country. That postcode lottery has to end now . . . Now the NHS has record funding secured . . . in the five years to 2004, [funding] will rise by a third in real terms – it is time to tackle infertility.
>
> (Boseley, 2000)

Professor David Barlow, group leader of the NICE Fertility Guideline Development Group, said at its launch in 2004, 'current NHS provision of fertility services in England and Wales varies considerably from an incomplete and patchy provision to a poor provision' (Barlow, 2004).

At publication, the 'Key Priority for Implementation' that captured public attention was that couples should be offered up to three stimulated IVF treatment cycles (with an appropriately diagnosed cause of infertility, or with unexplained infertility of at least three years' duration). The woman must be aged between 23 and 39 years at the time of treatment. This recommendation meant that for the first time, eligible couples, wherever they lived, could expect their local NHS provider to pay for their IVF treatment. The recommendations as a whole were broadly welcomed by the UK's fertility treatment providers and celebrated by many patients. The major limiting factor acknowledged by both sides of the debate was that the guidance was not accompanied by any specific increase in funding for implementation. The announcement had a mixed reception in the media, some welcoming uniformity of provision, others fearing that increased fertility provision might cut funding elsewhere in the NHS. The clinical guidance on IVF (but no other aspect of Guideline 11) was given an implementation date by the Government in England and Wales of 1 April 2005. Even though its implementation advice referred to fewer IVF cycles than NICE had recommended, this still raised voices questioning NHS capacity to cope with the projected levels of new referrals.

What is NICE guidance intended to do?

In 1999, the then Secretary of State for Health, Frank Dobson, hailed the launch of the National Institute for Clinical Excellence:

> In our Manifesto we promised that ... access to [the NHS] will be based on need and need alone, not on where you live. The creation of NICE is part of keeping that promise ... NICE is being created to help ensure that access to quality treatment is made fairer and faster. For the first time in its history, the NHS has a body dedicated to ensuring that every NHS patient in the country gets fair access to quality treatment.
>
> (Department of Health, 1999)

The National Institute for Clinical Excellence (Establishment and Constitution) Order 1999 (SI 1999 No 220) (as amended by SI 1999 No 2219) lays out the functions of NICE:

> 3. [. . .] the Institute shall perform such functions in connection with the promotion of clinical excellence and the effective use of available resources in the Health Service as the Secretary of State may direct.

As NICE is constituted to provide guidance for practitioners on best practice, while at the same time appraising the clinical and cost effectiveness of new and existing medical treatments and technologies, clearly these aims may conflict where resources are constrained.

The intention for NICE to produce national guidance to improve the quality of healthcare across England and Wales accords with the 'duty of quality' required by the Health Act 1999, s 18(1), which states that 'it is the duty of each Health Authority, Primary Care Trust and NHS trust to put and keep in place arrangements for the purpose of monitoring and improving the quality of health care which it provides to individuals'.

According to the 'Explanatory Notes' to s 18 of the Health Act 1999,

> ... a fundamental component of these [arrangements] ... will be the implementation of clinical governance arrangements ... a comprehensive programme of quality improvement systems ... (*including*

supporting and applying evidence-based practice, implementing clinical standards and guidance . . .) (at 173, my emphasis)

It would thus appear that 'supporting', 'applying' and 'implementing' the clinical guidance of NICE could potentially be seen as a requirement for Primary Care Trusts under the 1999 Health Act.

The contribution of the NICE Guideline towards improving equity of access to IVF in England and Wales remains limited, in that it gives solely clinical guidance and NICE is not equipped to tackle 'social' eligibility criteria. 'Notes on the scope of the Guidance' S.2 states that 'the guidance does not address . . . social criteria for treatment (for example whether it is single women or same-sex couples who are seeking treatment, or whether either partner in a couple already has children)'. In this omission, it could be said that the Guideline fails NICE's own aim of 'supporting' health professionals' decision-making, as expressed in its public information document 'The Legal Context of NICE Guidance':

NICE's purpose is to help reduce uncertainty for health professionals and their patients. NICE guidance sits alongside the knowledge and skills of experienced health professionals. It is not the intention of NICE guidance to replace the clinician's knowledge and skill, rather to support it.

In June 2004, shortly after the publication of the NICE Guideline, the charity Infertility Network UK (IN UK) surveyed 50 English PCTs. They found that of these PCTs, 'more than half believe that it fails to provide much needed guidance on the social eligibility criteria for provision of fertility treatment' (IN UK, 2004). In July 2005, the Welsh Assembly issued standardised social criteria for use in Wales, after more than a year's development and a public consultation. The Department of Health has not made a similar commitment to develop guidance on social criteria for use in England, despite political and professional calls to do so.

In fact, the NICE clinical guidance on fertility does make covert social references by virtue of the fact that the needs of only some patient groups are included in its recommendations. In which case, NICE should more properly have included their deliberation on this omission explicitly. For example, the central definition of infertility in fn 12 at p 10 is '. . . failure to conceive after regular unprotected sexual intercourse for 2 years in the absence of known reproductive pathology'. The clinical guidance also recommends the earliest point for NHS treatment as infertility of three years' duration. This blanket recommendation of earliest NHS treatment provision would appear to be inappropriate given the range of patient needs at issue. While a heterosexual couple might well conceive spontaneously within three years, a similar delay before treatment will be of no clinical benefit to the lesbian couple or a woman without a partner. NICE's omission of consideration of these groups' needs specifically cannot ensure that their treatment will be either clinically or cost effective. Although these groups will usually entirely self-fund their treatment, even within NHS institutions, on the point of cost effectiveness it has been argued that:

> If pregnancy is the outcome that matters for cost effectiveness, then there is no obvious reason why publicly funded fertility treatment should not be provided to lesbians and single women ... In fact it might be that lesbians and single women are more cost effective to treat than infertile heterosexual couples, because they are less likely to have a physiological cause for their unwanted childlessness.
>
> (MacMillan, 2003)

The marginalisation of this group is also out of step with the legislation on the adoption of children, for example. The Adoption and Children's Act 2002, applicable in England and Wales, does not specify that prospective adoptive parents have to be heterosexual. It refers to partners, and therefore same-sex couples will be able to become joint adoptive parents.

Guidance as to the treatment of lesbian couples and single women becomes particularly important with reference to use of intra-uterine insemination (IUI). Lesbian couples and single women are expected to form the largest group of IUI users in the future. As a patient group (depending on the woman's age) they may be less likely to be as frequent users of IVF than their heterosexual counterparts.

Heterosexual couples with male factor infertility are increasingly taking up the option of IVF with intra-cytoplasmic sperm injection (ICSI), a technique where the sperm head is injected directly into the egg. This technique allows the male partner to be the child's genetic father, removing the need for a sperm donor. This can also be important in terms of waiting time, as sperm donor numbers have steadily decreased in the years up to the removal of gamete donors' anonymity in the UK in April 2005, and a drastic shortage of sperm donors has been reported by professionals and the media since then. According to HFEA data, ICSI now accounts for 44 per cent of all UK IVF treatment cycles and more than 3,650 babies are born every year in the UK as a result of IVF with ICSI (HFEA, 2005). Despite the widely anticipated changing demographic of IUI patients, in 'Key Priorities for Implementation' in the NICE Guideline 11 the needs of different patient groups are not explored.

NICE guidance recommendations on IVF

The NICE Guideline on Fertility recommended in point 4 of its 'Key Priorities for Implementation' that:

Couples in which the woman is aged 23–39 years at the time of treatment and who have an identified cause for their fertility problems (such as azoospermia or bilateral tubal occlusion) or who have infertility of at least 3 years' duration should be offered up to three stimulated cycles of IVF treatment.

Azoospermia is the absence of sperm in semen or the failure to form any sperm. In bilateral tubal occlusion, the woman has two blocked fallopian tubes. Women younger than 23 were also recommended for three cycles with an absolute indication for IVF (such as prior treatment for cancer). Three cycles of IVF was recommended as the most likely way of achieving live births balanced against the health costs for the woman and scarce NHS resources. Success rates (resulting in a live birth) for a single cycle are generally about 20–25 per cent using fresh embryos and 12 per cent if using frozen. Three cycles of IVF will produce a 50 per cent live birth rate.

It should be noted that the NICE Clinical Guideline on Fertility forms just one part of NICE's guidance structure. Clinical guidance covers the treatment of people with specific diseases and conditions within the NHS in England and Wales only. 'Interventional procedure guidance' (IPG) considers whether procedures of diagnosis and treatment are safe and effective for routine use in Scotland, England and Wales. 'Technology appraisal guidance' (TAG) recommends the use of new and existing medicines and treatments in England and Wales.

The Secretary of State for Health has powers under primary legislation conferred on him by the National Health Service Act 1977, ss 17, 97C(8) and 126(4), to issue legally binding NHS Directions in relation to TAG, including on funding and the timescale of implementation. Clinical guidance and IPG have no mandatory requirement for NHS funding. Thus, NICE could set no date for implementation of the Clinical Guideline on Fertility, simply stating in s 3.1 that 'it is in the interests of people with fertility problems, and their partners, that the implementation timeline is as rapid as possible'.

NICE's public information document 'The legal implications of NICE Guidance' says, 'if it appears there may be issues around funding or resourcing of a guidance, then the Health departments of England and Wales can issue advice to the NHS on this, at the same time as the guidance itself is published'. In February 2004, on the same day as the publication of the NICE Guidance on Fertility, the Secretary of State for Health issued his advice on IVF implementation, as did the Welsh Assembly Minister for Health and Social Services. The then Secretary of State for Health, John Reid, said of English services:

> Our immediate priority must be to ensure a national level of provision of IVF is available wherever people live. As a first step ... by April next year I want all PCTs, including those who at present provide no IVF

treatment, to offer at least one full cycle of treatment to all those eligible. In the longer term I would expect the NHS to make progress towards full implementation of the NICE guidance.

(Department of Health, 2004)

This was the first time that a minister had issued such advice on any NICE clinical guidance. The Welsh Assembly Minister for Health and Social Services, Jane Hutt, issued very similar advice in a simultaneous press release (Welsh Assembly Government, 2004a) but with an even less generous emphasis, substituting Dr Reid's '*at least* one full cycle of treatment' with 'one cycle of treatment'. This was to be provided by Health Commission Wales, the commissioning body from April 2003 for Welsh IVF services.

The major dissimilarity between the English and Welsh government announcements was that in Wales, national eligibility criteria were established for IVF and other specialist fertility treatments to complement the implementation of the NICE guidance after 1 April 2005. The Minister in Wales announced a new All Wales Assisted Fertility Working Group to develop these social criteria 'and any additional access criteria the Assembly may wish to apply' (Welsh Assembly Government, 2004b). This action to provide consistent, considered treatment criteria marks a positive step towards overcoming the problem of equitable resource allocation.

Is there a legal requirement for doctors to follow NICE clinical guidance?

There is no legal requirement on clinicians to follow NICE clinical guidance; however, they should be aware of it, and consider it in their decision-making. 'The legal implications of NICE guidance' on the NICE website states that:

> ... health professionals are expected to take [the guidance] fully into account when exercising their clinical judgement. However, NICE guidance does not override the individual responsibility of health professionals to make appropriate decisions, according to the circumstances of the individual patient ...

The clinician may thus recommend an alternative treatment with no legal barrier to the NHS funding it. The Medical Defence Union (MDU) says 'a reasoned and reasonable decision to reject the guidance ... together with a good record, made at the time, may be acceptable'.

The NHS clinician is, therefore, technically, legally free to treat women excluded from the NICE Clinical Guideline or to omit to treat a woman included in it. However, the NICE website recommends that 'any health professional who is considering departing from the NICE guidance may wish to discuss the issue fully with the patient . . . and should keep a record of his/her reasons for taking such a decision in the patient's notes'.

However for some legal commentators, strong reasons will be needed for deviation from NICE clinical guidance:

> Increasingly, NICE guidance will be taken to set the quality and standard of care that a patient is entitled to expect. Thus, while not determinative of a duty of care in negligence, these standards are likely to be seen by the courts as an *expected* level of care, such as that departure will require some demonstrable justification relating to the individual patient's particular circumstances.
>
> (Kennedy and Grubb, 2000, p 32)

Anecdotally, patient groups have reported that GPs in England and Wales may be ill-informed about the content of the NICE guidance on fertility, and thus may not refer patients on for treatment. This could give PCTs a false impression of low patient demand for fertility services. NICE has formed a joint working group with the Royal College of General Practitioners on the implementation of NICE guidance in primary care. GPs also have no accreditation programme for fertility, so there is little incentive for busy GPs to raise their own awareness in the area.

Scarce resources as a reason for non-implementation of NICE clinical guidance

Regardless of the Secretary of State for Health's advice to the NHS in England to provide 'at least one' cycle of IVF by 1 April 2005 (crucially unaccompanied by dedicated additional funding), some English PCTs have since refused any funding for IVF, for example within Cornwall, a historically under-served area for NHS fertility treatment. Additionally, 10 PCTs within the Hampshire and Isle of Wight Strategic Health Authority were reported by the BBC in July 2005 to be refusing to fund any IVF except in 'exceptional' circumstances. What would constitute 'exceptional' need for IVF was not explained. Two of these PCTs, North Hampshire and Blackwater Valley & Hart, announced they would make no further IVF provision at all once they had funded their patients to complete any treatment they had already been accepted for. In one of these PCTs, North Hampshire, this action could deny around 48 new couples each year the opportunity of IVF.

A spokeswoman for both North Hampshire PCT and Blackwater Valley & Hart PCT said that following a lengthy review, they had decided IVF was a low priority. No indication was given as to when even one cycle might be provided. The spokeswoman said that 'the decision was not taken lightly and was absolutely necessary to ensure we have sufficient funds to invest in other important areas of care' (BBC News Online, 2005).

In September 2005, Cambridge City and South Cambridgeshire Primary Care Trusts announced they would be jointly suspending all funding for IVF treatment until April 2006. Eighteen couples who had already been given confirmation that funding was available would be treated before April 2006, plus three other eligible couples on their waiting list where the woman was soon to turn 40. The suspension of IVF treatment to all others was reported to save the PCTs £230,000. The waiting list of 42 couples was expected to rise to at least 70 couples by April 2006, yet any plans for subsequent renewal of funding were not reported (*Cambridge Evening News*, 2005).

The data on national implementation come from the survey of PCTs by the APPG on Infertility and NIAC, conducted in March 2005. The survey had a 70 per cent response rate across all English PCTs, with 22 per cent of responding PCTs reporting that they were already meeting the one-cycle requirement and a further 58 per cent stating that they had taken the steps necessary to achieve it by 1 April 2005. However, in February 2005, 16 per cent reported that they were still assessing the steps needed to meet the April implementation date or did not comment on progress. As about 30 per cent of PCTs did not respond to the survey at all, their progress remains unknown.

In a worrying consequence of the Secretary of State's advice to the NHS that it should implement 'at least one cycle' of IVF after 1 April 2005, 20 PCTs previously funding more than one IVF cycle confirmed they would reduce provision to just one cycle after 1 April 2005. Eighteen PCTs failed to confirm that they would maintain their previous funding levels and eight said they would place their own age restrictions on couples granted more than one cycle. However, 40 PCTs said they would not reduce their current provision, 28 PCTs would continue to fund two cycles and a further eight would continue to fund three cycles. Fourteen PCTs stated that their policy on IVF disinvestment had still not been decided. NICE guidance also emphasises that IVF with ICSI should be offered, a more expensive, but sometimes more effective treatment. The survey also identified 30 PCTs funding IVF, but not ICSI (All Party Parliamentary Group on Infertility, 2005).

Where no reasons specific to the individual patient exist to exclude them from the recommendations of NICE but the NHS purchaser declines to fund treatment altogether on the grounds of scarce resources, it is possible that the PCT's decision might be challenged by means of judicial review. Although resource allocation cases have been historically difficult for claimants to win, the existence of expertly developed, evidence-based NICE guidance could go some way to bolster their claim.

The courts have tended to avoid making a direct review of the allocation of scarce resources, regarding the distribution of economic resources to be a political rather than legal question, more appropriate for Parliament to answer. The classic statement of this judicial reticence is Lord Donaldson MR in *R v Central Birmingham HA ex parte Walker* (1987) 3 BMLR 32: 'It is not for this court, or indeed any court, to substitute its own judgment for the judgment of those who are responsible for the allocation of resources'. This case involved essential postoperative aftercare capacity, which was impossible to provide due to lack of resources. This lack of resources prevented a baby being able to undergo non-emergency heart surgery, especially as other emergency cases had taken priority for treatment. The delay in provision of the operation, it had been submitted, was a breach of the Secretary of State's duty in Art 3 of the National Health Service Act 1977 to give 'effective provision of health services'.

Sir Stephen Brown LJ famously stated in the case that it was not 'for the courts of this country to arrange the lists in hospital'. The court reiterated its preference for resource reallocating to be undertaken at a political level. Further, the court was unable to resolve another resource dilemma in *R v Cambridge Health Authority ex parte B* (1995) 1 WLR 898, although in fact in this case, the treatment proposed was essentially medically ineffective and so not in the best interests of the child patient concerned. Bingham MR explained that 'difficult and agonising judgments have to be made as to how a limited budget is best allocated to the maximum advantage of the maximum number of patients. That is not a judgement which the court can make' (at 907).

Questions of resource allocation at judicial review are not justiciable when made on the basis of resource alone, the court having no power to examine whether the PCT has the necessary funds available. However, the courts will intervene if they find a public authority's rationing policy decision-making process is not fair, consistent and coherently reached, using the principles of 'legality', 'rationality' and 'procedural fairness'. The 'legality' test might assist in a situation where the decision made was beyond the power of the decision-maker or in contravention of the law in another way; or the decision was made in bad faith, for an improper purpose, took account of an irrelevant consideration or ignored a relevant one.

The 'rationality' test sets a high standard. In *R v Central Birmingham HA, ex parte Collier* (1988) (unreported), Sir Stephen Brown LJ found that to come within the jurisdiction of the court, the Health Authority would have had to have made a decision that no reasonable body would have reached, saying:

> The courts of this country can not arrange the lists in the hospital and [if] there is [no] evidence that they are not being arranged properly due to some unreasonableness in the *'Wednesbury'* sense on the part of the authority, the court cannot and should not be asked to intervene.

Rational decisions must be based on the consideration of appropriate factors, so where NICE guidance or other guidance (perhaps from the Secretary of State) exists, the decision-maker must show it has considered this, and if it rejects this that there were clear reasons to do so. In *R v North Derbyshire HA ex p Fisher* (1997) 8 Med LR 327, the failure to consider a Department of Health Circular suggesting that hospitals should initiate and continue pre-scribing a drug, beta-interferon, for patients with multiple sclerosis required the Heath Authority to re-make their decision to restrict it. However, the court was not, of course, able to order that the treatment should, or should not be funded.

In *North West Lancashire HA v A, D and G* [1999] Lloyd's Rep Med 399, there was no evidence that the Health Authority had given the issue of fund-ing gender reassignment surgery the degree of careful and rational consider-ation of the individual's case which should be given. The Health Authority did not believe that this treatment was effective, precluding the patients' dem-onstration that their case was exceptional and required funding. The Health Authority's policy, however, appeared to accept that transsexualism was an illness, which would indicate that the treatment would be effective. Therefore, the policy not to treat on the grounds that treatment was ineffective was irrational. The policy on not funding the treatment was quashed on the basis of irrationality, and the decision had to be re-made.

Discrimination against particular groups is also 'irrational' and may also be otherwise illegal. In *R v Ethical Committee of St Mary's Hospital (Manchester) ex p Harriot* [1988] 1 FLR 512, the applicant was refused IVF because she was deemed unsuitable due to her sexual and criminal history, as the clinic judged this by the same criteria used by local adoption agencies. The court decided that in fact she had not been discriminated against in this respect, but stated that had the decision not to offer treatment been founded simply on the fact that she was Jewish, or black, they would have found discrimination. However, in that case she would already be protected by the Race Relations Act 1976.

The 'procedural fairness' test seeks to judge that cases have been con-sidered impartially by the decision-maker. Courts may not look at the worthiness of the policy underlying the decision unless the policy itself was arrived at in a way beyond that authority's power, or in contravention of the law. In that case, the court can order a decision to be re-made, but may not influence the decision reached. For example, in *Seale*, Auld J found it reason-able for the PCT to have taken into account financial implications, alongside their assessment of the clinical merits of a treatment for which they were deciding funding, where this affected a group of patients uniformly.

However compelling the strictures of scarce resources, it seems that where these restrict full provision, greater harm may be done by wasting NHS finances on a non-cost-effective, partial provision of a treatment. It would be interesting to see whether, in IVF provision, this argument might add substance to any claim for judicial review of a one-cycle-only funding decision. Single-cycle provision contradicts the latest clinical evidence about best IVF effectiveness. The Secretary of State, under Art 3 of the National Health Service Act 1977, must ensure 'effective provision of health services'.

NICE guidance is also compelled to promote 'the effective use of available resources', a responsibility introduced by an amendment in August 1999 (Art 3, National Institute for Clinical Excellence (Establishment and Constitution) Order 1999 (SI 1999 No 220), as amended by SI 1999 No 2219, Art 2 (2)).

The NICE IVF guidance also considered the most cost-effective way of providing IVF treatment. PCTs' limitation of provision to less than the recommended 'up to three' cycles could be said to be 'irrational' in funding a non-cost-effective treatment inconsistent with the NHS duty of quality, using scarce NHS resources to fund a less effective treatment against the opinion of an expert body. NICE intends to set national standards, and so local variation in IVF provision would now seem to require strong local reasons to be justified (Kennedy and Grubb, 2000, p 125). Disinvestment in IVF provision by PCTs offering more than one cycle prior to April 2005 would seem difficult to legally justify unless they could demonstrate that they had acquired specific local priorities precluding funding for IVF treatment at former levels. Certainly, 2004's advice from the Secretary of State to PCTs to offer at least one full cycle of treatment to all those eligible does not constitute any limitation on former provision, so PCTs might exercise caution in relying on this to justify disinvestment.

Many commentators have criticised the provision of one cycle only as a waste of funds. For example, *The Times'* science correspondent commented:

> By ignoring the NICE recommendations, Dr Reid has missed the chance to establish a funding system that promotes best practice ... [and] steered a meaningless middle course, the worst option open to him. If the government truly believes that IVF is worth funding on the NHS, it has to do it properly and offer three cycles. Otherwise it should spend the money elsewhere.
>
> (Henderson, 2004)

There may also be health costs to the patient in the single-cycle approach to funding. The comparatively decreased single-cycle success rate may result in more requests from NHS-funded patients (as with many private patients) for dual-embryo transfer based on economic necessity. For women aged 40 or over, the regulatory maximum for transfer is three embryos. Twin and triplet births can seriously endanger the health of mothers and babies. The best practice approach for younger patients is single-embryo transfer (SET) over two cycles. This gives similar chances of pregnancy to one cycle of dual-embryo transfer but without risking twins.

A recent review by the HFEA on the question of moving to single-embryo transfer in the UK was greeted with dismay by some sections of the patient body because of the one-cycle approach to NHS funding – even though the principle of avoiding multiple births had widespread support (Brown, 2005).

A decrease in multiple births where IVF patients are given financial support is widely seen. According to Tarun Jain, in the USA, 'state-mandated insurance coverage for [IVF] services is associated with increased utilisation of these services, but with decreases in the number of embryos transferred per cycle . . . and decreases in the percentage of pregnancies with three or more fetuses' (Jain et al, 2002).

The legal status of the Secretary of State's advice to the NHS

As previously indicated, on the same day in February 2004 that the NICE Guideline on Fertility was published, the then Secretary of State for Health, John Reid, issued advice to the NHS that the new guidance might be only partially implemented, with no timescale given for full implementation. He made no comment on NICE's recommendations for other lower-profile, less politically contested fertility treatments. His comments to the press (as mentioned above) were followed by an even shorter note the following day in the NHS *Chief Executive Bulletin* to NHS and Council chief executives and directors of social services, alerting them to new publications, circulars and announcements from the Department of Health. It said:

> NICE's guidance on NHS fertility treatment services was published on 25 February. The Secretary of State has welcomed the guidance and advises as follows:
>
> – the Department will be looking to PCTs who provide no IVF treatment to meet a minimum national level of provision of one cycle of IVF by April 2005
> – in the longer term he would expect the NHS to make progress to full implementation
> – the priority is to help those in greatest need – that must mean couples who have no children living with them
> > (Department of Health *Chief Executive Bulletin*, 2004)

The instruction to prioritise 'those in greatest need . . . by giving local priority to couples who do not have any children living with them' is particularly punitive towards step-parents, some of whom will be women who have not borne children. In any case, many couples would wish to have more than one IVF child and might not be able to afford to attempt this privately. Blanket deprioritisation of couples because their 'need' is judged to be less will cause delay in their treatment of an unpredictable length. This is not legally identical to refusing to treat a couple at all, but in many cases, because of the individual's own biological time-limits combined with NICE's upper age limit, the outcome will be the same. Deprioritising a group may also be in conflict with the prima facie meaning of s 13(5) of the HFE Act 1990, which requires each case to be considered individually before treatment.

It is within the Secretary of State's power to make mandatory instructions to the NHS. The National Health Service Act 1977, s 1(1) obliges the Secretary of State to:

> [c]ontinue the promotion in England and Wales, of a comprehensive health service designed to secure improvement –
>
> (a) in the physical and mental health of the people of those countries, and
> (b) in the prevention, diagnosis and treatment of illness
>
> and for that purpose to provide or secure the effective provision of services in accordance with this act.

This definition is clearly very broad, and so some of these functions are now delegated to Special Health Authorities like NICE. The Department of Health's 'Explanatory Notes to the Health Act 1999' explain at Pt 28 that 'he may also give direction about the exercise of functions by ... a Special Health Authority'. However, Directions are mandatory, unlike 'advice', as has been given in the case of IVF.

The European Convention on Human Rights and patients seeking NHS-funded IVF treatment

The European Convention on Human Rights and Fundamental Freedoms (ECHR) gives citizens basic protections by means of a series of fundamental human rights. However, absent in these provisions are a specified 'right to healthcare' or 'right to reproduce'. Persons attempting to compel public institutions to provide them with fertility treatment would thus need to rely on other provisions within the ECHR.

The Human Rights Act 1998 (HRA) came into force on 2 October 2000, incorporating the ECHR into UK law. The HRA in s 2(1) obliges domestic judgments to comply with the ECHR, also taking into account Convention jurisprudence. The HRA in s 6(1) created a means of action against public authorities in stating that 'it is unlawful for a public authority to act in a way which is incompatible with a convention right'. Public authorities are defined in s 6(3)(b) as 'any person certain of whose functions are functions of a public nature', which includes the judiciary, but not Parliament. Public authorities may only act incompatibly with the ECHR, as seen in ss 6(1) and 6(2) of the HRA, if the law of their jurisdiction requires them to do so. Where this is the case, and a declaration of incompatibility is made against the public authority by the court, the legislation must then be reviewed by the relevant minister. Here, public authorities of relevance to questions of fertility treatment access might include the Department of Health, NICE, the HFEA, NHS Trusts, local and district health authorities, and possibly even private fertility clinics treating patients funded by the NHS.

It is a matter of some academic debate whether those relying on the ECHR in a legal case about a delay in NHS treatment provision on the grounds of resources will be much assisted. In respect of this, and of the various social criteria imposed on prospective IVF patients, a potentially relevant ECHR right is found in Art 3: 'No one shall be subjected to torture or to inhuman or degrading treatment or punishment'; an absolute prohibition. It might be possible to argue of breach of Art 3 regarding waiting lists as unconscionable delays in medical treatment, for example in the 'deprioritisation' for IVF of those with children living with them. The treatment in question does not have to be of an emergency or lifesaving nature. In the breach of Art 3 found in *Hurtado v Switzerland* (1994) Series A, no 280-A, there was a delay in treatment in failing to x-ray a fractured rib quickly enough. However, the standard of 'inhuman' and 'degrading' is high, and UK courts have not previously been swayed by claims to Art 3 in the context of resource allocation.

North West Lancashire HA v A, D, and G (1999), although it predates the coming into force of the HRA 1998, shows judicial reluctance to rule using Art 3. Auld LJ stated: 'It is plain in my view that Art 3 was not designed for circumstance of the sort where the challenge is to a Health Authority's allocation of finite funds between competing demands.' In the same case, Buxton LJ is similarly dismissive: 'Article 3 . . . has never been applied to merely policy decisions on the allocation of resources . . .' Outhwaite contends that:

> this case gives a very strong indication that, as in the past, the public authority alone would determine the nature of the treatment to be given with limited resources. If this is so, at least under Article 3, a lack of resources would continue to be a defence. However, it is possible that a differently constituted Court might have had a different approach . . . The art 3 obligation to be given 'proper medical care' may have been underestimated . . . The safety-net defence of 'lack of resources' may not be that safe a net.
>
> (Outhwaite, 2001, p 62)

The patient would need to prove that very significant damage had been done by remaining on the waiting list to render this 'inhuman' and degrading'. However, it might be possible to argue that where the delay takes a woman beyond her realistic reproductive age limit, this could constitute 'inhuman' treatment.

It could also be argued that the rights conferred by Art 8(1): 'Everyone has the right to respect for his private and family life . . .', might constitute a right to assisted reproduction treatment. The infertile couple's right to privacy might be said to be curtailed by non-provision of fertility services, as fertile couples can make their own reproductive decisions freely within their own zone of privacy. However, Art 8(2) allows Art 8(1) rights to be legitimately interfered with by public authorities, 'such as . . . is necessary in a democratic society in the interests of . . . public safety or the economic well-being of the country . . . for the protection of health or morals, or for the protection of the rights and freedoms of others'. This was found to be the case in *R v Secretary of State for the Home Department, ex parte Mellor* [2001] 2 FLR 1158, where a prisoner's access to reproductive technology was legitimately denied, even after judicial review. Art 8 is a negative right of non-interference with fertile people, creating no corresponding duty to assist in the founding of families for those who cannot do so naturally. According to Auld LJ in *North West Lancashire HA v A, D, and G*:

> Article 8 imposes no positive obligation to provide treatment . . . if the respondents have no case under Article 8 of failure to respect their private and family life, they could not, *a fortiori*, establish that they were victims of inhuman or degrading treatment under Art 3 since the same essential issues arise.

Buxton LJ goes on to say in the same case that breach of Art 8 occurs only where there is:

> interference with either the applicants' private life or with their sexuality. ECHR jurisprudence demonstrates that a state can be guilty of such interference simply by inaction, though the cases . . . do not seem to go beyond an obligation to adopt measures to prevent serious infractions of private or family life . . . Such an interference could hardly be founded on a refusal to fund medical treatment.

Kennedy and Grubb describe this view of respect for family life as a solely negative obligation as a 'fairly narrow reading' of Arts 8 and 3 in the medical law context, but find that 'it suggests rather strongly that "claim rights" will not easily be accepted by the courts' (Kennedy and Grubb, 2000, p 32).

According to Art 12, 'Men and women of marriageable age have the right to marry and to found a family . . .'. This suggests that there is a prohibition on interference with those who can found a family naturally, but no positive right to assistance in founding a family is generated. The right to found a family by adoption has also not been recognised by the European court, in the case of *X & Y v United Kingdom* [1978] 12 DR 32.

In *Mellor*, an attempt to use Art 12 failed to establish a prisoner's positive right to found a family by using his sperm to artificially inseminate his wife. It could be said that the judgment in this prisoner's case somewhat turns on its own facts, but it does appear in consequence that Art 12 can give no positive right to assisted reproduction to either prisoners or free people.

It might, however, be contended that the denial of fertility treatment to the 'medically' and 'socially' infertile amounts to discrimination, which is addressed in the ECHR, as Art 14 states: '[t]he enjoyment of the rights and freedoms set forth in this convention shall be secured without discrimination on any ground such as sex, race, colour, language, religion, political or other opinion, national or social origin, association with a national minority, property, birth, or other status'. However, Art 14 cannot be engaged, as it applies only to 'rights and freedoms set forth in this convention' and no positive right to fertility treatment has yet been drawn from the ECHR.

Outside the European Union, there is no legal right to a child. For example, in the American case of *Lifchez v Hartigan* 908 F.2d 1395 (8th Cir 1990), the federal district court found that it might be unconstitutional to block access to fertility treatment:

> . . . it takes no great leap of logic to see that within the cluster of constitutionally protected choices, that includes the right to have access to contraceptives. There must be included in that cluster the right to submit to a medical procedure that might bring about, rather than prevent, pregnancy.

But various legal exceptions to this right are permitted, including those relating to lack of resources. Similarly, in Canada, the Nova Scotia Court of Appeal has found that the infertile were unfairly treated, in being denied an appropriate medical treatment (*Cameron v Nova Scotia (Attorney General)* [1999] NSJ No 297 (CA) (unreported)). However, the denial was found to be justifiable, because it was founded on the basis of scarce resources, despite also finding that unequal treatment of the infertile was discriminatory.

The move to full three-cycle IVF implementation

Patients with dwindling fertility are clearly severely disadvantaged by the continued vague governmental commitment to full three-cycle implementation of the NICE guidance. The APPG on Infertility and NIAC survey of PCTs in February 2005 found that while 56 per cent of responding PCTs reported 'working towards full implementation', nearly half of these PCTs had no timeline for completion. Of those that did have a projected implementation date, 37 PCTs reported an estimated implementation period of two years or more and 26 PCTs estimated that they would require three years or more to implement the guidance in full.

Despite Prime Minister Blair's assurance that 'over the next couple of years we shall see at least very substantial progress towards implementation of the full NICE guideline' (Prime Minister's Question Time, 25 February 2004), 60 PCTs (or 28 per cent of the 214 responding PCTs) reported no plans at all to work towards full implementation. Reasons given included the need to assess the feasibility of moving to greater provision, insufficient funds to increase current provision, or deciding not to fund more than one cycle at present. Four PCTs said they were awaiting further instruction from the Department of Health before they would implement in full.

For patients denied repeated NHS IVF cycles, or accepted for treatment but risking running out of time on waiting lists, the options are limited. Those young and healthy enough could attempt to secure subsidised IVF treatment by becoming a non-anonymous egg donor in an egg-sharing programme, which entails other serious considerations. Those with the financial means to do so may travel abroad for cheaper and swifter private treatment. IVF treatment abroad is not subject to HFEA inspection, which brings potential issues of variation in clinical standards. Clinics outside the UK may also have differently regulated payment to gamete donors and the majority of jurisdictions retain gamete donors' anonymity. These factors may provide much swifter availability of eggs and sperm than is currently possible in the UK.

It is to be hoped that the move to English and Welsh three-cycle implementation will not follow that of Scotland. In Scotland, the recommendation to provide three cycles has been in place since February 2000, after the publication of the 'National Service Framework for the Care of Infertile Couples in Scotland' from EAGISS. However, at the time of writing, this has yet to be fully implemented.

CONCLUSION

The NICE Clinical Guideline on Fertility is to be welcomed in preventing unnecessary or outdated treatment regimes being offered to NHS patients. It is to be hoped that the publication of NICE guidance on IVF and consequent advice on implementation by the Government will encourage every PCT to fund clinically eligible couples' treatment in future. However, it is questionable as to when every individual PCT might be willing or able to allocate the resources to make this possible. There is no clear legal means by which the Department of Health could compel PCTs to do so. PCTs reported debts running into millions of pounds in 2005–6 and announced new cuts across all aspects of healthcare provision. Subsequent to the advised 1 April 2005 implementation date for PCTs to provide 'up to one' IVF cycle, some PCTS have announced that they will not fund any IVF at all.

If, at a future date, there is full NHS implementation of 'up to three' IVF cycles for those who need them, access to NHS and private IVF provision in England and Wales may still not be equal, due to different interpretations of s 13(5) of the HFE Act. It is to be hoped that the new HFE Act expected in 2008 will revise this ambiguous and, in practice, discriminatory section (see Jackson, this volume).

Wales and Scotland have developed their own uniform social criteria for NHS IVF treatment. It is as yet too early to know to what extent the Welsh social criteria will increase equity in accessing IVF in practice. The Scottish Programme for Clinical Effectiveness in Reproductive Health (SPCERH), commissioned by the Chief Medical Officer, is at present reviewing the current social eligibility criteria advised by EAGISS (Expert Advisory Group on Fertility Services in Scotland 1999). However, there is not yet any guarantee that the Scottish review will touch on some of the more contested parts of these criteria, with widespread effects which include denying treatment to couples who have a child living with them or where either partner has previously had a sterilisation. In England, unless the Department of Health develops standardised social criteria for NHS IVF eligibility in consultation with professional and patient groups, the IVF 'postcode lottery' will remain, leaving otherwise clinically suitable couples subject to their local PCT's clinical and social criteria.

NICE has no responsibility for the implementation of its guidance beyond disseminating it to the NHS, but its success will be measured by its ability to assist the improvement of clinical practice. NICE recognises this, saying that it will be directing its 'attention towards supporting implementation. As part of this work we want to become the primary repository of information about how the NHS is using [NICE] guidance' (Implementation Tracking; NICE, 2005b). This information will be crucial to gather in order to progress implementation. The Department of Health does not collect these data, a task which has historically been left to the voluntary sector.

However, in the summer of 2005, NICE started work to review the implementation of Clinical Guideline 11, including a survey of PCTs and clinics to assess implementation progress. This is the first time that clinical guidance implementation has been reviewed by NICE. It is thought that the review was instigated partly because of the high media profile of fertility treatment and because the IVF guidance was unique in NICE's history, being accompanied with implementation advice from the English and Welsh Governments. A key question in the review will be the extent of use of the various tools that NICE issued to assist PCTs with implementation, such as costing templates. Such a review could also show clinicians' support for the guidance, revealing if the reason for non-implementation was because clinicians dispute its recommendations or because resources were lacking.

Since the completion of the NICE review at the end of 2005, it is possible that the Healthcare Commission (legally known as the Commission for Healthcare Audit and Inspection) may be able to play a role in assessing IVF provision and implementation of NICE guidance. The Healthcare Commission, formed by the Health and Social Care (Community Health and Standards) Act 2003, was launched on April 1 2004 to 'promote and drive improvement in the quality of healthcare and public health'. As part of this, it will be able to carry out and publish reviews into various aspects of treatment areas, which could include the implementation of NICE guidance. Potential IVF patients and health professionals will be hoping that the history of uneven NHS IVF provision will cease to be repeated if political and governmental will can be harnessed accordingly. With a dedicated increase in spending in place, it is to be hoped that despite the severe financial constraints faced by NHS purchasers, fair, accessible, uniformly distributed, evidence-based and cost-efficient fertility services will be achievable in England and Wales.

REFERENCES

All Party Parliamentary Group on Infertility and National Infertility Awareness Campaign (2005) 'Survey of Primary Care Trusts'

Ashcroft, R (2003) 'In vitro fertilisation for all?' 327 *British Medical Journal* 511

Barlow, D (2004) 'New guidance aims to end postcode lottery for fertility treatments' Press release, 25 February, National Collaborating Centre for Women's and Children's Health

BBC News Online (2005) 'NHS refuses couples IVF treatment', 19 July http://news.bbc.co.uk/1/hi/england/hampshire/4695773.stm

BBC News Online (2006) 'IVF "need for father" rule may go', 13 July http://news.bbc.co.uk/1/hi/health/5175640.stm

Boseley, S (2000) 'End in sight for infertility treatment lottery' *Guardian*, 1 December

Boseley, S (2004) 'Coming of age: baby born from 21 year old frozen sperm' *Guardian*, 25 May

Brown, C (2005) 'Single embryo transfer must go hand in hand with adequate funding' BioNews, 1 August

Cambridge Evening News (2005) 'Childless couples face agonising wait for IVF', 1 October

Department of Health (1999) 'Government keeps its promise for fairer, faster, treatment for patients, the new National Institute for Clinical Excellence opens for business' Press release, 31 March, Department of Health ref number 1999/0193

Department of Health (2004) 'Health Secretary welcomes new fertility guidance' Press release, 25 February, Department of Health ref number 2004/0069

Department of Health *Chief Executive Bulletin* (2004) Under 'NHS interest' 1 NICE Fertility guidance (Gateway ref 2845) issue 207, 20–27 February www.publications.doh.gov.uk/cebulletin27february04.htm

Expert Advisory Group on Fertility Services in Scotland (1999) s 3.5.2 Treatment in Level III 'Eligibility criteria for assisted conception' in *Evidence and Equity – A National Service Framework for the Care of Infertile Couples in Scotland* Issued by the Expert Advisory Group on Fertility Services in Scotland

Hall, C (2004) 'Baby born by sperm frozen 21 years ago' *The Daily Telegraph*, 25 May

Henderson, M (2004) 'Junk medicine: funding fudge' *The Times*, 29 May

House of Commons (2004) Uncorrected transcript of oral evidence, to be published as HC 599-iii 'Minutes of evidence taken before Science and Technology Committee, Human Reproductive Technologies and the Law', Wednesday 30 June 2004

www.publications.parliament.uk/pa/cm200304/cmselect/cmsctech/c599-iii/
uc59902.htm

House of Commons Science and Technology Commitee (2005) *Human Reproductive Technologies and the Law: Fifth Report of Session 2004–5* Vol II http://www.publications. parliament.uk/pa/cm200405/cmselect/cmsctech/7/7i.pdf Vol II

Human Fertilisation and Embryology Authority (2003) *Code of Practice*, 6th edn London: HFEA

Human Fertilisation and Embryology Authority (2005) 'Fertility problems and treatments – facts and figures' Accessed September 2005, available at www.hfea.gov.uk/PressOffice/Factsandfigures

Human Fertilisation and Embryology Authority (2006) *HFEA Guide to Infertility 2006/7* London: HFEA

Infertility Network UK (2004) 'Launch of PCT survey at National Infertility Day' Press release 11 June, Infertility Network UK

Jackson, E (2001) *Regulating Reproduction: Law, Technology and Autonomy* Oxford: Hart

Jackson, E (2002) 'Conception and the irrelevance of the welfare principle' 65 *Modern Law Review* 176 doi: 10.1111/1468-2230.00374,Vol 65 Issue 2

Jain, T *et al* (2002) 'Insurance coverage and the outcomes of in vitro fertilisation' 347 *New England Journal of Medicine* 661

Kennedy, I and Grubb, A (2000) *Medical Law*, 3rd edn, London: Butterworths

MacMillan, J (2003) 'NICE, the draft fertility guidance and dodging the big question' 29 *Journal of Medical Ethics* 313

National Institute for Clinical Excellence (2004a) *NICE Clinical Guideline 11, Fertility: assessment and treatment for people with fertility problems* London: National Institute for Clinical Excellence

National Institute for Clinical Excellence (2004b) 'Implementation Tracking', Accessed August 2004, available at www.nice.org.uk/page.aspx?o=200009

National Institute for Clinical Excellence (2005) 'Legal context of NICE guidance' Accessed July 2005, available at www.nice.org.uk/page.asp?o=202213

Outhwaite, W (2001) 'The scope of impact of the Human Rights Act 1998 on healthcare and NHS resource allocation' in Garwood-Gowers, Austen and Tingle (eds) *Healthcare Law: The Impact of the Human Rights Act 1998* London: Cavendish Publishing

Welsh Assembly Government (2004a) 'Jane Hutt announces equal IVF treatment across Wales' Press release, 25 February, Welsh Assembly Government, available at www.wales.gov.uk//assemblydata/N00000000000000000000000017901.htm

Welsh Assembly Government (2004b) 'Consultation on the Proposed Access Criteria for Infertility Treatment in Wales' Public consultation document issued by Peter Lawler of the Community, Primary Care and Health Services Policy Directorate Health & Social Care Department, 13 January 2005, available at www.wales.gov.uk/subisocialpolicy/content/consultations/infertility-treatment-e.pdf

Zhu, Jin Liang *et al* (2005) 'Paternal age and congenital malformations' *Human Reproduction Advance Access* doi:10.1093/humrep/dei186

Chapter 6

Unforeseen uses of preimplantation genetic diagnosis – ethical and legal issues

Jess Buxton

INTRODUCTION

Since 1989, it has been possible to screen embryos produced using *in vitro* fertilisation (IVF) for certain genetic and chromosomal conditions. This technique, known as preimplantation genetic diagnosis (PGD), can help couples give birth to healthy children, but has also sparked fears over 'designer babies'. In recent years, the proposed use of PGD to help couples conceive tissue-matched babies who can help save the lives of sick siblings – a procedure known as preimplantation tissue-typing (PTT) – has triggered a challenge to the way this technology is regulated. As well as 'saviour siblings', other unforeseen uses of PGD – such as sex selection for non-medical reasons, testing for diseases that do not appear until adulthood and testing for 'pre-dispositions' to disease that may never result in illness – may lead to new ethical and legal dilemmas.

This chapter will present an overview of the science, applications and ethics of PGD and its current regulation in the UK. It will consider the case of *R (on the application of Quintavalle) v Human Fertilisation and Embryology Authority* [2002] EWHC 3000, which questioned the legality of PTT. Though ultimately unsuccessful, this challenge highlighted the difficulties of drawing up legislation to govern this fast-moving area of science. The ongoing Department of Health (DH) review of the Human Fertilisation and Embryology (HFE) Act 1990 provides an opportunity to update the regulation of assisted reproduction so that it is flexible enough to deal with unforeseen uses of the technology. This chapter will conclude that, in particular, it is time to reconsider the regulation of PGD, placing control over treatment decisions firmly back in the hands of patients and their doctors.

WHAT IS PGD?

PGD is almost exclusively used by couples who have a high risk of passing on a serious genetic disorder to their children. It was developed as an alternative to prenatal diagnosis (PND) to avoid the need for termination of an affected pregnancy. PGD cannot be used for all genetic conditions, but it is suitable for diseases where the single gene involved has been identified (for example cystic fibrosis) and for disorders that usually only affect males (for example haemophilia). PGD can also be used to avoid chromosomal conditions such as Down syndrome, by checking the number and appearance of the chromosomes in an embryo.

Aneuploidy screening

Another use of the technique, dubbed preimplantation genetic screening (PGS) or aneuploidy screening, has also been licensed for use in the UK. It allows doctors to select embryos with no apparent chromosome abnormalities (including aneuploidy, an incorrect complement of chromosomes, and chromosome structural abnormalities) and is suitable for IVF patients who would otherwise have a very small chance of becoming pregnant. However, it is unclear whether PGS will ever be used routinely in IVF and the importance of this technique is still being debated (Wilton, 2002; Gianaroli *et al*, 2002). One interesting side-effect of PGS is that if all chromosomes are examined, it inevitably reveals the sex of an embryo. This could have implications for the regulation of sex selection for non-medical reasons, an application of PGD which will be discussed later.

How is PGD carried out?

Both PGD and PGS involve taking a single cell from a 2–6-day-old embryo created using IVF, performing a genetic or chromosome test on that cell, and then returning one or two unaffected embryos (if any are identified) to the womb. PGD was first used in 1989 (Handyside *et al*, 1990) to select embryos free from either adrenoleukodystrophy or X-linked mental retardation – both conditions that usually only affect males. In this case, the scientists did not test for the gene mutation directly but looked for the presence of a Y-chromosome (females have two X-chromosomes, while males have one X- and one Y-chromosome). Since then, advances in molecular genetics have greatly extended the range of genetic tests available for use in both PND and PGD. In theory, it is now possible to test embryos for any known genetic mutation for which a diagnostic test has been developed, although in practice there are technical limitations. PGD requires highly skilled practitioners and, even when carried out by experienced individuals, the overall live birth rate is only around 15–20 per cent (ESHRE PGD Consortium, 2005). This is slightly lower than the average success rate for routine IVF, because there are usually fewer embryos available to transfer following PGD once affected embryos have been discarded.

The most commonly used method for carrying out PGD is known as blastomere biopsy, which involves growing IVF embryos for three days, at which point they consist of eight cells. At this stage, all eight cells are identical and all are 'totipotent', that is, they still have the ability to develop into any body part or tissue. Because of this, it is possible to remove one or two cells from the embryo, using a fine glass pipette, without affecting its normal development. Since all the cells are genetically identical, it can be assumed that any genetic mutation found to be present in the biopsied cells will reflect the genetic make-up of the embryo. However, in practice this is not always the case, which can occasionally lead to misdiagnosis of embryos. Before being tested for a mutation, the DNA from the biopsied cells must first be copied many times, so there is enough of it to detect. This is done using the polymerase chain reaction (PCR), a DNA amplification technique which, although it has been in routine use for the past 15 years, is still technically demanding when carried out on a single cell. If the embryo is being tested for a chromosomal abnormality, then a different technique called fluorescent *in situ* hybridisation (FISH) is used, which allows scientists to look directly at the chromosome complement of a cell. This technique is also used to determine the sex of an embryo, by looking for the presence of a Y-chromosome.

PGD can also be carried out on embryos grown for 5–6 days in the laboratory, at which point they consist of around 150 cells and are known as blasto-cysts. In this case, several cells can be removed, rather than just one or two, which means that more DNA is available for testing. However, the main drawback of this technique is that there is less time available for carrying out the test, since IVF embryos are generally replaced in the womb by day six. A third method of carrying out PGD is 'polar body analysis', which involves looking at the polar bodies – the cells left over after egg cell production. This technique can be used to detect genetic mutations inherited from the mother but, because it is not carried out on cells taken from the fertilised embryo, cannot detect those transmitted by the father. Polar body analysis is used in some countries where PGD is not permitted, such as Germany, since it does not involve testing the embryo itself and is therefore less ethically problematic.

AVAILABILITY OF PGD IN THE UK

A recent review concluded that PGD is still a 'technically challenging, multi-step, labour intensive procedure' (Kanavakis and Traeger-Synodinos, 2002). Because of its costly and specialised nature, PGD is not widely available and is currently offered at only eight centres in the UK. The majority of the £5,000–7,000 treatment costs are usually borne by the couples themselves. DH guidelines (DH, 2002) for National Health Service (NHS) commissioners on the use of PGD state: 'On current evidence PGD may be a good use of resources in some individual cases after careful counselling and assessment but should not be regarded as a standard service'. The guidance goes on to suggest alternatives for couples at risk of transmitting genetic disorders to their children which include: voluntary childlessness; PND followed by termination of affected pregnancies; adoption; or the use of donor eggs or sperm to start a pregnancy at low risk of the disorder carried by one or both of the biological parents. It is clear that cost is a major factor in health policy decisions concerning PGD, since all of these alternative options are cheaper for the NHS. However, for couples who wish to have a biologically related child free from serious illness, the only real alternative to PGD is PND, potentially followed by repeated terminations. For those who find terminating a pregnancy unacceptable, whether for cultural, religious or personal reasons, PGD is the only option available to them. But even for couples who are not opposed to abortion in principle, the main benefit of PGD is that it avoids having to make the difficult choice between giving birth to an affected child and terminating a wanted pregnancy (Pembrey, 1998). Instead, couples are able to embark on a pregnancy knowing the foetus is likely to be unaffected.

Given the limited availability, expense and low success rate of PGD, along with the lengthy and invasive nature of the treatment – which includes all the physical and emotional stresses of routine IVF – it is highly unlikely that there will ever be much demand from individuals wanting to use the technique for 'trivial' reasons. But it is precisely such fears – along with general concerns about carrying out interventions on human embryos – that have led to the tight regulation of PGD both in the UK and elsewhere.

REGULATION OF PGD

PGD is prohibited in several countries worldwide, including Austria, Germany, Switzerland and Italy. In most countries where it is permitted, its use is limited to detecting serious medical conditions. This is the approach taken by the Human Fertilisation and Embryology Authority (HFEA), which is responsible for licensing all activities involving human embryos in the UK. The US has a more permissive approach, in that PGD is unregulated. In theory, this allows clinics to provide PGD for any technically possible reason for which it is requested. In practice, clinicians in the US adhere to professional guidelines issued by the American Society for Reproductive Medicine (ASRM). As a result of these different approaches, the use of PGD to select babies of a particular sex is permitted in the US (ASRM, 2001), whereas it is currently banned in the UK (HFEA, 2004a) and in many other countries. These examples are representative of the variety of approaches taken to regulating PGD worldwide (Knoppers and Isasi, 2004).

Regulation of PGD in the UK

In the UK, PGD is regulated by the HFEA, which licenses all fertility treatment and embryo research. As such, PGD must only be carried out in centres licensed by the HFEA to carry out IVF treatment. PGD is not specifically mentioned in the HFE Act 1990 but is regulated under Sched 2, which covers 'Activities for which licences may be granted'. The only specific mention of genetic testing of embryos appears under para 3, which relates to licences issued for research: s (2)(e) permits the Authority to authorise research into 'methods for detecting the presence of gene or chromosome abnormalities in embryos before implantation'. This legislation reflects the fact that PGD was still an experimental procedure at the time the Act was drawn up – news of the first women pregnant with babies conceived using PGD broke while the issues were being debated by Parliament (Challoner, 1999).

Licensing of PGD services in the UK

Part 14 of the HFEA Code of Practice (HFEA, 2004a) provides detailed guidelines on the provision of PGD and PGS. Section 14.22 deals with the applications for which PGD should be made available, stating: 'It is expected that PGD will be available only where there is a significant risk of a serious genetic condition being present in the embryo', adding 'the seriousness of the condition is expected to be a matter for discussion between the people seeking treatment and the clinical team'. However, the Code also states, in s 14.21, that 'indications for the use of PGD are expected to be consistent with current practice in the use of (post-implantation) prenatal diagnosis'. Section 14.10 expressly forbids centres from using information for selecting 'embryos of a particular sex for social reasons'. Elsewhere in the Code, s 14.2 deals with PGS, stating that it should only be used for women over 35; those with a history of recurrent miscarriage; those with several previous failed IVF attempts; or women with a family history of aneuploidy. No mention is made anywhere in this edition of the Code of using PGD to establish HLA-tissue type (PTT).

In terms of providing a clinical PGD service, two other parts of the HFE Act are also relevant. Section 13(6) deals with the requirement for clinics to provide counselling, saying that a woman shall not be provided with treatment services unless she, and her partner if she has one, 'have been given a suitable opportunity to receive proper counselling about the implications of taking the proposed steps, and have been provided with such relevant information as is proper'. In terms of PGD, counselling is expected to include non-directive genetic counselling, according to s 14.13 of the Code. Secondly, s 13(5) of the Act requires clinics to take account of 'the welfare of any child who may be born as a result of the treatment', as well as any other child who might be affected by the birth (see Jackson, Chapter 3 in this volume; Blyth, Chapter 2 in this volume). When providing PGD, s 14.23 of the Code says that this assessment should include consideration of the likely degree of suffering associated with the condition, the availability of effective therapy, the view of the people seeking treatment and their family circumstances.

PGD is licensed on a case-by-case basis, with s 14.7 of the Code stating that 'Centres must submit an application to the HFEA for each new condition for which they wish to test and for each new test they wish to use'. Anecdotal evidence suggests that many practitioners are frustrated by the bureaucracy surrounding this licensing process. Before being granted a licence to use PGD to test for a particular disease, the clinic must first 'work up' the test in the laboratory and then submit an application containing details of every step of the procedure – a process that can take several months. Clinics then some-times have to wait up to six further months to receive a response from the HFEA (Progress Educational Trust, 2004).

To address some of these delays, the HFEA recently streamlined the appli-cation process, so that centres can get 'fast-track' licences for conditions already tested for elsewhere in the UK (HFEA, 2005b). However, this does not apply to PTT, late-onset conditions or other 'unusual' applications of PGD. It also does not include testing for a type of chromosome abnormality known as a translocation. This means, for example, that even if a clinic is licensed to test embryos for one chromosome translocation, it still needs to make a full-length application to look at a different translocation, even though the techniques used are practically identical.

SAVIOUR SIBLINGS

In recent years, PGD has hit the headlines following its application in select-ing a 'tissue-matched' embryo that is not only free from a disease but is also a potential cord blood stem cell donor for a seriously ill sibling – a so-called 'saviour sibling'. In the UK, a request from a couple who wished to use PGD in this way resulted in a legal challenge to the powers of the HFEA by Josephine Quintavalle, backed by the pro-life pressure group Comment on Reproductive Ethics (CORE) (*R (on the application of Quintavalle) v Human Fertilisation and Embryology Authority* [2002] EWHC 3000).

First use of PTT

The first recorded use of PTT was in the US in October 2000, at the Reproductive Genetics Institute in Chicago, for the Nash family (Verlinsky *et al*, 2001). Their daughter Molly, aged six at the time of treatment, has Fanconi's anaemia. This rare hereditary blood disease primarily affects the bone marrow, resulting in decreased production of all types of blood cells. The lack of white blood cells predisposes the patient to infections, while the lack of platelets and red blood cells may result in bleeding and anaemia, respectively. Fanconi's anaemia is inherited in an autosomal recessive way, which means that only children who inherit two copies of the faulty gene (one from each parent) are affected. People with just one faulty gene are healthy carriers, but if both parents are carriers, they have a one in four chance of passing on the disease to each of their children. Bone marrow transplantation can cure the blood problems associated with Fanconi's anaemia and a 'tissue-matched' sibling is the best donor source. Alternative sources are matched umbilical cord blood cells from a sibling and/or bone marrow from an unrelated, tissue-matched donor.

Doctors treating the Nash family used PGD to identify an embryo that was both free of Fanconi's anaemia and also able to provide tissue-matched cord blood cells. After four attempts, the couple conceived a healthy son, who was able to provide his sister with a blood stem cell transplant from his umbilical cord. Doctors described the procedure as 'a complete success', and Molly's health was reported to have improved dramatically (Borger, 2000).

The embryo tissue-typing procedure

A tissue-matched donor can be identified by carrying out a blood test to determine which antigens they possess – proteins found on the surface of body cells that flag up a tissue as 'self' to the body's immune system. It is possible to look at these 'HLA' antigen proteins (or the genes that make them) to identify a likely tissue match between two people. This procedure is routinely used to check compatibility between a tissue or organ donor and the patient, to ensure that transplanted tissues or cells are not destroyed by the recipient's immune system. Its use to look at embryo genes to identify a potential cord blood stem cell donor, in conjunction with testing to avoid a serious condition, has now been reported by several groups worldwide (Fiorentino et al, 2004; Kahraman et al, 2004; Rechitsky et al, 2004; Van de Velde et al, 2004).

UK requests for PGD with tissue-typing

The Nash family's story attracted worldwide media coverage (for example, Borger and Meek, 2000, Weiss, 2000), and several UK families subsequently applied to have similar treatment. Doctors at the Centres for Assisted Reproduction (CARE) clinic in Nottingham treating the Hashmi family were granted a licence by the HFEA to use PTT in 2001, to help them conceive a healthy baby whose cord blood could help save the life of their son Zain, who has beta-thalassaemia (HFEA, 2001). As in the case of the Nash family, the embryos were to be tested to avoid the genetic mutation responsible for the existing child's illness, as well as to determine their tissue type.

In a decision criticised by many commentators (for example, Gavaghan,

2004; Sheldon and Wilkinson, 2004a, b; British Medical Association (BMA), 2004), the HFEA later turned down a request from the Whitaker family, who wished to conceive a child who would be able to provide compatible cord blood for their son James, who has Diamond-Blackfan anaemia (DBA). The Authority said it refused the application because the Whitakers wanted to screen their embryos for tissue type only, and not to also determine whether or not they were free from disease (HFEA, 2002). Some cases of DBA are caused by a mutation in a known gene, but for most, including James Whitaker, the gene or trigger responsible remains unknown. The family subsequently travelled to have the procedure carried out at the Reproductive Genetics Institute in Chicago in October 2002. The treatment was successful, and Charles Whitaker, a potential matched cord blood donor for his ill brother, was born in June 2003. Just over a year later, James underwent a successful bone marrow transplant operation using the cord stem cells and in October 2004 was pronounced 'effectively cured' by his doctors at Sheffield Children's Hospital (Walsh, 2004).

The Chicago group has now treated several families who wanted to use PTT only, without concurrently testing embryos for a genetic condition. The couples involved wanted to conceive babies who could provide matched cord blood transplants for existing children affected by acute lymphoid leukaemia, acute myeloid leukaemia or DBA (Verlinsky et al, 2004a). Because cord blood contains blood stem cells, which can give rise to both red and white blood cells, it can potentially be used to treat any disease in which these cells are affected.

Legal challenge to embryo tissue-typing in the UK

After the HFEA had allowed the Hashmis to begin treatment, a High Court judge then ruled that the Authority did not have the legal powers to grant IVF clinics licences to carry out PTT. The ruling followed a judicial review brought by Josephine Quintavalle, backed by CORE, at the end of 2002 (*R (on the application of Quintavalle) v Human Fertilisation and Embryology Authority* [2002] EWHC 3000). The House of Commons Science and Technology Committee (STC) also criticised the HFEA during this time, questioning its authority to license embryo tissue-typing (Gavaghan, 2004). But the HFEA successfully appealed against the ruling, and the ban was overturned by the Court of Appeal in April 2003 (*R (on the application of Quintavalle) v Human Fertilisation and Embryology Authority* [2003] EWCA Civ 667). CORE launched a further appeal, but the House of Lords ruled in favour of the HFEA in April 2005 (*Quintavalle (on behalf of Comment on Reproductive Ethics) v HFEA* [2005]).

Details of the judicial review of embryo tissue-typing

In *R (on the application of Quintavalle) v Human Fertilisation and Embryology Authority* [2002] EWHC 3000, Quintavalle claimed that the HFEA had acted *ultra vires* of the powers vested in it by the HFE Act of 1990. She argued that PTT was illegal under s 3 of the HFE Act, which states in Pt (1)(b) that no person shall 'keep or use an embryo except in pursuance of a licence'. The crux of her case lay in the contention that PTT could not actually be licensed, since Sched 2 of the Act provides that a licence may only be issued if it appears to be 'necessary or desirable for the purpose of providing treatment services'. Treatment services are defined as 'medical, surgical or obstetric services provided ... for the purposes of assisting women to carry children'. Quintavalle claimed that PTT could not be included in this definition of treatment services, since its purpose was not to enable a woman to carry children but to relieve the suffering of another child.

Initially, the HFEA responded by saying that PTT could indeed be licensed on the basis that it was 'necessary or desirable for the purpose of providing treatment services', but then changed its primary submission to argue that PTT did not actually require a licence because the procedure was carried out on cells removed from the embryo, not the embryo itself – effectively arguing that PTT was not governed by the HFE Act. Once cells have been removed from an embryo pursuant to a licence for the purposes of PGD, it said, further tests on those cells do not amount to further use of the embryo. Mr Justice Maurice Kay was not convinced by this argument, which could actually be applied to any application of PGD, not just PTT. He pointed to the fact that the HFEA itself had referred to PTT in its press release concerning the Hashmi licence as 'an additional step whereby the *embryo* is simultaneously tested for its tissue compatibility with an affected sibling'. He also pointed out that s 3 of the Act concerns prohibitions '*in connection with embryos*', which would guard against such splitting of hairs. Third, Kay J found it 'inconceivable' that Parliament had intended to leave an activity such as PTT outside the direct control of the Act (at para 12).

Kay J also disagreed with the HFEA's alternative submission, that PTT fell under the remit of 'treatment services' for the purposes of assisting women to carry children. He said that 'the sole purpose of tissue typing is to ensure that any such child would have tissue compatibility with its older child', and concluded that 'the language of the Act does not bear the strain which would be necessary to read "with particular characteristics" into the carrying of a child' (at para 17). While expressing his great sympathy for the Hashmi family's predicament, he said that on any reading of the HFE Act, 'the legislation has been so tightly drawn so as to ensure that the ground rules within which the HFEA operates restrict the potential for misuse of science and technology' (at para 20).

Quintavalle in the Court of Appeal

The HFEA appealed against Mr Justice Kay's decision in a case supported by the Secretary of State for Health, which was concerned that the judgment could have implications for PGD in general, and not just for PTT (*R (on the application of Quintavalle) v Human Fertilisation and Embryology Authority* [2003] EWCA Civ 667). In the Court of Appeal, the Authority argued that treatment 'for the purposes of assisting women to carry children' could embrace procedures designed to ensure that a child would not be affected by a genetic disease, or would possess stem cells matching that of a sick child – in effect, any characteristics that would otherwise inhibit or prevent a woman from bearing a child.

The appeal court judges agreed, ruling that 'Parliament envisaged the possibility or likelihood of future developments (even though it could not know precisely what they would be) and positively intended to bring all such procedures within the sphere of the HFEA, with the exception of those specifically prohibited' (at para 144), reversing the first instance decision. In reaching this decision, the Master of Rolls, Lord Philips of Worth Matravers, appears to have been particularly impressed by the fact that when the 1990 Act was drawn up, para 3(2)(b) of Sched 2 permitted licensing of research into 'developing methods for detecting the presence of gene or chromosome abnormalities in embryos before implantation'. If Parliament had intended for research into PGD to be permitted, then it would have been strange indeed for PGD itself to be prohibited, the argument went (Gavaghan, 2004).

In his detailed analysis of this case, Colin Gavaghan (2004) suggests that, although the definition of 'treatment services' can reasonably be considered to include PGD for genetic disorders, its encompassing of embryo tissue-typing is open to debate. Nothing in the background materials looked at by the court, or in other provisions of the Act, makes any direct or indirect references to PTT, he points out, concluding that categorising this procedure as part of 'treatment' seems to stretch the definition 'beyond reasonable usage'.

However, given that the court *did* find that the HFEA was rightfully entitled to issue licences for PTT, both Gavaghan and others (Sheldon and Wilkinson, 2004a) feel that the HFEA was wrong to distinguish between the Hashmi and Whitaker applications. Both papers conclude that the HFEA, in refusing to grant the Whitakers a licence, made the wrong decision from both an ethical and a legal point of view.

The House of Lords decision on embryo tissue-typing

CORE appealed against the Court of Appeal's decision in January 2004, and the case was heard by the House of Lords in March 2005 (*Quintavalle (on behalf of Comment on Reproductive Ethics) v HFEA* [2005] UKHL 28). Lords Steyn, Hoffmann, Scott, Walker and Brown unanimously found in favour of the HFEA, concluding that allowing the Hashmis' request did indeed fall within its authority. Lord Hoffman described PTT as a way to save the family 'from playing dice with conception', but did not further address the wider ethical issues surrounding saviour siblings. In effect, the Lords agreed with the Court of Appeal that the HFEA is legally entitled to make decisions of this nature. Although the Hashmis' lengthy legal battle is now over, it has highlighted the fact that 'the wording of the HFE 1990 Act has been found to provide limited or ambiguous guidance on a number of issues that were not foreseen by its drafters' (Sheldon, 2005).

Following the appeal court's decision in 2003, Raj and Shahana Hashmi were free to continue with their attempts to conceive a healthy child who could also act as a cord blood donor for Zain. In November 2004, the Hashmis were reported to be continuing with their attempts to conceive a matched donor baby, following a total of six IVF attempts and five miscarriages (BBC News Online, 2004). Meanwhile, the HFEA reversed its earlier policy decision on saviour siblings and in July 2004 announced that it would now license PTT in cases where searches for an existing matched donor prove unsuccessful (HFEA, 2004b). The first family to benefit from this policy change was the Fletchers, who in September 2004 were given permission to try to conceive a matched donor sibling for their son Joshua, who also has DBA. The birth of Jodie Fletcher, a baby girl who is a tissue match for Joshua, was announced in July 2005 (Gould, 2005).

Why did the HFEA change its policy on saviour siblings?

Prior to the legal challenge, the HFEA's own ethics committee had recommended that couples should be allowed to use PGD for tissue-typing only – cases like the Whitakers, as well as the Hashmis – a recommendation which the HFEA then ignored (Gavaghan, 2004; HC STC, 2005). Even when given the go-ahead to license such treatment by the Court of Appeal, it still did not issue a license – a decision that many feel was a serious error on the Authority's part (Gavaghan, 2004; Sheldon and Wilkinson, 2004a).

Once the Court of Appeal had ruled in the HFEA's favour, it could have confidently proceeded to authorise PTT requests, secure in the knowledge that it was qualified to make such decisions. However, it refused the Whitakers permission to have treatment, and did not change its policy (to that approved by its ethics committee) for a further two years. The HFEA then explained its change of heart as the result of a comprehensive review of the latest research, into the general safety of PGD, the psychological effects of being a 'saviour sibling' and the success of blood stem cell transplant treatments (HFEA, 2004b). In this report, published on its website, the HFEA said that it initially took a precautionary approach to allowing the procedure, balancing the theoretical risks of embryo biopsy against the lack of any direct benefit to a child conceived using PGD for tissue-typing only, and not to avoid any genetic condition. It is not clear how the data on the long-term outcomes of PGD have substantially changed in four years, although a recent study (published after the HFEA reversed its policy) shows that there is no increased risk of birth defects associated with the technique (Verlinsky *et al*, 2004b). But in truth there is not much more relevant scientific evidence in this area than there was in 2002, and it is tempting to view the HFEA's retrospective rationalising of its decisions partly as a 'face-saving' exercise.

GENERAL CONCERNS OVER PGD

There have been concerns that IVF in general, and particularly PGD – since it involves embryo biopsy – could affect the future health of any child conceived in this way. Although there is still a recognised need for more long-term follow-up studies of children born following assisted reproduction technologies (ART), there is no evidence as yet that they cause any major health problems (ASRM, 2004; Ponjaert-Kristoffersen *et al*, 2005). The largest study of children born following PGD carried out so far looked at 754 babies conceived at three different centres and concluded that they were no more likely to be affected by birth defects than children conceived naturally (Verlinsky *et al*, 2004b). Of course, as with any new medical technique, it is vital that the outcomes of PGD continue to be closely monitored.

There are several ethical objections to PGD, some of which are rooted in a general concern for the moral status of the human embryo while others reflect worries over the potential misuse of this technology. The first of these objections is that PGD involves selecting and discarding some embryos, a concern that is generally articulated as 'playing God' or 'interfering with Nature' (Human Genetics Alert (HGA), 2004). However, embryos are also selected (and some discarded) in routine IVF, to choose those most likely to implant in the womb. Indeed, this specific concern about PGD is generally raised by individuals and pressure groups opposed to any application of IVF, for this very reason. But it could be argued that selecting IVF embryos judged to be most healthy is mirroring (albeit in an imperfect way), rather than interfering with Nature, since it is known that many fertilised eggs never get as far as implanting into the womb – a process which occurs around six days after natural conception. The rest are lost, presumably because they contain genetic errors incompatible with normal development.

Another objection to the use of PGD is that it is an inherently eugenic procedure that raises the spectre of Nazism, which sought to breed a genetically superior 'race' of people (HGA, 2004). However, there is evidently a world of difference between a State-controlled effort to eliminate certain types of living people and personal reproductive decisions aimed at having a healthy child. Indeed, the US ethicist Arthur Caplan has argued that when commenting on areas of contemporary biomedicine, 'the cavalier use of the Nazi analogy in an attempt to bolster an argument is unethical' (Caplan, 2005). A related objection is that PGD (and PND) encourages discrimination against disabled or seriously ill people already living (Shakespeare, 1999; Watt, 2004) – an argument which is not borne out by studies of families who already have, and cherish, one child affected by a genetic disorder but wish to avoid the disease in future children (Genetic Interest Group (GIG), 1996; Tizzard, 1999).

SAVIOUR SIBLINGS: ETHICAL ISSUES

One of the main objections to saviour siblings is an extension of a further concern raised over PGD in general, namely that a child conceived in this way is not valued for itself but that parental love is conditional upon certain characteristics it has – being free from a particular disease or being able to provide tissue-matched cells for a sibling (King, 2003a; Watt, 2004). Many ethical arguments against PTT, whether used in conjunction with PGD to avoid a genetic disease (the 'Hashmi' situation) or alone (the 'Whitaker' situation), cite Immanuel Kant's dictum that one should 'never use people solely as a means but always treat them as an end'. Ethicists in favour of PTT say the key word in this argument is 'solely' – providing a child is loved and valued for itself, it is of no consequence that it is *also* a source of donor tissue (Boyle and Savulescu, 2001; BMA, 2004; Pennings *et al*, 2002; Sheldon and Wilkinson, 2004b). Indeed, it has been pointed out (in another, related context) that people may have children for a variety of reasons – to provide companionship for another child, to inherit a family business or to prop up an ailing marriage – none of which preclude the parents from loving and caring for their offspring (Savulescu, 1999).

Another concern raised by those opposed to PTT is that it represents the first step down a 'slippery slope' at the bottom of which are parents with a 'shopping list' of non-medical traits they would like their babies to have. However, even if this were scientifically possible (which it is not at present, and might never be), an inexorable slide down the slope is not inevitable – even if there were any demand for such a service, which seems highly unlikely, for reasons given earlier.

A further argument against saviour siblings is that a tissue transplant might not work and the ill sibling may die despite receiving matched blood stem cells. But, as Boyle and Savulescu (2001) point out, the resulting effect on the surviving child and its family is unlikely to be so harmful that it would have been better for the saviour sibling not to have been born at all. Their conclusion is that 'we must avoid the trap of interfering with individual liberty by preventing such procedures for no good reason, simply out of the "genophobia" that grips much of society today' (Boyle and Savulescu, 2001).

In another paper defending PTT, Merle Spriggs says that 'in a situation that requires an intervention involving no sacrifice and no inconvenience by one child to save the life of another, parental consent is morally acceptable', and adds that it may even be 'morally required' (Spriggs, 2005).

One final objection is that PTT is a costly procedure which may divert resources away from more pressing cases. However, given the lifetime costs of caring for a seriously ill child (an estimated £50,000 per year for someone with beta-thalassaemia), the £7,000–10,000 required for two or three cycles of PGD pales into insignificance (see Templeton, 2004).

OTHER UNFORESEEN APPLICATIONS OF PGD

Although PTT is the only application of PGD that has so far resulted in a challenge to UK law, there are other uses of this technology that have triggered controversy, or uncertainty about what is permitted. Sex selection for non-medical reasons, while currently banned by the HFEA in the UK, has been the subject of much debate, as has the use of PGD to test for diseases that do not cause symptoms until teenage or adulthood.

PGD for late-onset disorders/predispositions

In November 2004, the HFEA granted a licence to a team at University College in London to use PGD to test embryos for familial adenomatous polyposis (FAP) – a form of hereditary bowel cancer (HFEA, 2004c). This decision triggered much media debate, with pressure groups CORE (Henderson, 2004b) and GeneWatch UK (Boseley, 2004) both voicing their objections to this use of the technology. CORE argued that because the symptoms of FAP are not present at birth, this use of PGD is a qualitatively different use of the technology, since such a child would have several years of life unaffected by the disease. GeneWatch described the licence as 'a disgrace in a democratic society' and criticised the HFEA for making such decisions 'behind closed doors', with no public discussion.

Clinicians also called upon the HFEA to explain its decision-making process when considering such applications, which fall outside the new 'fast-track' licensing system described earlier. In the case of the licence issued to use PGD for FAP, a spokesperson for the HFEA referred to two important factors: the earliest age at which the cancer could develop (10 years) and the almost 100 per cent certainty that inheriting a mutated gene would cause the disease. More such information would help patients and doctors decide whether or not to apply for a licence to carry out a particular test, given the current absence of a clearly stated policy in this area, it was argued (Taranissi and Lawford Davies, 2005).

The HFEA responded to these criticisms, and sought the public's views on the use of PGD for diseases such as inherited cancers, in which not everyone who inherits the gene mutation responsible will go on to develop the condition (HFEA, 2005a). In May 2006, the Authority announced that it will now consider granting PGD licences for gene mutations that confer cancer susceptibility, but not for those involved in milder conditions such as asthma or eczema or more genetically complex ones like schizophrenia (HFEA, 2006).

It is likely that more requests for PGD tests to detect late-onset diseases will now follow, particularly for tests involving BRCA1 and BRCA2 genes which, when faulty, confer a high risk of breast and/or ovarian cancer (Henderson, 2004b).

In the US, PGD has already been carried out for a couple at risk of passing on a rare, early-onset form of Alzheimer's disease (Verlinsky *et al*, 2002). This case was criticised because the woman being treated is very likely to develop Alzheimer's before she reaches the age of 40, so she 'most likely will not be able to care for or even recognise her child in a few years' (Towner and Lowey, 2002). Such issues do, of course, need to be considered when offering treatment, but each family's circumstances will be unique and it is likely that the child will have other caregivers. As one ethicist points out, to be consistent, if people at risk of developing a late-onset genetic disorder were to be denied access to assisted reproduction treatment, then so too should patients with HIV, or cancer patients who have had gametes frozen – both of which are deemed acceptable uses (Robertson, 2003a).

Requests to use PGD to avoid passing on late-onset disorders are a relatively recent development, both in the UK and elsewhere. However, the ethics and practicalities of testing for diseases that do not appear until adulthood have already been considered, in the context of PND. In 1998, the Advisory Committee on Genetic Testing (ACGT, later subsumed by the Human Genetics Commission) published a report on testing for late-onset disorders which recommended that prenatal genetic testing for these disorders 'should only be undertaken in the context of full genetic counselling' (ACGT, 1998). It also points out that requests for such testing are likely to be fairly uncommon, and limited to families who have experienced particularly adverse effects of the disorder. If it is deemed ethically acceptable to terminate a pregnancy on the basis that a foetus is at risk of a late-onset disorder, then surely PGD for the same purpose is just as acceptable, if not more so.

In making the decision to allow PGD for hereditary bowel cancer, the HFEA abided by the conditions in its own Code of Practice (HFEA, 2004a): namely that when clinics are deciding whether or not to offer PGD, 'the seriousness of the condition is expected to be a matter for discussion between the people seeking treatment and the clinical team' (HFEA, 2004a). FAP is certainly a serious genetic disorder, which almost always causes bowel cancer between the ages of 20 and 40. The only treatment for those affected is to have large sections of the bowel removed, and even this drastic step cannot guarantee that the cancer will not return. For such families,

PGD offers a way to start a pregnancy secure in the knowledge that they have done all they can to avoid passing on a life-threatening disease to their child. GIG, which represents patients affected by genetic disease, makes no distinction between early- and later-onset diseases when considering both preimplantation and prenatal genetic diagnosis (GIG, 1996). It states that 'GIG firmly believes that individuals must be free to make their own decisions because they are the ones who will have to live with the consequences of those decisions'.

Non-disclosure testing for late-onset disorders

There is another ethical dilemma that may arise from using PGD to test for late-onset conditions which, again, has already been encountered in PND. There have been cases in which couples have requested prenatal testing for Huntington's disease (HD), but do not wish to know if the at-risk partner has already inherited the condition (Tassicker *et al*, 2003). HD is a serious disorder that affects nerve cells in the brain. Mild symptoms, which include forgetfulness, clumsiness and personality changes, first appear in middle age. Over the next 10–20 years, a person with HD gradually loses all control of their mental and physical abilities. There is no cure for HD at the moment, although some of the symptoms can be treated with drugs. HD is an example of a dominantly inherited disease, which means that it affects people who inherit just one copy of the faulty gene responsible. This means that someone with an affected parent has a 50 per cent chance of inheriting HD themselves, and in turn has a 50 per cent chance of passing the disease on to each of their children. In cases where a parent wishes to have a prenatal HD test but does not want to know whether they themselves have inherited the disorder, the parent's 'right to not know' has to be respected. One solution to this issue is simply not to tell them – so-called 'non-disclosure testing'.

Another way of dealing with such cases is to carry out 'exclusion testing', where geneticists test the foetus for the presence of one of the chromosomes inherited from the unaffected *grandparent*, neither of which carries the faulty gene – rather than looking at the faulty gene itself. The drawback of this approach is that although all foetuses with a chromosome inherited from the unaffected grandparent will be unaffected, around half of those with a chromosome from the affected grandparent will also be unaffected (those who inherit the chromosome that does not contain the faulty gene). This could result in the termination of a healthy pregnancy, a difficult ethical dilemma which can be addressed by using exclusion testing with PGD instead of PND (Sermon *et al*, 2002). However, there are also issues with using exclusion testing or non-disclosure testing with PGD, since it could mean carrying out repeated cycles of invasive and expensive treatment on couples who are not actually at risk of passing on the disease. In some cases, the clinician may be obliged to carry out faked embryo transfers if there are no unaffected embryos to return to the womb. Again, these are difficult clinical and ethical decisions that will vary according to different family circumstances.

Inherited predispositions to disease

As well as late-onset disorders such as HD, there are likely to be an increasing number of tests available for gene variants that increase a person's risk of developing a disease but which interact with other genetic and non-genetic factors in an unpredictable way. These conditions include late-onset Alzheimer's disease, diabetes and mental illnesses such as schizophrenia. How should requests for such tests be dealt with in the future, assuming that tests with significant predictive value can be developed? As with genetic conditions, only affected families can judge the true likely impact of a disease such as schizophrenia. It is unlikely that many couples will feel that a relatively small inherited risk is worth the cost, inconvenience and discomfort of undergoing PGD, but a small number might. It could be argued that as long as there are no proven long-term negative health effects of PGD, then its use to avoid an increased risk of future disease – however small – is justified. Any attempt to draw up a 'list' of medical genetic tests for which PGD is allowed, given adequate funding, would be at odds with the current law on abortion, which allows women to seek terminations for social as well as medical reasons. More importantly, such a list would make it impossible for doctors to take into account individual family circumstances, their previous experience of illness and their ability to cope with an affected family member.

PGD AND SEX SELECTION

Social sex selection – the use of PGD or other techniques to choose a baby's sex for non-medical reasons – is currently not permitted by the HFEA. This ban was challenged, unsuccessfully, by the Masterton family in 2000 (Scott, 2000). Alan and Louise Masterton wanted to use PGD to have a baby girl after their only daughter died in a bonfire accident. The couple, who have four sons, eventually travelled to a clinic in Italy to have the treatment, where the procedure was at that time permitted, but gave up after three unsuccessful attempts (Fracassini, 2005). It is unclear to what extent this ban will be challenged in the future, since couples who require this service are still free to travel to other European countries where sex selection is allowed. Although sex selection for non-medical reasons is banned by the Council of Europe Convention on Human Rights and Biomedicine drawn up in 1997, many European countries (including the UK) have not signed this document. In 2003, Nicola Chenery, mother of four boys, gave birth to a baby girl after receiving PGD treatment at a Spanish clinic (Savill, 2003).

Arguments surrounding sex selection

The HFEA conducted a public consultation on sex selection in 2002, triggered by the development of another technique for choosing a baby's sex. This procedure, called sperm sorting, is offered by US firm Microsort. The technique involves separating fresh sperm on the basis of whether they carry an X- or a Y-chromosome, and so does not fall under the HFEA's remit since it does not involve either embryos or frozen gametes. The success rate of sperm sorting – about 91 per cent for females and 76 per cent for males, according to the company's website – does not match that of PGD (almost 100 per cent), although it is much cheaper and less invasive. The consultation asked if people should be permitted to choose the sex of their child and if sperm sorting should become regulated by the HFEA. The subsequent report (HFEA, 2003) recommended that the ban on social sex selection using any method should be maintained, partly because around 80 per cent of those who replied to the consultation did not think it should be permitted.

The report also concluded that 'we are not persuaded that the likely benefits of permitting sex selection for social reasons are strong enough to outweigh the harms that may be done' (HFEA, 2003). The HFEA's views contrast with that of the Ethics Committee of the American Society for Reproductive Medicine (ASRM), which, although it counsels against its widespread use, concludes that 'sex selection aimed at increasing gender variety in families may not so greatly increase the risk to children, women or society that its use should be prohibited or condemned as unethical in all cases' (ASRM, 2001). Although this particular report referred to sperm sorting, an earlier report on sex selection using PGD also concluded that while such a practice should not be encouraged, neither should it be banned (ASRM, 1999). This view is perhaps surprising, given the perceived 'conservative' approach in the US to other procedures involving human embryos.

Some ethicists condone the use of sex selection for family balancing but not for choosing the sex of a first child (Robertson, 2003b). Others argue that while many people may disagree with the use of reproductive technology for social sex selection, to ban it in a democratic society represents an unacceptable curb on an individual's liberty (Harris, 2005; McCarthy, 2001; Savulescu, 1999; Tizzard, 2004).

Apart from the apparent lack of public support for allowing social sex selection in the UK, other arguments against using PGD for this reason include the concern that it will lead to a societal gender imbalance, that it is inherently sexist (neither of which applies to couples seeking gender variety) and that it represents a 'slippery slope' into a world in which babies are increasingly viewed as consumer 'objects' (King, 2003b; Shakespeare, 2002). Such children, it is argued, will not be valued for themselves and will carry an unacceptable weight of parental expectation to behave in a way that befits their gender. However, some parents will always have certain expectations of their children, rightly or wrongly, and it is not clear how banning sex selection addresses this issue.

It seems likely that even if social sex selection were allowed, most people will continue to leave reproduction to chance rather than face the inconvenience, uncertainty and cost of assisted reproduction techniques. However, some research has been carried out to see if allowing couples to choose the sex of their child would alter the sex ratios in either Germany or the UK (Dahl *et al*, 2003a,b). In the UK survey, the vast majority of respondents (68 per cent) said they wanted an equal number of boys and girls in their family, with only 3 per cent and 2 per cent respectively saying they would prefer only boys or girls. Overall, the results of both studies suggested that the effects on the sex ratio of allowing sex selection would be negligible. The two UK cases described earlier support this finding, in that both families wanted to use embryo sex selection for 'family balancing' reasons and were not expressing an absolute preference for one gender over the other.

If PGS – which can be used to look at all of an embryo's chromosomes, including the X and Y 'sex chromosomes' – ever becomes a routine part of IVF, then information about the sex of embryos may become widely known by clinicians, who will then be legally unable to pass this information on to their patients. It could be argued that there is little harm in offering such patients – who are, after all, likely to be paying for at least some of their treatment – a choice of whether male or female embryos are returned to the womb, especially given the survey results mentioned above. Furthermore, if it is found to be acceptable to offer IVF patients this choice, then, to be consistent, this option would also have to be made available to fertile people.

THE CHALLENGES FOR FUTURE REGULATION

This chapter has outlined the current state of the science, applications and regulation of PGD and has looked at past and possible future challenges to this legislation. What can be learnt from the legal confusion caused by the use of PGD to conceive saviour siblings, and how should this technology be regulated in future? The HFE Act has recently been the subject of an inquiry by the House of Commons Science and Technology Committee (STC). The resulting report, Human Reproductive Technologies and the Law (House of Commons STC, 2005), will feed into an ongoing review of the Act by the DH (DH, 2004), which has recently launched its own public consultation (DH, 2005).

On the subject of PGD, the STC said that 'the regulation of preimplantation testing is highly unsatisfactory'. In its recommendations, it concluded that it saw 'no reason why a regulator should seek to determine which disorders can be screened out using PGD'. It also criticised the HFEA's response to the requests for PTT, saying that 'the development of the

HFEA's policy and licensing decisions on preimplantation tissue typing has been highly unsatisfactory'. The general tone of the report was one of devolving clinical decisions in reproductive medicine down to medical professionals and patients. It is unclear to what extent the DH will take into account the STC's recommendations, however, since only half the committee members signed the controversial report. As part of its review, the DH is also seeking the views of the public on issues such as 'the rules governing screening and selecting embryos for medical purposes' and the scope for a 'lighter touch' regulation of IVF (DH, 2005).

Medical applications of PGD

Some of the responses to the STC inquiry were from groups who seek tighter regulation of this area, limiting PGD to the detection of serious medical conditions present from birth and banning other applications such as tissue-typing and the avoidance of late-onset disorders (Christian Medical Fellowship (CMF), 2004; HGA, 2004). However, in his initial ruling on the judicial review of the Hashmi 'saviour sibling' decision, Mr Justice Maurice Kay implied that the situation had arisen precisely because the legislation had been 'tightly drawn' to prevent any misuse of IVF technology – no one had envisaged that reproductive and genetic technologies might one day make 'saviour siblings' a possibility. But in the 27 years since the birth of Louise Brown, the world's first 'test-tube' baby, there has been little evidence of anyone in the world wanting to use IVF for anything other than helping infertile couples have babies and, using PGD, to have healthy babies. This area of science is continually evolving, and while it is highly unlikely that it will ever be possible to carry out PGD for characteristics such as intelligence, there could be other unpredicted beneficial uses of the technology that do not fall within the remit of 'avoiding serious genetic diseases'. Tightening the regulation to prevent hypothetical misuse of PGD would be short-sighted, especially since there is no evidence of any demand to use this technology for 'trivial' reasons.

Some clinicians, including fertility expert Robert Winston, feel that the current strict laws governing PGD are particularly at odds with UK abortion law (*The Times*, 2004). Abortion is currently legal up to the 24th week of pregnancy, but if there is a substantial risk to the woman's life, or if there are foetal abnormalities, there is no time limit (see Jackson, Chapter 3 in this volume). To comply with the 1967 Abortion Act, two doctors must give their approval, stating that to continue with the pregnancy would present a risk to the physical or mental health of the woman or her existing children. So, the decision to terminate a foetus found to be affected by a genetic condition can be made by two doctors and a patient, whereas the decision to select one embryo over another for implantation must be approved by the committee of a regulatory body – a process than can sometimes take months. This odd state of affairs – in which a three-day-old embryo is apparently accorded more importance than a nine-month-old foetus – was thrown into sharp relief by Jayson Whitaker when he gave oral evidence to the STC inquiry (HC 599-v, 2004). He and his wife were told that they could not use PGD for tissue-typing only, to conceive a saviour sibling to help treat their son Jamie, but they could legally try to conceive naturally and then terminate all pregnancies that were not a correct tissue match. Jayson told the STC that he felt this suggestion, as a legal, NHS-approved alternative, was 'disgusting', even though he described himself as 'not anti-abortion'. The Whitakers chose instead to go abroad for treatment.

Clearly, families who already have to deal with the stress of a serious illness should not have to go abroad or, as in the case of the Hashmi family, fight lengthy legal battles to obtain the treatment they need. Tighter regulation of PGD would merely make things more difficult for people who could benefit from the technique, and it is already an expensive, time-consuming procedure with a low success rate. Indeed, a recent survey of US PGD patients and providers found that they were 'more concerned about overzealous government regulation of PGD creating barriers to access than potential abuses of this technology' (Kalfoglou et al, 2005). A less restrictive approach to regulating PGD, entrusting medical decisions to clinicians and their patients, would allow for new, as yet unforeseen applications of this technology. Many UK clinicians are also known to favour such an approach, in which a regulatory body is still responsible for 'quality control' issues and collecting data for long-term follow-up studies but not for individual treatment decisions (British Fertility Society (BFS), 2000; House of Commons STC, 2005). Winston has actually called for the HFEA to be scrapped (The Times, 2004), but this view is not shared by most of his peers, who favour some regulation of IVF and its associated practices (Hagan, 2004). It is likely that some form of regulation is essential to maintain standards and, equally importantly, public confidence in reproductive technologies and those who practise in this area of medicine. However, the current remit of the HFEA, which includes ethical and policy decision-making as well as the role described above, needs revisiting.

The STC – following the advice of Richard Kennedy, chair of the BFS – has recommended the creation of a new Human Genetics, Fertility and Tissue Commission (House of Commons STC, 2005). Such a body would incorporate the existing Human Genetics Commission (HGC) but would also consider societal issues currently covered by the HFEA and the new Human Tissue Authority. Such a system would separate 'policy' from 'policing', as the BFS has suggested, and permit, for example, a more flexible approach to regulating PGD. The BFS also told the STC that professional bodies should draw up their own guidance, to incorporate and replace the current HFEA Code of Practice. In the case of providing PGD, adhering to professional guidelines instead of consulting a regulator over every new application of the technology would cut down on the time-consuming bureaucracy that currently plagues this area of medicine.

Extending the uses of PGD

Currently, it is accepted that in countries where it is permitted, PGD should be available for any condition for which PND is allowed. But there are also some instances where the use of PGD is deemed acceptable by many even though PND for the same reason is not. One example is using PGD to distinguish between healthy 'carrier' and 'non-carrier' embryos in cases where there are enough unaffected embryos to choose from. Some ethicists feel that social sex selection – particularly for 'family balancing' reasons – falls into this category. But the STC triggered much media debate in the UK when it concluded in its report that 'the onus should be on those who oppose sex selection for social reasons using PGD to show harm from its use'.

Many geneticists are opposed to the use of PGD for this purpose, arguing that allowing non-medical uses of this technology will reduce hard-won public confidence in genetics (Flinter, 2001). Flinter also argues that allowing social sex selection could draw resources away from an already underfunded area of medicine. The ethicist Guido Pennings has proposed a potential solution to this problem, in the form of a 'social compensation tax' levied at couples who want to use PGD for social sex selection – this money could then help provide treatment for couples awaiting PGD for medical reasons (Pennings, 2005).

So should PGD for sex selection be allowed for the small number of patients who might desperately require such treatment, and would be prepared and able to pay for it? Currently, the main reason given by the HFEA for banning sex selection is the lack of public support for such a service, but how much weight should be given to this argument? We may not always approve of or understand other people's reasons for seeking medical help – for example, those who have extensive, seemingly unnecessary cosmetic surgery – but, provided their actions are not harming others, particularly if they are paying for their treatment and are not draining resources away from people with a greater need, then should their requests actually be banned? The STC thought not, recommending that 'on balance we find no adequate justification for prohibiting the use of sex selection for family balancing'.

While there is a clear role for regulation in the field of assisted reproduction, restrictive legislation that triggers a legal challenge every time a new technique or unforeseen application emerges is costly, counterproductive and undermines the credibility of such a law. It is time to start trusting doctors and their patients to make their own decisions about their use of reproductive genetic technologies, as is commonplace in other areas of medicine. The model set out in the STC report – in which a regulator is responsible for technical standards, professional guidelines govern treatment decisions and conduct, and an extended HGC provides ethical oversight – is one way in which this could be achieved. The review of the HFE Act provides a unique opportunity to ensure that people continue to reap the benefits of advances in reproductive medicine, including current and future uses of PGD.

REFERENCES

Advisory Committee on Genetic Testing (1998) 'Report on Genetic Testing for Late Onset Disorders'

American Society of Reproductive Medicine (1999) 'Sex selection and preimplantation genetic diagnosis' 72 *Fertility and Sterility* 595–8

American Society of Reproductive Medicine (2001) 'Preconception gender selection for nonmedical reasons' 75 *Fertility and Sterility* 861–4

American Society of Reproductive Medicine (2004) 'ASRM comments on release of report on outcomes study of ART children' Press release, 19 October

BBC News Online (2004) 'Boy wants minority marrow donors', 24 November http://news.bbc.co.uk/1/hi/health/4035685.stm

Borger, J (2000) ' "Designer baby" cures sister' *Guardian*, 20 October

Borger, J and Meek, J (2000) 'Parents create baby to save sister' *Guardian*, 4 October

Boseley, S (2004) 'Critics attack landmark decision on gene screening' *Guardian*, 2 November

Boyle, R and Savulescu, J (2001) 'Ethics of using preimplantation genetic diagnosis to select a stem cell donor for an existing person' 323 *British Medical Journal* 1240–3

British Fertility Society (2000) 'Response to the HFEA and ACGT consultation document on preimplantation diagnosis', March 2000

British Medical Association (2004) Select Committee on Science and Technology Written Evidence, Appendix 12, May 2004

Caplan, A (2005) 'Misusing the Nazi analogy' 309 *Science* 535

Challoner, J (1999) *The Baby Makers: The History of Artificial Conception* London: Channel Four Books

Christian Medical Fellowship (2004) Select Committee on Science and Technology Written Evidence, Appendix 10

Dahl, E *et al* (2003a) 'Preconception sex selection for non-medical reasons: a representative survey from Germany' 18 *Human Reproduction* 2231–4

Dahl, E *et al* (2003b) 'Preconception sex selection for non-medical reasons: a representative survey from the UK' 18 *Human Reproduction* 2238–9

Department of Health (2002) 'PGD – Guiding principles for commissioners of NHS Services', September

Department of Health (2004) 'Review of the Human Fertilisation and Embryology Act 1990' Press release, 21 January

Department of Health (2005) 'Health Minister launches consultation on Human Fertilisation and Embryology Act' Press release, 16 August

ESHRE PGD Consortium (2005) 'Best practice guidelines for clinical preimplantation genetic diagnosis (PGD) and preimplantation genetic screening (PGS)' 20 *Human Reproduction* 35–48

Fiorentino, F *et al* (2004) 'Development and clinical application of a strategy for preimplantation genetic diagnosis of single gene disorders combined with HLA matching' 10 *Molecular Human Reproduction* 445–60

Flinter, F (2001) 'Preimplantation genetic diagnosis' 322 *British Medical Journal* 1008–9

Fracassini, C (2005) 'Couple abandon battle for baby of their choice' *The Times*, 23 January

Gavaghan, C (2004) ' "Designer donors"?: tissue-typing and regulation of preimplantation genetic diagnosis' 3 *Web Journal of Current Legal Issues*

Genetic Interest Group (1996) 'A briefing paper on antenatal and preimplantation genetic diagnosis, embryo research and contemporary abortion issues'

Gianaroli, L *et al* (2002) 'The role of preimplantation diagnosis for aneuploidies' 4 Suppl 3 *Reproductive Biomedicine Online* 31–6

Gould, N (2005) 'Born to save her big brother's life' *The Belfast Telegraph*, 18 July

Hagan, P (2004) 'UK scientists defend HFEA' *The Scientist*, 13 December

Handyside, A *et al* (1990) 'Pregnancies arising from biopsied human preimplantation embryos sexed by Y specific DNA amplification' 344 *Nature* 768–70

Harris, J (2005) 'Sex selection and regulated hatred' 31 *Journal of Medical Ethics* 291–4

Henderson, M (2004a) 'First "designer baby" could save his brother' *The Times*, 29 November

Henderson, M (2004b) 'How embryo screening might be the new way to beat cancer' *The Times*, 1 November

House of Commons (2004) 'Minutes of evidence taken before Science and Technology Committee inquiry into Human Reproductive Technologies and the Law', HC 599-v 8 September 2004

House of Commons Science and Technology Committee (2005) *Human Reproductive Technologies and the Law*, 24 March

Human Fertilisation and Embryology Authority (2001) 'HFEA to allow tissue typing in conjunction with preimplantation genetic diagnosis' Press release, 13 December

Human Fertilisation and Embryology Authority (2002) 'HFEA confirms that HLA tissue typing may only take place when preimplantation genetic diagnosis is required to avoid a serious genetic disorder' Press release, 1 August

Human Fertilisation and Embryology Authority (2003) 'Sex selection: options for regulation' www.hfea.gov.uk/AboutHFEA/Consultations/Final%20sex%20selection%20main%20report.pdf

Human Fertilisation and Embryology Authority (2004a) *Code of Practice*, 6th edn, January www.hfea.gov.uk/HFEAPublications/CodeofPractice

Human Fertilisation and Embryology Authority (2004b) 'HFEA Report: Preimplantation tissue typing', July www.hfea.gov.uk/AboutHFEA/HFEAPolicy/Preimplantationtissuetyping

Human Fertilisation and Embryology Authority (2004c) 'HFEA licenses PGD for inherited colon cancer' Press release, 1 November

Human Fertilisation and Embryology Authority (2005a) 'Should embryo screening help parents prevent passing on a wider range of inheritable diseases?' Press release, 1 August

Human Fertilisation and Embryology Authority (2005b) 'HFEA announce new process to speed up applications for embryo screening' Press release, 19 January

Human Fertilisation and Embryology Authority (2006) 'Authority decision on PGD policy' Press release, 10 May

Human Genetics Alert (2004) Select Committee on Science and Technology Written Evidence, Appendix 30, June 2004

Kahraman, S *et al* (2004) 'Clinical aspects of preimplantation genetic diagnosis for single gene disorders combined with HLA typing' 9 *Reproductive Biomedicine Online* 529–32

Kalfoglou *et al* (2005) 'PGD patients' and providers' attitudes to the use and regulation of preimplantation genetic diagnosis' 11 *Reproductive Biomedicine Online* 486–96

Kanavakis, E and Traeger-Synodinos, J (2002) 'Preimplantation genetic diagnosis in clinical practice' 39 *Journal of Medical Genetics* 6–11

King, D (2003a) 'Why it is wrong to select embryos to be tissue donors' Unpublished, Human Genetics Alert, 20 June www.hgalert.org/topics/geneticSelection/pgdcommentary.html

King, D (2003b) 'The case against sex selection' BioNews 8 October www.bionews.org.uk/commentary.lasso?storyid=1843

Knoppers, B and Isasi, R (2004) 'Regulatory approaches to reproductive genetic testing' 19 *Human Reproduction* 2696–701

McCarthy, D (2001) 'Why sex selection should be legal' 27 *Journal of Medical Ethics* 302–7

Pembrey, M (1998) 'In the light of preimplantation genetic diagnosis: some ethical issues in medical genetics revisited' 6 *European Journal of Human Genetics* 4–11

Pennings, G *et al* (2002) 'Ethical considerations on preimplantation genetics diagnosis for HLA typing to match a future child as a donor of haematopoietic stem cells to a sibling' 17 *Human Reproduction* 534–8

Pennings, G (2005) 'A "social compensation tax" for social sexing' BioNews, 11 April www.bionews.org.uk/commentary.lasso?storyid=2519

Ponjaert-Kristoffersen, I *et al* (2005) 'International collaborative study of intracytoplasmic sperm injection-conceived, in vitro fertilisation-conceived, and naturally-conceived 5-year-old outcomes: cognitive and motor outcomes' 115 *Pediatrics* 283–9

Progress Educational Trust (2004) Select Committee on Science and Technology Written Evidence, Appendix 33

Rechitsky, S *et al* (2004) 'Preimplantation genetic diagnosis with HLA matching' 9 Reproductive Biomedicine Online, pp 210–21

Robertson, J (2003a) 'Extending preimplantation genetic diagnosis: the ethical debate' 18 *Human Reproduction* 465–71

Robertson, J (2003b) 'Extending preimplantation genetic diagnosis: medical and non-medical uses' 29 *Journal of Medical Ethics* 213–16

Savill, R (2003) 'Twin girls for mother of four boys who always wanted a daughter' *The Daily Telegraph*, 28 June

Savulescu, J (1999) 'Sex selection: the case for' 171 *Medical Journal of Australia* 373–5

Scott, K (2000) 'Bereaved couple demand right to baby girl' *Guardian*, 5 October

Sermon, K *et al* (2002) 'Preimplantation genetic diagnosis for Huntington's disease with exclusion testing' 10 *European Journal of Human Genetics* 591–8

Shakespeare, T (1999) In: 'The Saturday debate – Could embryo screening lead to genetic cleansing?' *Guardian*, 20 November

Shakespeare, T (2002) 'Birds, bees and laser beams' *New Scientist*, 16 November

Sheldon, S (2005) 'What the House of Lords Hashmi ruling really means' BioNews, 7 May www.bionews.org.uk/commentary.lasso?storyid=2553

Sheldon, S and Wilkinson, S (2004a) 'Hashmi and Whitaker: an unjustifiable and misguided distinction?' 12 *Medical Law Review* 137–63

Sheldon, S and Wilkinson, S (2004b) 'Should selecting saviour siblings be banned?' 30 *Journal of Medical Ethics* 533–7

Spriggs, M (2005) 'Is conceiving a child to benefit another against the interests of the new child?' 31 *Journal of Medical Ethics* 341–2

Taranissi, M and Lawford Davies, J (2005) 'Why treat PGD for late onset disorders differently?' BioNews, 4 May www.bionews.org.uk/commentary.lasso?storyid=2550

Tassicker, R *et al* (2003) 'Prenatal diagnosis requests for Huntington's disease when the father is at risk and does not want to know his genetic status: clinical, legal, and ethical viewpoints' 326 *British Medical Journal* 331–3

Templeton, S (2004) 'NHS pays for first "designer baby"' *The Sunday Times*, 21 March

The Times (2004) 'Abolish fertility watchdog, says IVF expert', 10 December

Tizzard, J (1999) In: 'The Saturday debate – Could embryo screening lead to genetic cleansing?' *Guardian*, 20 November

Tizzard, J (2004) 'Sex selection, child welfare and risk: a critique of the HFEA's recommendations on sex selection' 12 *Health Care Analysis* 61–8

Towner, D and Lowey, R (2002) 'Ethics of preimplantation diagnosis for a woman destined to develop early-onset Alzheimer disease' 287 *Journal of the American Medical Association* 1038–40

Van de Velde, H (2004) 'Novel universal approach for preimplantation genetic diagnosis of beta-thalassaemia in combination with HLA matching of embryos' 19 *Human Reproduction* 700–8

Verlinsky, Y *et al* (2001) 'Preimplantation diagnosis for Fanconi anemia combined with HLA matching' 285 *Journal of the American Medical Association* 3130–3

Verlinsky, Y *et al* (2002) 'Preimplantation diagnosis for early-onset Alzheimer disease caused by V717L mutation' 287 *Journal of the American Medical Association* 1038–40

Verlinsky, Y *et al* (2004a) 'Preimplantation HLA testing' 291 *Journal of the American Medical Association* 2079–85

Verlinsky, Y *et al* (2004b) 'Over a decade of experience with preimplantation genetic diagnosis: a multicenter report' 82 *Fertility and Sterility* 292–4

Walsh, F (2004) 'Brother's tissue "cures" sick boy' BBC News Online, 20 October http://news.bbc.co.uk/1/hi/health/3756556.stm

Watt, H (2004) 'Preimplantation genetic diagnosis: choosing the "good enough" child' 12 *Health Care Analysis* 51–60

Weiss, R (2000) 'Test-tube baby born to save ill sister' *The Washington Post*, 3 October

Wilton, L (2002) 'Preimplantation genetic diagnosis for aneuploidy screening in early human embryos: a review' 22 *Prenatal Diagnosis* 512–18

Chapter 7

Parenting genetically unrelated children

A comparison of embryo donation and adoption

Fiona MacCallum

INTRODUCTION

Embryo donation is the process whereby infertile couples undergo IVF treatment using embryos donated by another couple. Thus, embryo donation children are raised by two parents with whom they lack a genetic relationship, creating a situation that structurally at least is similar to adoption. For this reason, some practitioners have argued that embryo donation should be considered as a form of 'prenatal adoption'. However, the Human Fertilisation and Embryology Act 1990 ('the 1990 Act') treats embryo donation as identical to gamete donation, requiring only consideration of the 'welfare of the child' according to s 13(5), rather than drawing parallels with adoption. This chapter examines the disparities in approach taken towards embryo donation and adoption, particularly in regard to the selection process applied for adoptive parents compared with embryo donation parents. It explores how these disparities have arisen, considering similarities and differences between embryo donation and adoption from a psychological, legal and social perspective. Following this comparison, it concludes that while there is good cause for applying different criteria to embryo donation and adoption, the magnitude of the current disparity is not justified. Therefore, the suggestion is that, in the reform of the 1990 Act, s 13(5) should not be abolished but should be reformatted. In regard to embryo donation families, the new format should take into account the similarities to adoption. One possibility is to follow the example of current practice in adoption by reframing s 13(5) to include an educative and preparative component rather than placing a strong emphasis purely on assessment of parenting capacity.

BACKGROUND

In 1983, an Australian team reported the first successful transfer of a donated embryo in a human. After a female patient had undergone 22 cycles of donor insemination with no success, embryo transfer was attempted using an embryo created using a donor egg and donor sperm (the egg donor and the sperm donor were unknown to each other and to the recipient couple) and a pregnancy was established. The clinicians involved likened the process to egg donation and sperm donation, and believed it could even be an advantage if both gametes were donated on the basis that 'the contribution of the couple to the conception is more balanced than in artificial insemination by donor' (Trounson *et al*, 1983). However, Sauer and colleagues, in a report on the use of donor eggs and donor sperm, viewed the transferring of donor embryos somewhat differently, referring to the process as 'preimplantation adoption' since 'conceptions resulted from embryos conceived *in vitro* without any genetic ties to the recipients' (Sauer *et al*, 1995).

The refinement of embryo freezing techniques, along with the reduction in multiple embryo transfers, has resulted in thousands of IVF embryos being held in storage, with couples having to decide whether to retain them, dispose of them, donate them for research or donate them to another couple. Therefore, in the large majority of modern embryo donation treatments, the embryos used had originally been produced by another couple in their own attempts at conception through IVF. Thus, if the treatment is successful, the recipient couple will raise a child that is genetically that of the donor couple and who may have genetic full siblings being raised by the donor couple; a family structure analogous with adoption.

Despite this similarity, embryo donation and adoption differ in the reasons for their origin and in how the nature of the procedures has been perceived. Throughout human history, adoption has been used as a means of creating families. It evolved as a social practice with two functions: first, to provide families for abandoned and orphaned children, and second, to provide heirs for childless couples. Over time, the process has become regulated by law and formal selection criteria have been set for adoptive parents, most of which are social or psychological, in recognition of the needs of the adopted child (Triseliotis *et al*, 1997). By contrast, embryo donation is a relatively new procedure, having only been possible for the last 20 years. It arose through a combination of the technologies of other assisted reproductive techniques, namely IVF and gamete donation. Thus, embryo donation can be seen as driven by the technological imperative – the assumption that scientific progress is good in itself and should be pursued (Widdows and MacCallum, 2002). As the technology required to perform embryo donation has become available it has been implemented. Embryo donation is therefore viewed as one medical procedure among others that can be attempted when 'treating' infertility (although, like gamete donation, embryo donation does not cure the cause of the infertility but rather allows childless couples to become parents). From this perspective, embryo donation is a medical solution to a medical problem, whereas adoption is a social response to a social problem

John Robertson, an expert on reproductive ethics and law, has considered whether ethically and legally the process of embryo donation more strongly resembles gamete donation or adoption. He came down on the side of gamete donation, concluding that 'the procedure of embryo donation is not equivalent to postnatal adoption of a born infant' (Robertson, 1995). The European Society of Human Reproduction and Embryology agrees, stating in its guidelines on embryo donation that 'the ethical concerns related to the technique are general to the donation of gametes' (ESHRE Task Force on Ethics and Law, 2001).

Others contend, however, that embryo donation does strongly resemble adoption, with a group of mental health professionals arguing in response to Robertson's analysis that 'embryo adoption should receive the same safeguards as adoption' (Bernstein *et al*, 1996). In the United States, 'embryo adoption' services, such as the Snowflakes Embryo Adoption Program, have been established where donors are able to set criteria for selection of the recipient couple and may keep in contact with the recipients following the birth of the child (Laurence, 2003; Stolberg, 2001). Headlines in the media in the United Kingdom such as 'Embryo adoption register planned' (Norton, 1999), 'Orphan embryos up for adoption' (Souter, 1999) and 'This little girl was adopted when she was just an embryo in a freezer' (Langton, 2003) reinforce the perception of a process synonymous with adoption. Indeed, Baroness Warnock, one of the main architects of the policies surrounding assisted reproduction treatment in the UK, referred to embryo donation as 'a better way of adopting' (Ballantyne, 1991). Nevertheless, in the UK, the two methods are currently approached very dissimilarly with respect to the legal status of embryo donation versus adoption and the selection processes used for adoptive parents compared with embryo donation parents. The next section examines these disparities and explores whether such different approaches to these two methods of family creation are justified. If embryo donation and adoption are indeed more similar than they are currently treated, the reform of the Human Fertilisation and Embryology Act 1990 should take this into account when considering whether and how to apply parenting criteria for prospective embryo donation patients.

COMPARISONS OF EMBRYO DONATION AND ADOPTION: DISPARITIES IN APPROACH

Legal status

In the UK, embryo donation is treated legally in the same way as sperm or egg donation, with the recipients of donated embryos being the sole legal parents (Human Fertilisation and Embryology Act 1990, ss 27(1) and 28(2)). When agreeing to donate embryos, donors automatically give up all legal rights and responsibilities to the resulting child. The same is true in those other European countries that allow embryo donation (including Finland,

France, Greece and Spain; it is not allowed in Austria, Germany, Italy, Norway or Switzerland; Jones and Cohen, 2004). In the United States, there are currently only eight states that have statutes explicitly recognising embryo donation and they too have generally modelled their laws regarding embryo donation on sperm donation laws, making the recipient woman and her spouse the legal parents for all purposes (Crockin, 2001). In contrast, adoption laws in all countries are complex, with protections inserted for all parties. Virtually every adoption law bans relinquishment of a child before birth and often for a set period of time after birth, in order to protect the birth parents from making decisions they come to regret. In the UK and the US, the child has to be in the adoptive placement for a minimum of three months before the adoption becomes final. Adoption requires either the consent of the birth parents or a judicial termination of parental rights; thus, birth parents are allowed to contest adoptions. No such laws exist with regard to embryo donation and it is highly unlikely that any patient would consider using donated embryos, then carrying and giving birth to a child if there was a proviso that consent for adoption had to be sought from the genetic parents (and was not guaranteed) after the birth. As Crockin (2001) explains, 'embryo "adoption" is a term that may be endearing and may even be accurate in a bio-psycho-social sense, but it is not accurate in a legal sense'.

To some extent, the legal framework depends on whether an embryo is viewed as having the status of 'person' or 'property'. Those who maintain that life begins at fertilisation, such as the Catholic Church, believe that the embryo should be regarded as a human being, stating that 'the human being is to be respected and treated as a person from the moment of conception' (Ratzinger and Bovone, 1987). From this perspective, embryo donation should have the same legal safeguards as adoption, since both involve the integration of a human being into a new family and should thus be treated in the same way. On the other hand, there is the opposite point of view that embryos are like property and therefore those who 'own' them are free to make decisions affecting them. Therefore, embryo donation involves transfer of property and does not resemble adoption.

There has often been reluctance to categorically define embryos legally, with policy-makers generally opting for a position in the middle, treating embryos as somewhere between person and property. For example, the Warnock Report declared that 'the human embryo . . . is not, under the present law in the UK, accorded the same status as a living child or an adult', but did grant the embryo 'special status' due to its potential to become a human being (Warnock, 1984). The American Fertility Society similarly concluded that an embryo cannot be regarded as a person but that it is different from other human tissue (American Fertility Society, 1990). The consensus among those involved in assisted reproduction seems to be that practitioners have to be seen as 'showing respect' for the embryo (ESHRE Task Force on Ethics and Law, 2001) but not the same level of respect as is shown to actual persons. From the legal perspective, then, embryo donation undeniably differs from adoption; embryos are not 'persons' so cannot be adopted.

Selection criteria for parents

In addition to legal differences, there is a conspicuous disparity between the parent selection procedures in embryo donation and adoption (Widdows and MacCallum, 2002). The selection process for adoption is lengthy and detailed, and focuses on social and psychological factors. In the UK, prospective adopters are assigned a social worker who visits their home several times over a period of months. A two-part form (Form F) must be completed. Part I asks first for factual information concerning characteristics such as age, marital status, ethnic origin and occupation. It also asks for two personal references for the applicants, who give their views of the applicants' parenting capacity. Part II of the form is a descriptive report made by the social worker based on observations of the household members during the home visits. A great amount of detail is obtained about the applicants, including their present relationship, their previous relationships, their attitudes towards being childless, their understanding of child development and their own childhood experiences. Emphasis is placed on the personalities of the individual applicants and the nature and quality of their relationships (The British Agencies for Adoption and Fostering, 1991). If, having completed Form F, the social worker considers the applicants to be suitable to become adopters, their recommendation is then put to an adoption panel of independent assessors who have the final say on whether the applicants should be approved for consideration as adoptive parents. Prospective adopters must attend courses with other couples with the aim of preparing them for all possible aspects of adoption. In addition, couples are matched with children according to the specific needs of the child, so even having been approved as adopters, a couple may have to wait a long time to be considered suitable parents for an *available* child. The contemporary emphasis of the adoption process is supposedly to educate rather than to evaluate, although many couples still feel that they are being judged and find the procedure intrusive and anxiety-provoking. However, it is regarded as essential to protect and support the child. The focus is on the needs of the child and on finding parents appropriate to fulfil those needs.

In contrast, the selection process for embryo donation parents focuses on medical criteria, with the emphasis on whether the mother is 'medically suitable' to carry the child rather than on whether the couple are psychologically suitable to be parents. Decisions on who should be allowed access to the treatment are made by medical practitioners, with little involvement of professionals trained in making social and psychological judgements. Prospective embryo donation recipients in the UK are treated in the same way as couples applying for any form of assisted conception, in that the only social criteria they are expected to meet are those laid down by the 1990 Act. Section 13(5) of the Act states that a woman 'shall not be provided with treatment services unless account has been taken of the welfare of any child born as a result of the treatments (including the need of that child for a father)'. This places providers of assisted conception services under an obligation to consider the prospective parents in terms of the child's future wellbeing. However, the Human Fertilisation and Embryology Authority (HFEA) Code of Practice asserts that clinics must consider both the 'wishes and needs of those seeking treatment and the needs of any children involved' (HFEA, 2004). Unlike adoption, where the child's needs are of primary importance, fertility clinics must give equal weight to the prospective parents' wishes.

Regarding the collection of information relevant to the future 'welfare of the child', the Code of Practice suggests that this should be done by taking medical and family histories and seeing the couple together and separately. Counselling should be offered but is not mandatory. Thus, there is little in the way of preparation or education, which is compulsory for prospective adoptive parents. The clinic is also required to contact the couple's GP to check if there is any reason why they should not be offered treatment. If the result of any of these inquiries causes concern, the clinic should approach the relevant authority or agency, such as the police or social services, for further information. However, an approach can only be made with the consent of the couple, and refusal to grant such consent is not automatic grounds for refusing treatment. In effect, the psychological components of the current selection process are relatively superficial, and it seems that only couples who are at risk of actually harming the child will be refused on social reasons. What Jackson (Chapter 3 in this volume) refers to as the 'thick' interpretation of the welfare principle, where factors such as the commitment to raise a child and the ability to provide a stable environment are considered, does not seem in practice to be applied in most clinics, and certainly is not applied consistently. (This applies only to heterosexual couples and not to single women or lesbian couples, for whom selection is often more complicated due to the inclusion of the phrase referring to the child's 'need' for a father in s 13(5).) The emphasis on the number of live births achieved, for example on the HFEA website information for patients, increases the need of clinics to maximise their 'take-home' baby rate. Therefore, those couples who are medically unfit or for whom successful conception is doubtful are most likely to be refused.

Thus, compared with adoption, the selection of embryo donation parents is far less involved:

> Selection for adoption is concerned with whether an applicant will be a fit parent and every effort is made to discover this, for medically assisted reproduction the effort is fairly minimal and is designed to exclude only those who might seem grossly unfit.
>
> (Campion, 1995)

The fundamental principle in adoption is that the child is the client, whereas in embryo donation the client is the would-be parent and the child is a product of a service created to meet the needs of these clients.

Summary of differences in approach

Treatment with donated embryos is clearly viewed by both the legal system and the social authorities as a very different process from the adoption of a child. The legal difference between the processes is irreducible under current UK law. Any change in the legal status of embryos would have far-reaching, and possibly undesirable, consequences for legislation surrounding other issues such as abortion and stem cell research. However, the fact that the embryo is required to be treated with 'respect' could be interpreted to entail giving more consideration to embryo donation than to other forms of assisted conception. For example in donor insemination, sperm is not stipulated to command the same 'respect', although it is (arguably) still 'different from other human tissue'. Despite this, the criteria applied to couples wishing to conceive through embryo donation are the same as those for any assisted conception treatment, and are vastly less stringent than the selection criteria for adoptive parents. To investigate the justifications for the size of this disparity, the underlying similarities and differences between embryo donation and adoption will now be examined.

COMPARISONS OF EMBRYO DONATION AND ADOPTION: UNDERLYING SIMILARITIES AND DIFFERENCES

Genetic relationships

Attitudes towards genetic parents

Embryo donation and adoption are undeniably similar in the genetic structure of the resulting family; the child is reared by two parents with whom they lack a genetic relationship and, in both cases, the child has genetic parents elsewhere. However, from a practical perspective, the majority of embryo donation programmes differ greatly from adoption arrangements in their attitude towards these genetic parents. A relatively recent phenomenon in adoption is that of the 'open adoption' arrangement, where there is some amount of direct or indirect contact between adoptive parents and birth parents. In the UK, particularly if the birth parents are voluntarily relinquishing the child for adoption, meetings will often be arranged between the birth parents and the prospective adopters prior to the placement of the child. Adoptive parents are encouraged to maintain mediated contact post-adoption with the birth parents, generally through letter contact via the adoption service. In some states in the US, the involvement of birth parents in the adoption process has been taken further, with the establishment of 'directed adoption', where the birth parents (usually the mother) choose the family with which their child will be placed.

In contrast, the majority of embryo donation programmes run by fertility clinics have involved anonymous donors with no contact between donors and recipients. New legislation came into force in the UK in April 2005 allowing children born through gamete or embryo donation access to the identity of the donors when they reach the age of 18 (the HFEA (Disclosure of Donor Information) Regulations 2004). However, from the recipients' point of view, anonymity will remain since they themselves will not receive identifying information about the donors prior to their children requesting it. There are organisations in the US that take a very different view of the transfer of embryos from one couple to another, for example 'Snowflakes', which styles itself as an 'embryo adoption' service. Here, contact is encouraged between donor and recipient families both prior to and following the 'adoption', with donors allowed to set criteria for the 'adopting' couple (Braid, 2003). However, these types of arrangements are the exception rather than the rule, and certainly in the case of the Snowflakes agency, the framework stems from the strongly pro-life religious principles backing the agency. In the UK, this type of 'embryo adoption' arrangement is not allowed.

One line of reasoning for the different attitudes towards the genetic parents in embryo donation and adoption relates to the fact that in embryo donation, the recipient parents' intent to parenthood is causal: it has caused the child to come into being and without it there would not have been a pregnancy. The same is not true of adoption, where the adoptive parents intend to take over the care of someone else's already existing child. This notion of intentionality is a factor in other issues surrounding assisted reproduction in UK law (excluding the situation of surrogacy). Thus, in gamete donation, it is considered that the intent of the gamete donors is to provide their gametes for the use of others to become parents, and therefore donors are not legally or morally responsible for the upbringing of their genetic offspring. In these terms, embryo donation is closer to assisted reproduction than to adoption; the intention of the embryo donors is to provide an embryo to allow another couple to create a child who would otherwise not exist. Following the example of gamete donation, where parenthood is determined primarily by intent rather than by genetics, the embryo donors are not seen as having any importance in the child's future life.

In one of the first controlled studies to examine the experience of families created through embryo donation in comparison with adoptive families, the varying significance placed on the genetic parents was reflected in the attitudes of the families (MacCallum, 2004). Embryo donation parents rarely talked about the donors, did not generally want information about the donors and, in the main, did not feel the need to inform the child of the donor's existence. The donation of embryos was generally viewed by these recipients as being on a par with blood or organ donation. In contrast, adoptive parents often talked about the birth parents, particularly the mother. Those who were in contact with the birth mother were keen to let her know the child was well and happy, acknowledging how difficult it must have been for her to relinquish the child. Thus, the adoptive parents saw the genetic relationships as relevant to family life, whereas embryo donation parents did not. It is worth noting, though, that these views contrast with those reported by some offspring of donated sperm, who considered information about the genetic father as highly important to their sense of self-identity (Donor Conception Support Group, 1997; Turner and Coyle, 2000).

Generally then, despite the similarity between embryo donation and adoption in terms of the lack of genetic links between parents and children, in adoption these genetic relationships are considered highly important while in embryo donation they are considered much less so. The significance of the role of the genetic parents in embryo donation has not been emphasised to the same extent as adoption has acknowledged the role of the birth parents. Therefore, embryo donation parents do not have the added complication of the involvement in the child's life of a second set of 'parents'.

Genetic parents' views of embryo donation or adoption

Related to how adoption services and embryo donation programmes view the genetic parents is the question of how the genetic parents themselves, either the embryo donors or the birth parents, perceive the process. It is well documented that birth parents suffer negative and long-lasting effects, such as grief and depression, as a result of relinquishing their child (for example, Hughes and Logan, 1993; Winkler and van Keppel, 1984). It is believed that the option of open adoption can ameliorate these consequences for the birth parents (Baran and Pannor, 1993; Chapman *et al*, 1986). One study found that the majority of birth mothers were not in favour of continued contact with the adoptive family but that they were very interested in having periodic updates on the child's progress so as to reassure themselves as to the child's welfare (Hughes and Logan, 1993). How do these views compare to those of embryo donors?

Those donors who approach the Snowflakes programme seem to consider their embryos as potential children, with one donor describing the prospect of maintaining contact with the recipients once the child is born as 'an exciting extended family' (Stolberg, 2001). A study by Newton *et al* (2003) that assessed attitudes of infertile couples towards the process of embryo donation seems to support this position. They found that those couples who expressed a willingness to seriously consider donating their embryos held 'views more congruent with a model of "embryo adoption" than with a model of traditional medical donation' (Newton *et al*, 2003). These potential donors were more comfortable with providing information about themselves to the recipients and more receptive to the idea of future contact from the child than were couples who were less sure about donating their embryos. However, it is important to remember that these were only potential donors and this position is not necessarily shared by the majority of those who actually donate embryos for use by infertile couples. A Finnish study evaluated the attitudes of 46 couples who had donated their embryos and found that only 35 per cent of them were willing to register identifying information for the child to access in the future (Soderstrom-Antilla *et al*, 2001). Less than half of the donor couples (47 per cent) felt that the child should be informed about the donor conception. One woman said about the donation: '[it] is the same as if I would have donated blood or some organ to another human being'. Similarly, a UK study found that 75 per cent of embryo donors did not want to know the outcome of their donation (Marcus *et al*, 1998). Clearly, from a psychological perspective, for a large proportion of donors, the process is not akin to adoption and should not be approached in the same way.

Consequences of genetic relationships for parenthood

Another important consideration is that of how much influence genetic links have on the experience of parenthood. From an evolutionary psychology perspective, it has been argued that one of the paramount reasons why parents invest so much time and effort in their children is because 'children are a parent's most direct route to genetic immortality' (Bjorklund *et al*, 2002). Thus, it might be expected that non-genetic parents would be less invested in their children and therefore show lower quality of parenting. For prospective adopters, one of the first challenges to accomplish is the letting go of the idea of themselves as achieving this 'genetic immortality'. Failure to confront the reality that biological parenthood will not be possible, or an inability to come to some sort of resolution regarding their infertility, increases the risk of encountering later difficulties in the adoptive parent–child relationships (Brodzinsky, 1997). However, research suggests that when adopted children are placed early, there is no difference in the closeness of mother–infant relationships between adoptive and non-adoptive families (Singer *et al*, 1985).

Prospective embryo donation parents also have to accept the loss of the prospect of their own genetic child before they consider conceiving a child using donated embryos. In the study of embryo donation and adoptive families mentioned above, findings indicated that embryo donation parents were able to accept this loss and to form warm and affectionate relationships with their children. In comparison with parents of genetically related children, embryo donation parents (and adoptive parents) did not show less positive parenting (MacCallum *et al*, in press). This supports previous research which found high-quality parenting in families created through egg and sperm donation, with no negative consequences for children (for example, Golombok *et al*, 1999). Since embryo donation parents seem to be functioning well, with good-quality parent–child relationships, this suggests that the lack of genetic relationships does not create psychological grounds for further screening of embryo donation recipients.

Conclusions regarding the genetic relationship

The structural similarity of embryo donation and adoption, where parents raise children to whom they are not genetically related, could be an argument for equating the two processes, meaning that this procedure would in fact be taken outside of the remit of the 1990 Act and placed in the context of adoption law. Such extreme action would be unnecessary, as well as undesirable; for most participants in embryo donation programmes, whether as donors or recipients, the exchange of an embryo is not equivalent to the relinquishment and adoption of a child. Furthermore, in spite of the lack of stringent psychosocial selection criteria, embryo donation parents have been found to provide good-quality parenting. However, concerns should be raised about, for example, the treatment of the role of the donors in embryo donation. Although recipients do not seem to view the donors as important, it is possible that children conceived in this way would benefit from the donors being accorded some significance, more analogous to the way in which birth parents are treated by adoptive parents. Again, the experiences of some offspring of gamete donation suggest that the donors certainly have some significance for them (Donor Conception Support Group, 1997; Turner and Coyle, 2000). Indeed, the need of donor offspring to have full access to their genetic background and the possible negative consequences for their psychological wellbeing of lacking this information was one of the key arguments that led to the changing of the law regarding donor anonymity. Since, unlike in donor insemination or egg donation, embryo donation children are not raised by either of their genetic parents, this issue may be especially pertinent for these offspring, particularly those conceived from April 2005 onwards, who will have the legal right to identifying information about their donors when they reach the age of 18. The suggestion is therefore that the reform of the Human Fertilisation and Embryology Act should have built into it more emphasis in relation to embryo donation recipients on obligatory information sessions as to how best to communicate about these issues with the child, which could be based on the compulsory preparation courses for adoptive parents. There should also be a legal requirement for clinics to establish post-treatment services to support parents in this course of action, similar to the post-adoption services made available to all adoptive families. Overall, the aspects identified as relating to the absence of genetic relationships do seem to justify some difference between approaches to embryo donation and adoption. However, they also make a case for bringing the two closer together in terms of the provision of counselling and support services for parents.

The gestational relationship

The most obvious difference between embryo donation and adoption is that in embryo donation there is a biological link to one parent, through gestation. The parents experience the pregnancy and the birth, allowing them to bond to the child prenatally as well as the opportunity to regulate the prenatal environment. It can be argued that the gestational mother has made the greatest contribution of work to the child, sometimes referred to as 'sweat equity' (Annas, 1988), which may be one reason why in the UK she is always legally regarded as the mother of the child. The gestational relationship leads to differences between embryo donation and adoption for several reasons: legal, psychological, social and practical (Widdows and MacCallum, 2002).

Legal issues

As has already been discussed, the difference between the legal status of embryo donation parents and adoptive parents is clear. In UK law, according to ss 27(1) and 28(2) of the 1990 Act, regardless of genetic relationship, the woman who gives birth to the child is the legal mother and, if she is married and her husband agreed to the procedure being carried out, he is the legal father (if he did not consent, the child will be legally fatherless since the donor cannot be regarded as the legal parent). In adoption, parental rights and responsibilities have to be legally transferred from the birth parents to the adoptive parents following birth. This does not happen immediately on placement of the child with the adoptive parents and may in fact take several months, or longer if the birth parents contest the adoption. Therefore, until the adoption is finalised, the adoptive parents are in the precarious position of caring for a child who is not yet legally theirs, and some adopters may not feel 'fully parental' until this legal process is complete (Sandelowski, 1995).

Psychological issues

Having a gestational link allows the woman to consider the child as 'hers' psychologically as well as legally from the outset. Some view the gestational link as equally important to the genetic link, if not more so. Research by Mahowald found that 'for some, the inability to gestate and give birth represents a greater loss than the inability to have a child whose genetic complement comprises 50 per cent of their own genes' (Mahowald, 2000). The experience of gestation can be seen as conferring on the mother the perception of self as mother. Over the last 20 years, there has been increasing recognition that attachment between mother and infant begins before birth, with the mother forming a relationship to the foetus (Laxton-Kane and Slade, 2002). This prenatal attachment is important in that it has been shown to be associated with the postnatal relationships of infants and their mothers (Muller, 1996), and mother–child relationships in early infancy are a significant factor in the healthy psychological development of children (for example, Erickson *et al*, 1985). Therefore, as Eisenberg and Schenker (1998) point out, from a psychological perspective, in addition to the benefits to the mother, 'unlike adoption, the child born through pre-embryo donation also benefits from the additional bond of being gestated in its future mother's womb, with the support of its future father' (Eisenberg and Schenker, 1998). This notion that prenatal attachment influences parental bonding to children was explored in the previously mentioned study of embryo donation families and adoptive families (MacCallum *et al*, in press). Comparisons showed that adoptive mothers were no different from embryo donation mothers in terms of the warmth they showed towards their child or the sensitivity with which they responded to their child. Contrary to expectations, the experience of pregnancy and childbirth did not seem to result in the development of more positive mother–child relationships than adopting a child in infancy.

Social issues

The fact that embryo donation parents go through pregnancy and birth allows them to present the pregnancy to the outside world as a 'natural' conception if they so desire. Unless the couple choose to tell family and friends of their assisted conception, no one will know. This contrasts with adoption, where there is no pregnancy to be seen and the couple must explain the arrival of a child who will already be at least a few months old. The gestational relationship also allows the parents to keep the non-genetic relationship secret from the child. Adoptive parents as a rule disclose to the child the circumstances of their birth from a young age, for example by keeping 'life-story books' containing photos and information about the adoption. In contrast, parents who have conceived using donor gametes have tended not to disclose the donor conception to the child, although there are signs that attitudes may be changing (Golombok *et al*, 2004). With respect to embryo donation, Soderstrom-Antilla *et al* (2001) found that 69 per cent of couples who had been treated with donor embryos in their programme thought that a child conceived in this way should be informed about the manner of his/her conception. However, only 11 of these couples (41 per cent) had actually had a child at the time of study and less than half of these (46 per cent) had definitely decided to inform the child. In MacCallum *et al*'s (in press) study of 21 couples with a child conceived by embryo donation, only two (9 per cent) had already told their child about the method of their conception, with a further five couples (24 per cent) reporting that they were planning to tell in the future. This compared with 100 per cent of the group of adoptive parents who had told their child something about the adoption.

It could be argued that disclosure is more necessary in adoption, since it may affect psychological issues that arise with respect to children as they develop. For example, the child may have already formed a relationship with the genetic parent prior to the adoption. Adopted children may need to know the circumstances of the adoption in order to feel that they have a complete 'life story'. Indeed, a study by Howe and Feast (2000) of adopted adults who were trying to trace their birth families found that, for the majority of adoptees, the psychological need for more autobiographical information was the major motivating factor for the search. Although embryo donation children do have a gestational link to their rearing parents, and therefore do not have the same gap in their life stories, information about their genetic parentage may also be important for their sense of identity. Therefore, they may also feel the psychological need to search for details of the donors.

Practical issues

One essential consideration is that, due to the gestation process, embryo donation parents do not have the same practical obstacles to overcome as adoptive parents. The first of these practical issues is that adoptive parents must meet not only selection criteria that mark them as fit to parent a child in general, but also selection criteria specific to an individual child. The already existing child has an individual personality, a specific history and particular needs arising from that history. Adoption services must select from all prospective adopters the couple who are most suitable for all these aspects, making it 'not just a matter of finding people who would be fit to look after children, but fit to look after the particular children available' (Campion, 1995). A child who is placed for adoption may come from a difficult background and have experienced neglect or abuse, necessitating the screening of a couple for their ability to cope with any ensuing child problems. Thus, the child's needs and not the parents' wishes are paramount in the selection of adoptive parents. As discussed above, in embryo donation, the only stipulation is that the future welfare of a potential child must be taken into account, a concept seen by some as meaningless (see Jackson, Chapter 3 in this volume, but also see Blyth, Chapter 2 in this volume, for a contrasting argument). Importantly from a practical viewpoint, unlike in adoption, at the point of parent selection the embryo donation child has no *specific* needs to be met since it is not yet a child at all.

The second practical issue that must be overcome in adoption is that of the child's separation from and relinquishment by the birth parents. The assumption is that adopted children have a 'significant wound' to resolve (Percy, 1999), and that in order to achieve this resolution they must receive the best possible parenting. Thus, 'adoptive parents need to be not just ordinary parents but extra-ordinary parents – with an emphasis on the "extra" ' (Campion, 1995). In terms of the children themselves, distinctions have been drawn between the psychological experiences of adoptees and those of the offspring of donor conception on the basis of the initial parental rejection in adoption. Therefore, for children born through donor conception, 'the fact that a child has always been a wanted child may constitute a very important difference' (Golombok *et al*, 1995). This may be true for children born using either donated sperm or donated eggs who still have a genetic link to one parent, but embryo donation children have the additional considerations that both their genetic parents are unknown to them and that they may have full genetic siblings born to the donor couple. It is possible that these factors may make embryo donation children, more than other assisted reproduction children, feel that they have been 'given up' by their 'parents'. This has led to some arguing that there is a parallel in embryo donation to the 'history of rejection' in adoption. For example, Bernstein and colleagues proposed that embryo donation children 'may see themselves as "spare" or "surplus" goods and may indeed have the same need for information – for access to their story – as other adoptees' (Bernstein *et al*, 1996). This conclusion seems extreme in that donating an embryo does not equate to placing a child for adoption, since it can be viewed more as an altruistic act than a necessary one, but it does highlight the fact that embryo donation children may be more similar to adoptive children in this aspect than are other assisted reproduction children.

Conclusions regarding the gestational relationship

The gestational link is the most compelling distinction between embryo donation and adoption and the primary justification for embryo donation being contained within the Human Fertilisation and Embryology Act rather than being governed by adoption law, since it gives rise to legal, psychological, social and practical differences between the two processes. However, do these factors provide good grounds for the *magnitude* of the inequality with which embryo donation and adoption are treated? The legal aspect could be important initially for adoptive parents' experience but may not continue to have an effect once the adoption is legalised. From this point on, parental responsibility is exactly the same as that of embryo donation parents, so there is no reason why the two should be approached so differently. From a psychological perspective, carrying the child could have the effect of creating more secure attachments in embryo donation families than in adoptive families, although research evidence collected so far does not support this hypothesis. Furthermore, gestation does not in itself guarantee bonding between mother and child, with some 'natural' conception mothers failing to bond immediately with their child. Although gestation may give embryo donation parents an initial psychological advantage, there is no evidence that adoptive parents cannot bond with their children as effectively, or that this will have any long-term effect on the parent–child relationship. Therefore, this is not an argument for maintaining the disparity in treatment of prospective adopters and prospective embryo donation patients. Socially, the fact that the embryo donation parents are able to present as a 'normal family' is likely to have an impact on their experience of parenthood. Unlike adoptive parents, embryo donation parents can choose not to disclose the circumstances of the child's birth. Whether this can be seen as beneficial for either the parents or the child depends on how one views the idea that the ability to keep the child's genetic origins secret is desirable; an assumption that has been the subject of considerable debate. As discussed previously, this could actually be seen as a reason for expanding the preparation process for embryo donation parents, to assist them in their decision regarding disclosure. It may be preferable to encourage parents as far as possible to be open with their child, particularly in light of the fact that the UK Government's change to an 'identity-release' donor system is intended to create a more open climate surrounding donor conception.

More pronounced are the practical differences that arise as a result of gestation; it is undeniable that the specific needs of the adopted child, and the 'rejection' experienced by adoptees, are likely to have long-lasting effects on the experience of adoptive families, particularly in terms of the child's social and emotional development. Adoptive parents need to be capable of providing support for the child to resolve these issues. Embryo donation children will not require the same support in regard to coming to terms with a difficult background. It is not yet known to what extent embryo donation children will also feel some sense of 'rejection' and will have to resolve their own sense of having been relinquished by their genetic parents. Research on embryo donation families has found children to be psychologically well adjusted, with no indication of problems with social and emotional development (MacCallum *et al*, in press). Nonetheless, the children studied were only five years old or younger, so it remains to be seen how these offspring will fare as they grow older, especially if they become aware of the unusual way in which their family was created. Again, the establishment of post-treatment services for embryo donation parents and offspring could be beneficial for dealing with any problems that do arise. As a whole, the factors arising from the presence or absence of a gestational relationship in embryo donation and adoption, respectively, provide justification for not equating the two processes, but do not justify the magnitude of the current disparities.

CONCLUSIONS

There are a number of similarities and differences between the processes of embryo donation and adoption. The key similarity is that, in both cases, there is no genetic relationship between the parents and the child. The main differences are the legal status of the embryo compared to that of an existing child and the gestational link which exists in embryo donation but not in adoption. The question is: to what extent do these differences justify the wide disparity in approach to the two procedures? While the differing legal status of embryo donation and adoption is probably inflexible (and rightly so), there is scope for change in regard to the different criteria set for prospective embryo donation and adoptive parents.

In general, the magnitude of the disparity in the criteria applied to embryo donation parents and to adoptive parents seems difficult to justify from an ethical viewpoint (Widdows and MacCallum, 2002). This is not to propose that embryo donation should be equated with adoption, bearing in mind particularly the additional practical challenges faced by adoptive parents. However, while differences in processes of selection and preparation for parenthood should remain, they should be proportional and representative, as opposed to the marked disparity that currently exists. In both situations, parents are raising a child who has other genetic parents and thus, if psychosocial factors are primary in selecting adoptive parents, they should also play a part in the screening of embryo donation parents. The review of the 1990 Act should consider revising s 13(5). First, the vague reference to the 'welfare of the child' should be replaced by clear guiding principles to protect any resulting child from foreseeable harm which would apply to all forms of assisted conception (for an in-depth discussion of possible principles, see Blyth, Chapter 2 in this volume). Second, the reformatting should allow specific provisions for different types of assisted reproduction, depending on the family structure resulting and the possible issues arising. For example, IVF patients who conceive using their own gametes do not have to consider whether or how to communicate with the child about their genetic parents, and therefore should not be required to attend information sessions on disclosure. On the other hand, as shown here, embryo donation parents do face some potentially difficult issues and need to be equipped to deal with them. As with adoption, however, it should be viewed as an educative process rather than as purely proscriptive. Adoptive parents are obliged to attend courses designed to prepare them for any obstacles that may crop up in consequence of the adoption. Embryo donation parents should similarly be alerted to issues which may arise in their families as a result of their unusual transition to parenthood. They should also be supported by the provision of post-treatment services, so that if they wish to have future discussion or counselling regarding these issues the facilities are available. This provision may be particularly important from 2023, when the first cohort of donor conception children born since April 2005 will be legally able to access the identity of their genetic parents.

The stipulation in the current formulation of the Human Fertilisation and Embryology Act 1990 regarding the welfare of the child does necessitate taking social factors into account when vetting would-be embryo donation parents, but at present these social criteria are not uniformly enforced in a systematic way. As Jackson (Chapter 3 in this volume) argues, s 13(5) may indeed in its present format be unworkable. However, that does not mean we should not attempt to develop a method of consideration of the 'welfare of the child' that can be put into practice in a transparent and consistent manner. Clarification of this framework would benefit assisted reproduction practitioners and would-be parents, as well as the children conceived through these treatments.

REFERENCES

American Fertility Society (1990) 'Ethical considerations' 53 *Fertility and Sterility* 34S–35S

Annas, GJ (1988) 'Death without dignity for commercial surrogacy: the case of Baby M' 18 *Hastings Center Report* 21–4

Ballantyne, A (1991) *The Sunday Times*, 15 December

Baran, A and Pannor, R (1993) *Lethal Secrets*, 2nd edn New York: Amistad

Bernstein, J, Berson, A, Brill, M, Cooper, S, Ferber, G, Glazer, E *et al* (1996) 'Safeguards in embryo donation' 65 *Fertility and Sterility* 1262–3

Bjorklund, DF, Younger, JL and Pellegrini, AD (2002) 'The evolution of parenting and evolutionary approaches to childrearing' in Bornstein, M (ed) *Handbook of Parenting*, Vol 2 Mahwah, NJ: Lawrence Erlbaum Associates

Braid, M (2003) 'Frozen dreams' *The Observer*, 16 November

Brodzinsky, D (1997) 'Infertility and adoption adjustment: considerations and clinical issues' in Leiblum, S (ed) *Infertility: Psychological Issues and Counselling Strategies* New York: Wiley

Campion, MJ (1995) *Who's Fit to be a Parent?* London: Routledge

Chapman, D, Dorner, P, Silber, K and Winterberg, T (1986) 'Meeting the needs of the adoption triangle through open adoption: the birthmother' 3 *Child and Adolescent Social Work* 203–13

Crockin, SL (2001) 'Embryo "adoption": a limited option' 3 *Reproductive Biomedicine Online* 162–3

Donor Conception Support Group of Australia Inc. (1997) *Let the Offspring Speak: Discussions on Donor Conception* Sydney: Donor Conception Support Group of Australia Inc.

Eisenberg, VH and Schenker, JG (1998) 'Pre-embryo donation: ethical and legal aspects' 60 *International Journal of Gynaecology and Obstetrics* 51–7

Erickson, MA, Sroufe, LA and Egeland, B (1985) 'The relationship between quality of attachment and behaviour in preschool in a high risk sample' in *Growing Points in Attachment Theory and Research*, Vol 50 (No. 1–2, Serial no. 209) pp 147–66

ESHRE Task Force on Ethics and Law (2001) 'The moral status of the pre-implantation embryo' 16 *Human Reproduction* 1046–8

Golombok, S, Cook, R, Bish, A and Murray, C (1995) 'Families created by the New Reproductive Technologies: quality of parenting and social and emotional development of the children' 66 *Child Development* 285–98

Golombok, S, Lycett, E, MacCallum, F, Jadva, V, Murray, C, Abdalla, H *et al* (2004)

'Parenting children conceived by gamete donation' 18 *Journal of Family Psychology* 443–52

Golombok, S, Murray, C, Brinsden, P and Abdalla, H (1999) 'Social versus biological parenting: family functioning and the socioemotional development of children conceived by egg or sperm donation' 40 *Journal of Child Psychology and Psychiatry* 519–27

Howe, D and Feast, J (2000) *Adoption, Search and Reunion: The Long-Term Experiences of Adopted Adults* London: The Children's Society

Hughes, B and Logan, J (1993) *Birth Parents: The Hidden Dimension* University of Manchester Department of Social Policy and Social Work

Human Fertilisation and Embryology Authority (2004) *Code of Practice*, 6th edn London: HFEA

Jones, HW and Cohen, J (2004) 'IFFS surveillance 04' 81 *Fertility and Sterility* Suppl 4

Langton, J (2003) 'A new parenting phenomenon is sweeping America' *London Evening Standard*, 6 March

Laurence, C (2003) 'Childless couples "adopt" America's leftover embryos' *Daily Telegraph*, online edition, 30 March

Laxton-Kane, M and Slade, P (2002) 'The role of maternal prenatal attachment in a woman's experience of pregnancy and implications for the process of care' 20 *Journal of Reproductive and Infant Psychology* 253–66

MacCallum, F (2004) 'Families with a child conceived by embryo donation: parenting and child development' Unpublished PhD thesis, City University, London

MacCallum, F, Golombok, S and Brinsden, P (in press) 'Parenting and child development in families with a child conceived through embryo donation' *Journal of Family Psychology*

Mahowald, MB (2000) *Genes, Women and Equality* Oxford: Oxford University Press

Marcus, SF, Appleton, T, Marcus, MK and Brinsden, P (1998) 'Attitudes of donor couples toward embryo donation' 13 *Human Reproduction* (suppl) 238

Muller, ME (1996) 'Prenatal and postnatal attachment: a modest correlation' 25 *Journal of Obstetric, Gynaecologic and Neonatal Nursing* 161–6

Newton, CR, McDermid, A, Tekpety, F and Tummon, IS (2003) 'Embryo donation: attitudes toward donation procedures and factors predicting willingness to donate' 18 *Human Reproduction* 878–84

Norton, C (1999) 'Embryo adoption register planned' *The Independent*, 5 July

Percy, M (1999) 'Adoption is a wound that can be healed' *The Independent*, 11 October

Ratzinger, JC and Bovone, J (1987) *Instruction on respect for human life in its origin and on the dignity of procreation* Vatican: Congregation for the Doctrine of the Faith

Robertson, JA (1995) 'Ethical and legal issues in human embryo donation' 64 *Fertility and Sterility* 885–94

Sandelowski, M (1995) 'A theory of the transition to parenthood of infertile couples' 18 *Research in Nursing and Health* 123–32

Sauer, MV, Paulson, RJ, Francis, MM, Macaso, TM and Lobo, RA (1995) 'Preimplantation adoption: establishing pregnancy using donated oocytes and spermatoza' 10 *Human Reproduction* 1419–22

Singer, L, Brodzinsky, D, Ramsay, D, Steir, M and Waters, E (1985) 'Mother–infant attachment in adoptive families' 56 *Child Development* 1543–51

Soderstrom-Antilla, V, Foudila, T, Ripatti, U and Siegberg, R (2001) 'Embryo donation: outcome and attitudes among embryo donors and recipients' 16 *Human Reproduction* 1120–8

Souter, T (1999) 'Orphan embryos up for adoption' *Red* 79–80, November

Stolberg, SG (2001) 'Some see new route to adoption in clinics full of frozen embryos' *New York Times*, online edition, 25 February

The British Agencies for Adoption and Fostering (1991) Form F

Triseliotis, J, Shireman, J and Hundleby, M (1997) *Adoption: Theory, Policy and Practice* London: Redwood Books

Trounson, A, Leeton, J, Besanka, M, Wood, C and Conti, A (1983) 'Pregnancy established in an infertile patient after transfer of a donated embryo fertilized in vitro' 286 *British Medical Journal* 835–8

Turner, AJ and Coyle, A (2000) 'What does it mean to be a donor offspring? The identity experiences of adults conceived by donor insemination and the implications for counselling and therapy' 15 *Human Reproduction* 2041–51

Warnock, M (1984) *The Warnock Report on Human Fertilisation and Embryology* London: HMSO

Widdows, H and MacCallum, F (2002) 'Disparities in parenting criteria: an exploration of the issues, focusing on adoption and embryo donation' 28 *Journal of Medical Ethics* 139–42

Winkler, R and van Keppel, M (1984) *Relinquishing Mothers in Adoption* Melbourne: Institute for Family Studies

Chapter 8

Unconsidered inconsistencies

Parenthood and assisted conception

Kirsty Horsey

INTRODUCTION

The review of the UK's Human Fertilisation and Embryology Act 1990 ('the 1990 Act') offers a timely and welcome opportunity to regulate areas of assisted reproduction and embryo research that were unconsidered at the time the legislation was passed, as well as to include regulations on new forms of technology that escape the provisions of the 1990 Act due to having been either omitted or unimaginable at the time. However, the review also allows an opportunity for legislators to *re*consider some areas of the law that time has shown could be better formulated. While there are a number of areas covered by the legislation that fall into this category, one aspect of the UK's regulatory structure that has so far received little critical attention is the way it ascribes legal parenthood following the use of assisted reproductive technologies. Notably, the way parenthood is legally ascribed has been debated and challenged more frequently in other jurisdictions, mainly as a result of real-life case law (for example, *Johnson v Calvert* 286 Cal Rptr 369 (Cal Ct App 1991); *In Re the Marriage of Buzzanca* (1998) 61 Cal App 4th 1410 (Cal CA); *Re Evelyn* [1998] Fam CA 55), but also evidenced in recent public consultations moving towards a more open and direct challenge to traditional views (Victoria Law Reform Commission, 2005; New Zealand Law Commission, 2005; New Zealand Ministry of Justice, 2006). In the UK, challenges to parenthood *per se* have been few and far between. In the majority, challenges centre on parentage in terms of asking who should have legal *custody* of a child, particularly in cases that have involved a dispute over surrogacy. As a result, challenges to the actual definitions and ascription of legal parenthood itself have not, until recently (and only then because circumstances dictated that these issues be faced: see *Re R (A Child) (IVF: Paternity of Child)* [2003] EWCA 182; *In Re D (A Child Appearing by Her Guardian ad Litem) (Respondent)* [2005] UKHL 33; *The Leeds Teaching Hospitals NHS Trust v Mr A, Mrs A and Others* [2003] EWCA 259 (QBD)), gained as much critical attention.

This chapter will explain how legal parenthood is determined by the 1990

Act and on what circumstances this depends, before moving on to show that inherent faults and inconsistencies currently exist in the way this is accomplished. Arguably, the provisions on legal parenthood are some of the most important within the Act – after all, people seeking (and paying for) assisted reproductive technologies are exercising a deliberate autonomous choice to become parents. Thus, a convincing argument can be made that those people who seek to become parents in this way should be legally recognised as the parents of any children they are lucky enough to have, as they are the ones who intentionally caused those children to come into being as well as the ones who will raise them. But for the purposive actions of such individuals (although perhaps born out of necessity), the children in question would not exist.[1] This chapter will show that while the 1990 Act has taken into account *some* of the parenthood situations that may arise, it does not recognise the social reality of all family situations, which should therefore be one of the aspects of the legislation taken into account by the legislative review. In general terms, the 1990 Act can be described as trying to fit alternative family forms (where the primary causative functions of bringing a child into being have been disrupted or fragmented) into a basic, symbolic nuclear family model. In so doing, it makes the assumption that this family vision is the best model (Sheldon, 2005): the nuclear family, or something closely approximating it, is represented, implicitly if not explicitly, as the Holy Grail of family formation. After discussing on a general level how the 1990 Act fails – although it sometimes tries, depending on how close to the nuclear family structure the situation is – to encompass unconventional family forms, the chapter will discuss three individual cases where legal parenthood was central to the argument, even if not always unequivocally so. It will show that a different legal definition of parenthood – a presumption based on the intention to create and actively parent a child – would have enabled each of these cases – and other, future, hypothetical cases – to be decided more justly and, on this basis, will make the assertion that the review of the 1990 Act should encompass modifications to the way legal parenthood is ascribed.

Assisted reproduction and parenthood

Historically, when a child was naturally conceived, little doubt could have existed as to who its parents were. Modern assumptions made in such circumstances highlight and maintain this historical and cultural throwback,

---

1 Of course, in assisted conception, there will be many parties – not only the intending parents – who will be causally relevant to the creation of a child. Throughout this chapter, causation should be taken as the intention to cause a child to be born, coupled with the intention to be its parent(s). I thank Sally Sheldon for this point.

reflecting presumptions held for many hundreds of years. A woman giving birth once could not have done so without having conceived through sexual intercourse with a man.[2] So, common law has long understood the woman who gives birth to a baby to be its mother. In order for a child to avoid the invidious label of 'bastard', a woman's husband has long been culturally and legally presumed to be the father of any child born to her, notwithstanding hearsay or other evidence to the contrary such as indications that she might have been having an affair. Unmarried women faced the stigma of having a bastard child, destined to be buried in an unmarked grave. Children born 'out of wedlock', to a couple not united as one in the eyes of the community, were simply fatherless, even if it was well known, or at least well indicated, who the biological father might be.

Gradually, as society has developed towards something like that we know today, it has become apparent that these cultural and legal assumptions simply do not always stand up. First, fewer stigmas were attached to children born out of wedlock, as not all couples married before they had children. There has been a steady increase in the number of children born into unmarried families or to single women. Correspondingly, there has been an increase in divorce and second marriages, leading to a number of differently shaped families (Summerfield and Gill, 2005). Second, the development of technologies that assist procreation – as well as our entry into 'the genetic age' – has led us to alter our perceptions, in some way at least, about what makes a mother a mother or a father a father. Arguably, many see a difference between biological parenthood and social parenthood, not least because of the increase in the rate of divorce and the formation of second families. Saying this, however, does not mean that *all* perceptions have changed. It is still, for the most part, a fact that the woman who gives birth to a child is the woman who will raise it. Indeed, it is arguable that this may hold an increased level of truth, given the lessening of stigma attached to single mothers, who were once more likely to be coerced into giving up children they conceived, willingly or not, in order to hide their 'predicament'. And there is no doubt that a woman's husband (or partner) is still perceived (socially and legally) to be the father of her child – although there is, in modern times, the means of disputing this via DNA paternity tests. Anecdotally, DNA tests of this sort are used to disprove paternity on a regular

---

2 Although it is interesting to note that biblical references are made to situations, often characterised as surrogacy arrangements, where (powerful) men 'naturally' impregnated slave girls in order that their own (barren) wives could raise the child as if it were their own (see the stories of Abraham and Jacob in Genesis 16: 1–16 and 30: 1–25, respectively). Furthermore, it is suggested that 'inter-familial surrogacy is historically a reasonably common practice' (Morgan, 1989, p 67) and possibly relatively common in some cultures, in which it would be regarded as quite normal for a woman to have a child for a sister or friend who was not able to do so herself (Harding, 1987, p 54).

basis, in order to avoid paying child support. Recently, a study has shown that a quarter of all men who demand paternity tests for suspected infidelity have their worst suspicions confirmed, using statistics that show that as many as one in 25 men are bringing up children mistakenly believed to be their own (Bellis *et al*, 2005). Of course, the reverse is also true – DNA tests can be used to try and *prove* biological fatherhood where there is some issue or dispute about who the father might be. A number of celebrities, including the actress Liz Hurley and David Blunkett, the former Home Secretary, are cases in point (see *Blunkett v Quinn* [2004] EWHC 2816 (Fam)).

IVF and donor insemination (DI)

Many forms of assisted conception separate the physical functions and biological necessities of reproduction from the actual process of parenting. For this reason, the 1990 Act had to define parenthood in a number of different situations. The development of *in vitro* fertilisation (IVF) and its related technologies, and of insemination using donated sperm (DI) and surrogacy as 'modern' reproductive technologies, has created familial situations outside of the norm. In traditional IVF, it is usual that the couple seeking treatment are heterosexual partners who intend to raise any resulting children together. Thus, it would seem that IVF poses no problems to the legal definition of parenthood, as the woman who gives birth will be genetically, gestationally and socially fulfilling the role(s) of 'mother'. The man who provided the sperm, her partner, will be both genetically and socially the 'father'. The law recognises this and unequivocally provides (in s 27(1) of the 1990 Act) that any woman, and 'no other woman', who has carried and given birth to a child 'as a result of the placing in her of an embryo or of sperm and eggs' will be the legally recognised mother of that child. Common law presumptions remain operative in respect of her husband or partner, as (re)stated in ss 28(2) and (3), which define the father as the party to the marriage with the woman giving birth or her partner ('unless it is shown that he did not consent to the placing in her of the embryo or the sperm and eggs or to her insemination'). However, the need for IVF is not always as simple as requiring a means to circumvent a glitch in one couple's internal reproductive ability. It may also involve, for example, the use of donated sperm (or eggs), thereby requiring an alternative examination of parenthood. Furthermore, IVF using donor sperm may be sought by those wishing to procreate in more 'unconventional' ways; for example, two women.

Following DI, it is usually the case that the woman who gives birth is the woman who will raise the child; this is the reason she was inseminated – using the sperm of a man other than her partner is simply the means of having a family that externally appears to have been created 'normally', as both parties can be involved throughout the gestation and birth of the child.[3] Only the male biological element is 'missing'. The definition of motherhood from s 27(1) of the 1990 Act is sound here as it reflects the intention of the woman to become the mother of the child, albeit through the use of sperm donated by a man who is not her partner (it is also worth noting that if a donor egg were to be used, the lack of a genetic link is overridden by the provision of s 27(1), again recognising the woman's intention to become the mother). If parenthood were defined biologically, following DI the 'father' would be the man who provided sperm and no other man. Fortunately, as stated above, s 28(2) provides that the married partner of the woman giving birth will be recognised as the father of the child born unless 'it is shown that he did not consent to the . . . insemination', even if his sperm was not used to inseminate her. If the woman has no married partner, then a man 'treated together' with her (although not having provided his sperm) can still be treated in law as the father of the child, by virtue of s 28(3). Here, too, the intention of the couple to become parents is implicitly recognised by the law. However, like IVF, DI can also be – and is – requested for 'unconventional' reasons, such as to create a pregnancy within a lesbian couple, or for a single woman. Here, too, the law proves to be inadequate.

Surrogacy

When surrogacy is used to create a family, the legal definitions of parenthood become much less stable. In surrogacy, the woman giving birth is *not* the woman who intends to raise the child, yet the law is rigid on motherhood, s 27(1) applying to all situations. Neither does the husband or partner of the woman giving birth intend to raise the child, yet he will be legally recognised as the father, by virtue of s 28, unless he can show that he did not consent to whichever procedure was used to create the pregnancy. Evidently, therefore, the couple who commissioned the surrogate to have a child for them (one or both of whom may be genetically related to the child) are *not* legally recognised as the parents of that child. In my view, this creates a less than ideal situation, which must stem from an overarching distaste for surrogacy more generally when the 1990 Act (and the prior Surrogacy Arrangements Act 1985 – which mysteriously did not deal with legal parenthood) was framed (as is evident from the later retraction of the idea of surrogacy as inherently distasteful by Baroness Mary Warnock in her later writings: see Warnock, 2002, pp 88–9).

The current provisions leave us with some technically bizarre situations. Depending on whether the commissioning/intending father provided a gamete

---

3 Note this perceived normality captures the essence of the status provisions of the 1990 Act, which appear to both implicitly and explicitly designate the nuclear heterosexual family as the preferred model (Sheldon, 2005).

for artificial insemination into the surrogate, whether the surrogate became pregnant through sexual intercourse with him or whether the surrogate was married, 'the child's legal father could be a woman's husband/partner, the sperm donor, or no-one' (Blyth, 1993, p 254; also see Douglas, 1991). Moreover, this is despite the fact that there is a man willing to take this legal role, and who intended to do so prior to conception. Protecting the right of the birth mother to keep any children born to her and to be legally recognised as their mother seems to be a 'non-negotiable' part of the law on parenthood following assisted reproduction (Jackson, 2001, p 266). These outcomes only seem correct, however, if surrogacy is viewed – as it is by some – as the taking of a child away from its 'real' parents to be given to someone else; if it is seen to be more akin to adoption, then the fact that the commissioning parents initially go legally unrecognised fits. Indeed, until the 1990 Act, all commissioning parents could do to achieve parental status in law was adopt the child. Yet, if surrogacy is properly viewed – as I believe it should be – as a form of assisted conception, enabling infertile couples to cause a child to come into being, then, as with DI, the realities of the situation created should be more accurately reflected in the parenthood provisions of the law.

In surrogacy, motherhood could be allocated according to the biological alternative: by recognising the woman who provided the egg and who is therefore the genetic mother of the child born. However, it is arguable that this too would distort the social reality of the situation and the pre-conception agreement actually entered into (see Mackenzie, forthcoming; Horsey, 2003). If the surrogate's own egg was used, she would still be the legal mother. This might, in some cases, leave 'the woman least likely to want to raise the child' having legal recognition as its mother (Jackson, 2001, p 266). This is particularly the case if a third woman – an egg donor – enters the frame. Therefore, in relation to legal motherhood following surrogacy, it is arguable that the 1990 Act fails to remove any ambiguities. Instead, because of the separation of the physical and social processes involved in having a child by surrogacy or another form of assisted reproductive technique, it can be argued that it *creates* or maintains ambiguity by failing to recognise and legally acknowledge the visible social family unit that is intended to be formed. Despite the fact that s 30 of the 1990 Act allows for a 'parental order' to be granted which provides 'for a child to be treated in law as the child of the parties' to a surrogacy arrangement, this is subject to a number of conditions which do not make a parental order available to *some* parties who enter surrogacy agreements; this, arguably, is not consistent with the fact that others who *intend* to be parents can be so treated in law.

Thus, while legal provisions ascribing parenthood following the use of assisted conception were included in the 1990 Act, solving some of the problems created by the division of sex from family creation, it seems that little attention was given to the inconsistencies that these provisions *create*. Or, as previously mentioned, it may simply be that surrogacy was not seen as a legitimate form of assisted conception but rather as a species of adoption, meaning that parenthood following the use of surrogacy *did not need* to be consistent with that following IVF or DI for example.

All in all, it seems that we may be forgiven for thinking that 'the rules created by the Human Fertilisation and Embryology Act 1990 have to deal with almost impossibly complex circumstances', and that 'they can no doubt be justified on the basis of a pragmatic assessment of what is expedient in the majority of cases' (Cretney, 2000, p 200). Yet pragmatism and expediency may not be good enough reasons for preventing those whose intention it is to be parents of a planned and wanted child from being legally recognised as such. In a technical, medical sense, achieving a family through assisted reproduction (including surrogacy) is relatively 'easy' to do, and an argument based on pragmatism and expediency can be challenged by stating that the circumstances that are created by the usage of artificial means of conception are, although complex, not 'impossibly complex' at all. If legal parenthood mirrored social reality and we did not rely on pre-existing and arguably outdated cultural and legal presumptions in this area, and instead based the law on different criteria (that can readily be found in other areas of law – promise, intention, expectation and reliance, for example), the social reality of the families created would be better reflected. Indeed, this would fit nicely with developments in other areas of law which are intertwined with assisted reproduction, such as adoption (where unmarried and same-sex couples can legally adopt children jointly), civil partnerships (where the lifelong commitment of same-sex couples to each other has been formally recognised, albeit not classified as marriage) and transgender issues (on how these developments potentially affect and inform legal parenthood following assisted conception, see Sheldon, 2005a). Basing legal parenthood following all forms of assisted conception on these suggested different criteria would achieve a level of consistency not present in the law as it currently stands. Thus, the Government, while reviewing the 1990 Act, should pay close attention to its provisions on parenthood. However, though the Department of Health consultation document had a section entitled 'Status and legal parenthood', and mentioned that 'the Government intends to consider the extent to which changes may be needed to better recognise the wider range of people who seek and receive assisted reproduction in the 21st century' (Department of Health, 2005, para 8.12), the questions asked to the public were limited to whether unmarried men should continue to be treated differently, whether parental orders should be available to unmarried couples, and whether civil partners should be treated in the same way as married partners (88–89). Other questions relating to parenthood escape mention in the consultation, suggesting that these issues are viewed by the Government as closed.

THE IMPACT OF THE CURRENT LAW

The complicated yet limited facilities of the 1990 Act to recognise parenthood following assisted conception have led to cases in which, arguably, incorrect outcomes have been reached. Below, I will consider how three cases (*Re R (A Child)(IVF: Paternity of Child)* [2003] EWCA 182, later *In Re D (A Child Appearing by Her Guardian ad Litem)(Respondent)* [2005] UKHL 33; *The Leeds Teaching Hospitals NHS Trust v Mr A, Mrs A and Others* [2003] EWCA 259 (QBD); and *Natallie Evans v Amicus Healthcare Ltd and Others* [2004] EWCA (Civ) 727) could have been decided differently given a different emphasis of the law. If parenthood following assisted conception was determined in an alternative way – that is, by basing it on the positive intentions of the parties – the decisions in these cases could have better reflected the realities of the families (to be) created. The outcomes – often sad – of these three cases can be used to further illustrate the faults within the current system. They demonstrate that the rules currently defining legal parenthood following assisted reproduction are unjust and inconsistent, both within themselves and held up against natural conception. The review of the 1990 Act could therefore have provided an opportunity for government to revisit legal parenthood and the way it is ascribed following different reproductive methods and an opening for those of us who believe the inconsistencies are unjust – or can lead to injustice – to demand an explanation, if there is no change, for why different forms of assisted conception are treated differently in law.

The decisions in *Re R/Re D, Leeds* and *Evans* all appear to highlight missed potential for the application of a presumption of intention in determining parenthood. Perhaps this is because this was initially (deliberately) missed by the drafters of the 1990 Act. Nevertheless, it is arguable that judicial interpretation of the statute could have allowed for this different approach to be taken. All three cases – none of which involve surrogacy – can be used to illustrate the potential of recognising intention, rather than relying on outdated presumptions. In each case, recognising a presumption of intention would have produced consistency without detrimentally affecting the welfare of the children born. Given that the current welfare of the child assessment under s 13(5) requires treatment providers to consider the familial situation a child will be born into, with an obvious bias towards two parents (preferably heterosexual), it is hard to see why a proposal that would give each child brought into existence two legally recognised parents *before* birth (or more than two parents, see Sheldon, 2005a; Mackenzie, Chapter 9 in this volume), as well as providing a consistency between *types* of treatment and with natural conception, could be argued not to be in a child's best interests. Indeed, in this sense, it is merely an alternative presumption. Moreover, given that the use of assisted reproductive techniques generally does not cause dispute and, despite tabloid anecdote and horror stories, very few surrogacy arrangements end in dispute and very few accidents happen in fertility clinics, it is possible to argue that the presumption should favour the intending parents in all such situations, as this would better reflect the reality of the majority of outcomes and would be more consistent with the acquisition of parenthood for fertile people. Where there is dispute, such as if a surrogacy arrangement goes wrong or if the wrong sperm sample is used in a fertility clinic, the presumption could be challenged by those in a position to do so, such as the birth mother or genetic parent.

Denying fatherhood

In *Re R*[4] (now *In Re D (A Child Appearing by Her Guardian ad Litem)* [2005] at the House of Lords – for a full account of the case's progression through the courts, see Sheldon, 2005b), a woman succeeded in her attempts to have legal fatherhood denied to her ex-partner, an infertile man with whom she had begun fertility treatment. Using IVF with donated sperm, they produced a number of embryos, two of which were unsuccessfully transferred to the woman's womb while others were stored at the clinic for future use. The couple separated after this initial unsuccessful attempt. Later, the woman, who by then had a new partner, went to the clinic and had some of the stored embryos transferred to her womb. She became pregnant and subsequently gave birth to a girl. She had not informed the clinic that she was separated from her former partner, nor indeed that she was then with a new partner. Had she done so, the treatment would not have gone ahead. Nor did she inform her former partner that she was continuing the treatment. On application to the High Court, Hedley J granted her original partner – the intending father – a declaration of paternity, pursuant to s 28(3) of the Human Fertilisation and Embryology Act 1990. This is the section that provides that a man who is neither the genetic father of a child nor married to the mother can be treated in law as the father in circumstances where the mother and that man (the intending father) had 'treatment services provided for [them] together by a person to whom a licence applies'. The phrase 'treatment services together' was interpreted by Hedley J for the purposes of s 28(3) as meaning that the provision of services continued until either party or the clinic expressly withdrew from the understanding that the parties were being treated together. This had not occurred on the facts of the case and so the intending father was recognised as the legal father on this basis.

The issue for the Court of Appeal in *Re R* was whether the 'treatment services together' rule applied where a man had participated as the mother's partner during much of the treatment provided but had separated from her by the time that the embryo which led to the child's birth was transferred to her. The Court of Appeal, in a judgment given by the then Lady Justice Hale, ruled that:

4 *Re R (A Child) (IVF: Paternity of Child)* [2003] EWCA 182.

the wording of section 28 makes it clear that the time at which legal paternity is created is the time when the embryo or the sperm and eggs which subsequently result in the birth of the child are placed in the woman ... Section 28(3) also focuses on the act of placing the embryo or sperm and eggs in the mother, further suggesting that the question whether this is done 'in the course of treatment services provided for her and a man together' should be answered at this time and no other.

(*Re R (A Child) (IVF: Paternity of Child)* [2003]
EWCA Civ 182: para 21)

In effect, this decision stripped the man of his paternity, despite the fact that it can be argued he initially had as much (in terms of intention) to do with bringing the child into the world as her mother (who admitted misleading the clinic and lying to the judge in the initial hearings), in that it was only, in the particular circumstances, with both of their actions that any embryos were created at all. While it is possible that the mother could have created similar embryos using donor sperm had she sought treatment from the clinic on her own, it is likely, given the welfare provisions in s 13(5) of the 1990 Act, that attending the clinic as a couple seeking treatment made it more likely that those embryos were ever created. Furthermore, while the Court of Appeal did not remove the contact order (which was not appealed against), it stressed that the parties should carefully consider whether the child continuing to have contact with the intending father would be beneficial to her. One reason why it might, it was suggested, was that 'the [intending father] might have an important role in helping the child to understand and come to terms with her origins' (at 34). This suggests both an implicit and explicit understanding of the importance of the intending father's role in the child's creation.

In the House of Lords, the man's appeal was dismissed 'with some hesitation' (Lord Hope, at 4). Lord Hope, while recognising that the wording of s 28(3) required that treatment must be provided for a man and woman 'together' before the (unmarried and biologically unrelated) man can acquire fatherhood, pointed out that:

[i]t is, of course, true that the use of these techniques does not require the participation by the man in any way in the treatment which is being given to the woman. In the physical sense, as the subsection refers to a man whose sperm was not used in the procedure, it is the woman only, and not the man who is being treated. But the subsection assumes that this is in reality a joint enterprise – that the treatment is being sought by the woman and the man together because they both wish to receive the benefit of the treatment to bring a child into being jointly as their child. It is the infertility of the man and woman *as a couple* that is being treated by the treatment that is being given to the woman.

(at 11, my emphasis)

Seeing the treatment as a 'joint enterprise' being provided for the couple would give a court leeway to (re)interpret what being 'treated together' actually means. In fact, this part of the judgment leads one to assume that His Lordship was thinking exactly that (despite going on to refuse the appeal on lesser grounds). He later explains that 'the test is not whether the man consented either to be deemed in law to be the father of the prospective child or to become legally responsible for him' (at 14), saying that this 'would have been a simple and convenient test'. No doubt, he says, this was not the test built into the 1990 Act, despite its simplicity and convenience, 'because it was *too* simple' (my emphasis). Nevertheless, with slightly altered wording, the test sh/could have been framed in the 1990 Act as one of intention, with the result that 'treatment together' would have a meaning exactly as Lord Hope described. This would have enabled the intending father in this case to have acquired legal fatherhood: he *did not intend* to withdraw his intention to be the father of this child, nor did the clinic have the perception that he had done so (Lind, 2003). This hypothetical, however, seems to have been one of the persuasive issues in the decision to *deny* this man's fatherhood (both at the Court of Appeal and in Lord Hope's judgment): it is clearly stated, in justification for the outcome, that 'the question of whether the treatment should be continued ought to be reviewed in the child's best interests if and as soon as it is known that the man is unwilling to continue to be a party to it' (at 19). Fair enough. But what if the situation is, as here, reversed: where the man is, by the actions of the woman, rendered *unable* to continue to be a party to the treatment? We should not simply dismiss him by saying that although he had intention in the past, his intention no longer remains when the woman (deliberately) continues her treatment in his absence. Either we should impose a further administrative burden on clinics, to confirm the status of each couple's relationship at every stage of treatment, or we should require patients to shoulder the consequences of their actions, which, in this case, should have meant that when the woman continued treatment to have the child that she *and this man* intended to create, this had the consequence of her becoming the mother and him becoming the legal father.

As Lord Hope points out, the 'treatment together' provision raises a question of fact: 'The question is how this crucial fact – crucial, as the question of whether or not the relationship of fatherhood is established in law is wholly dependent on it – is to be proved if there is a dispute about it' (at 14). Moreover, because of the emphasis on only one type of mother in the 1990 Act, fatherhood had to be defined in a more complex manner (see, for example, references to Lord Mackay's amendment to the Act, in *Re D*, at 9), which inevitably fails to take into account alternatives that might arise – such as what happens when intending parents, who were being 'treated together', separate and one implicitly but effectively deceives the clinic that this is not the case.[5] As Lord Hope laments, 'the lack of clear guidance in s 28(3) on such an important issue is regrettable' (at 19).

Lord Walker, who gives the most elaborate judgment, describes the wording of s 28(3) as 'rather compressed' and therefore giving rise to 'associated problems' (at 23). Likewise, Craig Lind, in a critique of the Court of Appeal's judgment, says the terms of the section are 'very peculiar' and that satisfying them has become 'an intractable problem' (Lind, 2003, p 327). It seems, therefore, given the criticisms of it, that s 28(3) can be said to have been inadequately drafted when the 1990 Act was passed, meaning that it is ripe for redrafting following the review of the Act and its consequences.[6] As Lind points out, the section 'does not speak of a woman and a man receiving treatment services together but of treatment services being provided for a woman and a man together', adding that while the woman may have been treated alone, the treatment *services* were, in the eyes of the clinic, being provided for both partners (Lind, 2003). Lord Walker similarly criticises the 'half-hearted' guidance contained in para 5.8 of the relevant fourth edition of the HFEA's Code of Practice, which he calls 'an inadequate recognition of the importance of establishing whether or not a child born as a result of licensed treatment has a father', adding that 'clinics should take steps to ensure . . . that acknowledgements are renewed at regular intervals, and in any case before the embryo replacement' (at 36, also noting that the next edition of the Code of Practice stipulated exactly that, at para 6.36, possibly as a direct result of this case). As he points out, 'more robust procedures' might have prevented the distressing outcome in this case. However, as indicated above, why should clinics shoulder this burden rather than patients accept responsibility for their own deliberate acts? Notably, in *Re D*, the woman concerned did not challenge the intending father's paternity when it was assumed in the original trial relating to parental responsibility; in fact, she conceded it (Lind, 2003) – it was only the Court of Appeal that questioned this concession. This may be because she had not been well advised, but may possibly equally be taken to demonstrate that in her own mind she considered him to be the father.

That the clinic ought not to bear the burden is especially true because, as

5 It is worth noting here that the opposite situation could not have occurred, thus the Act continues its bias towards motherhood, rather than the creation of *parents* or *families*. A man, separated from a partner with whom he had began to have 'treatment together', would not have been able to turn up at the clinic with another partner and have embryos transferred to her. In any case, in *Re R*, the intending father signed consent forms at 30 months and nine months before his former partner became pregnant. These said 'I am not married to [D] but I acknowledge that she and I are being treated together, and that I intend to become the legal father of any resulting child'. When did they cease to be treated 'together'?

6 Indeed, as Craig Lind points out (Lind, 2003), the fact that the 'awkward' wording of the Act might cause confusion was first pointed out when the Act appeared in its draft form by Morgan and Lee, writing in the *Law Society Gazette* in 1990, who wondered what 'together' would be taken to mean.

Lord Walker admits (at 36), 'it must be accepted that no system can be proof against deliberate deception'. In conclusion, he goes on to say that:

> important though legal certainty is, it is even more important that the very significant legal relationship of parenthood should not be based on a fiction (especially if the fiction involves a measure of deception by the mother). Infertility treatment may be very protracted and a general rule of 'once together, always together' (absent express withdrawal of his acknowledgement by the male partner, or review by the clinic) could produce some very undesirable and unjust consequences.
>
> (at 42)

Arguably, this is *exactly* what happened: due to the deception of the mother, the *denial* of fatherhood is a fiction, which is both undesirable and unjust. The decision only 'exacerbates the effects' of the woman's deception, by allowing the child to become legally fatherless by virtue of a circumvention of the welfare provisions (Lind, 2003; although note points made on *why* this deception may have taken place in Sheldon, 2005b).

Although this case was confined by statutory construction (though judicial interpretation of this could have been different), the argument may nonetheless be made that had parenthood been statutorily defined in terms of intention, the intending father would have been regarded as the child's legal father from birth. If the woman wished to challenge this (for example on the grounds that this was not in the child's best interests), then it would have been for her to do so. Recognising intention in this circumstance would not only have provided this child with two parents, including a legal father who intended to take on this role (as it seems is desired by s 13(5) of the HFE Act 1990 and, as Lind (2003) points out, s 28 itself, taken as a whole, is 'riddled with devices that militate against fatherlessness'), but also would not be so remarkably different to circumstances in which a child was conceived naturally before its parents separated, thus making the law relating to assisted reproduction more consistent with that relating to fertile parents. Such reasoning could be extended to situations like those in *Re D*. Although another man may act *socially* as the father of the child, this too is no different to many situations faced by fertile parents: step-parents, for example, have no legal tie to the children they care for unless they adopt, and it is well established that parental responsibility does not have to follow legal fatherhood.

Defining fatherhood

In *Leeds Teaching Hospitals NHS Trust v Mr and Mrs A and Others*,[7] a case that followed almost immediately after the Court of Appeal's decision in *Re*

---

7 *Leeds Teaching Hospitals NHS Trust v Mr and Mrs A and Others* [2003] EWCA 259 (QB).

R, the issue again centred on the legal fatherhood of children born after the use of IVF procedures. This case came to light after a procedural accident at a fertility clinic: a white women (Mrs A) undergoing IVF procedures with her husband had been negligently fertilised with the sperm of a black man (Mr B) undergoing treatment with his wife on the same day. The question for the court was whether Mr A (the husband of the woman inseminated and the intending father of her child) or Mr B (the man whose sperm was accidentally used and therefore the genetic father) was the legal father of the mixed-race twins born as a result. The judgment handed down by Dame Elizabeth Butler-Sloss confirmed that the children, YA and ZA, should remain with Mr and Mrs A but, in order to establish the legal parentage of the twins, it was necessary to determine how ss 28 and 29 of the 1990 Act applied. If s 28(2) or (3) applied to the facts of the case, Mr A would have been the legal father. However, in deciding that both sections did not apply, Mr B, proved to be the biological father by a DNA test, became the legal father, despite not intending to have caused the birth of those particular children (although he did not have automatic parental responsibility as he was not married to the children's mother, nor was he named on their birth certificate). While Mr B intended to create *a* child (with his wife) and can also be said to have a factually causative role in the twins that were born to Mrs A, it can be argued that any child(ren) born to Mrs A were not the ones that he intended to *be* a father *to*.

The legal issue turned on interpretation of s 28(2)[8] and the meaning of 'consent' within this section, as elaborated on in Schedule 3 of the 1990 Act. Because of the rigidity of the 1990 Act and the definitions contained within it, this instance could only be treated as a situation in which donor sperm was used: this meant that the relevant issue was consent. Because Mr A did not 'consent' to the use of 'donor' sperm in the treatment of his wife, the default position was that the biological father was therefore the legal father. Dame Butler-Sloss pointed out that 'there was no intention to have sperm donation from a third person' (at 15). This was because Mr B had not 'waived' legal fatherhood by donating his sperm to Mr and Mrs A in the first place – if he had, the possibility of his establishing paternity would have been excluded – but the presumption of legitimacy of a child born to a married woman (that her husband would be the legal father) *had* been rebutted by genetic tests

---

8 Human Fertilisation and Embryology Act, s 28(2): If –
   (a) at the time of the placing in her of the embryo or the sperm and eggs or of her insemination, the woman was party to a marriage, and
   (b) the creation of the embryo carried by her was not brought about with the sperm of the other party to the marriage,
   then ... the other party to the marriage shall be treated as the father of the child unless it is shown that he did not consent to the placing in her of the embryo or the sperm and eggs or to her insemination (as the case may be).

showing Mr B to be the biological father. Again this points to the rigidity of the statute (and moreover does not seem to reflect its intention): situations not covered by its provisions are still discussed in those terms (for example 'sperm donation') when perhaps it is the terms themselves which should be questioned. Dame Butler-Sloss herself clearly states that 'the present situation where the sperm of a man has been placed in the eggs of a woman by mistake was not in the minds of those drafting the Bill or in Parliament's mind when passing s 28' (at 21).

It is arguable, however, that although on one level the interpretation of the law in *Leeds* is correct, because the law does not apply directly to the factual situation, the case was open to a different interpretation. While Mr A had not given consent to the use of sperm from a third party in the procedure, he *had* consented to the procedure and done so under the assumption that the sperm used was his own; he still *intended* to be the father of any resulting child. Additionally, he was the *psychological* father of the children, particularly having been involved in preparing for their birth throughout the pregnancy (Douglas, 1991, p 146; Stumpf, 1996, p 196; also see van Niekerk and van Zyl, 1995, p 347; Jackson, 2001, p 269).

The argument can again be made that had parenthood been statutorily defined in terms of intention, Mr A could have been regarded as the children's legal father from birth.[9] It is certainly not inevitable that regarding Mr B as the legal father is in the children's best interests. Although it will be physically obvious to the children that one of their parents is not their biological parent, it does not follow that Mr A, who will raise the children as his own, should not be legally recognised as their father merely because he lacks a biological connection. This is simply one of those cases where openness about the circumstances of the conception is to be encouraged. Recognising intention would again have recognised social (rather than biological) reality: if then Mr (and Mrs) B wished to challenge that presumption (again, for example, on the grounds that this was not in the children's best interests), then they could do so. It appears to me that it is – at least – strongly arguable that it is in a child's best interests for social (encompassing intentional causation of the birth of the child, as well as the intention to parent the child) rather than biological circumstances to be taken into account when the two 'realities' have been separated. As currently formulated, s 13(5) of the 1990 Act reflects the desirability of children having fathers. These children have a father who intended them to be born and is happy to raise them. The only argument that their best interests would be better served by recognising Mr B as their legal father must be based in greater weight being given to biological parentage

---

9 Or, because statutory interpretation of the HFE Act 1990 did not quite fit this situation, intention could have been used as a 'tie-break', as it was in the US surrogacy case of *Johnson v Calvert* 286 Cal Rptr 369 (Cal Ct App 1991).

over social parenthood. It might legitimately be surmised in this case that biology was prioritised to reflect the racial difference between the potential parents (despite this issue being noticeably absent from the majority of the judgment). Dame Butler-Sloss commented that '[t]o refuse to recognise Mr B as [the twins'] biological father is to distort the truth about which some day the twins will have to learn through knowledge of their paternal identity' (at 57). Mr B had already been confirmed as the children's biological father, but it does not follow that he must be their legal father. It is perhaps commendable that in this case it was thought that the twins ought to have knowledge of their biological 'paternal identity', but again this does not necessitate the award of legal fatherhood to Mr B. It was open to the court to interpret this case differently *because* it fell outside the provisions of the HFE Act 1990. Arguably, here too, an opportunity to redefine parenthood was missed.

Denying motherhood

In *Natallie Evans v Amicus Healthcare Ltd and Others*,[10] a woman began IVF treatment with her partner, Howard Johnston, after she was told she would need to have her ovaries, which were cancerous, removed. Eleven eggs were harvested before the operation and were fertilised using Mr Johnston's sperm before being placed in frozen storage. The embryos created, therefore, represented Natallie Evans' only chance of having a child biologically related to her. Later, after successful cancer treatment and the breakdown of the couple's relationship, but before the frozen embryos had been removed from storage, thawed and transferred to Ms Evans, Mr Johnston wrote to the clinic and told them that he no longer consented to the use or continued storage of the embryos. On hearing of this, Ms Evans issued proceedings, seeking an injunction requiring consent to be restored and declarations saying that consent could not lawfully be withdrawn; that she may have the embryos transferred to her during treatment; that not to allow this would breach her human rights under Arts 8, 12 and 14 of the European Convention on Human Rights and Fundamental Freedoms; and also that the right to life of the embryos themselves was protected by the Convention (a full description of the declarations sought can be found in Alghrani, 2005). This was the first time that the courts had been asked to consider who and what should decide the fate of an embryo created by two people who later separate.[11]

In the High Court, Wall J dismissed her claims, having interpreted the

10 *Natallie Evans v Amicus Healthcare Ltd and Others* [2004] EWCA (Civ) 727.
11 But not the only time; the *Evans* case was initially taken alongside the case of *Hadley v Midland Fertility Services Ltd* [2003] EWHC 2161, where Lorraine Hadley, a woman facing a similar situation, was also asking to be able to use stored embryos.

consent provisions of the 1990 Act and (following *Re R*) found that the couple had each only given their consent for 'treatment together'. Thus, when the couple were no longer being treated 'together', there was no consent. Natallie Evans appealed. The Court of Appeal, in refusing the appeal, again interpreted the consent provisions of the 1990 Act, agreeing with the findings of Wall J. Further, the court(s) found that under Sched 3 of the Act, a man had an unconditional right to withdraw or vary his consent up until the point at which the embryos were 'used'. This, they said, was the point at which the embryo was transferred to the woman. In addition, no breaches of Ms Evans' human rights (or those of the embryos) were found.

What makes this case more poignant is the fact (which came out in court) that Ms Evans had inquired into the possibility of freezing her eggs, rather than embryos created with Mr Johnston's sperm. Had she done so, she could later have requested that her eggs be inseminated using donor sperm and had any resulting embryos transferred to her, subject only to welfare considerations emanating from s 13(5) of the 1990 Act. Alternatively, embryos could have been created using donor sperm – instead of Mr Johnston's sperm – at the time. Either way (as proved by *Re R*), she would have been able to continue her attempts to have the child she desired. Unfortunately, following the clinic's refusal to freeze her eggs and Mr Johnston's attempts to 'reassure' her (despite her apparent realisation of the implications of freezing their jointly created embryos) that they would not separate (see Miola, 2004, pp 70–1), this is not what happened, leading to 'horrendous and unjust consequences' (Miola, 2004, p 68).

Evans could have been decided differently. A more inspired interpretation of the wording of the law, coupled with a lesser reliance on the previous case of *Re R* – or even distinguishing it – would have enabled the judges to fix the meaning of 'treatment together' at the time the embryos were created rather than transferred. In so doing, this would have enabled a reading of the withdrawal of Mr Johnston's consent not as consent to her undergoing the embryo transfer procedure (it is interesting that he can veto her consent to have a medical procedure performed *on her*) but consent to his (legal) parenting of the child. In effect, he would have been withdrawing his intention to parent. Though it appears that this is not something he would have wanted to do (he argued that he had fundamental, not merely financial, objections to having genetic offspring born – see Sheldon, 2004, p 449; BBC News Online, 2003; and *Evans* (CA), at 32), this seems like an argument carefully constructed to make his case unassailable. Even if this is not the case, shouldn't we say that his claim (not to have a genetic child) needs to be treated at least as seriously as Natallie Evans' claim (to have her own genetic child), particularly when these diametrically opposed but equally strong feelings are attached to the importance of the genetic link by the two parties? After all, Natallie Evans could use donor embryos to have a child. However, it is arguable that moral comparisons can be drawn between this case and those situations in which men who – deliberately or misleadingly – create pregnancies (rather than embryos) with fertile women later seek either for the pregnancy to be terminated or to abstain from all responsibility for the child. There the law does not let men withdraw their consent so easily – and here, where both parties (albeit without perhaps fully understanding the implications of the consent they gave, see Sheldon, 2004, pp 446–7) entered an intentional parental project together, perhaps the law should more consistently reflect this. Instead, the courts' decision means that Mr Johnston retains 'ultimate control not just of his ability to have a child with [Natallie Evans], but of hers with *anyone*' (Miola, 2004, p 71, my emphasis).

In March 2006, Natallie Evans' case was heard by the European Court of Human Rights (ECHR, 2006),[12] after she was refused leave domestically to appeal the case to the House of Lords. She asked whether the law, as it currently stands, violated her human rights under Arts 8 (right to respect for private and family life) and 14 (freedom from discrimination) of the European Convention on Human Rights. She also asked the ECHR to consider whether the embryos themselves had a right to life under Art 2. The Court unanimously ruled that there had been no violation of Art 2 concerning the actual embryos; unanimously that there had been no violation of Art 14 concerning the way Ms Evans was treated by the law; and, by five votes to two, that there had been no violation of Art 8. The ECHR found that the UK was not obliged to take positive legislative steps to ensure that a woman who begins IVF treatment in order to have a genetically related child should be permitted to implant embryos after the withdrawal of consent by her former partner, saying that the UK's legislation had achieved a fair balance between the competing interests at stake, including those of the community as a whole, which is entitled to have laws giving certainty in what is often a contentious area of medicine. It said that because there is little consensus across EU member states as to how this area should be regulated, the UK Government enjoys a wide margin of appreciation when deciding what its own laws should be (paras 54, 62). The Court pointed out that having a clear or 'bright line' approach – one that helps to create certainty and maintain public confidence in the law – is desirable (paras 55, 65). However, it also stated that this 'bright line' did not necessarily have to be drawn at the point of continued storage or use of frozen embryos but *could* be drawn elsewhere, such as at the point of creation of the embryo (para 68) (also noting that a number of other European states have, in fact, done exactly this). Or, that it would be possible to legislate to say that such consent should become irrevocable – in any case, this part of the decision indicates that the Court thought that a 'fairer balance' could arguably have been struck.

The Court went on to conclude that because there had been no violation of

---

12 *Evans v United Kingdom* (Application no 6339/05).

the right granted under Art 8, it was unnecessary to consider whether – as a result of the breach of her Art 8 rights – Natallie Evans had in fact been discriminated against. Interestingly (and tellingly), however, two of the seven judges – Judges Traja and Mijovic – dissented on the Art 8 point, saying that the majority decision 'gave excessive weight to public policy considerations and to the State's margin of appreciation without paying due attention to the nature of the individual rights in conflict' (dissent, para 1). They said that the right to IVF procreation had a 'higher ranking value' and therefore deserved 'a fairer balancing than that struck by the 1990 Act' (dissent, para 1) and that the exceptional nature of Ms Evans' case – the fact that it affects 'the very core' of her right – should have warranted a 'deeper consideration' (dissent, para 2), as not to have done this is 'a total destruction of her right to have her own child' (dissent, para 2). In short, they argued that 'the dilemma between Natallie's right to have a child and her former partner's right not to become a father should not be resolved on the basis of such a rigid scheme and the blanket enforcement by the UK law of one party's withdrawal of consent' (dissent, para 3) – the withdrawal of one party's consent should generally be taken to prevail, except in situations where the other party has no other means to have a genetically related child and has no existing children (dissent, para 9). However, as enlightened as the dissenting judges may have been, Natallie Evans lost her case – although at the time of writing she has made one final attempt, having asked for the Grand Chamber of the ECHR to also hear her case.

While it may be argued that the 'treatment together' provision was introduced to the 1990 Act in order to deter or prevent large numbers of single women having children by assisted means, the Act evidently recognises that there are some situations in which this will be 'acceptable' by clearly stipulating when and in what circumstances an unmarried man will be a father, as well as providing married fathers with a 'get-out' clause if they did not consent to their wife's treatment. Furthermore, the welfare consideration that must be undertaken only entails consideration of a prospective child's 'need for a father', as opposed to the lack of a father being a definitive reason for the refusal of treatment. This clearly allows single women and lesbian couples to at least be considered for parenthood before being rejected. The 'acceptance' that single women may in some (albeit undefined) circumstances be eligible for treatment cannot therefore be a reason to deny treatment to Natallie Evans. The only reason is the absolute veto that Mr Johnston holds over the treatment by virtue of the consent provisions. That the law has been correctly read is undeniable; what is suggested is that had the 1990 Act determined parenthood in a different way – by intention – the consent provisions could have been built into this, meaning that a withdrawal of consent would only mean a withdrawal of one party's intention to parent the child. The other party could continue with treatment (a man would need to use a surrogate) subject to the proper welfare assessments being made and appropriate counselling being given. This might shake one of the 'twin pillars' of the legislation (Sheldon, 2004), but would not destroy it.

CONCLUSIONS

While one might have sympathy for the plight of Natallie Evans, it is fairly hard to criticise the legal decision the domestic judges made in this case – however, illumination may be drawn from the dissenting judgments at the ECHR. Mr Justice Wall and subsequent judges, while sympathetic, literally followed the letter of the law on consent. In so doing, they also, as did the judgments in *Re D* and *Leeds*, highlighted that the assignation of legal parenthood following assisted conception can be – and has been, more than once – a problematic area of the law. In the three cases analysed above, the courts have struggled to fit legal definitions of parenthood – particularly those that do not arise from having children in the 'normal' way – to the situations they faced. Whatever one thinks of the ethical and emotional issues involved, it is possible to argue that the cases were wrongly decided – and to propose hypothetical yet possible alternative outcomes. By this I do not necessarily mean that the judges involved misapplied the law – in fact, they only made literal interpretations of the (often rather strange) provisions of the 1990 Act regarding legal parenthood after the use of assisted conception. Rather, the wrong decisions were reached precisely because of the (assumed) rigidity of the legal definitions and the judges' reluctance in these cases to be more inventive and flexible in their interpretations.

Therefore, perhaps a better determinant of legal parenthood in these situations (and for all assisted conception treatments, including surrogacy) is one recognising the intentions of the parties to become legal (and social) parents. This would allow the courts more interpretive flexibility and freedom – and perhaps would even suggest it. Practically, what this would mean is that the intending father in *Re D*, despite not being the child's biological father, would be the legal father and could apply for parental responsibility and contact with her. He did not withdraw his consent/intention for this child to be brought into existence. Judicial and political rhetoric in plenty of other cases would support the contention that it is better for the child to have this man – who, it must be remembered, intended her creation – recognised as her father rather than no man at all (given that sperm donors are rightly not legally recognised as such). In the *Leeds* case, an intentional approach would mean that the man who underwent treatment with his wife, was with her throughout the pregnancy and who intended to and actually does in practice perform the role of social father is also recognised as the legal father. Why make a man who did not intend those *particular* children to be born (and who will not raise them) the legal father merely by virtue of a biological link?

The difference in *Evans* is that her former partner requested that the embryos be destroyed because he had no wish to be the father of any children born following the couple's separation. Because he withdrew his consent, the judges had little option but to respect his choice. But had parenthood been defined by intention, all withdrawing consent might mean is that he would have clarified that he had no intention to be either the legal or social father of any resulting children, while allowing her to go on (subject to a welfare of the child assessment under s 13(5)) to become a mother, as she intended to do. This might be an acceptable compromise regarding legal fatherhood, as it is evident that the provisions of the 1990 Act do not preclude 'fatherless' children in any case.

If parenthood had been defined by intention, Howard Johnston would, of course, be genetically related to a child he did not intend to father. However, so are many men, and it seems the law can treat them in whatever way it deems suitable (and in assisted reproduction in particular, it seems that the 'bright line' can be drawn anywhere within the wide margin of appreciation afforded to states). Men who get a woman pregnant by having sex with her but who do not intend to be the father are still treated as such by the law, which makes them pay child support. Men who donate their sperm are exempt, legally and socially, despite being biologically related to children. Men whose sperm is accidentally used to fertilise another woman in an IVF clinic fall somewhere in between: a legal father in name only. Why is it not possible for this kind of legal halfway house to be similarly applied to men who withdraw their consent? That way, the children can be born but these men will be neither their legal nor their social fathers.

The benefits of recognising intention

In surrogacy and other forms of assisted conception, registering intending parents as the legal parents would bring greater consistency. In *Re D* and *Leeds*, different outcomes would have been achieved which arguably would have been better for the families that were created, at least in terms of reflecting the reality of their situation. In *Evans*, the injustice of not allowing Natallie Evans the only chance she will have to become a genetic mother (and it is only a chance) would have been set aside. Although this would deny Mr Johnston some of his capacity for autonomy, it can be argued that 'given there is sufficient moral equivalency between doing so and denying Ms Evans her own autonomy . . . the potential for interpreting the law in this direction should have been more fully acknowledged' (Miola, 2004, p 76). Men do not always have control of their sperm, deliberately or otherwise, and women are often those left to make difficult reproductive choices on their own. There will always be some cases which are harder than others, but the benefits of the application of a consistent rule – an intention-based test for parenthood – far outweigh the disadvantages of having a system of rules which do not and cannot fit every situation, especially given that the number of disputes (and accidents) is relatively small.

In terms of surrogacy, for example, recognising intention may have the effect of deterring some potential surrogates from entering such an agreement in the first place, or serve as a constant reminder through the pregnancy term that the child is not that of the surrogate. This would not, however, be a negative outcome, as intention would bring greater consistency and, potentially, security. At present, whatever her motivations for entering a surrogacy arrangement, the woman acting as surrogate knows that she is safe to change her mind. If she wants to keep the baby when it is born then she can do so with impunity, as it is she who is both socially and legally recognised as the mother of the child. Although for this reason such a change to registration procedures might lessen the numbers of women who choose to become surrogates, it would also go some way to providing a better answer to the most important question that surrogacy raises before the process is even begun: who are the parents of the surrogate-born child? It would also mean that it would be the surrogate who would have to challenge this through the courts – a further deterrent. In surrogacy (as well as in all other forms of assisted conception), an operative presumption favouring the intending parents could be rebuttable if other parties object, and in such circumstances it could be replaced by a 'default rule, such as the conventional British definition of motherhood, or a "best interests" test' (Jackson, 2001, p 270). But it is unlikely that the numbers of willing surrogates would decline as rapidly as might be expected – although they draw a lot of publicity, the situations where surrogacy cases end in dispute and reach the courts are very much in the minority.

Those who intend and take action towards having a child by means of medically assisted conception or surrogacy are showing a form of commitment to parenthood that may often be lacking in the fertile world. For the infertile, conception is no accident. This is yet another reason why the law's reliance on outdated presumptions should be challenged. Not only could intention help to solve the question of parenthood, when 'but for' those with the intention a child would never have been born, but additionally if qualifications as to suitability are to be used or welfare of the child questions are raised, it goes some way to illustrating the commitment required from those seeking external help in enabling them to become parents. At present, the law is irregular and unacceptable. It remains inextricably linked to outdated concepts and constructs, when society, technology and medicine have changed the way a family can be created.

Redefining the family

Challenging the way families are defined may have the additional benefit of gaining further recognition and acceptance of alternative family creation. The 'idea that a family consists of one man, one woman, and the children they produce together is both a fairly recent concept and one that is prevalent primarily in Western middle-class culture' (Mahoney, 1995, p 35). The ideal of the nuclear family has been perpetuated in our modern society and serves as the standard with which all other families are compared (see O'Donovan, 1993, p 30). However, some 'unconventional' family forms have come to be accepted – such as step-parent or adoptive families, or single or unmarried parenthood – albeit sometimes with a certain degree of reticence in that they are not perceived to be 'ideal'. It is the truth that 'there are so many unorthodox forms of the family these days' (Warnock, 2002, p 67). Divorce and remarriage have become easier. Contraception has improved so that even married couples do not have to reproduce immediately and can choose to have children, if they want them, at a later date when, for example, they have paved a career for themselves and become financially secure. When a couple have problems having children naturally, they can be assisted to do so by technological developments in reproduction. IVF, in that it mimics, as far as is possible, the 'natural' creation of a family, has received little criticism on this front. DI, on the other hand, has only become accepted over time. Much of this is to do with changes in attitude as to what is acceptable in family formation. But where this leaves lesbian, gay or surrogate families, or post-menopausal or widowed women, for example, is not clear. These people may have equal desires to conform to the 'ideal' family form, but are deemed unconventional both by being unable to do so 'naturally' and for the method they have to use to do so. Many are also, in as far as is possible, trying to fit into the nuclear family ideal: two women and their children, for example, are really not very different to a man, his wife and their children.

If definitions of the family and of what makes a parent were changed, then all of the situations outlined above *could* be legitimate family forms. Recognition of the social, or intentional, element of parenting (including both the intention to create a child and the intention to parent it) would be desirable to all the parties concerned. Given that the western concept of parenthood has evolved from children being seen as the 'property' of their fathers, through a Victorian idealisation of motherhood, to a recognition that the best interests of children ought to be considered when determining what happens to them (Mahoney, 1995, p 36), it is time for the law in this area to be reconsidered. So viewed, the best interests standard ought not to be based on preconceptions of what a family is or ought to be. In a society where there is a multiplicity of familial relationships, the best interests test should recognise who that child has formed relationships (social bonds) with, or who intended to have the child's best interests as their own, and why. Thus, if two women have been raising a child together, the child will have formed 'parental' bonds with both of them and the genetic 'father' should have no claim to parenthood. The same would be the case when a child has been born after DI to a heterosexual couple – although at present the presumption is that the social father is recognised as the legal father (by s 28 of the 1990 Act), there is some element of doubt when the genetic (or natural) 'father' is referred to. There is no reason why this calculation cannot (and should not) be made before birth.

Currently, it appears that neither genetics nor social relationships create parenthood following assisted reproduction. Rather, it exists as is determined by the law. For example, the law determines who is granted legal parenthood following adoption; it creates the presumption that the social father is the legal father following DI and the presumption that the woman who gives birth to a child is always its mother:

> Neither legislatures nor courts seem to be eager to expand the definition of 'parents' to include other people who may be closely associated with a child and who may be viewed *by the child* as a parent, nor to legally acknowledge non-standard parental entitlements in such alternate arrangements as gestational surrogacy and same-sex parenting.
>
> (Mahoney, 1995, p 43, my emphasis)

In all, it can be argued that a number of the problems that have been associated with surrogacy, and have recently been highlighted in problematic assisted conception cases such as those critiqued above, would be countered by a reconceptualisation and redefinition of what constitutes a family and of what makes a parent. Current definitions of legal motherhood and fatherhood are limited in their extent and do not take into account either developments in medically assisted conception that enable genetic and social parenting to be separated or the fact that parenthood, as is well argued by a number of feminist and other scholars, can as equally be based on social connections as it can on genetics or gestation (see, for examples, Polikoff, 1990; Mahoney, 1995; Schultz, 1990; Bainham, 1999; Garrison, 2000; Andrews, 2000).

In a modern society, it would make for a more consistent approach to prioritise the intentional and social elements of parenthood. To do so would mean that the people who intended for the child to be born, and intended to care for it, would be recognised as the parents of any given child in all circumstances. It is argued, therefore, that we should recognise the intention to become (and act as) a parent as the legal basis of parenthood: that 'within the context of artificial reproductive techniques, intentions that are voluntarily chosen, deliberate and bargained-for ought presumptively to determine legal parenthood' (Schultz, 1990, p 323; see also Hill, 1991). In this suggested model, intention creates the *presumption* of legal parenthood, thus it may be able to be challenged. This would open the door, for example, for a genetic father to claim parenthood of a child being raised by a lesbian couple or a surrogate to claim parenthood of a child being raised by someone else. In both cases, the decision would have to be made on the basis of the child's best interests and, as has been argued, if one of the bases of best interests is the social bonds that have been formed and another is continuity, decisions may turn in favour of the social (intending) parents – and should – unless there is a clear welfare indication to the contrary.

REFERENCES

Alghrani, A (2005) 'Deciding the fate of frozen embryos: Natalie Evans v. Amicus Healthcare Ltd and Others' 13 *Medical Law Review* 244

Andrews, L (2000) 'Regulating reproductive technologies' 21 *Journal of Legal Medicine* 1–21

Bainham, A (1999) 'Parentage, parenthood and parental responsibility: subtle, elusive yet important distinctions' in Bainham, A, Day Sclater, S and Richards, M (eds) *What is a Parent? A Socio-Legal Analysis* Oxford: Hart Publishing, pp 25–46

BBC News Online (2003) 'Women lose embryo battle', 1 October http://news.bbc-.co.uk/1/hi/health/3151762.stm

Bellis, MA, Hughes, KE, Hughes, SK and Ashton, JR (2005) 'Measuring paternal discrepancy and its public health consequences' 59 *Journal of Epidemiology and Community Health* 749

Blyth, E (1993) 'Section 30 – the acceptable face of surrogacy?' *Journal of Social Welfare and Family Law* 248–59

Cretney, SM (2000) *Family Law*, 4th edn London: Sweet & Maxwell

Department of Health (2005) *Review of the Human Fertilisation and Embryology Act: A Public Consultation* London: HMSO

Douglas, G (1991) *Law, Fertility and Reproduction* London: Sweet & Maxwell

European Court of Human Rights (2006) Press release issued by the Registrar: 'Chamber Judgment Evans v The United Kingdom' http://www.echr.coe.int/Eng/Press/2006/March/ChamberjudgmentEvansvUnitedKingdom070306.htm

Garrison, M (2000) 'Law making for baby making: an interpretive approach to the determination of legal parentage' 113 *Harvard Law Review* 835

Harding, LM (1987) 'The debate on surrogate motherhood' 37 *Journal of Social Welfare Law*

Hill, JL (1991) 'What does it mean to be a "parent"? The claims of biology as the basis for parental rights' 66 *New York University Law Review* 353

Horsey, K (2003) 'Legally recognising intention: parenthood in surrogacy and assisted conception' Unpublished PhD thesis, University of Kent

Jackson, E (2001) *Regulating Reproduction: Law, Technology and Autonomy* Oxford: Hart Publishing

Lind, C (2003) '*Re R (Paternity of IVF baby)* – Unmarried paternity under the Human Fertilisation and Embryology Act 1990' 15 *Child and Family Law Quarterly* 327

Mackenzie, R (forthcoming) 'The potential of relational contract theory to resolve difficulties involved in the enforcement of surrogacy agreements'

Mahoney, J (1995) 'Adoption as a feminist alternative to reproductive technology' in Callahan, JC (ed) *Reproduction, Ethics and the Law: Feminist Perspectives* Bloomington: Indiana University Press, pp 35–54

Miola, J (2004) 'Mix-ups, mistake and moral judgement: recent developments in UK law on assisted conception' 12 *Feminist Legal Studies* 67

Morgan, D (1989) 'Surrogacy: an introductory essay' in Lee, R and Morgan, D (eds) *Birthrights: Law and Ethics at the Beginnings of Life* London: Routledge, pp 55–84

New Zealand Law Commission (2005) *New Issues in Legal Parenthood* Wellington: NZLC

New Zealand Ministry of Justice (2006) *Government Response to Law Commission Report on New Issues in Legal Parenthood* Wellington: NZMJ

O'Donovan, K (1993) *Family Law Matters* London: Pluto Press

Polikoff, N (1990) 'This child does have two mothers: redefining parenthood to meet the needs of children in lesbian-mother and other nontraditional families' 78 *Georgia Law Journal* 459

Schultz, MM (1990) 'Reproductive technology and intent-based parenthood: an opportunity for gender neutrality' *Wisconsin Law Review* 297

Sheldon, S (2004) *'Evans v Amicus Healthcare; Hadley v Midland Fertility Services* – Revealing cracks in the "twin pillars"?' 16 *Child and Family Law Quarterly* 437

Sheldon, S (2005a) 'Fragmenting fatherhood: the regulation of reproductive technologies' 68 *Modern Law Review* 523

Sheldon, S (2005b) 'Reproductive technologies and the legal determination of fatherhood' 13 *Feminist Legal Studies* 349

Stumpf, A (1996) 'Redefining mother: a legal matrix for new reproductive technologies' 96 *Yale Law Journal* 187

Summerfield, C and Gill, B (2005) *Social Trends 35* London: Office for National Statistics

van Niekerk, A and van Zyl, L (1995) 'The ethics of surrogacy: women's reproductive labour' 21 *Journal of Medical Ethics* 345

Victoria Law Reform Commission (2005) *Assisted Reproduction and Adoption Paper Two: Parentage* Melbourne: VLRC http://www.lawreform.vic.gov.au/ CA256902000FE154/Lookup/Assisted_Reproductive_Technology_and_ Adoption/$file/Position_Paper_2.pdf

Warnock, M (2002) *Making Babies: Is There a Right to Have Children?* Oxford: Oxford University Press

Chapter 9

Beyond genetic and gestational dualities

Surrogacy agreements, legal parenthood and choice in family formation

Robin Mackenzie

The agreement between the parties I hold as being against public policy. None can rely on it in any way or enforce the agreement in any way. I need only give one of the many grounds for saying this, namely that it was a purported contract for the sale and purchase of a child.

Comyn J, *A v C* [1985] FLR 445 at 445

The NECAHR's ideal was a continuing extended family wherein origins were known and rights and responsibilities were worked out by the parties early on, and continued to be negotiated. The law needs to establish a vehicle for the active recognition of a kind of parenthood where boundaries are fluid and roles continue to be negotiated.

Dr Rosemary De Luca, Foundation Chairperson of National Ethics Committee on Assisted Human Reproduction (New Zealand Law Commission, 2005, p 89)

INTRODUCTION

Agreements between women who agree to become impregnated and bear children in order that these children be raised by another or others currently in the United Kingdom fall under the Surrogacy Arrangements Act 1985 as amended by the Human Fertilisation and Embryology Act 1990 ('the 1990 Act'). Such women are known as surrogate, gestational or birth mothers, while those who intend to raise the children are called the commissioning or intentional parents. Agreements between the parties, or surrogacy arrangements, usually cover details of the impregnation, gestation and the handing over of the child.

How far and in what way the law should be involved here is far from simple. Whether there should be legal oversight in order to assign legal parenthood, ensure the wellbeing of the children involved and oversee agreements and, if so, what form this should take remain contested questions. Lee and Morgan have commented that, '[m]edical law is in (large) part about declaiming the values and virtues of a society. In the case of surrogacy, it is almost entirely concerned with that' (Lee and Morgan, 2001, p 191). How far such values and virtues might be seen as shared is a moot point. Even 20 years ago, when the first legislative attempts to control surrogacy were put in place, controversies over the new reproductive technologies ensured that their eventual regulation would represent compromise rather than consensus (Warnock Report, 1984). As outlined below, however, there was widespread agreement at that time that surrogacy should be condemned as unnatural and surrogacy agreements proscribed or at any rate rendered unenforceable. While the practice has achieved grudging acceptance in an increasing number of jurisdictions recently, there is still a wide variation in how it is treated by the law. Central here is the public policy issue of how far the State should permit private ordering of family life and to what extent protective measures should limit choice. This is part of a larger debate over normative regulation. Value pluralism today has resulted in what has been described as the triumph of autonomy read as choice over the dignitarian alliance. Brownsword questions the extent to which the regulation of reproductive technologies should seek to protect human dignity rather than merely to provide quality control mechanisms which ensure safety without restricting reproductive choice (Brownsword, 2004).

Certainly the regulation of surrogacy continues to be fraught with such considerations. I have argued elsewhere that such a precautionary approach is appropriate where unacceptable levels of evidential uncertainty surround the use of new technologies (Mackenzie, 2005). Recent research into surrogacy as a means of family formation, however, as elaborated below, suggests that many of the ethical concerns over surrogacy may be unfounded. In addition, the most recent official inquiry into the practice in the United Kingdom, the Brazier Report, stated that the practice was now accepted across a large spectrum of opinion, leaving the degree to which the State should intervene to protect the parties as the central remaining policy issue (Brazier Report, 1998). This chapter will explore what the appropriate policy here might be. In my view, protection of the parties would involve providing mechanisms whereby the wishes of the adults, the varieties of current families and the interests of the children all received legal recognition. I shall argue that court approval of pre-conception agreements among adults who had received separate legal advice and counselling, followed by automatic transfer of legal parenthood to the commissioning parent[s] should the gestational mother not object would serve this purpose, with all conflicts to be resolved post-birth according to the best interests of the child. Criteria associated with access to surrogacy arrangements in many jurisdictions, such as that the commissioning parent[s] should be married or heterosexual, are in my view unsustainable within the context of contemporary choices over family formation and would be eschewed.

It is a truism to say that the new reproductive technologies, especially surrogacy, have deconstructed notions of parenthood by separating gestation, genetics and social parenting. Yet, the fact that this disaggregation is mirrored in other neighbouring areas of law has implications for how the law should treat surrogacy arrangements and these implications have been insufficiently explored. Emotional partnerships associated with family life are no longer seen as based upon the norm of heterosexual marriage but incorporate de facto as well as de jure marriage, civil registration of same-sex partnerships and same-sex marriage. This plethora of possibilities is matched by a wealth of choices where the appurtenances of legal parenthood are concerned. Those who are single or in same-sex partnerships may now adopt or form families via new reproductive technologies. Orders assigning parental responsibility, child support obligations, residence orders and various variations on guardianship may be shared among an increasingly wide group of family members. This chapter will argue that these developments represent the law adapting to recognise increased private ordering and choice in our personal lives, and that this approach should be extended into the coming reform of the 1990 Act. In this light, the Act and the Surrogacy Arrangements Act 1985 should be amended to facilitate private ordering and reproductive autonomy where surrogacy is concerned. Those involved in a surrogacy arrangement should be able to choose the type of family they envisage creating by this means, such as an extended family with continuing contact between all potential parents and children or one with none. Prior court scrutiny and approval of such agreements should underlie a presumption of enforceability, while preserving the court's ability to assign legal parenthood on the basis of the best interests of the child post-birth should disagreements arise. Jurisdictions wherein the decision on the allocation of legal parenthood in surrogacy arrangements takes place via similar pre-conception agreements have generally chosen to restrict accessibility to commissioning parents who are married, genetically related to the child and where the wife has intractable infertility difficulties. This is not the position adopted in this chapter. Instead, I argue that the growing acceptability of private ordering in other areas of family formation should be matched within surrogacy arrangements, allowing for maximum reproductive autonomy as modified by considerations of the best interests of the child once born.

SURROGACY AND CHOICE OF KIN IN FAMILY FORMATION

While customary practices since biblical times have allowed the childless to raise offspring passed to them by fertile kinfolk, today's reproductive technologies and notions of legal parenthood render surrogacy arrangements more complex (Probert, 2004a). Thus they fall within wider policy decisions over how far family formation should be open to private ordering. State interests in this arena are usually seen as ensuring the protection of the vulnerable and fostering intimate partnerships within which domestic care takes place. Private ordering here has, until relatively recently, been restricted by legal standards many of which are now seen as outmoded. An obvious example is the growing ability of de facto, de jure, heterosexual and same-sex couples to have their partnerships treated alike by the State (DiFonzo, 2003; McClain, 2003; Morris and Nott, 2005). So far, this recognition is usually restricted to partnerships of two people, but calls for the acceptance of polygamy and polyamorous partnerships involving more than two adults represent a continuing pressure for increased autonomy here (Strassberg, 2003). A commensurate expansion of whom the law might regard as a family is also taking place (Fineman, 2004). Serious official consideration is being given to the possibility of granting legal recognition as a family to groups of adults who choose to form a kinship network based upon ties of affection which do not incorporate existing or past sexual relationships or child care responsibilities (Law Commission of Canada, 2001). This multiplicity of options as regards partnership and kinship, taken together with common parental choices involving serial monogamy and hence often serial parenthood of one kind or another, has also placed under tension classic notions of parenthood (Kavanagh, 2004). As partnerships dissolve and re-form over time, significant numbers of children may expect to have a number of parent figures to whom they are connected by blood, ties of affection or obligations of support enter and leave their lives. Which of these connections should be recognised by the law as entailing rights and responsibilities between the parties is far from self-evident.

The disaggregation of the appurtenances of legal parenthood into parental responsibility, residence, access, child support obligations, guardianship, step-parenthood and adoptive parent status has involved both choice (for example, one may choose to appoint another as a guardian) and a lack of it (parents whose children do not live with them are obliged to pay child support). Some aspects of legal parenthood are acquired via blood, as when a mother gives birth to her genetic child, others via ties of affection, as when an unrelated de facto partner is granted access rights to a child after the partners' relationship has ended, and others by the ability of the law to deem that some state of affairs should be so, as where a child is deemed to be the lawful offspring of her adoptive parents. How far we should be able to exercise autonomy here is problematic. For example, it is far from clear whether each of a succession of unrelated partners who have assumed responsibility for children should have parental responsibility but child support obligations are placed upon only the genetically related, no matter how tenuous a connection this might be in real terms. Whom the law should recognise as a legal parent, or to whom it should grant some or all of the salient rights and responsibilities, and upon what grounds, is thus an evolving and contested arena.

Reproductive technologies have rendered these dilemmas more complex in that they allow for the separation of genetic heritage, gestation and childrearing. Donors of eggs and sperm are simply deemed by the law not to be legal parents, although their genetic offspring are now seen as having the right to know who they are since a policy change in 2005 curtailing donor anonymity after *R (on the application of Rose) v Secretary of State for Health* [2003] Fam L 19. The fate of embryos, a joint creation, is regulated by consent procedures which may allow them to be 'adopted' by others receiving infertility treatment where those whose gametes are involved agree (see MacCallum, Chapter 7 in this volume). Where there is disagreement, the choice of one party not to become a parent prevails over the desire of the other to do so, as in *Evans v Amicus Healthcare Ltd and Others, Hadley v Midland Fertility Services and Others* [2005] Fam 1 (Lin, 2004). However, simple reliance on intention and consent, whenever this might be manifested, is insufficient to resolve conflict over the appropriate allocation of the appurtenances of legal parenthood, as when women receiving infertility treatment have given birth to children whose genetic heritage has resulted from mistakes in IVF treatment, as in *L Teaching Hospitals v Mr A, Mrs A, YA, ZA, the HFEA, Mr B, Mrs B* [2003] Fam L 396 and *Robert B v Susan B* 109 Cal App 4th 1109 (Cal Dept 4th Dist 2003), or when there are several sets of prospective parents who each believe themselves to have commissioned the same child to be born via a surrogacy arrangement (Johnson, 2004; Probert, 2004a).

This combination of claims to the appurtenances of legal parenthood based upon genetics, gestation, ties of affection and the ability of the law to deem that a person is a legal parent is crucial where surrogacy is concerned. There are six potential parents of a child born as a result of a surrogacy arrangement: the birth mother, her partner, the commissioning parent[s] and the providers of the egg and sperm. While there may be fewer potential parents, as when the gestational mother or the commissioning parents provide gametes, the allocation of legal parenthood is nevertheless far from straightforward when there are rival claimants, as when disagreement between the parties to a surrogacy agreement arises. Most of the case law surrounding surrogacy centres upon the courts being required to decide which of the parties should be the children's lawful parents, and the grounds upon which they should do so, given that in most jurisdictions such agreements have been deemed to be unenforceable.

One of the things at stake here is the appropriate choice of analogy. Where surrogacy is viewed as akin to adoption, the birth mother and her partner would be seen as the lawful parents and the child as appropriately adopted subsequently by the commissioning parent[s] only when the lawful parents so wish. However, where the birth mother and her partner are genetically unrelated to the child, commissioning parents who are so related have been seen as possessing a stronger claim to legal parenthood, as in *Johnson v Calvert* 851 P 2d 776 (Cal 1993), and may in an increasing number of jurisdictions in the United States be deemed to be the legal parents once the child is born (Appleton, 2004). Here the analogy relied upon is between gestation and gamete donation: a surrogate mother simply provides an essential component for treatment which allows an infertile couple to become parents. Nonetheless, this primacy of genetics over gestation is called into question when the sperm and eggs have been supplied by donors, whereupon the intention of the commissioning parents has been deemed to give rise to legal parenthood and hence child support obligations, as in *In Re Buzzanca* 72 Cal Rptr 2d 280. Yet there are self-evident difficulties involved in relying upon intention as a basis for assigning legal parenthood, not least when minds are changed or where gestational and genetic claims to motherhood are shared between lesbian partners who subsequently separate, as in *KM v EG* 13 Cal Rptr 3d 136 (Ct App 2004). In addition, when conflict between potential or actual parents arises over the allocation of legal parenthood, the proper relation between intention and the doctrine of the best interests of the child, enshrined as paramount in the law relating to children, is likely to be highly complex.

This sketch of the troubled terrain of surrogacy in relation to legal parenthood has been provided in order to illustrate the complexities of mapping appropriate pathways forward. In addition, the view that surrogacy raises specific ethical issues over the potential for the commodification of children and economic exploitation has proven highly influential (Radin, 1987). Similar concerns underlie much of the regulation of adoption, which prohibits agreements for the transfer of legal parenthood between mothers and unrelated would-be adopters in order to prevent economically vulnerable mothers giving up their children for financial reward and to ensure that transfers of legal parenthood take place only in the child's best interests (Lewis, 2004). Thus the current legal oversight of surrogacy arrangements in the United Kingdom depends upon treating surrogacy as most like adoption and subject to very similar ethical concerns. Hence it has as its focus excluding marketplace mechanisms, protecting those who are seen as vulnerable from exploitation and protecting the interests of children born as a result of surrogacy agreements through providing mechanisms which assign legal parenthood with certainty.

The central difference between adoption and surrogacy is that in the latter, the agreement of the birth mother to give her child to another or others to raise takes place before that child is conceived. At the time that the current regulatory structure was being put in place, this ensured that surrogacy was perceived as a sordid and unnatural practice akin to baby-selling. As a consequence, the presumptions underlying the law at present seek to contain or discourage the practice. One means of doing so has been to ensure that commercial surrogacy agreements would be unlawful and non-commercial agreements would not be enforceable. Section 36 of the 1990 Act, which inserts s 1A into the Surrogacy Arrangements Act 1985, specifies that such agreements are not enforceable against any of the parties to them. In addition, the birth mother and her partner, if any, are deemed to be the legal parents of children born as a result of a surrogacy agreement. Under ss 27 and 28, the woman who gives birth to such a child is its legal mother, and, where conception has taken place via assisted donor insemination with the consent of her husband or male partner, he will be regarded as the legal father.

Section 30 of the 1990 Act recognises that surrogacy is not equivalent to adoption in that it provides a procedure for streamlining the transfer of legal parenthood to those who have commissioned the pregnancy and wish to raise the child. The court may make such a parental order where the child has been born from the gametes of at least one of the commissioning parents, who must be married and at least 18 years old. The legal mother, at least six weeks after the birth, and, where possible, the legal father must give their consent to this. The application must be made within six months of the birth of the child, who must be living with the applicants. The court has the power to refuse to grant such a parental order where money, other than reasonable expenses, has been given to the woman who gave birth to the child. However, this power is inherently undercut by considerations of the welfare of the child, which have led the court to authorise payments of several thousand pounds retrospectively rather than interfere with the continuity of care and upbringing which is accepted as being in children's best interests, as in *Re an Adoption Application (Surrogacy)* [1987] Fam 81 and *Re MW (Surrogacy)* [1995] 2 FLR 789. Section 30 thus represents a conceptual mixture of conceiving of surrogacy as analogous to adoption as well as with the infertility treatment model, in that genetic ties achieved via assisted reproduction are linked with an entitlement to legal parenthood.

These provisions of the 1990 Act were added in order to address some of the perceived shortcomings of the insufficiently considered legislation outlawing commercial surrogacy passed in haste five years previously. After the British media encouraged the moral panic which accompanied Kim Cotton's surrender of Baby Cotton to an anonymous American couple for the then substantial sum of six and a half thousand pounds, public concern over baby-selling provoked the swift passage of the Surrogacy Arrangements Act 1985, wherein the central concern was to criminalise the making of surrogacy arrangements on a commercial basis. Non-commercial agencies, medical practitioners, licensed fertility clinics and the principals involved in a surrogacy agreement remain free from potential criminal liability. This means that surrogacy agreements arranged on an altruistic basis are lawful, but unable to be enforced, on the assumption that those prepared to act as gestational mothers and commissioning parents are less likely to enter into such agreements without the safety net of enforceability (Jackson, 2001, p 308). Where surrogacy involves IVF, it is subject under the Human Fertilisation and Embryology Authority Code of Practice to quality control provisions over the sperm used, as well as to criteria for treatment and supervision by the clinic or hospital's independent ethics committee, and is provided only after the welfare of the child-to-be, and the children of the gestational mother and those commissioning the pregnancy has been taken into account. Surrogacy without IVF, however, remains for the most part unregulated. In addition, under s 30, arrangements for the transferral of legal parentage are keyed to specific genetic links in a fashion which perpetuates legal uncertainties, as in the three years taken to resolve who should become the legal parents of twins born from donated embryos to a grandmother who carried them for her infertile daughter (Rogers, 2004). Inconsistencies and legal uncertainties are hence undesirable features of the present law. These are explored further below.

The forthcoming review of the 1990 Act, as announced by the Government in January 2004, thus provides a timely opportunity to reconsider both that Act and the Surrogacy Arrangements Act 1985. The House of Commons Science and Technology Committee's Report on Human Reproductive Technologies and the Law has recommended that surrogacy arrangements form part of this review (House of Commons Science and Technology Committee, 2005, recommendation 79). This chapter sets out to make a modest contribution to that enterprise. After placing surrogacy arrangements within their medical, legal and social contexts, I will argue that surrogacy is most fruitfully regarded not as analogous to adoption or infertility treatment, but as a means of forming flexible families where there is 'active recognition of a kind of parenthood where boundaries are fluid and roles continue to be negotiated' (New Zealand Law Commission, 2005, p 89). I will then suggest reforms as outlined above.

Surrogacy agreements in their medical, legal and social contexts

Many commentators have remarked upon the infelicity and inaccuracy of the popular designation of the woman who gives birth to a child for another as the surrogate mother (Morgan, 1989). It has been forcefully condemned as derogating from her rights to a continuing relationship with the child (Jaggar, 1994). Terms such as contract motherhood and baby contracts are favoured by some feminists (Ketchum, 1989; Dickenson, 1997). However, in this chapter I use the term surrogacy as established nomenclature within English legal scholarship. I refer to the woman who gives birth as the birth or gestational mother, the woman whose egg is involved as the genetic mother, the woman or women (if any) who raise the child as the social mother(s) and the woman or women (again, if any) involved in commissioning the pregnancy as the commissioning mother(s). This section of the chapter will explore the contested discursive contexts within which surrogacy remains contentious.

Surrogacy consists of an arrangement whereby one woman becomes pregnant with the ultimate aim of passing the child when born to another or others to raise. In traditional surrogacy, a woman will become pregnant, either through artificial insemination or intercourse, with the sperm of the man who intends to raise the child with his partner, so that the birth mother will also be the genetic mother. This form of surrogacy has now largely given way to gestational surrogacy. Here the birth mother will be impregnated via IVF (*in vitro* fertilisation), where the egg may belong to a commissioning mother or another woman whose identity is known or anonymous. The sperm may belong to a commissioning father or to a known or anonymous donor. Debates over how far surrogacy should be acceptable thus fall within the wider reformulation of family relations catalysed by reproductive technologies. Surrogacy remains contentious in that its potential to disrupt notions of kinship exceeds that of other means of treating infertility. Gamete donation and IVF, after initial social misgivings, are more readily normalised. Their social acceptability has hinged upon analogies made with praiseworthy altruistic and socially valued activities such as blood or organ donation and medico-surgical procedures. The routines of daily life also make it easier for most people to accept the severing of relations between a person and a renewable body part such as sperm. We often choose to remove, discard or transfer body parts such as hair, fingernails and various bodily fluids.

This is not, however, how we treat children. Instead, the bond between mother and child is widely conceptualised as natural, instinctive and sacred. Hence surrogacy arrangements have been equated with baby-selling, prostitution and slavery, and women who become pregnant with the intention of handing over the resulting children demonised. Yet regulation permitting only non-commercial surrogacy, framed in terms of mothers giving others 'the gift of life', does not deprive surrogacy of its disruptive potential. This is because surrogacy denaturalises parenthood not only in that it provides a means whereby the socially infertile such as gay men, single fathers, lesbian couples and transsexuals may become parents of babies to whom they may be genetically linked, but also as it demonstrates that cross-generational, same-sex and multiple parenthood are feasible legal forms. While some see this in a positive light, many jurisdictions either ban surrogacy outright or restrict its availability to infertile, heterosexual married couples.

Yet the activities involved in surrogacy arrangements, impregnation, childbirth and the formation of a family, might be regarded as quintessentially subject to private decision-making protected by human rights. Disagreements over surrogacy also form part of the wider debate over advances in medical technology which typically involve commercial interests and the human body. Issues concerning property rights over human body parts or their byproducts, one's ability to enter into contracts which assign monetary value to one's bodily products or services, the legality of certain medical procedures and the impact of such arrangements on children are thus bound to arise. Their resolution is essential, but hardly self-evident. In addition, surrogacy is embedded in ongoing controversies over the process of family formation as mediated by consumer choice, reproductive autonomy and increasing infertility (Brazier, 1999a,b). Finding a satisfactory regulatory structure is crucial, as demand will inevitably rise. Factors such as environmentally induced falls in sperm counts and the decline in fertility and gamete quality after the age of thirty-five taken together with the tendency towards delayed parenthood, rises in infertility due to sexually transmitted diseases, the wish of the socially infertile such as gay men and lesbians to have children (Hibbs, 2000), a cultural rejection of childlessness unless it has been consciously chosen (Deech, 2000) and the ever-decreasing number of children, especially babies, put up for adoption (Lowe, 1997) are among the more commonly acknowledged factors which are likely to remain influential, and will in all likelihood become more so.

Also relevant are the costs and difficulties of adopting children either locally or from overseas, the role of the new reproductive technologies for the biologically and socially infertile and contemporary thinking on parental responsibility, looked after children and adoption. As reproductive forum shopping is inevitably accompanied by intercountry exchange of children, any regulation associated with either reproduction or children must be evaluated in an international context if it is to prove effective. Further, would-be parents are increasingly likely to adopt a cost/benefit analysis approach to the acquisition of children where the usual means of ensuring their presence is viewed as problematic. From this perspective, surrogacy is highly likely to be the means of choice. In England, surrogacy arrangements are relatively cheap, result in the delivery of a newborn and afford a degree of control over the quality of the gametes as well as a streamlined means of acquiring legal parentage. The competing options are IVF and adoption. Whereas IVF may also result in the delivery of a newborn with control over the quality of gametes, its success rates are poor, its physical, emotional and financial costs are high, and its effectiveness diminishes sharply with advancing maternal age. Adoption in England is at present subject to suitability criteria which are by no means easy to meet, newborn babies are available only to the very few and the difficulties associated with adopting an older child with a fraught background from having been in care manifold. Arrangements for surrogacy or adoption may be entered into overseas but these will not necessarily prove fruitful, since under the Adoption and Children Act 2002 intercountry adoption regulation ensures that would-be parents wishing to bring children into the country from overseas are subject to strict criteria of suitability similar to those in place for adopting within this jurisdiction. Hence, claims that surrogacy has the potential to solve 99 per cent of infertility problems have some plausibility (Baker, 1999).

Given its promise, why is surrogacy seen as so problematic? Anyone beginning to write upon surrogacy can hardly hope to raise new philosophical questions. Indeed, many of the issues are all too familiar. Lee and Morgan tabulate the arguments for and against it as follows. Arguments for: it is the only chance for some couples to have a child; carrying a child for another is an act of generosity or virtue; women can and should decide for themselves how to use their own bodies; true voluntariness excludes exploitation; those who feel that surrogacy compromises the marital relationship should not impose this view on others; and there is no firm evidence of bonding between mother and child during pregnancy. Arguments against: surrogacy is an assault on the marital relationship; it is inconsistent with human dignity that a woman should use her uterus for profit; the relationship between mother and child is distorted by surrogacy; surrogacy is potentially damaging to both (a) the child and (b) the mother; the risks of pregnancy should not be run for money; and a woman should not be forced to part with a child against her will (Lee and Morgan, 2001, p 196). I have no desire to review the thoughts of so many eminent scholars again. Instead, I will consider the current legal regulation of surrogacy agreements and offer suggestions for reform.

The legal regulation of surrogacy agreements

As can be seen from the preceding material, surrogacy is inherently disruptive of normative categories and values. This conceptual upheaval continues where its regulation is concerned, as it cannot be restricted to a specific area of the law. Instead, it sits uncomfortably within the nexus between contract, property, medical and family law. All possess claims to theorise or colonise this territory, but none has so far succeeded in excluding the others. Nor do demarcation zones or peaceful coexistence seem possible. In that surrogacy arrangements involve agreements, contract law is involved. Concerns over commodification bring in property law, assisted reproduction medical law and the transfer of legal parenthood family law. It is noteworthy that the law regarding children is typically grounded upon the explicit statement that 'whenever the court considers a question relating to the upbringing of children, the paramount consideration should be the welfare of the children' (Herring, 2001, p 338). 'Paramount' has been interpreted by the House of Lords in *J v C* [1970] AC 668 as mandating that it constitutes the sole factor in decision-making here. This need to consider children's best interests is often seen as trumping other concerns, whether or not this is appropriate (Blyth, Chapter 2 in this volume; Jackson, 2001, Chapter 3 in this volume). Yet how this priority should enable the regulation of surrogacy given the competing claims located in human rights to privacy and family formation, contractual freedom and bodily autonomy is at the very least problematic. Regulatory authorities must decide how and when to assign legal parentage among up to six possible parents, how far to place reproductive autonomy in a context of compulsory safeguards and assess the place, if any, of apparently conflicting legal principles and mechanisms such as consideration, enforceability and best interests. Hence surrogacy destabilises regulatory governance by exposing internally contradictory theoretical positions within these areas of law which structure so much of our lives. It can be seen as the ultimate 'unruly technology' (Latour, 1993) in that it possesses the power to disrupt the shared societal and legal narratives which permit differing values to coexist.

This ability has been evidenced in the attitudes taken in the two official reports in the UK which have considered how the law should treat surrogacy arrangements. The Warnock Committee, chaired by Baroness Mary Warnock, was established to consider issues associated with the new reproductive technologies in the wake of the moral panic caused by the birth of the first IVF baby, Louise Brown, in 1978 (Warnock Report, 1984). Seeking to establish an ethical consensus over embryology and reproductive technology in a politically fraught situation, the Committee was anxious to present recommendations which would be acceptable to the public while permitting research on embryology and infertility to continue. In considering the Warnock Report and its eventual translation into the Human Fertilisation and Embryology Act 1990, feminists have drawn attention to how the symbolic figurations of women longing to become mothers enabled compromises over the regulation of the then controversial assisted reproduction technologies (Franklin, 1993, 1995a,b, 1997, 1998). Surrogacy proved paradoxical here in that the image of the mother yearning for a child which can be located in the commissioning parent[s] is matched by the distorted mirror reflection of the birth mother becoming pregnant and giving birth with the explicit intention of giving away her baby. Efforts to gain public acceptance of new reproductive technologies by grounding them in the natural, i.e. 'just giving nature a hand', faltered when allied with such 'unnatural' mothers. The rhetoric of naturalisation was also tainted when commercial surrogacy raised issues of commodification of children and childbirth. This vision of women who would undertake to give birth to but not raise children as somehow unnatural was commonplace not only among members of the public but also on the Warnock Committee itself. Baroness Warnock has courageously admitted subsequently that her 'very strong abhorrence' of surrogacy led to her 'being too emotional, not to say irrational' on the subject (Warnock, 2003, p 102). As a result, her view that the practice should ideally be prohibited, or at the very least stringently regulated, prevailed over the minority's proposal of a form of regulation similar to adoption which she with hindsight states 'now seems to me eminently sensible' (Warnock, 2003, p 104). The minority had proposed a limited, non-profit-making surrogacy service, subject to licensing and inspection, but this was rejected by the majority as implying an approval of the practice (Warnock Report, 1984). The majority of the Committee was also preoccupied with the possibility that commercial agencies would profit from the desperate desire of couples to have a child, and that impoverished women would be exploited by such agencies.

These concerns were seen as still salient by the members of the Brazier Committee. While that Committee favoured regulation, their stance has been characterised as a policy of containment of a process still somehow distasteful, associated with commodification and the commercialisation of assisted reproductive services Brazier has condemned elsewhere (Brazier, 1999a,b). The principal means of protection was seen as eschewing marketplace mechanisms and values. This approach falls within the tradition of Titmuss's work on the gift relationship, which provides a central theoretical grounding for the British health care system's reliance upon altruism as a means of fostering desirable social bonds (Titmuss, 1970). Excluding commercial agreements figures surrogacy as a 'gift of life'. This enables the inherently 'unnatural' element of surrogacy, a woman's agreeing to become a mother of a child she does not intend to raise, to be redeemed in part by framing it as an altruistic act. Hence, according to the Brazier Committee, payments were to be stringently limited to actual designated expenses, with the court's ability to retrospectively authorise additional payments removed. Recommendations that surrogacy agreements should remain unenforceable, with a restrictive code of practice limiting conditions under which such agreements could be made and those who could enter into them, were put forward as mechanisms to protect those who were prepared to act as gestational mothers and commissioning parents from exploitation. This orientation was also driven by the Committee's assumption that surrogacy should be primarily governed by family law values. The code of practice favoured would enshrine the welfare of the child as paramount and provide that surrogacy could take place only where the welfare of the child to be and other children of the gestational mother had been considered by the gestational mother and those commissioning the pregnancy.

These proposals have been criticised as unduly restricting women's autonomy (Freeman, 1999) and as compromising citizens' ability to engage in reproductive choice (Jackson, 2001). In addition, this application of the welfare principle has been condemned as inappropriate (Jackson, 2001, Chapter 3 in this volume). Space constraints preclude my engaging with these issues. Instead, I wish now to consider how some of the difficulties associated with surrogacy agreements might be ameliorated. My argument here is that as surrogacy agreements should no longer be seen as offending against public policy, they fall within permissible bounds of family formation. As such, the place of the law should be limited to pre-conception oversight of agreements allocating legal parenthood, with a presumption that these will be enforced unless overturned by welfare of the child considerations post-birth.

Public policy and surrogacy agreements

Much of the preceding material in this chapter has demonstrated the ability of surrogacy to destabilise established categories. Surrogacy agreements also manifest this characteristic when an attempt is made to fit them within the doctrinal requirements of classical contract law. A non-commercial pre-conception agreement lacks consideration so cannot be easily accepted as a bargain and may not evidence an intention to create legal relations. In addition, it is inherently unenforceable in that it involves a promise to make a gift. Given that the purpose of the agreement is that a child be handed from its lawful mother to another to raise, public policy concerns over the elements of legal parenthood arise. Under most countries' family law, parental rights and responsibilities may not be simply transferred or waived as a matter of private ordering, despite the fact that children may be brought up by various members of extended families. Similarly, a commercial surrogacy agreement may share many characteristics of standard contracts: consideration, intention to create legal relations, and so forth. But public policy is usually seen as preventing enforceability where surrogacy agreements are regarded as falling within adoption, as adoption provisions in most jurisdictions, as well as international agreements, prohibit the selling of children.

A central public policy objective of laws governing the transfer of children and associated parental responsibilities is the prevention of child trafficking (Anderson, 1990; Smolin, 2004). Current legislative provisions in the United Kingdom criminalise the private transfer of children for adoption unless this takes place between relatives, who may be grandparents, siblings, uncles and aunts but not non-genetically related commissioning parents: *Re WM (Adoption: Non-parent)* [1997] 3 FCR 132. It is also an offence to provide payment or reward for agreement or consent to an adoption, or the handing over of a child for adoption or the making of arrangements for an adoption. If viewed from this conceptual framework, surrogacy agreements between would-be adoptive parents who wish to commission a woman to become pregnant with a view to her passing the child to them to raise are, at the very least, suspect. In addition, under s 1A of the Surrogacy Arrangements Act 1985, the agreement would be unenforceable. This prohibition is usually attributed to public policy concerns (Hibbs, 2000).

It is in this light that English courts considering surrogacy agreements have repeatedly characterised them as against public policy. In *A v C* [1985] FLR 445, Comyn J held: 'The agreement between the parties I hold as being against public policy. None can rely on it in any way or enforce the agreement in any way. I need only give one of the many grounds for saying this, namely that this was a purported contract for the sale and purchase of a child' (at 445). Similarly, in *Re P (Minors) (Wardship: Surrogacy)* [1987] FLR 421, Sir John Arnold condemned surrogacy agreements, stating that they should be rejected by law as contrary to public policy.

Courts in common law and European jurisdictions where surrogacy arrangements are banned or tolerated on an altruistic basis have tended to take this stance. Arguments relying upon public policy have been commonly used to justify refusals to recognise or enforce surrogacy agreements. A typical case here is *Re Baby M* (1987) 525 A 2d 1128 (NJ Super Ct, Ch Div), where the New Jersey Supreme Court relied upon public policy arguments to proscribe payments to 'surrogate' mothers as 'illegal, perhaps criminal, and potentially degrading to women', though there was no offence when 'a woman, voluntarily and without payment agrees to act as a "surrogate" mother, provided she is not subject to a binding agreement to surrender her child' (at 1234–5). Interpreting public policy concerns as determining the best interests of the child, the Court held that a contract which made arrangements for the custody of the child before its birth was against the child's best interests, since the contract failed to inquire into the fitness of the commissioning couple as custodial parents and failed to consider the effect on the child of separation from its natural mother (at 1248). The Court further construed that public policy required that children remain and be raised by both natural parents (1246–7). Distinguishing between the right to procreation and 'the custody, care, companionship and nurturing that follow birth', the Court held that the right to procreation is 'qualified by the effect on innocent third persons of the exercise of those rights', so that biological parents could not use the right to procreate to make arrangements that were not in the best interests of the child (at 1254). Surrogacy agreements, then, may be condemned as unenforceable because they are seen both as illegal and as against public policy.

Yet the impact of doctrines such as illegality and public policy on contract law is neither simple nor static (Buckley, 2002). The doctrine of public policy is a means whereby judges might refuse to enforce contracts on the grounds that they were so inimical to the interests of the public that they should not be enforced. Classically, contracts which involved or tended to promote sexual immorality, along with those tending to undermine marriage, would be judicially viewed as unenforceable on public policy grounds (Beale *et al*, 2000). However, as the changing fortunes of cohabitation contracts and prenuptial agreements reveal, the heads of public policy evolve to suit the times (Kingdom, 2000; Probert, 2004b). Indeed, in *Sutton v Michon de Reya and Gawor & Co* [2003] EWHC 3166, Hart J explicitly stated that, 'I accept the submission that there is nothing contrary to public policy in a cohabitation contract governing the property relationship between adults who intend to cohabit or who are cohabiting for the purposes of enjoying a sexual relationship' (para 19). Similarly, in *Briody v St Helen's and Knowsley Health Authority* (2000) 53 BMLR 108, Ebsworth J agreed with Ms Briody's argument that a claim to include the costs of surrogacy within an award for damages should not be denied on grounds of public policy, holding that:

> I do not . . . find it necessary or desirable to exclude a claim for the 'costs of surrogacy' from the ambit of recoverable damage in an appropriate case . . . This is a constantly developing field in an area of science where the concept of surrogacy goes back at least to Biblical times.
>
> (at 37)

Nonetheless, recovery of the costs of a commercial surrogacy arrangement made lawfully in California were denied, partly because of Ms Briody's age and additionally because in this jurisdiction such a contract would be unenforceable and unlawful.

It is in this light that I wish to argue that the enforcement of surrogacy agreements should no longer be seen as against public policy. Marilyn Strathern has warned of the dangers of ideological preconceptions, unanchored by empirical and experiential findings, driving policy decisions (Strathern, 2000). It is noteworthy that at the time of the Warnock Report, the Surrogacy Arrangements Act 1985 and the collection of cases cited above, there was a paucity of extant research on surrogacy arrangements which would have enabled evidence-based policy-making here. As a result, for reasons explored above, surrogacy was viewed as a suspect practice akin to baby trafficking and hence inherently against public policy. This is now no longer the case. Empirical evidence provided by clinicians (Brinsden, 2003; Meek, 2002), the co-founder of the charity COTS (Childlessness Overcome Through Surrogacy) which has coordinated surrogacy arrangements since the mid-1980s in Britain (Dodd, 2003), counsellors (Appleton, 2003), psychologists (Ciccarelli and Beckman, 2005; Edelmann, 2003) and anthropologists (Ragone, 2003; Teman, 2003) documents a picture of all parties to surrogacy arrangements as capable of protecting their own interests and making responsible and realistic judgements. Evidence from several jurisdictions where surrogacy agreements are enforceable and payments to gestational mothers lawful suggests that the fears of exploitation and commodification are unlikely to be realistic (Andrews, 1995; Schutz, 2003). Professional bodies such as the British Medical Association have approved surrogacy as a means of last resort for treating infertility (British Medical Association, 1996). Large-scale surveys of public opinion such as the House of Commons Science and Technology Committee's recent online consultation on human reproductive technologies and the law also reveal that the public at large have come to accept surrogacy in the same light. In addition, the House of Commons Science and Technology Committee's Report on Human Reproductive Technologies and the Law cites evidence from Margot Brazier to the Committee to the effect that she 'would certainly like to see the regulation of surrogacy looked at again. The [Brazier Report] was issued in 1998 and a great deal has changed . . . It would be equally regrettable, I think, now just to pick it up six years later and say "Let's do something about it," because everything has moved at such a pace' (House of Commons Science and Technology Committee, 2005, p 138). The Committee also placed emphasis upon the views of COTS that payment should be permitted and contracts rendered binding.

Reasons of space preclude my traversing or summarising this material. Its significance has been to demonstrate that changed circumstances and results of research projects have led expert and public opinion to regard the ethical presumptions and legal structures associated with surrogacy agreements as ripe for reconsideration. Regulatory structures based upon evidence-led policies have become a plausible possibility. Yet, the recognition of surrogacy as an acceptable means of exercising reproductive autonomy in family formation does not overcome all the doctrinal difficulties associated with the enforcement of surrogacy agreements. I have argued elsewhere that relational contract theory has the potential to do so, and do not wish to focus on this aspect of the issues at hand here (Mackenzie, forthcoming). Instead, I shall explore pre-conception agreements, the allocation of legal parenthood and the appropriate relationship between these issues and court oversight of the best interests of the child when disagreements arise.

Pre-conception agreements, legal parenthood and the best interests of the child

My central argument in this chapter is that surrogacy arrangements might be most fruitfully treated by the law as an opportunity for those wishing to form a family to do so in a fashion which allows them to design a kin network as they see fit. This position is based partially upon a recognition of the disaggregation of elements of family life as exemplified in the current plethora of varieties and components of marriage, legal parenthood and the options offered as a result of reproductive technologies. Attempting to bind family life to an outmoded Procrustean bed of heteronormativity and permanence disregards the increasingly fluid boundaries and continually negotiated roles prevalent in today's families of chosen kinship networks (Fineman, 2004; Kavanagh, 2004; New Zealand Law Commission, 2005). Affording State recognition to the wide variety of family forms is essential if the care of dependants which takes place within them is to be most effectively supported. One possibility which has been mooted here is a kinship registration scheme, which might encompass not only sexual affiliation between adults and/or care-taking roles with children, but also close adult personal relationships involving neither element which move 'beyond conjugality' (Law Commission of Canada, 2001). The recognition of both the reality of kin networks in family life today and commensurate evolutionary developments within the regulation of this area of life as outlined above would support allowing parties to a surrogacy agreement to do so as they see fit where it comes to family formation in terms of the numbers of adults involved and the relations between them.

This approach stems not only from an assumption that kinship networks which represent increasingly common family forms should benefit from legal recognition but also an attempt to arrive at legal oversight of surrogacy arrangements which is evidence-based. The results of research as sketched out above suggest that the adults involved are capable of protecting their own interests while making reasoned and responsible decisions. What possible forms, then, would evidence-based legal oversight of surrogacy arrangements take?

There are some inevitable caveats here. The research suggests that where pre-conception counselling, legal advice and psychological assessment take place, those entering agreements are highly likely to fulfil them and to regard the outcome positively. This suggests that both for the benefit of the adults involved and hence the emotional stability of the children, the afore-mentioned safeguards should be viewed not as a fetter on reproductive autonomy but as appropriate ethical precautions. Nonetheless, the centrally decisive factor determining whether there is post-birth disagreement between the parties, as well as long-term satisfaction with the outcome, is the relation-ship between the surrogate mother and the commissioning couple during the pregnancy and continuing contact post-birth (Ciccarelli and Beckman, 2005). I have elaborated on the significance of this elsewhere (Mackenzie, forthcom-ing). In the present context, it foregrounds the importance of the pre-conception process incorporating a finely tuned matching of the surrogate mother and her family with those commissioning the pregnancy so that the expectations of all should match. Current thinking on open adoption, know-ledge of genetic heritage and disclosure to the children born from assisted reproduction techniques would support a presumption of continuing contact as beneficial for all concerned. Incorporating such measures in the initial agreement would certainly prove more effective than a reliance upon courts to adjudicate subsequently (Smith, 2004). However, mandating such contact seems inadvisable should the parties concerned not wish it.

An obvious and justifiable limit on adult autonomy here would be the wellbeing of any children involved in the families so formed. While the evi-dence now available on surrogacy arrangements may be seen as allaying ethical concerns over exploitation of vulnerable adults, research on the well-being of the children concerned is still tentative as many of those studied are still quite young (Ciccarelli and Beckman, 2005; Golombok, 2004). While the findings so far suggest that the children born as a result of surrogacy arrangements may receive better than average parenting, the State's interest in ensuring that appropriate safeguards are in place for all children remains. Where a transfer of legal parenthood of whatever nature is concerned, State oversight according to the best interests standard is in keeping with current normative standards and legal provisions. Those favouring flexibility in family formation would argue that surrogacy agreements which provided negotiated legal certainties over care-taking roles where the children were concerned would be the optimum means of fostering their best interests. It is for this reason that I would endorse court oversight of pre-conception agreements among the parties, with a presumption that legal transfer of parenthood from the surrogate mother and her partner (if any) would take place unless she objected after the birth, with disagreements to be resolved by the court on the basis of the best interests of the child. Continuing oversight by courts with an ongoing expertise in family law matters seems more appropriate than regulatory oversight by a body specifically formed for surrogacy arrangements, and more likely to circumvent disagreements arising post-birth.

Currently, however, the regulatory structures allocating the appurtenances of legal parenthood in relation to reproductive technologies allow for only a limited amount of private ordering. Potential parents are all too often placed in unhelpfully adversarial positions by regulations which mandate hetero-normativity and duality of parenthood. An obvious example here is the difficulties faced by known sperm donors and lesbian couples, where the lawful allocation of parental responsibilities, instead of allowing for a flexible sharing among several co-parents, entails the pitting of the biological mother's partner against the known sperm donor, as in *X v Y (Parental Rights: Insemination)* 2002 SLT (Sh Ct) 161 and *Thomas S v Robin Y* 209 AD 2d 298 (NY App Div 1st Dept 1994). Similarly, where various mistakes have been involved in the provision of IVF treatment, the allocation of legal parenthood according to strict construction of consent provisions has arguably proven to be less than ideal, as in *L Teaching Hospitals NHS Trust v Mr A, Mrs A, YA, ZA (By Their Litigation Friend, the Official Solicitor), the Human Fertilisation and Embryology Authority, Mr B, Mrs B* [2003] 1 FLR 1091 and *In Re R (A Child)(IVF: Paternity of a Child)* [2003] Fam 129. Moving beyond the mandate of two parents of opposite sexes seems a likely outcome for family formation in the future in an increasing number of jurisdictions. It would certainly be appropriate for the varieties of kinship networks that surrogacy agreements as sketched out in this chapter are likely to favour.

Nonetheless, this has not been the typical mechanism in the few jurisdictions where legal oversight of pre-conception agreements has preceded surrogacy arrangements and allocation of legal parenthood. In Israel, prior approval of a surrogacy agreement precedes the transfer of legal parenthood post-birth only where there are genetic links to the married commissioning couple, the intending mother has infertility problems and all parties have been medically and psychologically assessed (Schenker, 2003). In the United States, Art 8 of the Uniform Parentage Act 2000, as amended in 2002, provides that a surrogacy agreement may be recognised where there has been prior court approval. States may choose between this and the Uniform Status of Children of Assisted Conception Act 1988, which states that all surrogacy agreements are void, or construct their own legislation. Virginia and New Hampshire have adopted the UPA approach. Both states provide court approval of pre-conception surrogacy agreements where it has been ascertained that all parties have entered the agreement voluntarily, with a full understanding of its nature and effects, and have been assessed as suitable. In Virginia under Va Code Ann 20–160D (2004), a genetic relationship between the child and at least one of the commissioning parents must be proven and those intending to raise the child must notify the court of the child's birth within seven days, whereupon legal parentage will be transferred to them and a new birth certificate issued. Where prior court approval has not been obtained, this transfer of legal parenthood may take place provided the surrogate mother signs a surrogate consent form relinquishing her parental rights 25 days after the child's birth and at least one of the commissioning parents is genetically related to the child. In New Hampshire under NH Rev Stat Ann 168-B-23 (2003), prior court approval of the agreement automatically terminates the parental relationship between surrogate mother and child at birth, although the agreement must contain a clause which permits her to execute notice of her intention to keep the child up until 72 hours after the birth. However, most states have chosen not to take the option of prior court approval to enable the transfer of legal parentage. In Florida and Texas, surrogacy arrangements may be enforced provided that the commissioning couple is legally married, the wife is unable to carry a child and there is a genetic link between at least one of the couple and the child. In California, the commissioning parents involved in a gestational surrogacy agreement may obtain a pre-birth court order describing them as the legal parents of the child. In my view, these mechanisms for the transferral of legal parenthood embody the shortcomings of framing surrogacy as a method of infertility treatment to which access should be limited. Its potential to foster a variety of family forms is thereby curtailed in ways which are difficult to justify today. While the safeguards which ensure that all parties are assessed, informed and legally advised appear sensible, restrictions upon those who might make use of surrogacy represent, in my view, an unwarranted legislative attempt to curtail reproductive autonomy. How far such limits might survive the Supreme Court's equal protection finding in *Lawrence v Texas* 539 US 558 (2003) is a moot point (Rodgers-Miller, 2005).

CONCLUSION

It has not been my intention to provide an overall map of how various jurisdictions handle surrogacy agreements and allocate legal parenthood, as this may be found elsewhere (Ciccarelli and Ciccarelli, 2005). Nor has this chapter set out to explore the specific ethical aspects of surrogacy or the doctrinal minutiae of enforceability, as I have done so elsewhere (Mackenzie, forthcoming). Instead, I have sought to suggest that regulatory structures which frame surrogacy either as a type of adoption or as a means of infertility treatment are less than helpful. Instead, appropriate regulatory oversight would approach a surrogacy agreement as a method of family formation with the potential for creating an extended network of kinfolk. The surrogate mother and her immediate family, together with those commissioning the arrangement and their families, are involved in a matrix of the components of family formation: gestation, genetics, intention and ties of relationship. In the same way that openness in adoption, knowledge in gamete donation and flexibility in family form are being promoted increasingly by the law, pre-conception surrogacy agreements should be assessed in this light by the courts. Issues of post-birth relationships need to be addressed as part of all parties receiving pre-agreement counselling and advice. I have argued else-where that surrogacy contracts are most fruitfully viewed from a relational contracts perspective, and that the reasons they break down are typically quintessentially relational (Mackenzie, forthcoming). It is to be expected that there would be a spectrum of motives for entering surrogacy arrangements where post-birth contact was concerned, from a desire to foster a wider kin network to the reverse. The appropriate role for the law here is to promote private ordering insofar as this is compatible with protecting the best interests of the children born as a result of such agreements. I would suggest that the methods outlined above provide a promising means of its doing so and should be considered in the reform of the 1990 Act.

REFERENCES

Anderson, E (1990) 'Is women's labour a commodity?' 19 *Philosophy and Public Affairs* 71–83

Andrews, L (1995) 'Beyond doctrinal boundaries: a legal framework for surrogate motherhood' 81 *Va L Rev* 2342–65

Appleton, S (2004) 'Adoption in the age of reproductive technology' (2) *U Chicago Legal F* 393–437

Appleton, T (2003) 'Emotional aspects of surrogacy: a case for effective counselling and support' in Cook, R, Day Sclater, S and Kaganas, F (eds) *Surrogate Motherhood: International Perspectives* Oxford: Hart Publishing

Baker, R (1999) *Sex in the Future: Ancient Urges Meet Future Technology* London: Macmillan

Beale, H *et al* (2000) *Contract: Cases and Materials*, 4th edn London: Butterworths

Brazier, M (1999a) 'Can you buy children?' 11 *Child and Family Law Quarterly* 345–57

Brazier, M (1999b) 'Regulating the reproduction business' 7 *Medical Law Review* 166–84

Brazier Report (1998) *Surrogacy: Review for Health Ministers of Current Arrangements for Payment and Regulation* CM 4068 London: HMSO

Brinsden, P (2003) 'Clinical aspects of IVF surrogacy in Britain' in Cook, R, Day Sclater, S and Kaganas, F (eds) *Surrogate Motherhood: International Perspectives* Oxford: Hart

British Medical Association (1996) *Changing Conceptions of Motherhood: The Practice of Surrogacy in Britain* London: British Medical Association

Brownsword, R (2004) 'Reproductive opportunities and regulatory challenges' 67 *Modern Law Review* 304–24

Buckley, R (2002) *Illegality and Public Policy* London: Sweet & Maxwell

Ciccarelli, J and Beckman, L (2005) 'Navigating rough waters: an overview of psycho-logical aspects of surrogacy' 61 *J Soc Issues* 21–43

Ciccarelli, J and Ciccarelli, J (2005) 'The legal aspects of parental rights in assisted reproductive technology' 61 *J Soc Issues* 127–37

Deech, R (2000) 'It's OK not to have children' *The Times* www.thetimes.co.uk/article/0..30462,00.html

Dickenson, D (1997) *Property, Women and Politics: Subjects or Objects?* London: Polity Press

DiFonzo, J (2003) 'Unbundling marriage' 32 *Hofstra L Rev* 31–60

Dodd, G (2003) 'Surrogacy and the law in Britain: users' perspectives' in Cook, R, Day Sclater, S and Kaganas, F (eds) *Surrogate Motherhood: International Perspectives* Oxford: Hart Publishing

Edelmann, R (2003) 'Psychological assessment in "surrogate" motherhood relationships' in Cook, R, Day Sclater, S and Kaganas, F (eds) *Surrogate Motherhood: International Perspectives* Oxford: Hart Publishing

Fineman, M (2004) 'Progress and progression in family law' (2004)(1) *U Chi Legal F* 1–17

Franklin, S (1993) 'Making representations: the Parliamentary debate on the Human Fertilisation and Embryology Act' in Edwards, J *et al* (eds) *Technologies of Procreation: Kinship in the Age of Assisted Conception* Manchester: Manchester University Press

Franklin, S (1995a) 'Postmodern procreation: a cultural account of assisted reproduction' in Ginsburg, F and Rapp, R (eds) *Conceiving the New World Order: The Global Politics of Reproduction* Berkeley: University of California Press

Franklin, S (1995b) 'Romancing the helix: nature and scientific discovery' in Stacy, J and Pearce, L (eds) *Romance Revisited* London: Lawrence & Wishart

Franklin, S (1997) *Embodied Progress: A Cultural Account of Assisted Conception* London: Routledge

Franklin, S (1998) 'Making miracles: scientific progress and the facts of life' in Franklin, S and Ragone, H (eds) *Reproducing Reproduction: Kinship, Power and Technological Innovation* Philadelphia: University of Pennsylvania Press

Freeman, M (1999) 'Is there surrogacy after Brazier?' 7 *Medical Law Review* 1–25

Golombok, S (2004) 'Families created through surrogacy arrangements: parent–child relationships in the first year of life' 40 *Developmental Psychology* 2196–205

Herring, J (2001) *Family Law* London: Sweet & Maxwell

Hibbs, M (2000) 'Surrogacy: who will be left holding the baby?' *Family Law* 736–41

House of Commons Science and Technology Committee (2005) *Human Reproductive Technologies and the Law, Eighth Special Report of Session 2004–05*. HC 491 London: House of Commons

Jackson, E (2001) *Regulating Reproduction: Law, Technology and Autonomy* Oxford: Hart Publishing

Jaggar, A (1994) *Living With Contradictions: Controversies in Feminist Social Issues* Boulder, CO: Westview

Johnson, W (2004) 'Mother treated her baby as "a commodity" ' *Scotsman*, 21 May

Kavanagh, M (2004) 'Rewriting the legal family: beyond exclusivity to a care-based standard' 16 *Yale J L & Feminism* 83–128

Ketchum, S (1989) 'Selling babies and selling bodies: surrogate motherhood and the problem of commodification' 4 *Hypatia* 116–25

Kingdom, E (2000) 'Cohabitation contracts and the democratisation of personal relations' 8 *Feminist Legal Studies* 5–27

Latour, B (1993) *We Have Never Been Modern* London: Harvester Wheatsheaf

Law Commission of Canada (2001) *Beyond Conjugality: Recognising and Supporting Close Personal Adult Relationships* Toronto: Law Commission of Canada

Lee, R and Morgan, D (2001) *Human Fertilisation and Embryology: Regulating the Reproductive Revolution* London: Blackstone Press

Lewis, J (2004) 'Adoption: the nature of policy shifts in England and Wales 1972–2002' 18 *Int J L & Pol'y & Fam* 235–49

Lin, O (2004) 'Rehabilitating bioethics: recontextualising IVF outside contractual autonomy' 54 *Duke L J* 485–505

Lowe, N (1997) 'The changing face of adoption – the gift/donation model versus the contract/services model' 9 *Child and Family Law Quarterly* 371–80

Mackenzie, R (2005) 'Reprogenetics and pharmacogenetics: in whose best interests?' *Medicine & Law* 56

Mackenzie, R (forthcoming) 'The potential of relational contract theory to resolve difficulties involved in the enforcement of surrogacy agreements'

McClain, L (2003) 'Intimate affiliation and democracy: beyond marriage?' 32 *Hofstra L Rev* 379–408

Meek, J (2002) 'Surrogacy leads to better parenting' *Guardian*, 1 July

Morgan, D (1989) 'Surrogacy: an introductory essay' in Lee, R and Morgan, D (eds) *Birthrights: Law and Ethics at the Beginning of Life* London: Routledge

Morris, A and Nott, S (2005) 'Marriage rites and wrongs: challenges to orthodoxy' 27 *Journal of Social Welfare & Family Law* 43–57

New Zealand Law Commission (2005) *New Issues in Legal Parenthood* Wellington: NZLC

Probert, R (2004a) 'Families, assisted reproduction and the law' 16 *Child and Family Law Quarterly* 273–88

Probert, R (2004b) 'Cohabitation contracts and Swedish sex slaves: *Sutton v Michon de Reya and Gawor & Co*' 16 *Child and Family Law Quarterly* 453–68

Radin, M (1987) 'Market inalienability' 100 *Harvard Law Review* 1849–937

Ragone, H (2003) 'The gift of life: surrogate motherhood, gamete donation and constructions of altruism' in Cook, R, Day Sclater, S and Kaganas, F (eds) *Surrogate Motherhood: International Perspectives* Oxford: Hart Publishing

Rodgers-Miller, B (2005) 'Adam and Eve and Steve: why sexuality segregation in assisted reproduction in Virginia is no longer acceptable' 11 *William & Mary J Women & L* 293–310

Rogers, L (2004) Court lets parents keep the twins who have five parents' *Sunday Times*, 12 September

Schenker, J (2003) 'Legal aspects of ART practices in Israel' 20 *J Assisted Reproduction & Genetics* 250–62

Schutz, R (2003) 'Surrogacy in Israel: an analysis of the law in practice' in Cook, R, Day Sclater, S and Kaganas, F (eds) *Surrogate Motherhood: International Perspectives* Oxford: Hart Publishing

Smith, C (2004) 'Autopoietic law and the "epistemic trap": a case study of adoption and contact' 31 *Journal of Law and Society* 318–44

Smolin, D (2004) 'Intercountry adoption as child trafficking' 39 *Valparaiso U L Rev* 281–306

Strassberg, M (2003) 'The challenge of post-modern polygamy: considering polyamory' 31 *Cap U L Rev* 439–545

Strathern, M (2000) *Audit Cultures: Anthropological Studies in Accountability, Ethics and the Academy* London: Routledge

Teman, E (2003) 'Knowing the surrogate body in Israel' in Cook, R, Day Sclater, S and Kaganas, F (eds) *Surrogate Motherhood: International Perspectives* Oxford: Hart Publishing

Titmuss, R (1970) *The Gift Relationship* Harmondsworth: Penguin

Warnock, M (2003) *Nature & Mortality: Reflections of a Philosopher in Public Life* London: Continuum

Warnock Report (1984) *Report of the Inquiry into Human Fertilisation and Embryology* Cm 9314 London: HMSO

Chapter 10

Beyond health and disability
Rethinking the 'foetal abnormality' ground in abortion law

Nicolette Priaulx

[T]here are no entirely convincing arguments in favour of the distinction set out in s 1(1)(d) [of the Abortion Act 1967], this in itself provides a prima facie case for at the very least questioning its place in law – since, we would argue, there should be a presumption of equal treatment of women seeking abortion, one which can only be over-turned by the existence of a sound argument for differential treatment.

(Sheldon and Wilkinson, 2001, p 88)

INTRODUCTION

In the wake of the genetic revolution, definitions of parenthood, kinship, reproduction and risk have been thrown into a state of flux. Prenatal and preimplantation genetic diagnostic techniques offer 'new alternatives for action in fields which up to now were beyond human influence' (Hildt, 2002, p 69) and, arguably, expansion in reproductive 'choice'.[1] In the era of the gene, prospective parenthood no longer turns on quantitative questions alone ('how many children?'). As reprogenetics increases our ability to detect an ever greater range of 'harmful' genetic conditions, parents increasingly confront the issue of qualitative choice ('what *kind* of child?'). But the question of what kind of children to have, as Buchanan *et al* comment, is 'one of the most controversial components of reproductive freedom' (Buchanan *et al*, 2000, p 210). Disagreements exist here as to the justification for, and interests implicated in utilising reprogenetic and abortion practices to avoid the 'risk' of a disabled child. Seen by some as driven by cost-benefit analyses to avoid the State or individuals bearing the costs of disability (Bailey, 1996), or as 'confirming a general public hostility

---

1 Of course, some argue that rather than enhance reproductive autonomy, the availability of, and prevailing discourses surrounding such diagnostic techniques actually presents women with little choice and creates pressures to use the technology. See further Rothman (1988) and Shakespeare (1998).

towards those with impairments' (Barnes *et al*, 1999, p 222), reprogenetics is viewed as inherently discriminatory. An alternative perspective suggests that the avoidance of conception or termination of pregnancy might actually benefit the prospective child under circumstances where it would otherwise live with intolerable pain and suffering as a result of severe disability (Morgan, 1990).

Others, by contrast, support a 'parental choice' model, holding that the desire to have a child healthy and free from disability is 'natural'; nor is this position regarded as being incompatible with the 'generally accepted notion that an individual already born with that condition should receive appropriate respect with full civil and human rights' (Deech, 1998, p 713). But, 'natural' as that desire might be, Deech highlights that the fear still remains that 'modern genetics will create a society in which people are intolerant of anything less than perfection and in which the family becomes the focus of ensuring that that perfection is created in a new generation' (Deech, 1998, p 714). While reprogenetics raises a much wider series of concerns and criticisms, what becomes immediately apparent is the magnitude of the regulatory challenge in determining 'how much we leave to genetic chance and individual choice' (Brownsword, 2003, p 14). And ultimately, it might well be that the answer to this fundamentally depends on establishing what and whose purpose these technologies serve.

Yet, in the realm of abortion politics in the UK, such questions continue to receive a divided response. Despite some 16 years passing since the Abortion Act 1967 was amended by s 37 of the Human Fertilisation and Embryology Act 1990 ('the 1990 Act'), in creating a general upper limit of 24 weeks for lawful terminations, one of the exceptions to this gestatory time limit has become increasingly controversial. Under s 1(1)(d) of the 1967 Act, a pregnancy may lawfully be terminated *up to term* where there is a substantial risk that if born, a child will be seriously handicapped.[2] Although statistically very few abortions are actually performed under this ground,[3] this provision appears to attract greater public support than in other cases of termination (Lee and Davey, 1998). But while practice and public opinion suggest that the provision is fairly uncontentious, many have questioned, from distinct perspectives, not merely 'whose interests' are, and *should* be implicated in existing legislation, but whether there is *any* remaining

---

2 Although, as Gillon (2001) suggests, this provision was one of the *least* controversial clauses when David Steel's Abortion Bill was being debated.

3 In 2003, the total number of abortions performed in England and Wales was 190,660 (*Abortion Statistics Summary*, 2003), 87 per cent of which took place before 13 weeks' gestation. Terminations performed in accordance with s 1(1)(d) constituted a mere 1 per cent of the total figure. There is no report of any abortions being carried out in order to save the life of the pregnant woman, to prevent grave permanent injury to her physical or mental health or where the continuation of the pregnancy would involve risk to the pregnant woman's life.

justification for this exceptional provision at all. And this is far from surprising, since s 1(1)(d) creates a strict dichotomy in 'explicitly distinguishing between the termination of (presumed) disabled foetuses and (presumed) non-disabled foetuses in the sense of providing that the former is permissible whilst the latter, in the absence of other contraindications, is not' (Sheldon and Wilkinson, 2001, p 88).

Whether there is any 'convincing' theoretical justification for such differential treatment has already formed the subject-matter of a detailed examination by Sheldon and Wilkinson (2001). And their conclusion forms a useful starting point for analysis. While the authors find that an argument based on 'parental interests' provides the strongest rationale for s 1(1)(d), notably, that the strain of caring for a disabled child may be substantially greater than caring for a non-disabled child, they nevertheless recommend 'caution' when invoking it, because of 'the danger that in so doing one might be colluding with social discrimination against people with disabilities' (p 105). Such dangers, they suggest, might only be overcome by distinguishing between trivial impairment and those 'disabilities which have more substantial impairment elements and would be seriously harmful even in the absence of social discrimination' (p 107).

Yet, in one sense, it is the impossibility in practice of making such 'fine-grained' distinctions that lies at the heart of this chapter. Even if it were possible to exclude concerns over social discrimination, great caution is still required in invoking this justification; for what remains is the assumption that caring for a disabled child is *harmful*, and therefore sufficiently distinctive from the burden of caring for non-disabled children. In the context of abortion, where women for whatever reasons do not wish to continue a particular pregnancy, nor wish to undertake the burdens of parenthood, the assumption that 'disability' makes all the difference must be seen as deeply problematic. And, if others are correct in their assertion that s 1(1)(d) is premised on 'maternal' interests, would this not suggest that if it is lawful to terminate a pregnancy on the grounds of foetal disability after 24 weeks, then it should also be lawful on any other grounds?

As this chapter will argue, whether or not the existence of s 1(1)(d) is really justified by reference to 'maternal' (or 'parental') interests, it is now essential that we move beyond the binaries of health and disability towards a more contemporary approach based on the value of reproductive autonomy. Drawing briefly on the jurisprudence of Baroness Hale in her adjudication of wrongful conception cases in negligence law, it is argued that such an approach might better resonate with women's diverse experiences of reproduction and offer a different perspective by which to challenge the problematic health/disability dichotomy so readily embraced within existing abortion legislation. As this chapter concludes, once we begin to think about the complex conditions of women's lives, it is simply not possible to draw hard lines between the 'kinds' of harm that result from caring for either a disabled or a healthy child. Rather, if there is a difference, it will only be one of degree.

SECTION 1(1)(d): IN WHOSE INTERESTS?

> The decision to abort is not seen as an intrinsically acceptable one, as a choice which any woman could face at some time in her life. Rather, it is an option which may be justified only in certain cases by the individual circumstances (or inadequacies) of individual women, in the opinion of two doctors. Conceptually then, abortion stands as the exception to the norm of maternity. No women can reject motherhood.
>
> (Sheldon, 1997, p 42)

Out with permissive – in with divide and control

Gaining the freedom to decide whether or not to bear and nurture children through the wider availability of contraception and access to legal abortion remains high on the feminist political agenda. The supply of abortion services, as Leslie Bender comments, is 'one part of women gaining control of their reproductive lives, an essential prerequisite to women freeing themselves from male dominance' (Bender, 1993, p 1251). Not only is this central in securing a right to reproductive autonomy, but ultimately, an identity untied to reproduction. Yet, despite assertions to the contrary, existing abortion legislation far from reflects these (modest) goals. Although heralding the partial decriminalisation of abortion, in creating statutory defences to criminal offences under the Offences Against the Person Act 1861 and the Infant Life (Preservation) Act 1929,[4] as Sheldon argues, the 1967 Act simultaneously installed 'the medical profession as the gatekeepers . . . who could grant or refuse access to termination according to how deserving an individual case was felt to be' (Sheldon, 1997, p 24). Therefore, rather than being premised on a woman's right to self-determination, the thrust of the 1967 Act simply placed decisional control in the hands of the medical profession. As a result, a woman will only be entitled to terminate her pregnancy where *two* doctors, acting in good faith, are satisfied that an abortion is necessary in order to protect a woman's health or that of her existing children, or

---

4 Under ss 58 and 59 of the Offences Against the Person Act 1861, intentionally procuring a miscarriage in oneself or in another is a criminal offence which carries a maximum sentence of life imprisonment. Under the Infant Life (Preservation) Act 1929, s 1, it is an offence to destroy the life of a child capable of 'being born alive' unless this is done in 'good faith' for the purpose only of preserving the life of the mother. The Act contains a rebuttable presumption that a child is capable of being born alive at 28 weeks.

to prevent the birth of a child who would suffer from severe abnormalities.[5] Indeed, the very requirement that a woman must seek approval from *two* doctors also quickly dispels claims that existing abortion legislation is in any way permissive; as Lee comments of this requirement, Britain has one of the 'formally most restrictive abortion laws of those countries where abortion has been legalized' (Lee, 2003, p 533).

In so many respects, existing abortion legislation is deeply unsatisfactory. That British abortion law is underpinned by the assumption that doctors, rather than women, are best placed to make the abortion decision seems to lie at the heart of many, if not most feminist critiques on the subject. For example, while the decisional power afforded to doctors was premised on the basis that abortion is 'essentially a medical matter', as Emily Jackson rightly suggests:

> a legal requirement that only qualified medical professionals should carry out surgical abortions makes sense, [but] it is less obvious that their medical training equips doctors to decide *whether* a woman should terminate her pregnancy.
>
> (Jackson, 2001, p 81)

And, similarly, while the 1967 Act permits doctors to take account of 'the pregnant woman's actual or reasonably foreseeable environment' under s 1(2) in adjudging whether an abortion could be detrimental to the woman's mental or physical health or existing children of her family, this clearly demonstrates that the power wielded by the medical profession 'far exceeds that which would accrue merely on the basis of a technical expertise' (Sheldon, 1997, p 25).

While prevailing discourses surrounding abortion suggest otherwise, nor is the lack of decisional autonomy afforded to women and the apparent requirement for medical control under the 1967 Act *sufficiently* explained by

---

5 Section 1(1) of the 1967 Act states, 'subject to the provisions of this section a person shall not be guilty of an offence under the law relating to abortion when a pregnancy is terminated by a registered medical practitioner if two registered medical practitioners are of the opinion, formed in good faith:

(a) that the pregnancy has not exceeded its twenty fourth week and that the continuation of the pregnancy would involve risk, greater than if the pregnancy were terminated, of injury to the physical or mental health of the pregnant woman or any existing children of her family; or

(b) that the termination is necessary to prevent grave permanent injury to the physical or mental health of the pregnant woman; or

(c) that the continuance of the pregnancy would involve risk to the life of the pregnant woman, greater than if the pregnancy were terminated; or

(d) that there is a substantial risk that if the child were born it would suffer from physical or mental abnormalities as to be seriously handicapped.'

virtue of the need to achieve a balance between two competing sets of rights: 'the right to life of the foetus versus the right to choose' (Sheldon, 1997, p 42). As Sheldon convincingly argues, the 1967 Act instead entrenches rights only insofar as it vindicates the right to medical autonomy over that of a woman. In achieving this, she remarks that the 1967 Act is 'clearly predicated upon a particular understanding of the nature of the woman seeking to terminate a pregnancy' (p 33). And, as her analysis of the parliamentary debates leading up to the enactment of the 1967 Act illustrates, the woman who seeks a termination is generally viewed as a 'marginal and deviant figure who stands against a wider norm of women who neither need nor desire abortion' (p 35). Yet, the same discourses of maternity, while marking out the 'peripheral, deviant subject' (p 42), also serve to bring into view those women who are adjudged as particularly 'deserving':

> The only women who should be allowed to terminate pregnancies are those who can do so without rejecting maternity/familial norms *per se*, in other words those who have reasons to reject this one particular pregnancy without rejecting motherhood as their destiny in general.
>
> (Sheldon, 1997, p 42)

And, for present purposes, among these more 'virtuous' characters stands the woman who carries the 'wrong sort' of foetus; the woman who 'can reject this (abnormal) pregnancy without rejecting the whole institution of motherhood itself' (Sheldon, 1997, p 43). Although seemingly more virtuous than many of her counterparts, establishing *whose* or *what* interests the foetal abnormality ground really seeks to protect is far from straightforward. While Sheldon remarks that the original clause (s 1(1)(b) prior to the 1990 Act amendment) can be seen to display 'eugenicist considerations', it can also be interpreted with regard to the status of the woman, since it was justified:

> . . . in part on the grounds that to force a woman to carry an abnormal child to term will discourage her from future pregnancy . . . The disabled baby or child is not seen as being as desirable as a 'normal' one and does not feature in the romanticised family ideal.
>
> (Sheldon, 1997, p 43)

This does not illustrate, as Sheldon clearly acknowledges, a straightforward concern with women; the 'status' of the woman and any interests in permitting her access to abortion were clearly contingent upon the (un)desirability of (ab)normal children. However, while the 1967 Act in its original form may, as Furedi suggests, have been 'initially motivated by eugenic considerations', she comments that 'today it is very definitely the case that abortion is not seen by doctors, policy makers, or women themselves as within that tradition of social engineering' (p 16). Rather, the contemporary context for abortion is one where 'its provision meets the request of a woman who no longer wants to be pregnant' (p 16). While eugenicist policies might be seen as lying in the past, the question is, to what degree has the 1990 amendment to the 1967 Act centralised its concern with women, rather than 'foetal status'?

Objections and justifications

Prior to the reforms introduced by s 37 of the 1990 Act, there had been no time limit set for lawful terminations in the Abortion Act itself. However, such limits could be found by reference to the Infant Life (Preservation) Act 1929 (ILPA). The ILPA made it an offence to destroy 'a child capable of being born alive' and carried a rebuttable presumption that a child becomes capable of being born alive from 28 weeks' gestational development. One effect of the 1990 Act amendment was to disengage the Abortion Act from the ILPA and insert a general fixed limit of 24 weeks into the 1967 Act, except in those circumstances already noted: where there was a serious risk to the pregnant woman's life or health, or there was a substantial risk of serious foetal handicap. However, as Murphy comments, the s 37 amendments were largely 'cosmetic', since the substantive grounds were essentially the same as those contained in the original 1967 Act (Murphy, 1991, p 390). Moreover, in practice, not only had clinicians already been treating foetal viability as occurring around 24 weeks (Sheldon, 1997), but the ILPA itself permitted action necessary to save the life of the mother, even if this would entail the destruction of the child (Brazier, 2003). But, of course, the amendments were not wholly cosmetic; the most significant change was the removal of a time limit in respect of serious foetal handicap (Murphy, 1991). As Brazier remarks of this 'novel' provision:

> The impact of section 37 . . . is that in England, children capable of being born alive may be killed providing they are disabled. The protection afforded to the viable foetus by the Infant Life (Preservation) Act is withdrawn from the disabled foetus. A medical practitioner acting within the provisions of the amended and extended Abortion Act cannot be convicted of child destruction. The 1929 Act remains in force, but is applicable only to unlawful late abortions and those cases where a violent attack on a pregnant woman kills the child within her.
>
> (Brazier, 2003, p 330)

Responses to the extension of this ground illustrate little consensus. Noting the greater ambivalence surrounding terminations for foetal abnormality, even among those who 'most loudly oppose abortion', some appear to have construed this as a largely positive measure (McLean, 1999, p 86); and, as Sheldon notes, this provision situates British abortion legislation as one of the '*most* liberal of western abortion statutes' (Sheldon, 1997, p 157).[6] Others, perhaps largely in tune with this view, consider the 'foetal ground' as being directed to the 'effects on the mother resulting from the birth of a defective child' (Mason, 1990, p 100), a point to which I later return. By contrast, however, the greater recognition of the rights of the disabled, as Biggs and Lee suggest (1999), has given rise to a very different discussion surrounding the ethics of this exemption; and foetal life, rather than maternal interests, is the central concern.

Unsurprisingly, since it is as illegitimate to discriminate on the grounds of disability as it would be on the grounds of race or sex (Jackson, 2001), few disability rights activists readily conceptualise s 1(1)(d) as being in any way 'liberal', but attack it as discriminatory or eugenic. Along such lines, Morgan and Lee point to how this provision was the 'most clearly favoured ground for abortion' and suggest that Britain has actually embraced a 'much more explicitly based eugenic abortion policy than before 1990' (cited in Bailey, 1996, p 160). In similar force, Morris remarks that 'it is outrageous that, under [the amended 1967 Act] a foetus of more than 24 weeks' gestation is treated as having rights as a human being but loses these rights once it is diagnosed as being disabled' (Morris, 1991, p 75) and suggests that the same rules should apply to disabled and non-disabled foetuses. As the recent statement of the Disability Rights Commission illustrates, there is great pressure for change:

> [The provision is] offensive to many people; it reinforces negative stereo-types of disability and there is substantial support for the view that to permit terminations at any point during a pregnancy on the grounds of the risk of disability, while time limits apply to other grounds set out in the Abortion Act, is incompatible with valuing disability and non-disability equally.
>
> (DRC Statement, 2004)

While those like Furedi vigorously deny that the foetal abnormality ground can be seen as 'eugenicist' in nature, since 'women are not forced to have an abortion . . . rather doctors meet the woman's request' (Furedi, 1999, p 16), the related issue of whether the provision nevertheless 'discriminates' against people with disabilities is met by a slightly different response. And critical to this issue is the contentious question upon which the abortion debate frequently pivots: what legal (and moral) personhood is afforded to the foetus?

---

6 Although, as Sheldon further notes, since 'MPs refused to allow abortions prior to 12 weeks either on request or where authorised by only one doctor', such strict medical control also situates the 1967 Act 'amongst the *least* liberal of western abortion statutes' (Sheldon, 1997, p 157).

Of course, debates surrounding the moral status of the foetus afford little promise of compromise, and range from views that abortion is incompatible with respect for the moral value of the foetus to those which maintain that because the foetus lacks 'self-awareness', the notion that it is unethical to terminate the life of a foetus is unsustainable (Harris, 1999).[7] But, in relation to the *legal* personhood of the foetus, this is largely thought to be a matter of well-settled law, since English law affords the embryo and foetus *no* legal personality or independent rights until birth (*Paton v BPAS* [1979] QB 276). If this is so, it must certainly dispense with arguments that the foetal abnormality ground 'discriminates' against disabled persons, since 'if one accepts that a foetus does not have legal personality, rules that prohibit discrimination cannot apply *in utero*' (Jackson, 2001, p 481). Making a similar point, Furedi comments that 'the idea that abortion for abnormality represents discrimination against the disabled . . . elides the difference between foetal life and our respect for persons' (Furedi, 1999, p 17).

Yet, while such claims are entirely understandable, since maintaining a woman's superior legal status in abortion is a critical aspect of the feminist claim, there are difficulties with this approach. As Montgomery points out, it is misleading to say that the foetus in English law does not have *any* rights prior to birth and holding a separate existence from its mother (Montgomery, 2003, p 379). As he suggests, 'if that were true, then you would expect that the abortion decision would be governed only by the law of consent. In reality, foetuses are protected by the law even though they are not treated in the same way as they would be once born' (p 380). But more striking still, the logical effect of s 1(1)(d) is that 'disabled foetuses are denied any protection from destruction, even ones capable of surviving birth', while normal foetuses 'acquire a qualified right to birth at twenty-four weeks dependent on their survival posing no grave risk to the mother' (Montgomery, p 338). While there is reason to doubt the validity of Montgomery's claim that the 1967 Act confers a qualified 'right' to birth upon a 'normal' foetus, it is nevertheless true that it is afforded some protection under the law, whereas the disabled foetus is offered none.[8] Therefore, to suggest that 'the foetus' is afforded *no* protection is to ignore legal reality, for existing abortion legislation recognises

---

7 The varied arguments which surround the moral status of the embryo/foetus are beyond the scope of this chapter. For an excellent précis of these arguments, see Biggs and Lee (1999).

8 It is worth querying whether Montgomery is conflating the language of 'protection' and 'rights', since the two are not coterminous, particularly in this context. It cannot, for example, be argued that the terms of the 1967 Act confer any such foetal 'right' to birth, qualified or not; nor is the Act amenable to such a reading. Secondly, in the context of third-party attempts to prevent women from terminating their pregnancies, the courts have been forthright in rejecting such right-based assertions on behalf of foetal life on the grounds that a foetus is incapable of having any rights of its own until born and holding a separate existence from its mother (*Paton v BPAS* [1978] QB 276).

'two classes of foetus' (Montgomery, 2003). So, although it is possible to counter the claim that abortion law currently 'discriminates' against disabled *persons* on the ground that the same cannot be said *in utero*,[9] it is undeniable that there remains a pressing need to account for the 'distinction' that law at present draws, discriminatory or not.[10]

However, the most recent and detailed scholarly analyses of justifications for s 1(1)(d) do not come down in favour of maintaining this distinction in law. As Sheldon and Wilkinson's (2001) account illustrates, arguments deploying 'foetal interests' (that is, that abortion on these grounds prevents suffering) simply fail. Not only would this constitute an extremely restrictive reading of s 1(1)(d), which merely requires a 'substantial risk' of 'serious handicap', but it could only apply to a narrow range of cases where it is possible to say that if born, the child 'would, quite literally, be better off dead, or better off never having been born' (p 90). And, such a reading would be wholly out of line with abortion practice, since one of the most common grounds for termination is Down syndrome, where a person need not suffer at all (Radcliffe-Richards, 1999).[11]

Perhaps the most convincing justification must be that of the 'parental interests' argument, since this has mustered much greater support. As we saw earlier, Mason considered that the foetal abnormality ground was directed to the 'effects on the mother resulting from the birth of a defective child' (Mason, 1990, p 100). And, as Douglas comments, considerations of the impact on the parents 'seem[ed] to have qualified the compelling nature of the arguments that a handicapped child's right to life is as valid as that of any other' (Douglas, 1991, p 93). The effect in question, of course, is commonly related to the emotional, financial and caring burden which results from the birth of a disabled child and is well elucidated by Barnes *et al*:

> The justification offered is that a disabled child places an excessive

---

9 Note that such claims of 'discrimination' are also met with a further counter-argument: if abortion to prevent disability sends out a disrespectful message to disabled individuals, then it could be argued that abortion on the grounds of family size or poverty sends out the same 'disparaging messages to children of large families, or the poor, or to those who share with the foetus whatever properties that were the basis of the abortion' (Nelson, 2000, p 217). Nevertheless, these counter-arguments similarly fail to address the *unique* treatment of disabled foetuses in British abortion law.

10 The same arguments are also apparent in relation to the 'moral' status of the foetus; Savulescu comments that 'admitting a foetal disability ground, as UK legislation and practice do . . . probably cannot be supported by any plausible account of foetal moral status without significant revision of practice' (Savulescu, 2001, p 170). Contrast this view with Gillon (2001).

11 Since the case of *Jepson v The Chief Constable of West Mercia Police Constabulary* [2003] EWHC 3318, the question of how to interpret 'substantial risk' and 'serious handicap' has become increasingly controversial. See also Morgan (1990), Murphy (1991), Scott (2003).

burden on the woman/family/society – both in terms of additional time needed to support the child as well as the financial and emotional resources that must be devoted to its well-being – with a consequent deterioration in the quality of family life and relationships.

(Barnes *et al*, 1999, p 222)

On this account, parental/maternal interests certainly appear to have been the primary consideration in drawing up the foetal abnormality ground; the burden that every disabled child imposes justifies investing would-be parents with an ability to avoid that reproductive experience in law. But, if we think carefully about the *conditional* nature of parental interests, does this offer a complete or satisfactory explanation for the existence of s 1(1)(d)? Since 'women are seen as having the "right" to "late" abortions only on a special-case basis, where the status of the foetus so allows' (Sheldon, 1997, p 118), we should treat these so-called 'interests' as fairly circumspect. But, perhaps we can go further than this; as Janet Radcliffe-Richards' (1999) analysis of s 1(1)(d) suggests, it is nigh impossible to find an *acceptable* justification for the foetal abnormality ground.[12] She argues that even if we conceptualise the normal foetus, but not the abnormal foetus, as having a right to life, it is:

[S]trongly out of line with what we think about the rights of children and adults. We do not think that disabled *people* can be killed at will. So if we are to say that a disabled person has full human rights, while an abnormal foetus has not, we shall have to say those rights don't come into existence until birth. But if so, why can't the woman with the normal foetus have an abortion? Are we going to say that normal foetuses have full human rights all the way along but abnormal ones only after birth? If so, on what basis? The idea sounds quite arbitrary.

(Radcliffe-Richards, 1999, p 11)

And arbitrary it is. The s 1(1)(d) exception to the gestational period disrupts any possibility of developing a coherent justificatory account. Since there is a clear absence of 'serious reasons' for drawing gestational lines between abnormal and normal foetuses, 'serious reasons' are then required for restricting women's freedom to terminate up to term *only* in cases where there is a risk of foetal disability. If, as English law (formally) maintains, the foetus has

---

12 While Radcliffe-Richards fails to locate a coherent explanation for the distinction in law, she suggests an alternative: 'But if we [consider] *mothers* . . . there is a possible explanation . . . The idea makes sense – more or less – if you think that we shouldn't allow abortions to women who have only themselves to blame for unwanted pregnancies, but should allow an escape to respectable women who have had sex for the right reasons, and then, through no fault of their own, found themselves carrying the wrong sort of child. Again, this may sound preposterous, but what else fits?' (Radcliffe-Richards, 1999, p 11).

no legal personality or rights until birth, then not only does existing law lack internal coherence, and 'discriminate against some women', but it strongly implies that:

> [W]e should liberalise our approach to [late termination of pregnancy] and eschew considerations of foetal abnormality as a ground for [late termination of pregnancy]. If we are to give any weight to maternal interests, this should be the sole ground for justifying [termination of pregnancy], early or late.
>
> (Savulescu, 2001, p 169)

Savalescu's point is significant; even if the law cannot be said to discriminate against foetal 'life', it most certainly discriminates against particular *kinds* of women in restricting access to abortion where foetal abnormality is not at issue. Therefore, we should ask what 'serious reasons' might exist to justify the distinction currently drawn between women seeking abortion? If we assume for argument's sake that the driving force of s 1(1)(d) *is* to protect parents' interests so they may avoid the significant burden of caring for a disabled child, might this justify recognising parental interests in those cases, but not in others? Since some argue, in the context of abortion and wrongful birth cases, that these considerations provide 'serious reasons' for invoking parents' reproductive interests (Scott, 2003), perhaps this is precisely the justificatory power that s 1(1)(d) requires? However, as a more detailed examination of these claims reveals, not only do we find that 'serious reasons' lacks explanatory power for the differential treatment of women, but that there are good reasons for cautiously approaching the assumption that the emotional, financial and caring burden *only* 'seriously' arises in relation to disabled children.

SEARCHING FOR 'SERIOUS REASONS'

> Instinctively, the traveller on the Underground would consider that the law of tort has no business to provide legal remedies consequent upon the birth of a healthy child, which all of us regard as a valuable and good thing.
> (*McFarlane v Tayside HB* [2000] 2 AC 59: 82 *per* Lord Steyn)

As the recent history of the wrongful conception (and birth)[13] cases attests,

---

13 In 'wrongful conception' actions, parents seek damages from clinicians on the basis that they would not have conceived the child (whether healthy or disabled) but for the negligence in techniques such as sterilisation, or misinformation in postoperative testing. In cases where the child has been born disabled, this will have been largely coincidental. 'Wrongful birth'

the dichotomous treatment of health and disability has been absolutely central to the adjudication of these claims; but akin to abortion, it has also been one of the most problematic aspects of the law in this area. While for over a decade parents were able to seek damages from the courts following clinical negligence in family planning techniques resulting in the birth of a healthy or disabled child, in 1999 the House of Lords adjudication of *McFarlane v Tayside HB* [2000] 2 AC 59 brought one dimension of this trend to a close. Their Lordships reasoned that if parents had suffered any loss, then this was pure economic loss which was far outweighed by the considerable joys parents acquired as a result of the 'blessed' healthy child they took deliberate measures to avoid. In other words, in law, parents *raising* an unwanted healthy child were seen as suffering no actionable harm at all.[14] Yet in the case of the disabled child, 'harm' has been conceptualised quite differently indeed; and although the point was not raised in *McFarlane*, even Lord Steyn commented that the matter might need to be adjudicated differently.

Defying legal principle, largely as a result of no clear *ratio* emanating from *McFarlane*, courts finding themselves confronted with precisely this scenario awarded the additional costs of child maintenance to parents of a disabled child; but with varying levels of difficulty. Some, seeking to distinguish cases in the light of the 'blessings' rhetoric in *McFarlane*, found themselves, perhaps understandably, saying that while a disabled child was still a 'blessing', and carried the 'advantages' of a healthy child, these would be more 'difficult to discern' in the case of a disabled child (see Newman J in *Rand v East Dorset* (2000) BMLR 39). And, while the House in *McFarlane* also sought to *deny* damages in cases of healthy children on the basis of the third element of the duty of care principle, notably that it would not be 'fair, just and reasonable' to award such damages (see *Caparo v Dickman* [1990] 2 AC 605), lower courts have also utilised the flip-side of this somewhat hollow device to *justify* compensation: in the case of a disabled child, 'an award of compensation which is limited to the special upbringing costs with rearing a child with a serious disability would be "fair, just and reasonable" ' (see *Parkinson*

claims generally only involve the birth of a disabled child. Typically the negligence at issue includes failures in genetic counselling or diagnosis, which leaves parents under the false impression that the child is healthy. The crux of the claim is that, but for the negligence, the parents would have elected to terminate the foetus under s 1(1)(d) of the Abortion Act 1967.

14 While *McFarlane* rules out the possibility of recovering the potentially substantial costs of raising a healthy child, claimants are entitled to seek limited recovery under two further heads of damages. First, claimants can recover for the pain and suffering attendant upon the injury of pregnancy and childbirth; and secondly, following *Rees v Darlington* [2003] UKHL 52, a 'conventional' award, provided for the frustration of the claimants' desire to avoid reproduction, may be recovered in future wrongful conception actions. For the purposes of the argument, however, note that neither of these awards relate to the 'harm' of raising an unwanted healthy child.

v St James' [2001] 3 All ER 97: [50] *per* Brooke LJ). But, as is demonstrated by *Lee v Taunton* (October 2000, unreported), others were willing to go much further:

> I do not believe that it would be right for the law to deem the birth of a disabled child to be a blessing, in all circumstances and regardless of the extent of the child's disabilities; or to regard the responsibility for the care of such a child as so enriching in the ordinary nature of things that it would be unjust for a parent to recover . . . (*per* Toulson J).

Of course, this discourse of parental 'tragedy' emerges largely as a result of the *McFarlane* legacy and its celebration of health. Not only has the influence of *McFarlane* denied lower courts the ability to articulate more positive discourses around the experience of parenting a disabled child, but in the case of healthy children it has also denied 'the compatible social and legal reality that many conscientious responsible couples do not want children either at all or at particular times' (Dickens, 1990, p 87). However, the discourse of celebration/tragedy flowing from *McFarlane* denies much more than this; it is also saying something quite powerful about *particular* women. By contrast with the wrongful conception and birth cases involving *disabled* children where courts have emphasised women's emotional and caring role, in *McFarlane* rarely does one see any reference to the *mother*, or indeed her role as mother in caring for the healthy progeny in question. But in their denial of her caring role, we find that she is most certainly present in the judgment. Might it be significant that their Lordships repeatedly referred to the fact that the healthy child was 'loved', 'accepted' and 'welcomed'? Or, that their Lordships thought it 'absurd to distinguish between the claims of the father and mother' ([2000]:79)? Or that the House focused on the non-pecuniary benefits and *financial* costs of parenthood alone? Indeed, at the only point where a woman's role as 'mother' is explicitly acknowledged – and let us not forget that these are circumstances where she has taken invasive measures to avoid that very outcome – her labour merely becomes the inherent and non-compensable 'price of parenthood' (*per* Lord Millett: 114). As Atkins and Hoggett remark, this is:

> [A]n excellent illustration of how easy it is for the law to perceive the financial loss to the father who has to provide for an unplanned child, but not to the mother, who has to bring [the child] up . . . The law is not used to conceptualising the services of a wife and mother as labour which is worthy of hire.
>
> (Atkins and Hoggett, 1984, p 90)

Since *McFarlane* appears to embrace the notion that caring for (healthy) children is simply 'what women just do' (Graycar, 2002), this case might best be understood as fitting within a legal regime that has traditionally perpetu-ated the systematic devaluation of women's work within the family home.[15] However, since we are searching for 'serious' reasons to provide justificatory force for the exceptional treatment rendered to parents of disabled children in wrongful conception suits, and the differential treatment of women resulting from s 1(1)(d), such gendered assumptions (even if held by the 'commuter on the Underground') should be speedily dispensed with. So, once again, the question remains: what justifies the differential treatment of women in the cases of abortion and wrongful conception? While there are obvious differ-ences between these legal contexts, since s 1(1)(d) appears to have 'outcome' in mind, it seems fair to ask at a general level of both: what are the defining elements in law that make these particular outcomes serious, exceptional and harmful?

Of interest, a recent account by Rosamund Scott (2003) has attempted to address this question in a lengthy examination of the relationship between abortion and wrongful *birth*. Outlining her position, she notes that while accepting the value of reproductive autonomy ('broadly speaking'), 'the difficult question always concerns its limits' (Scott, 2003, p 300). In exami-ning the limits at present drawn in both wrongful birth and abortion, she argues that:

> [E]ven if the fetus is arguably not a moral person, unless we hold that it has no moral value there should be some moral justification for aborting it. This means that *reasons* should be offered to justify fetal demise. This can only plausibly occur when the reasons are of a good, that is, serious nature. Arguably, the question of the moral justification for aborting in such cases should be related to the seriousness of the condition which the prospective child might have. This is because serious conditions will significantly impact on parents' lives and hence seriously invoke their reproductive interests. In this way our perception of the appropriate extent of reproductive autonomy in this context might be related to the severity of the child's condition and the impact of that condition on the parents.
>
> (Scott, 2003, p 303)

Now these are truly intriguing claims; and at first sight, they appear fairly convincing. But the reason they appear initially convincing is that, ultimately, these are largely restatements, not justifications of the current position in wrongful birth, the law of abortion and the qualified version of the parental interests argument. Unsurprisingly then, many questions are left begging by this analysis. Why, for example, does Scott restrict 'serious reasons' to

15 See further Priaulx (forthcoming).

the 'serious' condition that the child might suffer from, if born? Furthermore, while it may well be true that caring for a seriously disabled child might significantly impact upon parents' lives, could this not be said of *any* unplanned child? And, even if committed to a 'gradualist view of foetal moral status' (Scott, 2003, p 303), might not the exercise of reproductive autonomy itself, by an individual already invested with full moral person-hood and legal rights, constitute a 'serious reason' for trumping the claim of a foetus who is 'arguably not a [full] moral person' (Scott, 2003, p 303)? Why then, morally speaking, should we be concerned about the presence of a serious foetal condition?

In truth, there is little here to provide us with an analytical tool by which to critique *or* justify existing law and the disparities between kinds of women under wrongful conception and the law of abortion. Without a careful and perhaps 'objective' explanation of what each instance of 'serious' actually means, it looks rather like a 'seriousness' loop. But Scott's analysis does demonstrate one useful point: the dangers of using 'serious reasons'. For example, what does it mean to invoke reproductive autonomy seriously? Do not all 'choices' to avoid reproduction matter, or deserve being taken seriously? And more specifically, how do we adjudge which choices are more important or 'serious' than others? If this question is to be answered by the consequences, as Scott's thesis implies, then it enters into very danger-ous territory, since what it does not answer is, who is the judge of 'serious reasons'?

At a more general level, however, arguably it is the failure to explicate such concepts which has seriously compromised women's reproductive autonomy, for all too quickly can the assumption of 'seriousness' become a mask to limit, override and control reproductive bodies. Beyond abortion, one can quickly point to alternative examples. The sterilisation of the intellectually disabled and enforced Caesarean section cases both provide examples where coercive medical practices were judicially authorised on the basis of prevent-ing some ulterior harm. Yet there is no doubt that at that time, judges con-sidered that the risk of a viable foetus's death, or of the world being 'swamped with incompetents' (*Buck v Bell* 274 US 200 (1927): 207), gave rise to conditions 'serious' enough to *override* autonomy interests. And similarly, as Emily Jackson's contribution to this collection illustrates, we can point to the hierarchical treatment of those seeking fertility services under s 13(5) of the 1990 Act; no doubt 'the need of that child for a father' also appeared to give rise to 'serious' enough concerns to render single and lesbian women's autonomy conditional.

As has been argued, few justifications for s 1(1)(d) appear convincing. So far, the only approaches that provide an internally coherent account are not only those that argue against the distinction in law but, more particularly, those that maintain that the maternal interests argument should allow abortion up to term irrespective of the foetal condition. And such a view,

I suggest, is more fully vindicated by an attention to context and a strong commitment to the value of reproductive autonomy.

TOWARDS A CONTEXTUAL APPROACH

> When considering the parenting of a child with a cognitive impairment, people seem to forget the fact that *every* child is more or less a burden to her parents. Children without impairments may cause stress to their parents due to problems . . . Families of children with impairments do not necessarily experience any more difficulties than families with so-called normal children – their problems are just different.
>
> (Vehmas, 2002, p 472)

Attempting to challenge notions of 'seriousness' is, perhaps, a thankless task; no doubt some at this stage may dispute a few of my claims: 'Of course the birth of a disabled child is more serious than a healthy child's birth!'. But to be clear at this stage, this chapter is not necessarily arguing otherwise. What *is* being argued is that the concept of 'seriousness', like 'harm', takes on an almost self-evident quality – we know what it is, or we'll know it when we see it. Yet, what I hope to have illustrated in part is that it is this very danger that should prompt us to ask a set of important questions: who decides what counts as 'serious', and by reference to what values? But it is not merely our tendency to rely on concepts which we think are 'intuitively' right that is the real problem; at the heart of the difficulty is the manner in which we measure notions of seriousness against what we think, by comparison, is 'non-serious' and draw rigid lines between them. And the wrongful conception case law provides a useful illustration of this.

As we saw earlier, Scott's analysis justified the existence of wrongful birth suits by virtue of the serious impact that a severely disabled child would have upon its parents. By comparison with the healthy children cases the outcome certainly sounds more serious, since in many cases parents will have a greater (and longer) caring, financial and emotional burden. Indeed, as the facts of the cases involving disabled children demonstrate, distinctions can be drawn. Take, for example, the facts of *Hardman v Amin* [2000] Lloyd's Rep Med 498, where the mother's caring burden involved 'spending almost all her waking hours attending to [the disabled child's needs]', or those of *Rand v East Dorset* (2000) BMLR 39, where the mother 'assumed almost total responsibility for the care and upbringing' of her disabled child, to the exclusion of her husband 'from all but very limited support and participation'; both provide female biographies which, as Janet Read suggests, are quite typical of the 'patterns of informal care provided by mothers and fathers of disabled children' (Read, 2000, p 52). And, as Hale LJ clearly recognised in her sensitive analysis in *Parkinson v St James' & Seacroft University Hospital*

NHS Trust [2001] 3 All ER 97, many of these cases do provide clear examples of where a disabled child raises a much more extensive burden, since s/he:

> [N]eeds extra care and extra expenditure. He is deemed on this analysis, to bring as much pleasure and as many advantages as does a normal healthy child. Frankly, in many cases, of which this may be one, this is much less likely. The additional stresses and strains can have seriously adverse effects upon the whole family, and not infrequently lead, as here, to the break up of the parents' relationship and detriment to other children.
>
> (*Parkinson* [2001]: [90])

If we now focus on the case of the healthy child and assume the opposite, we will have made our first mistake, albeit a simple one, because our intuition leads us to assume that health is the necessary opposite of disability and that it is the fact of disability that adds the additional burden, which is absent in 'other' cases. And, it is that very fact that tends to blind us to the real context of not only wrongful conception cases but also those of abortion: these individuals do not want *this* child at all. So, when these individuals' reproductive expectations fail, for whatever reason, quite simply, they all confront an additional financial, emotional and caring burden. A further dimension to these cases that we also tend to ignore – again possibly because we are so focused on finding the 'serious' case and weeding out its direct opposite – is that the legal subjects of the wrongful conception cases and of abortion law are individuals, with distinct biographies, different social circumstances, priorities and emotional make-ups. In the context of a wrongful conception case involving a disabled parent and *healthy* child, Waller LJ in *Rees v Darlington* [2002] EWCA Civ 88 elucidates the danger of forgetting this contextual dimension:

> Assume the mother with four children who had no support from husband, mother or siblings, and then compare her with the person who is disabled but who has a husband, siblings and a mother all willing to help. I think ordinary people would feel uncomfortable about the thought that it was simply disability which made a difference.
>
> (Rees [2002]: [53])

Parallels can be drawn. The hardship involved in caring for a child need not derive from the fact of 'disability' alone. Lone parenthood, coupled with a lack of social and familial support, typifies an analogous situation where individuals may honestly believe themselves to suffer exceptional hardship in caring for a healthy child, although to what extent will inevitably vary. So, in other words, if we can draw a distinction between the cases involving disability and those involving health, the difference lies not in the 'kind' of harm and burden these individuals suffer, but rather a contextual approach suggests that it can only be one of degree.

And this point cannot be emphasised enough; although Hale LJ remarks that 'the difference between a normal and a disabled child is primarily in the extra care that they need, although this may bring with it extra expenditure' (*Parkinson* [2001]: [94]), as she also acknowledges throughout her judgment in *Parkinson*, this is far from saying that caring for a healthy child is a harm-*less* experience. In a compelling essay, she details at length the severe loss of autonomy involved in pregnancy, childbirth and parenthood. Clearly critical of *McFarlane*, she comments that 'parental responsibility is not simply or even primarily a financial responsibility' ([2001]: [70]); but nor is it necessarily a shared responsibility. Illustrating that the burden of child care, 'in the greater majority of cases', typically falls upon women ([2001]: [93]), she emphasises that the burden of caring for *any* child is an extensive and enduring responsi-bility, since the 'obligation to provide or make acceptable and safe arrange-ments for the child's care and supervision lasts for 24 hours a day, 7 days a week, all year round, until the child becomes old enough to take care of himself' ([2001]: [71]). And this is a valuable point; as Amy Bernstein similarly argues, by contrast with the experience of pregnancy, motherhood is 'chronic' (Bernstein, 2001, p 173). Therefore, from a female perspective, the impact of *any* unwanted child endures well past childbirth; motherhood involves more than just biological capacity.

So, while the foregoing emphasises the need for context, where does this take us in the debates over s 1(1)(d)? As a consideration of the wrongful conception cases demonstrated, the categories of disability and health as indicators of harmful (or harmless) reproductive outcomes are deeply flawed; indeed, Scott's thesis of 'serious reasons', as we saw, failed to provide any explanatory power for maintaining a distinction between different kinds of women seeking abortion under s 1(1)(d). Not only is the logic of her thesis circular and dangerous, but more particularly, it fails to respond to one fun-damental criticism: even on a 'gradualist view' of foetal moral status, how can a foetus with no legal personality and a lesser moral claim to life ever trump the rights of the mother who is already invested with full legal rights and moral personhood?

Second, rather than assessing outcome by reference to foetal status, a closer attention to context and the actual differences between individuals serves to challenge the health/disability binary currently embraced within the existing law of abortion. But, that is not to say that the law has not been interested in context; it has. Not only does the law omit a consideration of social factors, through formulating abortion as a primarily 'medical phenomenon' (Sheldon, 1997, p 155), but when context does arise, 'it is often in extreme form: women who have been raped; living in poverty; whose health is threat-ened by additional children' (Boyle, 1997, p 114). What this suggests in the present context is that while abortion legislation has been preoccupied with the inevitable hardship that results from a medical conception of disability, a contextual and broader social view suggests that *any* unwanted child will bring about precisely the same kind of hardship: emotional, caring and financial. If any difference can be drawn between health and disability, in many cases (but not necessarily all) this will be one of extent.

But significantly, a further and final strand that arises out of this analysis is the degree to which the maternal interests argument currently embraced within abortion legislation is so deeply out of kilter with dominant ideas of reproductive autonomy elsewhere in medical law (Jackson, 2000). Indeed, even more recently in the field of wrongful conception, fairly promising lines of analysis are being developed to recognise that the failure of an individual's reproductive life plan constitutes a 'denial of an important aspect of their personal autonomy' (*Rees v Darlington* [2003] UKHL 52: [139]); and this analysis is notable in transcending the conceptual distinction drawn between health and disability. While in practice the approach has its problems, since the 'loss of autonomy' in question explicitly excludes the significant burden of caring for a child (Priaulx, 2004), it nevertheless illustrates a positive development in the field. Yet, in the law of abortion, we might reflect that existing legislation actually facilitates the denial of these important aspects of women's personal autonomy. Indeed, as Emily Jackson (2000) argues, judging a woman's reasons for seeking an abortion may be inconsistent with the 'priority currently granted to the common law principle of self-determination' (p 468). And, while a pregnant woman in labour is conceptualised as 'a patient with full rights of self-determination', even where her refusal to accept medical treatment may result in the death of a viable foetus (*St George's Healthcare NHS v S* [1998] 3 WLR 936), as Jackson asserts, a pregnant woman who has decided to terminate her pregnancy is constructed as:

> [A] woman whose potentially illegal act can be legitimized by the beneficent exercise of medical discretion. She has no right to make this particular decision about her medical treatment despite the fact that it is a firmly established legal principle that the choices of competent, adult patients must be respected even if they are foolish, misguided or immoral.
>
> (Jackson, 2000, p 478)

The varying levels of control afforded to pregnant women who, in principle, are no differently situated at all must surely give us good reason to rethink the shape of existing abortion legislation. And, insofar as this chapter has not touched on a wider variety of problems raised by existing abortion legislation, for example women's unequal access to abortion across the UK, or the 'gap' between abortion law and practice (see Lee, 2003), what has been demonstrated here, I hope, is that there are good reasons for thinking that the amended 1967 Act is not only flawed but is in need of significant revision.

Given the value of individual autonomy in all aspects of our lives, it is important that abortion is not left off the agenda, or worse, given a different agenda more restrictive than the one that currently exists. Therefore, if there is a commitment to creating a new framework, it is essential that its development not only reflects women's diverse and complex sexual lives, but importantly that the decision to have an abortion is one which can only 'properly be made by the pregnant woman herself'.

(Jackson, 2001, p 71)

CONCLUSION: BEYOND HEALTH AND DISABILITY

> When women have no duty to explain their reasons for terminating pregnancies, abortions based on disabilities do not exist in the eyes of legal authorities. In this situation, there is no need to frame an official policy stating that individuals with disabilities are inferior to individuals without them.
>
> (Häyry, as cited in Vehmas, 2002, p 474)

The absence of 'serious reasons' justifying the existence of s 1(1)(d) leaves the law susceptible to claims that it discriminates against particular *kinds* of women. Restricting women's access to abortion after the 24-week time limit is quite evidently based upon the assumed tragedy and potential hardship individuals will suffer if suspected foetal disability is realised at birth. And, on the face of these claims, the justification appeared to be one of 'maternal' interests. Yet, as this chapter has demonstrated, since English law maintains that 'the foetus' has no legal personality or rights until birth, this most certainly brings the maternal interests ground into question, since a woman's ability to terminate a pregnancy past 24 weeks is critically dependent upon which of the two classes of foetus *she* carries. In that sense, then, the 1967 Act is perhaps better described as recognising two distinct classes of women.

Yet, as the foregoing analysis has suggested, the justification for differential treatment of women is completely unsustainable, and this remains the case even if one deploys the idea that the birth of a disabled child will 'seriously impact' upon its parents. In this respect, in the context of abortion (and wrongful conception cases), it has been emphasised that the failure of a woman's reproductive desires will always necessarily result in an additional emotional, financial and caring burden if she continues to care for the child; and this is so irrespective of the child's health or disability. Therefore, if conceptions of 'hardship' guide the logic of s 1(1)(d), it is no longer possible, on either a 'maternal interests' basis or on categories of health or disability, to justify the continuing disparity of treatment between different kinds of women. As the analysis has shown, since notions of seriousness and hardship apply to any unwanted pregnancy that results in the responsibilities of parenthood, if there is a difference in the burden that does result, it will never be one of kind but of extent, contingent upon the individual's circumstances. If we think that there is value to providing women with real choices about their bodies and sexual lives, and are concerned about the lack of justification for s 1(1)(d), as well as the invidious (even if not discriminatory) premises which appear to underpin it, then an approach based on the value of reproductive autonomy which embraces these subtle considerations might well offer a more promising basis for future revision of the 1967 Act.

At the same time, there is a need to be conscious of the fact that some might take issue with where this analysis takes us, particularly where the political climate is increasingly geared up towards entertaining arguments supporting the *reduction* (rather than the removal) of the upper time limit for abortion.[16] Yet here, too, the reference point for such discussions is all too familiar: rather than an examination of women's lives and the inevitable repercussions such developments would wreak upon women's health, instead the argument centres on foetal viability and the ability of medical science to increase survival rates of premature babies. Therefore, the message that this chapter conveys must be seen as particularly important, for it is precisely this displacement of women's needs and lives that the argument takes issue with. Since a contextual approach based on reproductive autonomy coupled with the lack of legal personality afforded to the foetus strongly challenges the restrictive nature of maternal interests, there seems no convincing reason for maintaining a gestational time limit at all. But in addition to the claims made so far, there are at least three further reasons to argue that the removal of the gestational limit should be seriously considered. First, just because we 'dislike' the fact that women abort on grounds we strongly disapprove of, as Sharp and Earle argue, dislike 'has no moral force against her fundamental right' (Sharp and Earle, 2002, p 144). Second, as numerous commentators have pointed out (Jackson, 2001; Furedi and Lee, 2001), late abortion is not an easy 'choice' for women and in practice most seek terminations as soon as possible; very few abortions, beyond cases where foetal abnormality is detected at a typically late stage, take place after 24 weeks. But third, and connected to this, not only do 'women take pregnancy and parenting seriously', but 'the decision to end a pregnancy is one which is also taken seriously' (McLean, 1999). The culmination of these arguments suggests that anxiety on the basis that the removal of the gestational time limit will open the floodgates to late-term abortion is largely unfounded.

And one final note. Although recognising that this chapter relates to recent

---

16 Although note that British Medical Association representatives 'overwhelmingly' rejected a motion calling for the upper limit to be cut from 24 to 20 weeks in a recent vote (BBC News, 2005).

critiques of s 1(1)(d) by disability rights advocates who similarly contend that the law should not distinguish between the impaired and non-impaired foetus (Shakespeare, 1998), the intersection between the arguments developed here and those of the disability lobby is 'entirely accidental' (Sharp and Earle, 2002, p 141). In arguing from a feminist position, which also is committed to equal treatment between women, I should also note that my argument does not extend to denying women the opportunity to terminate on the grounds of foetal abnormality.[17] Rather, my view is that women should be entitled to determine precisely what happens to their sexual and reproductive bodies, at any point and on whatever grounds – it is simply a matter of a woman's individual choice. But, while this may constitute a significant point of departure from some disability rights critiques, this is not to say that I am unconcerned about the negative symbolism that the law maintains in treating disabled foetuses differently under s 1(1)(d). My sense is that even if this provision cannot be said to 'formally' discriminate *in utero*, it is nevertheless arguable that it does serve to discriminate against disabled individuals, since the policy of the law here is quite clearly shaped by *ex utero* considerations. Therefore, perhaps the removal of the gestational time limit offers the best way forward for both feminist and disability equality activists seeking to reframe existing abortion law. Although this will not remove many of the problems surrounding the continued differential treatment of either women or individuals with impairments in the field of reproduction, it does, I think, offer a valuable starting point.

REFERENCES

Abortion Statistics Summary, England and Wales (2003) *Statistical Bulletin* 2004/13

Atkins, S and Hoggett, B (1984) *Women and the Law* Oxford: Blackwell

Bailey, R (1996) 'Prenatal testing and the prevention of impairment: a woman's right to choose?' in Morris, J (ed) *Encounters With Strangers, Feminism & Disability*, London: Women's Press

Barnes, C, Mercer, G and Shakespeare, T (1999) *Exploring Disability* Oxford: Polity Press

BBC News (2005) 'Abortion time limit cut rejected' http://news.bbc.co.uk/go/pr/fr/–/–1/hi/health/4636991.stm (03/06/2005)

Bender, L (1993) 'Teaching feminist perspectives on health care ethics and law: a review essay' 61 U Cin LR 1251

Bernstein, A (2001) 'Motherhood, health status and health care' 11 *Women's Health Issues* 173

Biggs, H and Lee, E (1999) 'Editorial' in Biggs, H and Lee, E (eds) *Abortion, Ethics and the Law* Canterbury: University of Kent

---

17 For a discussion of the range of objections to abortions on these grounds, see Jackson (2000).

Boyle, M (1997) *Rethinking Abortion* London: Routledge

Brazier, M (2003) *Medicine, Patients and the Law* London: Penguin Books

Brownsword, R (2003) 'Regulating human genetics: new dilemmas for a new millennium' 12 *Medical Law Review* 14

Buchanan, A, Brock, D, Daniels, N and Winkler, D (2000) *From Chance to Choice, Genetics & Justice* Cambridge: Cambridge University Press

Deech, R (1998) 'Family law and genetics' 61 *Modern Law Review* 697

Dickens, B (1990) 'Wrongful birth and life, wrongful death before birth, and wrongful law' in McLean, S (ed) *Legal Issues in Human Reproduction* Aldershot: Dartmouth

Douglas, G (1991) *Law, Fertility & Reproduction* London: Sweet & Maxwell

DRC Statement (2004) 'Abortion Act "discriminatory" ', BBC News news.bbc.co.uk/1/hi/health/15–2827

Furedi, A (1999) 'Abortion for fetal abnormality' in Biggs, H and Lee, E (eds) *Abortion, Ethics and the Law* Canterbury: University of Kent

Furedi, A and Lee, E (2001) 'The case for "late" abortion' *Spiked On-Line*

Gillon, R (2001) 'Is there a "new ethics of abortion"?' 27 *Journal of Medical Ethics* 5–9

Graycar, R (2002) 'Sex, golf and stereotypes: measuring, valuing and imagining the body in court' 10 *TLJ* 205

Harris, J (1999) 'Ethics and abortion law' in Biggs, H and Lee, E (eds) *Abortion, Ethics and the Law* Canterbury: University of Kent

Hildt, E (2002) 'Autonomy and freedom of choice in prenatal diagnosis' 5 *Medicine, Health Care Phil* 65

Jackson, E (2000) 'Abortion, autonomy and prenatal diagnosis' 9 *Social and Legal Studies* 467–94

Jackson, E (2001) *Regulating Reproduction* Oxford: Hart Publishing

Lee, E (2003) 'Tensions in the regulation of abortion in Britain' 30 *Journal of Law and Society* 532–53

Lee, E and Davey, J (1998) 'Attitudes to abortion for foetal abnormality' Pro-Choice Forum

Mason, JK (1990) *Medico-Legal Aspects of Reproduction and Parenthood* Aldershot: Dartmouth

McLean, S (1999) *Old Law, New Medicine* New York: Pandora

Montgomery, J (2003) *Health Care Law* Oxford: Oxford University Press

Morgan, D (1990) 'Abortion: the unexamined ground' *Criminal Law Review* 687–94

Morris, J (1991) *Pride Against Prejudice* London: The Women's Press

Murphy, J (1991) 'Cosmetics, eugenics and ambivalence: the revision of the Abortion Act 1967' 5 *Journal of Social Welfare and Family Law* 375–93

Nelson, J (2000) 'Prenatal diagnosis, personal identity and disability' 10 *Kennedy Inst Ethic J* 231–8

Priaulx, N (2004) 'That's one heck of an "unruly horse"! Riding roughshod over autonomy in wrongful conception' 12 *Feminist Legal Studies* 317–31

Priaulx, N (forthcoming) *The Harm Paradox: Tort Law and the Unwanted Child in an Era of Choice* London: Routledge-Cavendish

Radcliffe-Richards, J (1999) 'Abortion on grounds of foetal abnormality' in Biggs, H and Lee, E (eds) *Abortion, Ethics and the Law* Canterbury: University of Kent

Read, J (2000) *The Family and Society, Listening to Mothers* Buckingham: Open University Press

Rothman, B (1988) *The Tentative Pregnancy* London: Pandora Press

Savulescu, J (2001) 'Is current practice around late termination of pregnancy eugenic and discriminatory? Maternal interests and abortion' 27 *Journal of Medical Ethics* 165–71

Scott, R (2003) 'Prenatal screening, autonomy and reasons: the relationship between the law of abortion and wrongful birth' 11 *Medical Law Review* 265–325

Shakespeare, T (1998) 'Choices and rights: eugenics, genetics and disability equality' 13 *Disability & Society* 665–81

Sharp, K and Earle, S (2002) 'Feminism, abortion and disability: irreconcilable differences?' 17 *Disability & Society* 137–45

Sheldon, S (1997) *Beyond Control* London: Pluto Press

Sheldon, S and Wilkinson, S (2001) 'Termination of pregnancy for foetal disability: are there grounds for a special exception in law?' 9 *Medical Law Review* 85–109

Vehmas, S (2002) 'Parental responsibility and the morality of selective abortion' 5 *Ethical Theor Moral Pract* 463–84

Chapter 11

The abortion debate today

Ellie Lee

INTRODUCTION

Abortion has become a hotly debated issue once again. A flurry of media comment attended a meeting in June 2006 between the head of the Catholic Church in England, Cardinal Cormac Murphy-O'Connor, and the Secretary of State for Health, Patricia Hewitt, where the former reportedly pressed for a re-opening of public debate on British abortion law (Vasagar, 2006). In 2005, there was extensive debate about whether politicians' stance on abortion should be an election issue. This politicisation of abortion has followed extensive media discussion about whether abortion after 12 weeks of pregnancy should be restricted because of 4D ultrasound images of a foetus apparently 'walking' and 'smiling', and of whether developments in the care of babies born very prematurely should lead to a reduction in the upper time limit for legal abortion. Abortion for foetal abnormality has also recently come under the spotlight because of claims that doctors acted unlawfully by aborting a foetus of 28 weeks' gestation diagnosed with cleft palate (Allison, 2003; Hume, 2003; Jepson, 2005; Palmer, 2005). There has been debate about the broadcast by Channel 4 in 2004 of an abortion procedure (Brown, 2004; Whittam Smith, 2004). 'Botched abortions', where 20- or 21-week-old foetuses have shown signs of life following abortion procedures, and allegations that abortion providers act illegally by providing women with information about a Spanish abortion clinic that will terminate pregnancies after 24 weeks' gestation have been the subject of controversy (Templeton and Rogers, 2004; BBC News Online, 2004; Foggo and Edwardes, 2004; Hume, 2004).

One central claim pressed in much of this discussion is that British abortion law needs to be changed. Under the current law, the 1967 Abortion Act, abortion can be legally performed up to 23 weeks and 6 days of a pregnancy (usually termed 24 weeks) where two doctors agree that the pregnancy, if continued, threatens the health of the woman or her family. After this point, it can only be provided where the life or health of the woman is at grave risk, or where there is substantial risk of serious abnormality in the foetus.[1] It is the legality of 'late' abortion that has attracted most recent criticism, with many who have commentated during most of the episodes mentioned above calling into question the legal provision of abortion up to 24 weeks.[2] After a long period of time when abortion law appeared to be a settled question in Britain (Lee, 2003a), it has thus re-emerged as a matter of public controversy. Public debate about abortion looks set to continue, in the media and also in the parliamentary arena.[3]

A striking aspect of current criticism of the abortion law is that it has not been only traditional abortion opponents that have provoked and encouraged it. Although the Catholic Church has provoked debate, the anti-abortion organisations SPUC and Life have played a relatively marginal role in turning

---

1 This is the 1967 Abortion Act (as amended by s 37 of the 1990 Human Fertilisation and Embryology Act), which states:

> A person shall not be guilty of an offence under the law relating to abortion when a pregnancy is terminated by a registered medical practitioner if two registered medical practitioners are of the opinion formed in good faith –
>
> (a) that the pregnancy has not exceeded its twenty-fourth week and that the continuance of the pregnancy would involve risk, greater than if the pregnancy were terminated, of injury to the physical or mental health of the pregnant woman or any existing children of her family; or
>
> (b) that the termination is necessary to prevent grave permanent injury to the physical or mental health of the pregnant woman; or
>
> (c) that the continuance of the pregnancy would involve risk to the life of the pregnant woman, greater than if the pregnancy were terminated; or
>
> (d) that there is substantial risk that if the child were born it would suffer from such physical or mental abnormalities as to be seriously handicapped.

2 A variety of alternatives have been proposed. These include 12 weeks by American feminist Naomi Campbell; 22 weeks by obstetrician Professor Stuart Campbell; 18 weeks by Secretary of State for Health John Reid; 20 weeks by Conservative Party leader Michael Howard; and 'as low as possible' by Conservative MP Anne Widdecombe.

3 Lord David Steel, who proposed the Bill that became the 1967 Abortion Act, has argued strongly this should happen. As part of its recommendations arising from its review of the 1990 Human Fertilisation and Embryology Act, the Parliamentary Science and Technology Committee has stated:

> We call on both Houses in the new Parliament to set up a joint committee to consider the scientific, medical and social changes in relation to abortion that have taken place since 1967, with a view to presenting options for new legislation. This committee should be broadly based and should include nominees from the Commons Select Committees for Science and Technology and Health and the Lords Science and Technology Committee.

In June 2006, Geraldine Smith, the Labour MP for Morecambe and Lunesdale, tabled a Commons motion calling on the Government to create a committee of MPs and peers to debate the abortion law and consider 'the scientific, medical and social changes in relation to abortion'. At the time of writing it had been signed by 31 MPs. The Government has, however, so far clearly rejected calls for such parliamentary debate. Health ministers and the Secretary of State for Health have stated unequivocally that the Government has no plans to re-open consideration of the abortion law.

late abortion into the issue it has become. Some journalists, in contrast, have acted as campaigning crusaders, presenting late abortion and those that provide it as unethical (Templeton, 2005; Day, 2004; Foggo and Edwardes, 2004; Templeton and Rogers, 2004; Gerard, 2004; Marsh, 2004). Drawing mainly on recent media coverage of this kind, the main purpose of this chapter is to offer a critical review of this abortion debate. We first provide some context for this review by considering the extent of and reasons for the demand from British women for 'late' abortion.

WHY DO WOMEN HAVE LATE ABORTIONS?

British law, unlike that of other jurisdictions, makes no distinction between abortions performed at any stage up to 24 weeks.[4] One response to the controversy about abortion being legal to this point has been that, in conjunction with a reduced upper time limit, abortion should be made legally available to women 'on request' in the first 12 weeks of pregnancy, on the grounds that this might considerably diminish demand for abortion at later gestations. Under this legal regime, where the woman is less than 12 weeks pregnant she would not need two doctors to agree 'in good faith' that an abortion should be provided, as the current law requires (see fn 1). Presumably her simple consent to treatment would become sufficient for the procedure to take place. After that, the law would stay as it is, but the upper time limit for abortion would be reduced.

Lord David Steel, who as an MP proposed the bill that became the 1967 Abortion Act, is one advocate of this reform.[5] In response to hostility to late abortion he has argued that abortion needs to be provided 'as early as possible', but that because of the 'two doctors' requirement, sometimes this does not happen. 'The requirement [that two doctors agree to all abortion requests] has led in some cases to delay,' he has claimed, thus pushing some abortions later into pregnancy (Steel, 2004). In other words, the law as it stands is presented as a reason why abortions after 12 weeks of pregnancy occur, and it is suggested that if it were changed there would be fewer of them. Lord Steel notes that the anti-abortion lobby will not agree with his solution to the incidence of late abortion. But he implies it could do much to defuse others' objections, since this way the need for late abortion could be minimised.

---

4 There is a great deal of difference in practice, however. While early abortion is provided across Britain in NHS hospitals, most only provide up to 18 weeks of pregnancy at most. After this, abortion is provided by specialist agencies, primarily the British Pregnancy Advisory Service, who sometimes have to turn away women who are within the legal time limit for abortion because of lack of appointments.

5 It has also been reported that the abortion provider Marie Stopes International would accept this kind of reform (Templeton, 2005; Marie Stopes International, 2005).

Steel is right that the contention that abortion should be provided to women as early as possible is unobjectionable to all except those who oppose abortion in principle, and this is now a small minority in Britain. For a variety of reasons, including growing concern about sexual health and teenage pregnancy and social anxiety about 'problem parents', there is widespread pragmatic acceptance of early abortion (Lee, 2004). Early abortion is generally considered 'wrong but the right thing to do'; it is disliked in the abstract but accepted in practice as a backup if contraception fails (Furedi, 1998). The claim that later abortions are mostly a product of the law allowing doctors to make it difficult for women to access earlier ones is not borne out by the evidence, however.

A legal question?

There is no doubt that in the past women experienced significant problems obtaining abortion because the law places access to the procedure in doctors' hands (Lane Committee, 1974). Both family doctors and hospital gynaecologists made it difficult for women to obtain abortion, and indeed the independent abortion provider British Pregnancy Advisory Service (BPAS) was established soon after the Abortion Act was passed to provide abortion outside the NHS because of this. Changes in medical opinion (Paintin, 1998) and developments in service provision (Lee, 2004) have made this a less significant part of women's experience, however. Over the past decade, as a result of policies pursued by the Royal College of Obstetricians and Gynaecologists (2000) and the Department of Health (2001), early abortion has become more accessible. Almost 90 per cent of women seeking abortion already terminate pregnancies within the first 12 weeks.

Arguably, it is the organisation of the abortion service rather than the law that is a more significant factor in generating the delays to women's access to early abortion that still pertain. Local NHS services are unable to meet demand and in a small number of places are all but non-existent (All-Party Parliamentary Pro-Choice and Sexual Health Group, 2004). It is not clear that legal change would address these outstanding problems, but they could be addressed within the current legal framework.

There is, most importantly, a demand for late abortion that neither legal nor service modifications will remove. Despite the changes that have taken place in the abortion service over the years, the proportion of abortions provided at 20 weeks and over has remained almost constant, at between 1 and 1.5 per cent (Clements, 2004). Taking the second trimester (weeks 13–24) as a whole, it has been found that only 13 per cent of abortions during this time could have been managed earlier by service improvements (George and Randall, 1996). This suggests that while some women will have abortion earlier if abortion services make it easier for them to access, most of the demand for late abortion will not 'go away' even if the law were to change.

Women who terminate pregnancies later in gestation fall into three categories, other than those affected by delays in obtaining abortion (Lee, 2005). There are women for whom the foetus is found to be seriously abnormal. Far more babies are born with abnormalities than are affected pregnancies terminated. At all stages of pregnancy, only just over 1 per cent of abortions are performed for foetal abnormality and more than 60 per cent of these take place before the nineteenth week. The number of abortions for this reason at around or after 24 weeks is thus very low. Termination rates for abnormality also reflect the severity of the condition. It is noteworthy that of just under 600 cases of cleft palate notified in 2001, only two were terminated pregnancies, the remainder being still or live births (Statham *et al*, 2004). (This calls into question the claim made in recent debate about an abortion carried out for cleft palate that there is a trend to 'eugenic' attitudes on the part of pregnant women and gynaecologists.)

More late abortions occur where women fail to recognise the pregnancy early on, largely because of issues associated with contraceptive use. There are also women who know they are pregnant but delay seeking an abortion because of indecision, apprehension, failure of anticipated emotional or economic support (from family, partner and employer) and unanticipated changes in circumstances. Recent research indicates how some of these factors result in second trimester abortions (Lee *et al*, 2004). One woman, aged 17, who had an abortion at 20 weeks, explained:

> I started on the pill about the end of August. I'd never been on the pill before. I didn't know what to expect. When I'd been to the GP I'd worked out I was two months pregnant, then I went in to have the internal examination and he [the doctor] was like, 'well actually you're more like four and a half months pregnant'. I hadn't known, 'cause I hadn't been having my periods normally.

Another, also 17, knew she was pregnant at eight weeks, but had an abortion at 19 weeks. She said:

> I told my partner, he seemed all right with it as well. But then I started getting mixed feelings about whether or not I should keep it and I started coming up with all the reasons in my head, it's from there it started to change.

An ongoing study (Lee *et al*, unpublished) highlights other aspects of women's experience. One counsellor who works for an abortion provider described the situation of a woman she had recently counselled this way:

> A recent one, that was a planned pregnancy, very much wanted. She was about 23 weeks. And her husband said he was leaving her for her best friend. She just couldn't continue. She just couldn't have his baby. She just wept, and wept and wept.

Most women who abort a pregnancy later on do not request abortion until they are more than 12 weeks pregnant. The proposal for abortion on request in early pregnancy is therefore unlikely to have the practical outcome its proponents assume it will. Implicit in the proposal for abortion on request to 12 weeks is another assumption too, that where women request abortion after 12 weeks, their request for abortion should be considered by the law as significantly different to that made before this point. There is also no self-evident reason why this should be the case, since a woman who is over 12 weeks pregnant is not necessarily less well equipped to undergo abortion at her request than the woman who is not. The claim that abortion later in pregnancy is significantly different to that earlier on has illuminated most recent controversy, however, and in the remainder of this chapter we discuss the case made by proponents of this view.

WHAT'S WRONG WITH LATE ABORTIONS?

The notion that there should even be consideration of the idea that, after 12 weeks of pregnancy, abortion could be made available at a woman's request runs contrary to the spirit of much recent debate. That women have abortions at later gestational stages *at all* has been widely presented as a source of discomfort, with the main legal recommendation being pressed that the upper time limit for abortion should be reduced. One main claim has been made to justify this case: developments in science and medicine, it has been argued, mean the existing limit is too high. 'Advances in the care of pre-mature babies mean that a handful now survive at 22 weeks' gestation. This change, and the photographs . . . of foetuses moving and even appearing to walk in the womb are behind the rethink [of the upper time limit]', explained *The Times* (Webster and Hawkes, 2004).

Some have thus argued that images of the foetus generated by 3D and 4D ultrasound, given high visibility through extensive media coverage of them, mean that the law should change. Others emphasise the significance of medical technology associated with premature babies (Day, 2004). As *The Sunday Times* put it of the latter issue, there is a 'reason for unease' about the abortion law because:

> Medical technology has advanced to the point where it is possible . . . to save the life of a baby at 24 weeks of gestation . . . Yet while a foetus is being saved in one operating theatre, a termination for 'social reasons'

may well be taking place in the next theatre on a foetus at exactly the same stage of gestation.

(Driscoll and Rogers, 2004)

Allison Pearson, columnist for the London *Evening Standard*, has made the same point in more sensationalist terms: 'How can we have a situation where premature units are spending thousands a day fighting to save 23-week foetuses while, down the same corridor, a baby of the same gestation is being induced, then chucked in the incinerator?' she asks (Pearson, 2005).[6]

Some also argue that law *should* be decided by what science suggests. Argued an editorial in the *Evening Standard* following its publication of 4D ultrasound images of the foetus, 'The arguments over the appropriateness of the 24 week limit will continue and it is right that debate over morality should follow advances in science' (*Evening Standard*, 2004). Mark Henderson (2004), science correspondent for *The Times*, has made this case particularly clearly, claiming that recent debate about abortion forces those of a 'liberal persuasion' to reconsider the abortion law.

Science, he contends, can provide 'a compassionate answer' to the abortion question which is 'considerably subtler than either traditional pro-choice or pro-life positions'. 'As scientists learn more and more about human gestation', he argues, 'it is difficult to hold that the choice to abort in the early weeks of pregnancy is qualitatively much different from contraception.' But, he continues, 'the science does not all point one way . . . it is increasingly hard to justify abortions after 20 weeks unless there is compelling medical need', because of what science tells us about foetal development at this stage. The 'subtle answer' to the abortion issue, therefore, would be one that finds existing law 'at once too liberal and too strict', and points instead to abortion being treated much like contraception early on but with access to abortion more restricted later in pregnancy.

Media discussion about abortion has reached a point where claims that science and medicine have run ahead of the law have been repeated so often they appear like 'common sense'. It is interesting that these claims have become dominant, since evidence suggests the impression they give of recent medical developments is hard to sustain.

6 This 'ethical problem' is in fact something of a fiction. A major development in abortion provision in Britain is separation of neonatal care and abortion procedures, the latter being almost entirely provided for in the independent sector (Clements, 2004). It is not therefore the case that in NHS hospitals doctors are routinely saving the life of just viable foetuses in one room while others 'take the life' of other foetuses of the same gestation down the corridor.

Science and foetal development

3D and 4D ultrasound images have been widely portrayed as a 'revelation' and 'astonishing', and it has been argued they show us that the foetus is more developed at an early gestational stage than had been assumed (Marsh, 2004; Smith, 2004). The notion that a foetus is more baby-like than has previously been considered is the implication, suggesting that abortion is more like infanticide than the law currently suggests. Yet while it may be the case that those who have not seen images of the foetus before find 3D and 4D foetal images a 'revelation', the novelty of what they indicate can be considered overstated.

It has been known for many years that the developing foetus has manifestly human characteristics from an early point. Fifteen years ago, Swedish photographer Lennart Nilsson's photographs tracking a pregnancy from ovulation to birth provided a 'window on the womb' and demonstrated the process of foetal development in great detail, indicating that these characteristics are apparent in the foetus in the very early weeks. If it is no revelation that the developing human foetus looks human, it has also been argued that 4D ultrasound does not contribute to medical understanding of foetal development. As Professor Alan Templeton of the Royal College of Obstetricians and Gynaecologists has explained it, while what new ultrasound images show us 'is of great interest physiologically', the images do not change 'anything about the time of viability' and do not change 'development stages of the foetus' (Adam, 2004).

One particular claim that has been made of the significance of these images is that they indicate early emotional development. Professor Stuart Campbell, who provided the press with 3D and 4D images, has thus argued of his images that show the foetus 'smiling', 'I can't believe a baby smiling in the womb is not showing happiness' (Smith, 2004). This claim, as Campbell's own phrasing makes apparent, is speculation based on his impressions of the movement of foetal facial muscles. Scientific evidence amassed through research about pain questions the basis for this interpretation of what ultrasound images have captured. As one pain specialist has pointed out, the difficulty with any attempt to assess foetal experience is that there is no 'painometer' that can be used to measure it accurately (Derbyshire, 2005). It has been argued nevertheless that the concept of 'foetal pain', and by extension that of 'foetal happiness', is misleading (Derbyshire and Furedi, 1996; Derbyshire, 2004).

The distinction, it is argued, should be made between foetal movement, reflexes and response to stimuli that occur in the womb and 'true pain experience' (Fitzgerald, 1995). The experience of pain involves anatomical responses the structures for which are in place by 26 weeks' gestation (RCOG, 1997). Pain, however, is much more than an anatomical response. This feeling, like other emotions, while dependent upon the neural system that is developed in the foetus, requires *psychological* development. Emotion is not simply biological, but is a complex aspect of human experience that requires interaction with the world 'beyond the brain and outside the womb' before it can exist (Derbyshire, 2004). It is, explains Derbyshire, 'an experience we have spent a good part of our psychological development learning to recognise'. 'True pain experience', as Fitzgerald (1995) has explained, is therefore not available to the foetus. '[It develops] postnatally along with memory, anxiety and other cognitive brain functions.'

The images that result from new ultrasound technology are fascinating and captivating because of their clarity, but claims about foetal development that have arisen from them appear, in this light, misplaced. The images show us in great detail the amazing process of foetal development. Over the 40 weeks of a pregnancy, a waking, aware baby emerges from a small ball of cells, and a whole range of points during this time are important developmental milestones. Regardless of how astounding foetal development is, however, 'there can be no question that foetal development is limited . . . seeking an equivalence between foetus and baby . . . is bound to produce disappointment and exaggeration' (Derbyshire, 2005).

What of viability? The British Association of Perinatal Medicine (BAPM) considers that infants born at 22–<28 weeks gestation (weighing approximately equivalent to 500–1000 g) have 'threshold viability' (BAPM, 2000). It is only at this gestational stage that foetuses stand any chance of survival beyond neonatal care. Much media coverage has been given to so-called 'miracle babies' born at 22 or 23 weeks, and it has been claimed in recent discussion that 'viability has come down' in recent years. The results of studies have, however, been described in contrast in far less certain terms as 'difficult to assess', since most involve relatively small numbers of infants, particularly at 24 weeks or less, and differ in their design (Rivers et al, 2004).

The picture overall seems to be that survival after birth at 24–28 or more weeks has improved since the early 1990s through developments in neonatal intensive care that include better provision of respiratory and circulatory support, surfactant usage and nutrition. There is no evidence of any increase in survival at gestations of 22 weeks or less (Evans and Levene, 2001; Macfarlane et al, 2003) and survival at 23 weeks is still rare. The inability of the foetal lungs to expand, and to permit oxygen transfer, prevents survival before 22–23 weeks and cannot be overcome with the technology currently available. The most detailed study of outcomes for premature babies shows that infants born in Great Britain and Ireland have survival rates of 0 per cent at 21 weeks, and about 1 per cent at 22 weeks, 11 per cent at 23 weeks and 26 per cent at 24 weeks, where survival is defined as discharge from hospital. One-quarter of children born at less than 26 weeks have severe disabilities at age two and a half and 40 per cent moderate to severe problems in cognitive development at age six (Costeloe et al, 2000).

As a result, the RCOG advises that it is professionally acceptable not to attempt to support life in foetuses expelled before 22 weeks' gestation, and that clinicians must distinguish between physiological movements and signs of life and be aware that movement of the expelled foetus may be of a reflex nature, not a sign of life or viability (RCOG, 1999). It is strongly emphasised in guidelines for clinicians dealing with parents of babies born at the point of 'threshold viability' that it is essential that they are encouraged to have 'appropriate and realistic' expectations regarding survival, and also later health outcomes (BAPM, 2000). Guidelines make it very clear that there are no certainties where babies are born so early, and that in all respects medical care in these situations is extremely taxing for all concerned.

The claim that 'science has run ahead of the law' appears overblown in the face of sober assessment. This suggests that the argument that science and medicine tells us the law needs to change is less an objective assessment of medical and scientific change than an argument about the problem of abortion couched in the language of medicine. It can be thought of as an approach that medicalises the abortion problem and its resolution. Why has this approach become so prominent?

Medicalisation

The medicalisation of the abortion argument is certainly not new. It has been identified as a relatively longstanding aspect of anti-abortion strategy (Franklin, 1991). Abortion opponents have emphasised for many years that 'abortion stops a beating heart' and have drawn attention to such medical facts as foetal response to stimuli such as sound. Anti-abortionists have made extensive use of ultrasound images for many years, albeit of a lower quality than those now available, to show that a developing foetus looks like a baby (Petchesky, 1987). Campaigns against abortion in the 1980s, for example that in support of MP David Alton's Bill that aimed to lower the time limit for abortion to 18 weeks, were accompanied by images of 'dancing babies'. Over the last decade anti-abortionists have frequently claimed that science has proven the foetus feels pain, and also that women suffer medical problems following abortion (Lee, 2003b).

The extent to which science and medicine have become the key motif in arguments about abortion is striking, however, and in particular it is notable how those with no formal association with the anti-abortion movement now justify legal restrictions in medicalised terms. Claims that make a medical case for changing the law are, as the discussion above has indicated, ubiquitous. The assumption that there are new developments in regard to foetal development that must be taken into account and the perception that the foetus is more like a born baby earlier on than was previously thought carry a great deal of social and cultural weight. Notably, even some feminists more known for their hostility to medicalisation have become advocates of a lowered time limit for abortion because of 'what medicine and science tells us' (Wolf, 2004; Pearson, 2005). If this widespread adoption of appeals to 'science' in the abortion debate cannot be accounted for by the reality of scientific and medical change, how can it be explained? It can perhaps best be understood as a reflection of a sensibility of discomfort with forms of moral authority that are perceived to have helped shape the abortion debate in the past.

One kind of moral authority now largely eschewed is religion. Religion is a minority preoccupation in Britain, and recent research shows that only 33 per cent of Britons believe the church offers answers to moral problems (Elliott, 2005; Davies, 1992). It is perhaps for this reason that in order to try and find some resonance with a waning audience, even churchmen adopt medical-sounding arguments to express their distaste for abortion. The Archbishop of Canterbury's contribution to discussion of whether abortion should be an election issue thus included the claim that a foetus is a 'natural candidate for "rights" of some kind' not for religious reasons but because of 'evidence about foetal sensitivity to outside stimuli (including pain), the nature of foetal consciousness [and] expanding possibilities of saving early foetal life outside the womb' (Williams, 2005).

Religion is also a mostly middle-class preoccupation, and thus influences a sector of society that has been, and remains, the least hostile to abortion (Furedi, 2005). One influence over the outcome of unplanned pregnancies is the effect that childbearing can have for women's educational and employment prospects. Middle-class women, especially young middle-class women, are, as a result, proportionately more likely to terminate pregnancies than those from less socially advantaged backgrounds (Lee *et al*, 2004). This means that many who describe themselves as 'religious' do not necessarily give their faith reflection in their attitudes to abortion. It is certainly the case that absolutist arguments against abortion, for example as espoused by the Catholic Church, have a small British audience receptive to them. The label 'pro-life' is one that few want to embrace, but it may be that those who oppose all abortion on moral terms consider their arguments will gain a wider hearing when couched in the language of science and medicine.

Ambivalence and discomfort about 'pro-life' claims is increasingly accompanied, however, by rejection of the other source of moral authority in modern abortion debate, that of the idea of individual choice. Indeed, because it is expressed by those who suggest they consider themselves broadly 'liberal', it is the vocalised discomfort about giving the pregnant woman the 'right to choose' that is the most striking development of the recent abortion controversy. As veteran anti-abortion MP Anne Widdecombe has observed, 'It is pro-choice people who have re-ignited the debate' (Curti, 2004). The distinctive aspect of the current abortion debate is the representation of the idea of choice as a problem by those who also self-consciously distance themselves from the 'pro-life' position.

The Times science columnist Mark Henderson's comments, for example, indicate a sensibility that it is desirable to find a 'third way' that accepts abortion but not the 'right to choose'. As noted above, he believes that science provides answers for liberals that are 'considerably subtler than either traditional pro-choice or pro-life positions'. What is 'subtle', he contends, is to argue women have rights – but only up to a point. What is 'traditional' (thus outdated and increasingly irrelevant) is a view which holds that a woman's right to choose holds so long as she is pregnant. Journalist Jasper Gerard is a self-described 'liberal' critic of abortion, and he provides a particularly good example of this approach. 'Those of us of broadly liberal opinion find ourselves painfully torn: we do not wish to fall into the cold, churchy dogma, lampooned by Monty Python, that "every sperm is sacred" ', he argues, expressing his sense of distance from religion. But, he continues, 'the glib feminist refrain, "it's woman's right to choose" has had a free ride for too long'.

Some feminists have come to agree, and now also draw on claims about medicine and science to reject this 'refrain'. Feminist novelist and journalist Allison Pearson has thus described the 'pro-choice camp' as 'belligerent' in its assertion that 'you have a right to choose and that's the end of it'. This, she argues, is untenable when foetuses can survive at 23 weeks. '[If] a foetus has the capacity to live outside the womb, then an abortion is killing it', she states: 'Who would defend the "right to choose" that?' She thus argues for the 'sensible, humane, move' of reducing the upper limit for abortion to 20 weeks. Feminist commentator Yasmin Alibhai-Brown argues that in the light of 4D ultrasound images, she wishes she'd 'been less casual about my abortions', that 'there was something callous, selfish and unnatural about prochoice rhetoric and the practice "of abortion" itself', and that abortion should be accompanied by 'remorse' (Alibhai-Brown, 2004).

American feminist Naomi Wolf is the feminist with the highest profile who has indicated her disenchantment with the idea of choice and argued for restricting access to late abortion on 'medical' grounds. Wolf (2004) has written for British newspapers in the light of Julia Black's documentary *My Foetus*, which showed footage of an early abortion and also images of foetuses aborted at later gestational stages. Julia Black had argued that the documentary would allow people, especially those who are pro-choice, to become 'more aware' of the 'reality' of abortion, namely that it involves the destruction of foetal life. Agreeing with the need for the consciousness of those who are pro-choice to be raised in this way, Wolf wrote of her own experience that she was previously 'uncritically in favour of abortion'. 'I had something of a conversion when I was pregnant', she continued, however, explaining that, 'The amazing technology now available in early pregnancy means that we know more about the development of the foetus. Abortion does end a beating heart.' Her conclusion, on this basis and because of developments in neonatal technology, is that the 24-week time limit is 'too generous'. Women's choice to have an abortion should therefore be restricted. After three months, 'a network of supportive adoption agencies should be on hand to help and sustain the pregnant woman and her baby', she argues.

Medicalisation, in the current abortion debate, thus seems to be a process driven in part at least by a reaction against the idea of choice. What should be made of this development? It can certainly be argued that there are problems with its proponents' consequent lack of accuracy and objectivity regarding medical developments. It does not help the abortion debate when the truth of what science suggests and what medical advance has generated is mis-represented. Other criticisms of this hostility to the idea of choice can also be made.

What's wrong with choice?

Taking claims made by some feminist commentators first, while presented in the language of medicine, it is their personal experience of a wanted pregnancy that animates their case. It was Naomi Wolf's own experience of being pregnant and seeing the foetus on a screen during an ultrasound scan, for example, that made her reject her previous support for choice. Allison Pearson similarly argues that it is the experience of women like her, who 'have modified our ideas about abortion after having our own babies', that means she had a case that there should be a change to the law. Julia Black's docu-mentary is tellingly entitled *My Foetus*, its making being motivated by her own experience of pregnancy. Feminists making claims against late abortion therefore do so on the basis of their own feelings and experiences of a wanted pregnancy.

This can be put another way: these claims are based upon a failure to recognise the experience and perceptions of other women whose pregnancy is unwanted, or where the pregnancy is wanted but foetal abnormality is diag-nosed. When Allison Pearson rhetorically asks, 'Who could want the "right to choose" to terminate that' of a 23 week pregnancy, this is precisely what she displays. It is this deficit in understanding that also accounts for her claim that it is a problem for doctors to both try to save the lives of premature babies and perform late abortions.

There are women with wanted pregnancies whose babies are born early. There are women with unwanted pregnancies or for whom there has been a diagnosis of foetal abnormality seeking abortion. These different groups of women have varying needs, but why should medicine only strive to address those of one group? It can be considered moral and right for medical practice to fight as hard as it can to save babies born early to women from the first group and also help women who do not want to be pregnant terminate their pregnancies.

An approach that cannot see this point demonstrates a very troubling inability to take seriously the concept of individual autonomy, this being apparently overwhelmed by self-absorbed emotionalism born of the experience of motherhood. In effect, what is being said on the basis of this experience is that the perceptions of those women who seek abortion count for little. Their feelings about the prospect of continuing a pregnancy they feel very negatively towards, of giving birth and becoming a mother should be ignored, indeed to the point that the woman concerned should be prosecuted under the criminal law if she acted upon her own feelings about her pregnancy and sought to terminate it.

This feminist sensibility has been rightly described as narcissistic in spirit – as the 'it's all about me' approach to abortion – and criticised on the grounds that such 'increasing subjectivism' provides no proper rationale for restricting the choices of others (Bristow, 2005; Aaronovitch, 2005). One of the difficulties in attempting to discuss the contemporary reaction against choice is, indeed, that it often appears driven more by inchoate feelings and sentiments of this kind than research and reason. Developing his case for rejecting 'the right to choose' further, Jasper Gerard, for example, explains his 'problem' with late abortion this way:

> There seems to be a culture where getting an abortion is just another side of our supermarket culture, where girls pop in for a packet of Marlboro Lights and a termination . . . The permissive society was meant to be life enhancing. Broadly I still support it. But as my wife prepares to give birth, just thinking of an abortion makes me shudder.
>
> (Gerard, 2004)

Again, a commentator's feelings about a wanted pregnancy continued to term are referred to as if they constitute valid grounds for restricting abortion when requested by women whose pregnancies are unwanted.

The other claim made here is that 'getting abortion is just another side of our supermarket culture'. In other words, it is necessary to restrict late abortion because it is symptomatic of moral slippage. This perception of late abortion is relatively commonplace. The editor of *The Sunday Times*, for example, writes of 'remarkable photographs of fetuses in the womb' and babies born at 24 weeks that survive. He indicates that while he is no opponent of legal abortion – 'there is an argument for making early abortions easier' he suggests – the case for a lower upper limit is a 'powerful one'. This is because later abortion signifies 'fecklessness', he argues, citing the fact that women have abortions after 12 weeks because 'they discover their boyfriend is having an affair' or 'it has taken a long time to make up their mind' as evidence that this is the case (*The Sunday Times*, 2004).

It is true that those women who have abortions later in pregnancy do so because they have specific circumstances, such as their partner's infidelity, that drive them to conclude that it is better if their pregnancy does not result in the birth of a child. The perception that what women experience when they choose to do so is feckless, thoughtless or similar to the experience of buying cigarettes is, however, bizarre.

As gestation proceeds, as has been noted already, requests for abortion decline dramatically in number, with around 2,500 of an annual total of 180,000 (about 1.6 per cent) performed at 20 weeks and over in Britain (Clements, 2004). This distribution of abortion procedures, weighted very strongly to the early weeks of pregnancy, occurs because women, together with those doctors who perform abortions, feel that abortion is less of an option as pregnancies proceed. The small demand for late abortion is a reflection of this feeling, not the law. (Indeed, were there to be no law at all, it is highly unlikely that the distribution of abortion procedures would change.) Pregnant women do not want late abortions. They are very aware of the process of foetal development taking place within their bodies and know what a late abortion will entail, and so do not request late abortion often or lightly. Those women who do seek late abortion are not 'feckless' and immune to these same feelings. They are, however, strongly compelled to end their pregnancy, since they consider abortion the most responsible option.

The claim that there is a 'powerful case' for legal change to restrict the 'fecklessness' of this small group of women is unsustainable. There is no need for the law to do more to restrain women's urges to terminate 23-week pregnancies. There are, however, compelling reasons for accepting that women should be able to have abortions at this stage. The right for women to make the choice to do so is certainly dissimilar to other rights for women. It will obviously not be experienced as liberating in the same way as, for example, the right to vote. When acted upon it will involve terminating a pregnancy that most likely will have been public knowledge, where foetal movements will have been felt by the woman and where she will then undergo labour and give birth to a dead foetus. Nonetheless, denying a woman the right to make this choice can be considered a negative act.

In direct contrast to the representation of choice as ethically suspect, it can be argued that just the opposite is true. As Furedi has argued, choice matters, 'because the ability to make choices, to weigh up values and decide on the rightness of them, is one of the things that differentiates us from animals; it makes us human and defines us as adults' (Furedi, 2005). To deny the woman this ability to choose – even where it means undergoing the process of a late abortion – would thus undermine entirely a central aspect of her existence as a responsible, adult human being. The current reaction against the idea of choice more than anything else indicates a loss of appreciation of what makes us human and what defines adulthood and responsibility.

CONCLUSIONS

It is right that society debates its abortion laws, and further debate is neces-sary and very welcome. It is hard to tell what the outcome of the current abortion debate for the law will be, but in order to take discussion further there is a need for contest over the unhelpful direction in which much media discussion has taken debate so far. It is important in particular that the medicalisation of the abortion debate is confronted.

The central issue for the law is: who decides? Who should be given the legal authority to judge whether a pregnancy can be terminated? The domin-ant answer in the abortion debate today, as this chapter has illustrated, is for the claim to be made that it should be medicine and science. While this answer may appear objective and even progressive, it brings with it some dangerous pitfalls. As Derbyshire has suggested, 'The question of who should and should not continue a pregnancy is not one that science can resolve. Trying to do so is likely to produce both bad science and bad law' (Derbyshire, 2005).

Bad science may result because, as indicated above, medicalisation is associated with a tendency to exaggerate and misrepresent scientific and med-ical change. It is to the benefit of no one – least of all to the project of science and to the work of clinicians – that overblown claims have become so domin-ant. The impression generated so far is certainly unhelpful for those who give birth to premature babies and for the doctors who care for them, as well as for women seeking late abortion.

Medicalisation is also bad for the law, since it encourages questions that need to be central to the law to be set aside. As this chapter has indicated, medicalisation is a product of cultural and social developments, not medical ones. It is discomfort with existing moral precepts that is driving medicalisa-tion, in particular, disenchantment with the idea of choice. While this dis-comfort and disenchantment takes the form of medicalised arguments, it is based in an incoherent and often irrational reaction against the idea of choice. Those who make arguments on this basis display perceptions of women who have abortions that are wildly inaccurate, and also often begin from a subjectivist starting point. Law based on this reaction against choice would not seem to have much to recommend it. If the law concedes ground to this anti-choice sensibility, it will also mean it proceeds in a direction entirely at odds with medical law in general, which more and more tends to accept the primacy of patient autonomy and individual choice.

In the recent debate, one response to this cultural development advocates a legal solution that attempts to defuse negativity about late abortion by argu-ing that there should be abortion on request at early stages of pregnancy, with access more restricted later. While this may seem appealing, it does not take into account evidence regarding why women seek abortion when they do. Like any proposal that includes a reduced upper limit for abortion, its consequence in practice would be that women who request abortion will be forced by law to continue unwanted pregnancies, and it is important to be honest that this would be the outcome. Further, this proposal accepts rather than confronts the claim that there should be a reduced upper limit. This proposal therefore also endorses what this chapter has argued is most significant of all about the turn away from choice, namely a weakening of understanding of the connection between the idea of choice and adulthood and responsibility.

The problem identified through the discussion above is that, above all, it is the loss of this connection that is the significant development of contemporary culture. The outcome of the abortion debate from now on – specifically, whether there is or there is not a reduction in the upper limit for abortion – will be indicative of what view is taken in this regard. It will tell us whether society agrees with the critics of late abortion that choice-making is dangerous for society and needs to be reined in, or whether, on the contrary, it considers choice-making a positive contribution to society that makes people more moral, adult and responsible.

REFERENCES

Aaronovitch, D (2005) 'Let women decide for themselves' *Guardian*, 15 March

Adam, D (2004) 'Scanner pioneer urges curb on abortion' *Guardian*, 29 June

Alibhai-Brown, Y (2004) 'I wish I'd been less casual about my abortions' *Evening Standard*, 29 June

Allison, R (2003) 'Outrage of a campaigner who survived painful childhood' *Guardian*, 2 December

All-Party Parliamentary Pro-Choice and Sexual Health Group (2004) *NHS Abortion Services*

BBC News Online (2004) 'Care call for abortion survivors', 23 June

Bristow, J (2005) 'Should abortion be an election issue? Vote no!', 16 March

British Association of Perinatal Medicine (2000) Memorandum (www.bapm.org/documents/publications/threshold.pdf)

Brown, H (2004) 'Bloody reality of abortion brought to our living rooms' *The Daily Telegraph*, 22 April

Clements, S (2004) 'Abortion at 20 or more weeks: trends and statistics' in Lee, E (ed) *Late Abortion: A Review of the Evidence* www.prochoiceforum.org.uk/pdf/pcf late abortion08.pdf

Costeloe, K, Hennesy, E and Gibson, AT (2000) 'The EPICure Study: outcomes to discharge from hospital for infants born at the threshold of viability' 106 *Pediatrics* 659–71

Curti, E (2004) 'Pro-lifers should "stay quiet" over abortion limit' *The Tablet*, 28 August

Davies, C (1992) 'How people argue about abortion and capital punishment in Europe and America and why' in Badham, P (ed) *Ethics on the Frontiers of Human Existence* New York: Paragon House

Day, M (2004) 'This two-year-old is the reason why the abortion law will change' *The Sunday Telegraph*, 11 July

Department of Health (2001) *The National Strategy for Sexual Health and HIV* London: Department of Health

Derbyshire, S (2004) 'Fetal sentience and the neurobiology of pain' in Lee, E (ed) *Late Abortion: A Review of the Evidence* www.prochoiceforum.org.uk/publications.asp

Derbyshire, S (2005) 'Why I see no place for science in the abortion debate' *Times Higher Education Supplement*, 21 January

Derbyshire, S and Furedi, A (1996) ' "Fetal pain" is a misnomer' 313 *British Medical Journal* 795

Driscoll, M and Rogers, L (2004) 'To be or not to be' *The Sunday Times*, 4 July

Elliott, J (2005) 'Laid-back Britain tolerates everything, except the state' *The Sunday Times*, 10 April

Evans, DJ and Levene, MI (2001) 'Evidence of selection bias in preterm survival studies: systematic review' 84 *Archives of Diseases of Childhood, Fetal and Neonatal Edition* F79-F84

Evening Standard (2004) 'Foetal questions' Editorial, 28 June

Fitzgerald, M (1995) *Foetal Pain: An Update of Current Scientific Knowledge* London: Department of Health

Foggo, D and Edwardes, C (2004) 'British Pregnancy Advisory Service helps women get illegal abortions' *The Sunday Telegraph*, 10 October

Franklin, S (1991) 'Fetal fascinations: new dimensions to the medical-scientific construction of fetal personhood' in Franklin, S, Lury, C and Stacey, J (eds) *Off-Centre, Feminism and Cultural Studies* London and New York: Harper Collins

Furedi, A (1998) 'Wrong but the right thing to do: public opinion and abortion' in Lee, E (ed) *Abortion Law and Politics Today* Basingstoke: Macmillan

Furedi, A (2005) 'Faith in the abortion debate' www.spiked-online.com

George, A and Randall, S (1996) 'Late presentation for abortion' 22 *The British Journal of Family Planning* 12–15

Gerard, J (2004) 'A blurring of the abortion battle lines' *The Sunday Times*, 18 April

Henderson, M (2004) 'Terminating pregnancy' *The Times*, 24 April

Hume, M (2003) 'Celebrity anti-abortionist' *The Times*, 8 December

Hume, M (2004) 'They're trying to shut us down' *The Times*, 20 October

Jepson, J (2005) 'Murder, even "in good faith", is still murder' *The Daily Telegraph*, 20 March

Lane Committee (1974) *Report of the Committee on the Working of the Abortion Act* Vol 1 London: HMSO

Lee, E (2003a) *Abortion, Motherhood and Mental Health: Medicalizing Reproduction in the US and Britain* New York: Aldine de Gruyter

Lee, E (2003b) 'Introduction' in *Abortion: Whose Right?* London: Hodder and Stoughton

Lee, E (2004) 'Young women, pregnancy and abortion in Britain; a discussion of law "in practice" ' 18 *International Journal of Law, Policy and the Family* 283–304

Lee, E (2005) 'Debating late abortion: time to tell the truth' 31 *The Journal of Family Planning and Reproductive Health Care* 7

Lee, E, Ingham, R, Clements, S and Stone, N (2004) *A Matter of Choice? National*

Variation in Teenage Pregnancy, Abortion and Motherhood York: Joseph Rowntree Foundation

Lee, E, Ingham, R, Clements, S and Stone, N (unpublished) 'Women's Experience of Abortion in the Second Trimester' Ongoing research project

Macfarlane, PI, Wood, S and Bennett, J (2003) 'Non-viable delivery at 20–23 weeks gestation: observations and signs of life after birth' 88 *Archives of Diseases in Childhood, Foetal and Neonatal Edition* F199-F202

Marie Stopes International (2005) 'Marie Stopes International restates its position on reducing the 24 week time limit' www.mariestopes.org.uk/uk/press/press-uk-040405.htm

Marsh, B (2004) 'Room in the womb for those first steps' *Daily Mail*, 29 June

Paintin, D (1998) 'A medical view of abortion in the 1960s' in Lee, E (ed) *Abortion Law and Politics Today* Basingstoke: Macmillan

Palmer, N (2005) 'They told me not to talk – now I'm an MP!' *Daily Mail*, 18 March

Pearson, A (2005) 'We know too much to leave abortion law as it is' *Evening Standard*, 16 March

Petchesky, R (1987) 'Foetal images: the power of visual culture in the politics of reproduction' 13 *Feminist Studies* 263–92

Rivers, R, Rapheal, E and Riley, L (2004) 'Foetal viability' in Lee, E (ed) *Late Abortion: A Review of the Evidence* www.prochoiceforum.org.uk/publications.asp

Royal College of Obstetricians and Gynaecologists (1997) *Foetal Awareness* London: Royal College of Obstetricians and Gynaecologists

Royal College of Obstetricians and Gynaecologists (1999) 'Foetuses and Newborn Infants at the Threshold of Viability: A Framework for Practice' Memorandum

Royal College of Obstetricians and Gynaecologists (2000) *The Care of Women Requesting Induced Abortion* London: RCOG Press

Smith, R (2004) '12-week foetus makes first kick' *Evening Standard*, 28 June

Statham, H, Dimavicius, J and Gillott, J (2004) 'Termination of pregnancy after prenatal diagnosis of foetal abnormality' in Lee, E (ed) *Late Abortion: A Review of the Evidence* www.prochoiceforum.org.uk/publications.asp

Steel, D (2004) 'We need to rethink my abortion law' *Guardian*, 6 July

Templeton, S-K (2005) 'Toll of babies aborted with life chances hits 1,000 a year' *The Sunday Times*, 17 April

Templeton, S-K and Rogers, L (2004) 'Babies that live after abortions are left to die' *The Sunday Times*, 20 June

The Sunday Times (2004) 'New limit on abortions' *The Sunday Times*, Editorial, 4 July

Vasagar, J (2006) 'Catholic church urges review of abortion laws' *Guardian*, 22 June

Webster, P and Hawkes, N (2004) 'Blair backs abortion review' *The Times*, 8 July

Whittam Smith, A (2004) 'Television: Broadcast and be damned: the death and the abortion we should not be spared', 18 April

Williams, R (2005) 'People are starting to realise we can't go on as we are' *The Sunday Times*, 20 March

Wolf, N (2004) 'Face to face with a horrible truth' *The Sunday Times*, 11 April

Index